ISLAMIC THEOLOGY

ENCYCLOPAEDIC SURVEY OF ISLAMIC CULTURE SERIES—1

Islamic Theology

Edited by
MOHAMED TAHER

ANMOL PUBLICATIONS PVT. LTD.
New Delhi-110 002

ANMOL PUBLICATIONS PVT. LTD.
4374/4B, Ansari Road, Daryaganj
New Delhi-110 002

Islamic Theology

First Edition 1997
ISBN 81-7488-535-8

PRINTED IN INDIA

Published by J.L. Kumar for Anmol Publications Pvt. Ltd., New Delhi-110 002 and Printed at Mehra Offset Press, Delhi.

Preface

The Encyclopaedic Survey of Islamic Culture is a unique reference source. This series seeks to anthologise the most important primary and secondary materials on a wide variety of topics and writers of Islamic culture and civilisation. The scholar, the student and the layman will find in various volumes not only a generous selection of reprinted articles, but original essays, bibliographies, and other materials brought for the first time in a comprehensive and exhaustive fashion.

The need for this collation grew out of our awareness that there is no comprehensive source of information for the study and research of the field. Other published works are too specialised in the topics discussed or neglect the institutional as well the individual role which the Islamic system plays. Few encyclopaedic works do exist, and few anthologies also have appeared. Fewer books, again, have systematically covered such topics as Islam in Africa, Islamic sociology, Islamic polity, Islamic thought, etc. Although these topics have been addressed separately, no attempt has been made to discuss them as part of a united treatment of the literature of the field.

Islam brought a total change in all spheres of life. It revolutionised many societies, both in the east and the west. But this is not always accepted and acknowledged. To quote Major Arthur Leonard from his work: Islam; her moral and spiritual value:

"Never to this day has Europe acknowledged in an honest and whole hearted manner the great and everlasting debt she owes to Islamic culture and civilisation. Only in a lukewarm and perfunctory way has she recognised that when, during the dark ages, her people were sunk in feudalism and ignorance, Muslim civilisation under the Arabs reached a high standard of social and scientific splendour that kept the flickering members of European society from utter decadence."

"Do not we, who now consider ourselves on the top most pinnacle ever reached by culture and civilisation, recognise that, had it not been for the high culture, the civilisation and intellectual, as well as the social splendours of the Arabs and soundness of their school system, Europe would to this day have remained sunk in the darkness of ignorance. Have we forgotten that the Muslim maxim was that, the real learning of a man is of more public importance than any particular religious opinions he may entertain, that Muslim liberality was in striking contrast with the then intolerant state of Europe? Does the magnificent valour of the Arabs, inspired as it was by a theism as lofty as it was pure, not appeal to us? Does not the moderation and comparative toleration shown by them to the conquered, notwithstanding the fierce and burning ardour to regenerate mankind that impelled them onward to conquest, also appeal to us? Does it not all the more appeal to us when we contrast this with the bitterness of the attitude of the Christian sects towards one another? Especially when we consider that in Christendom, as it was then constituted, extortion, tyranny and imperial centralisation, combining with ecclesiastical despotism and persecution, had practically extinguished patriotism, by substitution in its place schismatic and degenerate Church?"

Further the same writer continues to say:

"Is it possible that Europe is unmindful of, and has the ingratitude to ignore the splendid services of the scientists and philosophers of Arabic? Are the names of Assamh, Abu Othman, Alberuni, Albeithar, Abu Ali Ibn Sina (Avicenna) the great physician and philosopher, Ibn Rushd (Anempace) besides a host of others but dead letters? Is the great work that they have done and the fame they have left behind them in their books to be consigned to the limbo of oblivion, by an ungrateful but antipathetic Europe?

"It cannot be that already we have lost sight of the amazing intellectual activity of the Muslim world during the earlier part of the `Abbaside' period more especially. It cannot be that we have quite forgotten the irrecoverable loss that was inflicted on Arabian literature, and on the world at large, by the wanton destruction of thousands of books that was promoted by Christian bigotry and fanaticism? It cannot be surely said of Christian Europe that for centuries now she has done her best to hide obligations to the Arabs; yet most assuredly, obligations such as these, are far too sacred to lie much linger hidden."

This is one side of the story. The other side is that the West has definitely absorbed much of the Islamic contributions and is "unaware." To quote Marcus Marby and William Underhill "Bold new visions from ancient landscapes" (Newsweek May 29, 1995): Christian and Islamic civilizations have been in conflict for most of their history. But as often as they have clashed, they have enriched each other. In this ninth century, Moors brought advanced architecture, astronomy and medicine to occupied Spain. While Europe lingered in the Dark Ages, courtly poetry from Persia inspired the troubadours, whose verse evolved into the literature of the early French Renaissance. Even whiling away hours over coffee and conversation—the basis for the cafe—came from Arab culture... France's most popular dish today is not escargots but couscous. French slang is peppered with Arab words like kif-kif (50-50) and Insha Allah (God willing). The hottest new music is Arab-inspired rai" (p. 28). The list of Arabic borrowed words in English and Western usages are many more, not mere algebra, alchemy, azimuth, albatross, timbal, zenith, etc.

There is, in short, a lot of misinformation and incorrect representation about Islam. And more so there is a need today to describe and interpret the issues and express in clear terms what this thought actually deals with. Due to social and cultural changes, the salient aspects of the field require examination. The post cold war era has left the world with a unipolar political system. Islam is a system which promises the world that if applied in toto it would solve the multi-dimensional problems of the modern era. But is there any one who wishes to test this module and try it in a space and time to see the truth of the statement?

The primary purpose of this encyclopaedic survey is to serve as a basic handbook on significant topics of Islamic culture. To facilitate an understanding of the field, the series presents a survey and an analysis of the various socio-cultural forces that shape both the structure and functions of the field as well as by the way this society has changed. We also analyse the larger forces outside the community, such as assimilation and acculturation, and forces inside the community, like, role of the leadership, role of the social and cultural groups and the so much alleged 'imbalance' in the theory and practice of the faith.

We are confident that this work will make a permanent and significant contribution to the study of Islam. Its style is simple, and it is presented in a style accessible to a wide audience. Its target audience is faculty, students, and all concerned with the understanding of the faith of the second largest following in the world. While it has scholarly materials, it is nevertheless also of use to those who have no knowledge of the field, as well as to those who are working in related and allied fields. Most important, we hope that this series will be useful in teaching and learning as an educational resource in the academic world.

The series is planned to be both, multi-volume and multi-facted set, which will run into hundreds of numbers. The compilation of such a huge set is a gigantic task and requires the support and encouragement of all concerned. It requires feed-back and also support from the literary market place and literary circles all over.

A collection of articles, or an anthology, has many benefits, like, it renews our acquaintance with literature which we have neglected, it reveals to us material of which we were ignorant, and it exposes relationships where we did not suppose them to exist. This is the ultimate purpose of our efforts and we wish and pray that this is fulfilled.

A word of acknowledgement is due to the inspiration of the idea of a comprehensive, commulative and compact set of literary works on the Islamic culture. These inspirers are from all walks of life and their efforts must be acknowledged which includes, contributors, authors and editors, as well as the publishers who have graciously contributed to this project and we duly acknowledge their cooperation. The well wishers are many more and listing all the concerned by names is impossible here. Each must be duly rewarded for this gesture, and this is our sincere prayer.

Editor

Contents

1

The Theology of Alienation

JALALUL HAQ

> Alienation as used today implies a subject of it and an object—the former being a constant and the lattter being a variable... Whether one is in mosque or in market-place, one has to keep oneself close to the model life of the Prophet, which is, both in his person and preachings, a paradigm of a delienated being.

There seems to be in people a permanent and inherent tendency not to be satisfied with the natural and social conditions that surround their personal and interpersonal existence. Temporally, in all ages, people have subjected their environment to a severe examination and relentless criticism making, as a rule, their own egoistic pleasures the criteria for this examination and criticism.

Humanity has given expression to its tendencies of self-assessment and self-critique through its giant minds. Socrates, Augustine, Martin Luther, Erasmus, More, Marx, Russel were all, to consider the civilizational continuity of the Western part of human globe only, the great people who made accountable, through their writings and activities, the conditions prevailing in their respective times and places.

The above stated truth holds equally good in the case of our own contemporary cultural universe. Two differentiating points—one of the quantitative and other of qualitative nature—are nevertheless there which need mention. Firstly, the feeling of discontent and dissatisfaction is experienced today on a much wider scale and more consciously and expressly than at any earlier time in the past. Secondly—and this is more important than the first—whereas earlier the criticism made was on a horizontal plane, these days it is undimensional.

That is to say, whereas in the past, the critiques analysed their 'present' either with reference to their 'past' or with reference to 'future' (sometimes with reference to both), the present-day social-criticism understands present only in terms of 'present'. People like Hobbes and Rousseau nostalgically remembered and referred to a golden and glorious bygone past in which man lived a most happy life. While Plato, Marx etc., fixed their gaze upon a distant eschatological future when man, according to their hope, will realize all material and spiritual comforts he has been longing for since times immemorial.

As against this past/future-directed criticism of present, what marks the modern psyche is its unconcern for past or future and what it tends to be more and more enclosed in the immediate moments of present. In plain words, modern man is neither nostalgic to his past nor optimistic about future; he is just dissatisfied with 'present'—i.e. everything that makes up his ethos—his philosophy and science, his religion and technology, his politics and ethics etc. He is disoriented, uncommitted, cynic hopeless and what not.

The word that is considered to epitomize and express most perfectly this entire syndrome of modern attitude is Alienation. Thanks to the great richness of its meaning and its wide applicability upon the diverse phenomena and hyper-and epi-phenomena abounding to present human situation, it has come to have such great currency that no other word in modern scientific jargon can claim to match or compete it. It is, as many authors have said, 'the catchword of the day". The popularity and vogue that it enjoys can be imagined even by making cursory look at the recent literature pertaining to a variety of disciplines like philosophy, theology, sociology, psychology, political science, economics and even somewhat remoter subjects like medicine, physiology and physics.

Philosophers, philosopher-theologians and some philosophically oriented psychologists take this word as indicating to some deeper facts about man in which he is separated from some ultimate cosmic reality. It is a favourite of sociologists as they apply it to the most threatening of human problems namely individual's inability to accept and adjust himself with the established values, norms and institutions of society. Psychoanalyst-psychiatrists too find it meaningful to use it to describe many psychical illnesses like schizophrenia, schizoid, necrophylia etc. Its usage is equally popular in literature, newspaper columns, and political commentaries etc.

That the term 'alienation' fascinates and is adopted by the pandits in about all the disciplines of human sciences in a natural evidence to the fact that the phenomenon itself characterizes the entire gamut of activities we do in our personal and collective life. There is no aspect of our individual life which is not affected by it and there is no section of our society which is immune to its influence. Our love for our wives, respect for parents, affection to children, our treatment to our subordinates and superordinates, our way of earning livelihood, our political affiliation, our entertainments and our likes and dislikes in the matters of food, clothes etc., are all alienated.

In society, every segment of the people, whether it represents culture, sub-culture or counter-culture, is said to be alienated. Marx held the whole class of labour as being alienated and Erich Fromm, his ardent disciple, treated the class of bourgeoisie (constituted by capitalists, managers, bureaucrats etc.) as even more terribly alienated. Psychologists like Karen Horney see in many abnormal behaviours of psychotics the sign of their alienation from some deeper and more real aspects of their self. And sociologists like Middleton, McClosky, Dean, Richardson find in the defiant and problematic behaviour of ghetto people, immigrants, hippies, yippies, delinquents, drug-addicts etc., the sure fact of their alienation from the generally accepted social values and norms. What is important is that we are told that alienation had developed not merely as a deplorable by-product of our modern western culture, but that it is the very essence of this culture. Lo, verily, this is The Age of Alienation.

The most interesting thing in this connection is that the word 'alienation' with its contrast 'de-alienation' has replaced many categories of normative concepts like good bad, virtue, sin, happiness unhappiness, brave, coward etc. Thus a hippy is said to be neither lazy nor socially irresponsible, nor unhappy; he is alienated. The factory manager is neither oppressive nor dishonest; he is alienated. Similarly a prostitute is neither wicked nor a social; she too is alienated. And so on and so forth.

But, aside from the fascination and vogue that the term enjoys, there is a darker side of the picture too. Due mainly to the plethora of diverse contexts in which it is used and due also to its handling by people hailing from so diverse disciplines, it has come to be lacking in the clarity and specificity in its meaning which is otherwise a prerequisite for any term to be adopted in scientific vocabulary. Writers today confront great difficulty in their effort to conceptualize it and operationalize its connotation.

This lack of specificity and dysfunctionality in the term has made many cynic minds to take a reluctant attitude towards it and discourage and deprecate the overdramatization of its usage. Some have even been bold enough to suggest its removal from scientific vocabulary. All the same, as one writer puts it, "the peculiar attraction it exerts for intellectuals, students, social critiques and social scientists indicates that the idea of alienation will not easily or quickly yield its prominent position in contemporary thought."

The greatest factor contributing to the confusion, which may be aptly mentioned here, has its source in the paradoxical approaches of different alienationists regarding its symptomatology. That is, they often take contradictory stands in telling what according to their minds are the signs and symptoms of alienated behaviour. Certain phenomena which for a particular thinker are clear signs of the fact of alienation, are for other thinkers evidence of the opposite fact.

A difficulty of this kind is experienced when, for example, one tries to develop the implications of relationship that alienation has with its corresponding collectivistic counterpart "anomie". Anomie is the process whereby a society ceases to exert an effective control upon the behaviours of its members. It is, as is obvious, related with alienation in a circle-making chain of cause-effect-cause....Man's refusal to accept the authority of the established norms and values of society (alienation) leads to the latters' getting weakened which, in turn, causes further alienation of man from them. The circle goes on viciously and indefinitely. But this non-conformistic attitude in social behaviour is admitted as alienation only by some people. For others it is the conformism, instead of non-conformism, which points to the state of alienation.

It can however be said that the above difficulty and others like it are more a result of a lack of correct perspective on the part of scholars than due to there being an inherent lacuna in the concept. The line of approach adopted in this article, as would appear, easily removes them.

To start the discussion, it may be said that the term 'alienation', as it is used today, implies a subject of it and an object—the former being a constant and the latter being a variable. The subject (i.e. who is alienated) is always the individual and object (i.e. what one is alienated from) may be individual's self, another person, any institution, whole society or cosmos or God. The tendency among scholars is to treat all these kinds of alienation independently, although they admit a relative connection between them.

But opposed to this treatment, it is assumed here *ex hypothesio* that alienation is basically alienation from self and all other types of alienation follow it and stem from it. This hypothesis is based upon another assumption that individual's relations with the objective social and natural realities are rooted in and generated by the structure of his self and are inconceivable apart from self; (it will be substantiated in course of discussion).

At the outset, it will be seen that, our making alienation tantamount to self-alienation or alienation from self is consistent with the word's standard usages in Middle English. Richard Schacht, in his book *Alienation*, has analysed in detail the word etymologically and historically. According to his research its Latin origin in *alienatio* which derives its meaning from the verb *alienare* (to make something other's, to take away, remove). There were aboriginally two uses of the word *alienare* (and *alienatio*)—one legal and other medical.

In its first use it meant "to transfer the ownership of something to another person". And in medicine it was used to mean 'the paralysis or loss of one's mental power or senses—as, for instance, in an epileptic seizure, or as the result of a severe shock". Thus, in both of its uses it implied a state of being in which one lost what one once possessed e.g. his property, his consciousness etc. Therefore when we talk of man's alienation, we may mean by it man's loss of his self, his transferring his self to some external object, his being possessed or subjugated by something other, his not leading his own life etc.

It seems to be somewhat essential to elaborate the meaning of self-alienation, because much of the difficulties that are felt in operationalizing the alienation-concept are the result of our scholars' giving a very off-hand and superficial treatment to the concept of 'self'. They treat this word in a way which leads to the speculation that for them its meaning is some thing given and there is no need to make any philosophical study regarding its nature, its ontic structure or the modes and ways in which it functionally expresses itself. But this complacent attitude has its adverse repercussions on the attempt to have a satifactory solution of the problem and for this reason must be avoided.

When we speak of self-alienation or alienation of self we speak in other words 'self's alienation from self' or 'alienation of self *from* self.' This obviously involves an assertion about the duplicity of selves in the single personality of an individual. But is this a just and genuine assertion? Are there really two selves one which is that which is and which should not have been alienated from the other? From the strict scientific point of view, to be sure, any kind of ontological dualism in the personality of individual is inadmissible.

The cardinal principle of scientism is that we can assign an ontological status only to those things which are directly or indirectly experienced and which, for that reason, can be made a term of a meaningful logical proposition. Now the self whose idea emerges out of our perception of physiological constitution and is subject to its laws is certainly a real self. Any other self supposed to be concealed behind this empirical self is impossible to be asserted due to its inexperienced and inexperiencible character.

But whatever the decree of scientism, the duplicity of selves may be asserted on grounds no less secure and sound than the scientism can claim. A primary fact that points out to the possibility of there being two selves is the experience in our life of crises—crises of the nature of either/or as Kierkegaard would call it. Man placed in a complex social situation is often faced with the dilemma of choosing between the two or more than two courses open to him in regard to the solution of a certain problem. He very ostensibly perceives that what his physiological self wishes to do is resisted by some reality which lies deeper inside him. This reality may be weak or strong and accordingly the resistance may be a failure or success. But the very fact of resistance or clash or crisis leads to the inevitable conclusion that man lives a two-levelled life, one of which is constituted by the physiology of his personality and the other which transcends it. As against man, the animals never confront such cirsis or dilemma and are accordingly said not to possess any transcendental self besides their physiological self.

What is said above may not lead any one to confuse the transcendental self with what in common parlance is called "conscience". Apart from the fact that conscience is a socially made up faculty of human personality and which for that reason may itself be good or bad according to the training it has been given in the respective society, the crisis, though of different nature, is felt even when our actions are dictated by what we think are out "conscientious decisions". This happens not only when the decision is made under some pressure but also when it is free. A free moral act which does not have its roots in the spiritual self fails to give the sense of satisfaction and fulfilment which we expect from it and for the sake of which we sacrifice the urges of our physiological self.

It is the rootedness in spiritual self which gives the ethical actions their objective validity. When a person acts morally only due to his conscious or unconscious desire to conform with established norms of society and to avoid the risks which non-conformity may entail, or, in other words, when he acts morally without having any faith in the truth-value of his actions, he is certainly cut off from his self. He must experience in such circumstances a crisis, a certain feeling of anguish, a hollowness or emptiness in his being. He must feel as if he is not living a full life or he has lost something very important from his personality. These feelings, to be sure, go side by side with his full awareness that he has done what was morally worth doing. Here the truth-value in the proposition asserting the existence of a metaempirical self becomes most glaring and palpable. The great fallacy that underlies the approach of scientistic people (i.e., the people who believe in the postulates and assumptions of scientism, whether or not they are practical scientists) is their confining knowledge to sensory perception. Any proposition which is not analysable into sensory data or which is unverifiable by our sense experience is, for them, meaningless, is indeed not a proposition at all. Our inner subjectivity, obviously, does not come in the purview of our sensorily given knowledge; hence it is non-existent.

But this is to define knowledge, experience, meaningfulness etc. too narrowly. Our making a distinction between good acts and bad acts, true proposition and wrong proposition and beautiful object and not beautiful object which are based respectively upon our moral, rational and aesthetic senses are as genuine to us as genuine are the perceptual judgements.

The knowledge obtained through the moral, rational and aesthetic senses, although subjective as against the objective quality of perceptual knowledge, is never the less quite alike with the latter in so far as their conviction-carrying values are concerned. When I appreciate the beauty of a picture model or when I say charity is good or when I make some rational judgements, I am as much sure about the truth-value of my experience as I could be when, for example, I say that I see a table before me. It is perfectly meaningful for me to say that a certain picture is beautiful or a certain act is good even though the 'beauty' of the picture or the 'goodness' of the act is inexperiencible through out sense-organs. We of course sometimes err in our rational or ethical or aesthetic judgement but so we do in our perceptual judgements.

The moment the validity of the triology of rational-aesthetic-ethical truths is properly admitted, the belief in a trans-phenomenal self becomes irresistible. For these cannot be the functions of our physiological self as they are qualitatively radical unlike with the activities that that self generates. Animal too poses physiological self but there is a total absence of such activities in him. An elephant may know the property of the ball that if kicked it will rebound but it cannot be said to believe in the proposition that the ball has got a centre. Or a brid may construct a beautiful nest but it expresses no sign on the basis of which it could be said that she appreciates too the beauty of hernest; constructing the nest and living in it is simply a matter of course for her. Similarly a hungry man abstain from eating the food before him; but he will do it not on the basis of his thinking that God would punish him for his immoral act but simply for the reason that somebody is there around the food with a stick in his hand.

If this is a fact that rational-aesthetic-ethical senses are exclusive possession of humankind, then the inevitable conclusion that there is in man's personality a seat other than and qualitatively different from his phenomenal physiological self which acts as the fountain to generate those activities. The belief in this interior seat, or as otherwise called the spiritual self cannot be rejected merely on the plea that its knowledge is irreducible to perceptual data or that it is not amenable to experiment and analysis in laboratory.

We have indulged in proving the existence of a metaphysical psycho-spiritual self keeping in view the great popularity that the reductionist theory enjoys in various academic circles. Classical

Materialism, Evolutionism, Positivism and Behaviourism have joined hands to deny any ontological status to self except as an epiphenomenon of our physical-physiological body. Social analysts with their general allergy against metaphysical speculation and with their abject eagerness to follow the line of scientists inevitably give vent to this amorphous reductionism.

As a natural consequence their entire endeavour to understand and analyse the human phenomena is social perspective is marred. It is however a good sign that in past some decades quite a good number of eminent persons in *academia* have realized and revolted against this dehumanizing trend of sciences and scientism. The names of Erich Fromm, Julian Huxley, Arthur Koestler, Professor Perry may aptly be mentioned. These people recognised a human element in man's personality which although elusive and unanalysible is yet a fact and cannot be reduced into the phenomena explicable in scientific terms.

There emerges from the above theory a very important point which is vital to a correct understanding of the problem of alienation but which is not attended to by the above named anti-reductionist thinkers. It is that our acceptance of spiritualism on microscopic level in human personality leads to our acceptance of the same on macroscopic level in cosmos at large. The presence of finite spiritual selves in the bodies of so many people logically implies the presence of an infinte self in universe from which the former comes into existence and into which they are rooted. Thinkers who evade this conclusion due to their atheistic bias make thereby philosophy inconsistent. In as much as the spiritual element is inexplicable in naturalistic terms its explanation in terms of supernatural being is logically the only course left. In other words, theism is the only alternative of reductionism in explaining comprehensively the human and cosmic phenomena.

Another corollary that attends to the above theory and which has great bearing upon the problem at hand is this: When it is agreed that human selves have their source in God it would also not be disputed that they share their nature with God. This means that the properties and attributes which characterize human selves on finite level also characterize the Self on an infinite level. This is what in Judeo-Christian-Islamic parlance in expressed by the phrase that "man is created in the image of God." It follows that self-talk is essentially God-talk and God-talk, self-talk.

When a religious person speaks of his commitment with God, he, in other words, speaks of his commitment to self or when a philosopher speaks of alienation from self, he may be taken to mean alienation from God. Self-alienation, in this way, is tantamount to alienation from God and *vice-verse:* And accordingly self's de-alienation means our de-alienation from God.

The most outstanding feature that characterizes the spiritual self of man is its freedom. Traditionally the significance of human freedom was restricted to moral domain; man was said to be free to be moral or amoral in his social actions. But there is a deeper and more important sense in which man's freedom can be understood. It is the sense in which self's freedom has a reference to its own subjective reality. Man is free to accept his spiritual interiority and he is also free to deny it or accept it while occasionally betraying its command through his actions. In theological language the same would be conveyed by saying that man is free to believe or not to believe in God or believe while going against His commands.

Paradoxical though it may seem but it is a truth known to everyone intuitively that man is free to have or not to have faith in his freedom and for that matter in the spirit which is the seat and source of that freedom. There are of course people who deny spirituality but they do so only by admitting in their statement a self-contradiction. As one author put it: "We are told by man superbly equipped mentally that man has no mind." Somewhere above we have mentioned traditional materialists, Evolutionists and Behaviourists who certainly fall in the category of such men. It follows from the very structure of human freedom that he should have the power to contradict his own essential nature; otherwise, he would be a thing among other things.

Granted, however, the suggestion that man is at liberty to accept and deny his freedom and spirituality and that he sometimes does deny them, the important question arises that why at all he does so, what actually tempts him to deny what is essential to him and actually enables him to be called man. To answer in a word, it is his fear of uncertainty.

The realm of freedom and spirit is also the realm of uncertainty, quite contrary to the physical-physiological realm in which every thing is fixed and certain. There are the so-called laws of nature inexorably governing the movements of animals and other dead material bodies. It is absolutely denied to them to choose, to act according to their own decision or discretion, to act against what they have already been ordained and ordered to. But man being free always finds before him to or more than two courses open, from which he has to choose one. Given a very limited foresight, he, however, in most of the cases, does not know the likely consequences of the choice he is going to make. This fill him with a sense of hesitancy and uncertainty. He abhors, indeed dreads this uncertainty which often tempts him to deny altogether his freedom, his power to make choices and decisions and yield to the fixed and certain domain of physics.

The temptation to eat the "forbidden fruit" as illustrated by scriptures, indeed symbolizes the strong tendency in human nature to make a leap from the uncertainty to certainty, from the spiritual to mundane. Moreover, our fixation with mother (Oedipus complex), soil (nationalism), blood (racialism) etc., as stressed by psychologists are the manifestations of our fear from freedom.

The notion of freedom in human context should be understood in its two states—one in which it is merely potential and the other in which it becomes real or actual. A newly—born human baby is no better than a pup in being under the compulsions and constraints of his bodily instincts. But whereas in the course of time the former grows into a free agent, the latter retains his handicaps till the last. This points out to the fact that human child possesses a potentiality which the pup is deprived of. In the process of baby's becoming a man—the process of "hominization" as Teilhard De Chardin could call it—a variety of factors contributes, the chief one being the baby's social atmosphere. The actualization of freedom of man is very gradual; in a full-blooded sense he realizes it when he reaches his adulthood. Phylogenetically speaking, Adam's first "free act" was his eating the forbidden fruit which he could do only after having come into contact with Eve (which constituted his social atmosphere); until then he was merely an infant, a child, a youngster having his freedom only in a potential form.

The two states in which man's freedom is potential and actual may be called respectively as his essential and existential states. (The two terms have been extensively used by Paul Tillich, the great theologian of alienation of our times and a comparison of his position with our own will be made a little later). Man's essential state being yet immune from perversion of any kind which is made possible by man's exercising his freedom, is his de-alienated, or more correctly non-alienated state. But, at the existential level, he is entirely on his own to be faithful or unfaithful to his self which respectively constitutes his de-alienated and alienated states of being.

Given the fact that man's self is nothing but a microscopic prototype of God's Being, its essential non-alienated state is also the state in which it is in perfect harmony with God. For the same reason, in his existential state man's alienation and de-alienation depends upon the negative or positive attitudes that he takes towards God. The positive response which a person may exhibit by being faithful to his self/God is technically called *Imam* meaning literally 'the belief (in God)'. And his deliberate choice for not putting faith in his self/God is termed as *Kufr* that is unbelief. Paul Tillich has included 'unbelief' in the list of three which he calls 'marks of estrangement'. According to him

> "Unbelief.. is not the unwillingness or inability to believe the doctrines of Church, but, like faith, it is an act of the total personality, including practical, theoretical and emotional elements.......Unbelief...means the act or state in which man

in the totality of his being turns away from God. In his existential self-realisation he turns towards himself and his world and loses him essential unity with the ground of his being and his world.. Unbelief is the disruption of man's cognitive participation in God.."

But here seems to be the time to discuss, at least in brief the theological understanding of phenomenon of 'estrangement' (his substitute for 'alienation') as developed by Paul Tillich in his *opus Systematic Theology* and compare it with that of our own. As with us Tillich's theory of estrangement rests upon the ontological disparity between essence and existence. However, whereas in his system this disparity takes the form of dichotomy, nothing of the kind happens in the system presented here. That is to say that while, for Tillich, the existential state of man necessarily and compulsorily contradicts his essential state, to us no such necessity abounds. Man, on existential plane, has full freedom and power to be or not to be in harmony with the nature and urges of his essential state.

Man's essential state, according to Tillich, is what he calls 'the state of dreaming innocence" which, as he says, "is potentiality not actuality. It has no place, it is *ou topos* (utopia). It has no time; it precedes temporality, and it is suprahistorical". Clearly this definition of essential state is, in essence, not very different from our description of it as non-essential state i.e., the state is which man has not yet actualised his power to alienate himself from his essential self. Regarding existential state, however, he says that it is by an original necessity the state of estrangement. Estrangement characterizes "the human situation universally". Or more simply. "The state of existence is the state of estrangement". But as this determinism apparently absolves man from his having any responsibility what so ever of this evil, Tillich is landed in an special difficulty to reconcile it with the notion of freedom which he is constrained to employ in describing the human situation.

Tillich does not ascribe human self with full-fledged freedom. He, instead, speaks of "finite freedom.' Only god has infinite freedom. Man's potentialities, he says, "which constitute his freedom are limited by the opposite pole, his destiny". And in nature, "destiny has the character of necessity". Nonetheless, the list of powers that man, according to Tillich, possesses, having finite freedom, includes almost every power including the power of "contradicting himself and his essential nature".

But if man is free to contradict his nature, there should at least be theoretical possibility of his not contradicting his nature. The very notion of freedom demands that both of the two courses should be open. It would be meaningless and self-contradictory to say that man is free to contradict his self but not to do the same. A servant will not be "free" if he is given only the freedom of serving his master. Tillich does not see the logic of the situation and continues to assert the human (finite) freedom while at the same time rejecting the view that "each individual could always either contradict or not contradict his essential nature".

As may be clear, Tillich's dilemma arises due to his already having decided to remain faithful to the Christian dogmas while interpreting them in a new and more modern-sounding language. The notion of "Fall" of primordial persons (Adam and Eve), constitutes a very important ingredient of Biblical story of creation and Christian theology and Tillich too leans heavily upon it to explain man's transition from his essential to existential state.

The traditional theology interpreted the "Fall" as an event that happend once-upon-a-time in the lives of Adam and Eve and the consequences of which are still suffered by all the people. But since this has a clear deterministic implication, Tillich is constrained to reject it. He refuses to believe it as an "once-upon-a-time event". For him, the Fall happens to every man in his own personal life individually and collectively rather than being something inherited from his remote parents. "Theology", claims Tillich, "must clearly and unambiguously represent 'the Fall' as a symbol for the human situation universally, not as the story of an event that happend "once upon a time".

But does this shift from ontogeny to phylogeny in interpreting "the Fall,', helps in any way the real difficulty. Clearly, the determinism persists as the man is still being said to "fall" universally and necessarily. He is still said to be without help in plunging into the existential debasement from the essential state of dreaming innocence.

Commenting upon this patent inconsistency in Tillich's asserting on the one hand the human freedom and denying it at the same time on the other, Richard Schacht writes:

> "...The acknowledgment of both simultaneously may pose no problem for those accustomed to performing a similar feat in connection with the traditional Christian conception of 'original sin", to which Tillich's concept of estrangement is admittedly and obviously related. To the uninitiated mind, however, he appears to be proposing the acceptance of views which exclude each other. For both to be true would be every bit as mysterious as theologians traditionally have acknowledged 'original sin' to be."

After this little digression we may now pick up the thread of our discussion on alienation as represented by unbelief. Unbelief may be defined as man's deliberate choice not to commit himself existentially to his God which results in the disengagement of his self from self. But aside from this straight non-commitment there is another way of man's becoming unconnected with his self. This is the way in which man replaces the real god by some false god or gods making them the object of his concern and commitment. This replacement is done sometimes by denying blatantly the real God and sometimes with a vague acceptance and approval of Him. The process whereby man relates himself to fake and false gods and ruins his spiritual personality is technically called "Idolatry" (*Shirk*).

We have already said it that the realm of spirituality is the realm where fixity and certitude is absent and for that reason man dreads it and tries to evade and escape it. Only the people with deep convictions and strong power of will are expected to make a leap into this realm. It is more common for men to take refuge into the fixed domain of materiality. Dreading darkness and uncertainty, they perpetually make efforts to remain tied up with the physical-physiological conditions of their existence.

Speaking symbolically, 'I' breaks off its relation with the spiritual 'Thou' and becomes consequently subjugated by the brute and ruthless 'It'. The transition from "I-Thou" relationship to "I-It" relation brings disaster only to I's self since, as we have seen, in the former there is a complete concordance of natures while in the latter the terms of relation, in their ontic nature, are completely opposed to each other.

Man has given expression to his tendency to It-worship from oldest to the most recent times and into myriad forms. The polytheistic ethos of Indian antiquity is perhaps the richest of its kind to help us understand the various natural forces which may be taken shelter of by man after his escape from spirituality. Besides worshipping nature-object like sun, moon, rivers, animals etc., the Indians also made money, sex, power, lifeless stones, priests, saints, kings, etc., into gods.

Modern man, too, is frantically after money, sex and power. In that sense he is still the worshipper of Lakshmi, Indra and Kali. The big lifeless machines are modern expression of stone idols. File-stars, sport-stars etc., are our new rishis and munis whom we praise and adore with devotion. The kings have been replaced by our rulers whom we fear and hate but whom we, nevertheless, submit to. Political leaders are our new priests whom we obey as if they were paragons of virtue and wisdom, as if they were gods. Indeed modern man has added a lot more gods in his pantheon like 'nation', 'race', 'language', 'humanity' etc.

It is interesting to see that while the theist Paul Tillich has stressed unbelief as mark of estrangement, the atheist Erich Fromm sees in Biblical conception of idolatry a clear case of alienation. He delightfully writes:

> "...The Prophet of monotheism did not denounce heathen religions as idolatrous primarily because they worshipped several gods instead of one. The essential difference between monotheism and polytheism is not one of the *number* of gods, but lies in the fact of self-alienation. Man spends his energy, his artistic capacities on building an idol, and then he worships the idol, which is nothing but the result of his own human effort. His life forces have flown into a "thing" and this thing, having become an idol, is not experienced as a result of his own productive effort, but as something apart from himself, over and against him, which he worships and to which he submits. As the prophet Hosea says (XIV, 8): "Assur shall not save us; we will not ride upon horses; *neither will we say any more to the work of our hands, you are cut gods;* for in thee the fatherless finds love. "Idolatrous man bows down to the work of his own hands. *The idol represents his own life-forces* in an alienated form." (Italics by Fromm)

Unbelief, whether straight-forward or in the form of idolatry, is the chief source of self-alienation. Man, by refusing to relate himself with God, actually unrelates himself with his self. He becomes unconnected with what is the root of his existence, with what is most essential in his personal reality. Being no longer in touch with self, even his "good" actions cease to be good so far as their value as an aid to the self-enhancement is concerned. Moral worth of an action requires two things: First, it must stem from and be directed to one's essential self and second it must be socially useful. An action which is beneficial to society but which is done without reckoning to self is, by necessity, to loose its authenticity in man's existential perspective. For, when not stemming from the spiritual 'I', it necessarily has its source in the physiological self which is an 'It'. And can It-originated and It-oriented action, even when its effects are good for society, causes self-alienation.

Clearly, if unbelief is the chief source of man's self-alienation, it is 'belief' which is to be taken as its chief remedy. May must put his total faith in God denying forthrightly any other god as coobject of his faith in order to be a 'de-alienated'. An effort towards self-dealienation must start from a genuine acceptance of God as one accompanied with a straightforward rejection of any associate what-so-ever to Him. The first part of the first Islamic proclamation '*Kalimah*' (There is no god but Allah) epitomizes this attitude.

Belief in God, however, should not be taken to mean as an acceptance of His Being on intellectual or logical plane. It is much more than that. The Arabic word *Imam* for which the word 'belief' is taken as translation points out to a deeper and profounder meaning. It points out to man's self-involvement in God's Being. Man recognizes God as his root, as the giver of his existence unto whom he has ultimately to return. He derives the meaning of his being from the Being of God. He identifies himself with God and defines his existence in His terms. It is the realization of total dependence upon God for self's meaning and definition, which constitutes the real meaning of the word 'belief'.

A vigrous application of the meaning of the word 'belief' in man's life implies the involvement in God of man's total personality which includes its reflective, emotive and conative parts. Man must *think* god as his real god while denying godhood of everything other than God. And he should offer to Him all his love and devotion. And in the last, he must fully abide by His commands. Only when man submits himself to God on all these three planes, does he become real believer and only then can he be said to be living a de-alienated life.

That man should surrender himself to God completely and absolutely is emphasized in the Quran at various places. At one place it asks man to enter into Islam with the totality of his being. At another place the attitude of total submission and surrender has been expressed by the word which it is not possible to translate into English. It points out to man's commitment to god with complete single-mindedness and with fulness of the being.

But here objection may be raised that a complete surrender to an external authority may results into the loss of self, into self-alienation. Erich Fromm, in continuation to the paragraph quoted above, writes:

> "Monotheistic religions themselves have, to a large extent, regressed into idolatry. Man projects his power of love and of reason unto God; he does not feel them any more as his own powers, and then he prays to God to give him back some of what he, man, has projected unto God. In early Protestantism and Calvinism, the required religious attitude is that man *should* feel himself empty and impoverished, and put his trust in the grace of God, that is, into the hope that God may return to him part of his own qualities, which he has put into God."

This paragraph, when read in conjunction with the earlier one gives the impression that Fromm regards monotheism, overall, as a de-alienating factor, although, to him, certain form of it leads to the opposite situation. But the immediately following paragraph starts with the sentence: "Every act of submissive worship is act of alienation and idolatry in this sense". This makes Fromm's attitude unclear and ambiguous. He seems to be undecisive in his dual loyalties to his Judaic family background on the one hand and atheistic bias on the other. Monotheism, as far as it goes, certainly requires unconditional submission of man before God. But does this submission really lead to self-alienation? Perhaps not.

God of monotheism, as said above and as is admitted by Fromm, is the macroscopic reality of which man is a microscopic expression. There is a complete concordance between ontic nature and structure of God's Being and being of men. When man worships God he, in fact, is seeking the development of his own finer qualities of which God's Being is an infinite expression. Although in cosmological sense, God has His external and objective existence, for man. He also constitutes his interiority. Thus, existentially speaking, god is not "the Other" of Sartre but a "Subjectivity" of Kierkegaard. In the sense worship of God is de-alienating and by no means alienating factor. The more intensely we worship God, the more we come near to God/self and the more we are de-alienated.

As already said, it requires a total existential involvement in God for man to achieve complete de-alienation. He has to submit himself to God on all three—reflective, emotive, and conative—planes of his being. But there is discernible in man a strong tendency to confine his submission (when at all he decides) to one or two parts of his being alone. It is often found that, although intellectually aware of his spiritual roots, man allows the extraneous non-spiritual forces to influence his actions, thus, betraying a part of his essentiality. The phenomenon is what, in theology, is called 'sin'.

Sin is also a form of alienation but unlike 'unbelief' it is not absolute. In unbelief man is absolutely cut off from his self while in sin only a part of his existence is alienated. Moreover, whereas in unbelief self is permanently alienated, in sin, its alienation is confined to the period of time during which it is under the influence of alienating factor. As soon as man comes out of his sinning state and regrets it, he becomes free of alienation. It may, however, be said that the proneness to commit sin every time and other and the tendency to live a life in utter disregard of the urges and demands of self, lead to a gradual loosening of one's ties with his self and finally man reaches a stage which is, for all practical purposes the state of unbelief and the state of absolute and permanent alienation.

Sin, although almost universal, is however by no means a necessary condition of human existence. There is no ground for the supposition that a state of sinlessness is a logical impossibility or that it can be realized only of God' making direct descent into the human personality. The transformation of man from the essential to existential state, or in other words, the realization of the capacity of freedom to commit or not to commit sin, as already said, is a natural process wherein only two factors work, namely, the preexistent potentiality of freedom and social situation. This is not required, as Christian theologians believe, any betrayal or break-through on man's part to make him conscious of his freedom which, according to them, brings about an essential corruption in man's personality. Sin obviously is effect not the cause, is posterior and no anterior to freedom.

Sense of guilt and anxiety are two natural and necessary accompaniments of sin and consequently of alienation. On ontogenic plane, a child becomes conscious of his freedom and capacity to sin only gradually. He violates the command of his parents or teacher. This is negation of what to him or all—powerful authorities makes him fearful and anxious and a feeling of guilt comes to pervade his being. He regrets it and wishes to repent. It should, however, be said that a child's act of commission is not sin. In proper sense, sin is only that act which is committed when a sufficient degree of freedom is achieved which is possible only in the adult age. Adam might have committed a lot of mistakes before meeting Eve. But those mistakes do not constitute his sins because they were made when he was not yet free in actual sense; he was until that time an infant child or a youngster.

Adam's eating of forbidden fruit was a 'sin' because then he was living in a social situation (being in relation to Eve) which gave him the amount of freedom required from sin. His act, as in the case of human beings in general, was followed by the sense of guilt and anxiety. He wept, he regretted his act and wished to repent. By violating the command of God he has lost touch with his self, he had become alienated. But by repenting, by approaching to God he again became related to God and to his self. He again became de-alienated. Had he not repented, he would have remained in the state of alienation. Man too may remain in an alienated state or overcome it by his negative or positive decision to repent before God when he commits sin.

The propensity in human individual to commit sin is a rule which is, at any rate, not without exceptions. There has been in history a legacy of man specially chosen by Divinity, who lived a complete sinless life. Called "Prophets", these men were entrusted with the duty of showing the people the path travelling on which they could live a de-alienated life. Man's own intellectual powers are too feeble to enable him thrash out a sound and satisfactory programme which could save his existence from plunging into the drudgery of complete alienation.

Given this fact and also the proposition that unless man "knew" the solutions to his existential crises, he could not be held responsible for his (mis) deeds, the presence of Prophets becomes a necessity. (The absence of prophetic agency would obviously shift the responsibility of man's actions from himself to God).

Here comes the necessity of affirming the other half of the *Kalimah* which says that Muhammad is the messenger of God. But the belief in the prophethood of Muhammad does not mean the belief in his person alone; by implication it rather means the belief in the institution of prophet hood——the institution through the agency of which God absolves Himself of his responsibility to provide sufficient knowledge and training to man to enable him to live a de-alienated life. A muslim is asked to believe in the whole chain of prophets who appeared in different times and at different places and the end of which is the prophethood of Prophet Muhammad.

This kind of prophetology, obviously, invites some questions. For example, an uninitiated person may be tempted to ask who is the true prophet? or more primarily, how to judge what a Prophet is saying are really the words of God? and also why to regard Muhammad as the last prophet and not merely one of the links in the chain? The answers to these questions, although not very difficult, are however, not proposed to be given here as this will take us far off from our discussion. Suffice it to say that the similarity in the central teachings of the prophets with so diverse training and contextual background coupled with the fact that they were recognized by their people of having an absolutely impeccable character, at least lends some credence to their having been divinely inspired and that what they said was truth.

It is important it realize that a prophet's teachings, in order to be a genuinely life-enhancing force, a de-alienating factor, are needed to cover the whole of human life and not only parts of it. Religions (in its presently taken narrower sense) would risk involving an inner self- contradiction if it is merely a 'private' affair of man quite unconcerned with the 'collective' affairs. The distinction between 'private' and 'collective' or 'personal' and 'public', although in itself ingenious, has, however, been made to be dangerously misleading through the Christianity based modern secular culture.

Strictly speaking, there can be no aspect of human life which is personal without being public and *vice versa*. Man being an In-Dividual cannot admit any division or separation in his existence. Man's *person* (ality) is special not only in the sense that all of his activities presume a social context in respect to origin, content and direction but also in the deeper sense that social relations are indispensable preconditions to arouse in the person of man what is called his personality. Society is thus the very essence of man's self while being an external expression of it. Self and society are inclusive and not exclusive of each other. They are the interiority and exteriority of the same reality. They are as inseparable as inseparable are the two ends of a chalk or two sides of a coin. Schizophrenic secularism is outrageous to religion in as much as the latter is expected to given a full and integrated response to the ontological content and existential urges of human personality.

What we call society is the name of an inextricably intricate jumble of institutions which are all creations in the sense of being "expressions" of men's selves and which, in turn, regulate and regularise the latter's behavioural manifestations. The institutions are differentiated not in their essential nature, but in their modes of operations. Some influence human activity more directly some less directly and some others indirectly. For example, the state, the ethical precepts and the rituals are all institutions. Now whereas the effect of the first on life is more direct that of the second is less so and the last had only an indirect effect. But this by no means implies that the activities coming under the purview of the first are 'public' affairs of man while those pertaining to the latter two are more or less 'personal'. Moreover, institutions, in order to be properly responsive to human needs, are needed to be in harmony with each other and reciprocally, in order to be in harmony with each other, they must be properly responsive to human needs.

Aside from the theoretical necessity involved in the prophetic teachings as being comprehensive and covering all the aspects of human life, when he put a glance on Scriptural (Biblical and Quranic) records we find that prophets did preach things which were related to the so-called collective affairs of man. All of the prophets either taught their own "Laws" or those of their predecessors. These Laws, though different in amount and content in the case of each prophet, contained the same and similar doctrinal basis. This was necessitated by the fact that while the doctrinal aspects responded to the man's needs which were permanent to him, the Laws were meant for the society which changed continually. In this way, Religion took into consideration the whole of human life and guided it accordingly.

It the above understanding of the nature of relationship between self and society is correct, we may see that the apparent opposition between the alienation—and anomie—concepts of which we talked in the early pages of this essay gets resolved and along with it is broken the impasse which a social analyst was said to confront while disentangling the question that whether it is the conformism or dissent that constitutes alienation.

According to our theory, alienation and anomie are the two sides of the same coin. Alienation is self's inability to relate itself meaningfully to society and anomie is society's inability to relate itself meaningfully to self. But if society is nothing but the extension and expression of self, then it comes out to be the same thing. A society comprising the alienated selves can never be fully *nomic* while an anomic society can never produce completely de-alienated selves. Putting succinctly, we may say that anomie is the alienation of the society and alienation is anomie of self.

The point is that it all depends upon *how* a person reacts to his society. If he reacts *religiously* i.e. if he intellectually—emotionally-volitionally commits himself to God, then he would be considered de-alienated whether or not his actions conform to the prevalent social system. A society will be anomic when it is not regulated by the Divine Laws and in such a society one would be needed to rise above it by dissenting and defying its value-system. But if a society is nomic in being modelled upon the prophetic teachings, one must need conform to it in order to live a de-alienated life. Any dissent, any defiance will in this case be tantamount to being alienated.

The dissent or defiance however does not mean complete lawlessness; in fact no individual can afford to be a total conformist. But then no society can afford to be fully anomic either. Every social structure has its integrating as well as disintegrating factors. It is only when the latter come to dominate the former, we say that the society in question is anomic. A religious person is supposed to negate and re-form only those parts of system which are the chief factors of anomie. To the rest he may fairly give his assent. Negation or dissent, it should be emphasized, must go together with reform. A de-alienated person must constantly strive to change and replace the disintegrating factors by the integrating ones so that the whole society may become nomic. For example, if the political or economic institutions of a society are not modelled upon Divine Laws, one must try to change them properly.

This is what prophets really did in their respective societies. Moses participated in the normal economic activities of the then Egyptian society but questioned the authority of Pharoah who had exalted himself to the status of God, perverting thereby the whole populace of his society, which praised and prostrated before him as if he was really a God. There was obviously an alienating phenomenon and Moses was asked to stand against it even at the risk of his life.

Similarly Jesus did not generally criticise the Roman governors whose interference in the community life of Jaws was nominal and which made them not an important alienating or anomic factor of the society. The chief alienating factor was there where the priests were terribly vain, arrogant, hypocrite and money minded. Jesus criticised them tooth and nail and at the risk of his life.

Since in our own society it is the political and economic institutions which are chief factors of alienation, they are most in the need of reform and reconstruction. And in the conditions and requirements of our times, the best way to do this to work organisedly. One must relate himself to some organisation or party which aims at the reconstruction of the society on religious lines.

Our stress upon the essentially social character of our personality should, however, not blind us to the fact that there are moments is man's life when, although not asocial, he is not directly interacting with the social environment around him. These are the moments when he is secluded, when he is less in touch with others and more in touch with himself. On such occasions, he is afforded with the opportunity to make a dialogue with his Creator, to come in a more simple and intimate relationship with Him. Man praises God's glory and grandure, thanks Him for what He was vouchsafed to him through His grace and favour and asks more as His is the ultimate giver. He repents before HIm for his sins and seeks mercy for He alone is truly forgiver and merciful.

Prophetic way of relating one's self to god is both simple and institutionalised. Man can "talk" to God while he walking or eating or simply lying on the bed. But there has also been prescribed some definite modes which a believer is expected to observe regularly with sincerity of heart and mind. These are prayers (*Salat*)—some obligatory, some non-obligatory and some semi-obligatory.

Prayers are for man the simplest and surest means to attain the nearness of God which also, in other words, is the state of his self-dealienation. There is a Prophetic tradition which holds that prayer is the *Me'raj* (ascension) of the believer. Now apart from the historical significance of this phenomenal event, what is essential to it is the fact that through it the Prophet came close to God and talked to Him. Thus if prayer is the *Me'raj* of believers, it is because through it they obtain the company of God; they come close to God.

Although prayers are meant essentially to bring man face to face with his Creator, they are also important means of saving him from the alienating influence of the external environment around him. A man in action is a man pre-occupied with something—with other men or/and some natural objects. This preoccupation has an inherent tendency to become alienated unless it is illuminated with divine light. In other words, man's interactions with other man or objects and the satisfaction-giving purpose which is sought through the interaction tend to become ultimatised if he is not living in constant remembrance of God.

Prayers serve as an effective check against the danger of self's getting lost into the world, which amounts to its alienation from itself. World either can rule over man or be ruled over by him. The former possibility amounts to slavery and alienation while the latter to transcendence and dealienation. Man can enslave world only by being enslaved by the Being which is his root and the nature of which he shares with his own nature.

The fact of prayers being a delineating factor against the alienating universe justifies their regularisation and institutionalisation although this involves the risk of their being monotonised and routinised. It is man's determination to keep himself ready at the appropriate time for prayer that makes him conscious of his commitment to God. An irregular and uninstitutionalised mode of prayer can never bring the desired effect.

Besides, prayers observed only in solitude can hardly serve any useful purpose. Existentially speaking, man needs the company of God less when he is in a lonely and secluded place and more when he is, for example, "politicking". In moments of man's intense preoccupation with his daily mundane affairs, the caller calls;

> God is Great, God is Great,
> I witness there is no God but He,
> (and) I witness Muhammad is God's messenger,
> Rush for prayer, rush for prayer,
> Rush towards success, rush towards success,
> God is Great, God is Great,
> There is no God but He.

The Call makes a shaking effect upon man's attitude towards the object with which he is preoccupied, 'It' being concrete and tangible is powerful enough to overwhelm man and consequently subjugate him, even though he, in some remote corners of consciousness, "thinks" he believes in God. But the call strikes man at the very moment when he is most vulnerable; it comes to the rescue of the self at the point when it is most exposed to be overpowered by "non-self". The call that Allah is great reminds him of the existential truth that neither man nor his objects and the petty satisfaction that he is extracting from them is absolute. They are all abject and humble things and it is only God Who is really great and Who is the object really worth being pursued after.

Man is asked to rush for prayers leaving aside all his involvements and indulgences, because therein lies his success, his dealienation. He is asked to sever his relationship with the world of 'It', where he is a stranger and come back to the house of Gods which is his own real home. Man comes face to face with God by standing before Him and expresses him humbleness and humility by bowing and prostrating before Him. Through all these gestures he re-unites himself with the self and with the God; he makes himself dealienated.

Whether one is in mosque or in market-place, one has to keep oneself close to the model life of the Prophet, which is, both in his person and preachings, a paradigm of a dealienated being. A prophet is what Tillich would call a "New Being" as he lives in perfect harmony with God and his self and in whose life the existential actualities are genuine and authentic depression of his essential potentialities. Man's dealienation, his turning his existence into New Being is ensured by his following the footsteps of the Prophet. The more one observes he obeys the commands of the Prophet, the more he is dealienated.

To conclude, it may be remarked that the principle of freedom in each individual soul is quite sufficient to enable it to overcome its alienated state. There is not at all the need of God's making a descent into human body and then sacrifice Himself upon the Cross to remove the obstacle in the transition from essence to existence, to create the New Being in whose "participation" lies man's salvation as Tillich has said. Nor is necessary the Grace which as Tillich says, 'does what freedom under the condition of existence can not do, namely, it reunites the estranged". Grace has its value only in being a succour to freedom and cannot be taken to be the sole antidote for alienation. Grace can help only so long as man is potentially free; only if the transition from essence to existence is *theoretically possible*. If man is universally *conditioned* to be estranged, it would be a contradiction to say that he can ever be saved from estrangement.

Revised and edited; originally published in Islam and the Modern Age, Feb., 1980.

2

Shuhud Vs Wujud: A Study of Gisudiraz

S. S. KHUSRO HUSSAINI

Shuhud-unity of witnessing, and Wujud=unity of being, are two different philosophical doctrines in Muslim Philosophy which have generated much debate on proving or disproving one against the other. Gisudiraz, the Sufi of Deccan, is viewed in the light of the ensuing debate on the two doctrines.

Wahdat al-wujud is the mystical doctrine expressed by Ibn al-`Arabi (b. 560/1165 in Murcia, and d. 638/1240 in Damascus). His mystical theories not only came to be supported by a large following, but also became a target of severe criticism from the orthodoxy (*`ulama'-i zahir*), for whom the expounder of such theories was an heretic and an apostate. Surprisingly, his theories were criticised by some Sufi circles also. 'Ala' al-Dawlah al-Simnani (d. 736/1336) of Iran, Sayyid Muhammad al-Husayni-i Gisudiraz (b. 721/1321 in Delhi, and d. 825/1422 in Gulbarga), Shaykh Ahmad Sirhindi (d. 1034/1624) both of India *et al.* were, for instance, critical of Ibn 'Arabi. Professor Hermann Landolt rightly questions the attitude of Simnani, for instance:

> But what shall we say if such opposition to and condemnation of Ibn 'Arabi comes from the side of someone who was himself, as everybody agreed, a great mystic? Does it not mean that while criticizing Ibn 'Arabi's *wahdat al-wujud* or "unity of being," Simnani was in fact attacking the very basis of his own mystic endeavours, for, we may ask, whether it is possible to conceive of any mysticism at all without assuming the perception or realization of some kind

> of unity in Being, including what theologian call Creator and creature or God and world? Or does it perhaps mean that Simnani had an alter native solution to offer to the problem of mystical Union?

The above questions posed by the Professor regarding Simnani, who lived in Iran approximately 85 years before Gisudiraz, are quoted here because of their relevance to this paper and Gisudiraz himself. It is the contention of this paper of show that Gisudiraz offered an alternative solution to the problem of *wahdat al-wujud*, and that he belonged to the same mystical tradition as that of Simnani, a tradition often labelled as *wahdat al-shuhud.*

Both the Sufis had been very harsh on Ibn 'Arabi. Gisudiraz writes,

> if he (Ibn 'Arabi) were alive during my times, I would have made him conscious of "beyond-the-beyond" by taking him up (into the spiritual realm), and would have revived his belief (*imam*) and converted him into a Muslim.

On reading Ibn 'Arabi's praise of the Divine Being in *al-Futuhat al-Makkiyah*, "Praise be to the One who made things appear and who at the same time in the things" (*subhana man azhara al-ashya wa Huwa 'aynuha*), Simnani seems to have reacted bitterly,

> O Shaykh! If you heard someone saying that the excrement of the Shaykh is identical with the existence of the Shaykh, you certainly would not accept this from him; no, you would be angry... Return to God by sincere repentance, so that you may get out of this dangerous intricacy, for which even the materialists, the naturalists, the Greeks (i.e., the 'Philosophers') and the Buddhists have only disdain! Peace upon those who follow the Right Guidance.

The two Sufis in fact criticized the same point; a point so central to Ibn 'Arabi's doctrine, upon which the whole theory of "unity of being" is built. Let me briefly analyse the salient features of the world-view of Ibn 'Arabi, before I talk of Gisudiraz.

Ibn 'Arabi and the Three Metaphysical Categories

Ibn 'Arabi distinguishes three types of ontological categories':

(1) The Absolute Being (*al-Wujud al-Mutlaq*) which he identifies in his treatise, *Kitab Insha' al-Dawa'ir,* as God or Allah the Creator. God qua Absolute Being, he describes as that which exists through itself and through which everything else exists. It has no equal. According to 'Abd al-Razzaq al-Kashani (d. 736/1335), the identification of God as the Absolute Being is the essential point of Ibn 'Arabi's doctrine. Simnani criticized this identification, and Gisudiraz also aimed his refutation at the same idea.

(2) The second category is that which stands opposite to the first. In other words, this is the "limited being" (*al-wujud al-muqayyad*). It is "limited" because it cannot exist by itself, but necessarily needs the Absolute to exist through. Ibn `Arabi identifies it as the material world and all that it contains.

(3) The third metaphysical category is the most important one. According to Ibn 'Arabi, it is joined to both, the first, i.e., the Absolute, and the second, i.e., the world. In short, it is both God and the world, and, at the same time, it is neither God nor the world. It is described as being existence and non-existence. It contains in itself the first and the second categories. Among the many terms used to describe it are, "breath of the compassionate" (*nafas al-Rahman*), "reality of all realities" (*haqiqat al-haqa'iq*), "permanent archetypes" (*al-a'yan al-thabitah*), "perfect man" (*al-insan al-kamil*), "reality of being Muhammad" (*al-haqiqat al-Muhammadiyah*) and others. The main idea behind this entity is that everything that belongs to the world takes its form first in it, before becoming concrete things. It is, therefore, a link between God qua Absolute and the "limited being."

Relationship Between the First and the Third Categories: Manifestation (Tajalli)

The relationship, however, of the first category "Absolute

Being" with the third category "reality of realities" is more interesting because of the mystical nature of the latter. It is, no doubt, given a status somewhat similar to the first metaphysical category; that is to say, it is, in the words of Professor Landolt, "in some sense 'absolute.'" Ibn 'Arabi himself does not elucidate this relationship clearly.

Nevertheless, it can be said that the idea of manifestation (*tajalli*) plays a signal role in this regard. This manifestation is based upon the famous divine tradition so popular among the Sufis: the Prophet David asked God as to why He created the creation, and God replied, "I was a hidden treasure. I loved that I be known. So I created to be known." Thus, Ibn 'Arabi divides divine manifestation basically into two types:

(a) *tajalli-i shuhudi* or the visible manifestation which signifies the world, and that which a mystic experiences;

(b) *tajalli-i ghaybe* or the hidden manifestation, also called *tajalli-i dhati* or the essential manifestation, which takes place in the unseen. It is implied that the essential or hidden manifestation is that which takes place in the form of the third category "reality of realities," while the visible manifestation is in the appearance of concrete entities in the present world.

These two levels of manifestation, however, are one in reality. This is so because for Ibn 'Arabi,

> theophany in visible forms is essential or hidden theophany; for the divine Essence, just because it is essentially hidden and absolute, has no other means to show itself than in the very form of the one of whom it shows itself (*al-mutajalla lahu*). In other words: because the divine Essence has no form in its absolute oneness (*ahadiyah*) and therefore can never appear as such, its form is identical with the forms of the things.

In short, Ibn 'Arabi says in his *Fusus al-Hikam* that the Truth (*al-Haqq*) is in reality limited by all limits, for "to isolate the Absolute from the limited means precisely to limit the Absolute."

This naturally brings before us a new aspect of the Absolute, which is basically different from the first category God quo Absolute Being "unlimited." Thus, the transcendence of God safeguarded in the first instance becomes ambiguous. These two contradictory aspects of the Absolute tended to confuse the issue. It was, presumably, one of the reasons for Simnani's and Gisudiraz's criticism of the identification of God as Absloute Being.

Application of the 3 Aspects of Quiddity (Mahiyah) to Existence

The commentators Sadr al-Din Qunawi (d. 672/1273) and al-Kashani philosophized the two-fold concept of the Absolute. In trying to clarify this duality, they applied the three Avicennian (Ibn Sina, d. 429/1037) aspects (*i'tibarat*) or quiddity (*mahiyah*) to the notion of existence (*wujud*).

These 3 aspects are:

(a) *la bi-shart shay* (absolutely unconditioned), i.e. if a concept is considered as having the possibility of being predicated of any particular species, or as being undetermined.

This aspect comprises of the other two:

(b) *bi-shart la* (negatively conditioned), i.e. if a concept is considered as being impossible to be mixed with anything else or being exclusively itself; and

(c) *bi-shart shay'* (positively conditioned), i.e., if a concept is considered as being determined by mixture with one particular other quiddity.

Thus, we see that Ibn 'Arabi's first category corresponds to negatively conditioned, the second to positively conditioned, and the third category to absolutely unconditioned aspects.

The commentators, however, identified pure existence with the aspect of *la bi-shart shay'* or absolutely unconditioned. Thus, existence itself from the above point of consideration became the third category of Ibn 'Arabi. Besides, Kashani seems to have also identified divine Essence as pure existence; with in turn being absolutely unconditioned became the

> origin (*mansha'*) of both the "negatively conditioned" or "exclusive" aspect of divine Unity (*ahadiyah* as meaning *bi-shart la*) and the "positively conditioned" or "inclusive" aspect of divine Unity (*Wahidiyah* as meaning *bi-shart shay'*), that it to say of both the "exclusive" Unity of the divine Essence considered in its stage "before creation," as it were (*kana Allah wa lam yakun ma'ahu shay'*) and of the "inclusive" Unity of the Essence considered together with its names or "after" creation, as it were.

Another problem was, perhaps unintentionally, created due to the application of these considerations. As the aspect *la bi-shart shay'* of the quiddity was generally related to Ibn Sina's natural universal (*kulli tabi'i*), the transcendence of God could not be saved, because the natural universal exists in reality as a part of its every particular which exists, and a part of what exists has existence, for example, the animality of "animal" is a part of every animal that exists. This is the reason why Gisudiraz, particularly, emphasizes in his criticism that besides identifying God with Absolute Being, Ibn 'Arabi and his followers have turned Him into a "natural universal." He writes,

> Muhyi al-Din Ibn 'Arabi and his followers say that beyond this existence (*wujud*) there is not other existence, on which account they have called Him "Absolute" (*Mutlaq*) and "limited" (*muqayyad*), and have made God into something similar to natural universal (*kulli tabi'i*).

With all this in mind, let us analyse the world-view of Gisudiraz.

The World-View of Gisudiraz

The World-view of Gisudiraz is also based on theophany (*tajalli*), as that of Simnani and Ibn 'Arabi. The divine tradition—

I was a hidden treasure. I loved that I be known. So I created to be known—which we have quoted earlier, contains the reason for God's self-manifestation. This theophany of God is presented from two points of view: the first kind of manifestation is through the process of creation, while the second is related to the individual mystical experience.

The Cosmic Process of Creation

According to Gisudiraz, God wanted to create that individual who could fully recognize His manifestation in direct vision. God is reported to have said: "I sat for a thousand years with My head between My knees, My eyes closed, thinking and investigating for a form and a structure which could know Me and perceive Me through the manifestations and openings. I could not think of anything but the form of Man. For this reason and purpose I fermented the clay of Adam with My own two hands for forty days, (so that) he becomes a representative (*khalifah*) on My earth and a marrow in My heaven. Necessarily, that form had to comprise in itself all the manifestations or had to be comprehensive of all the categories and species of the universe so as to know Me in himself and perceive Me in his own individual being."

By introducing this Arabic quotation in the form of an otherwise unknown variant of the famous *hadith qudsi* mentioned above, Gisudiraz intends to stress a point central to the world-view. The purpose of creation is not only manifestation of God's attributes in the multiplicity of things, but also recognition of His own individuality, possible only through self-cognition of another individual being, the perfect human person (according to the anonymous commentator, the "light of Muhammad" which is man's *walayah*) summing up the totality of things. Therefore, Gisudiraz adds in Persian, "as long as the person does not perceive a thing in himself and taste it such as it is, he will not really perceive it."

The commentator of *Asmar al-Asrar* thinks that the "individual" is the "light of Muhammad" which is the beloved of the Truth. This light comprehends everything that exists and every other light is from it. It is the first and the last, the external and the internal for it is the manifestation of the Essence. The term "direct vision" is explained by the commentator of God's placing His own Eye and Essence in the eye and essence of Muhammad.

The form of man which was perceived by God as the only one which could perceive God in himself in return was given a comprehensive shape. All the attributes found in potential in God were manifested in actual through man. Thus all the entitles were composed in the framework of man. Gisudiraz insists that the implication here is more than a mere philosophical recognition that man as microcosm reflects the universe. God cannot be known through the world. Rather, for the Sufis it is the opposite. Thus they say, "travel while staying at home" and "search solitude while in community." In other words, the universe is present in the very essence of man's being. "Travel in yourself (not in the world) and everything will be witnessed by you."

The anti-philosophic and pro-religious attitude of Gisudiraz becomes clearer when he stresses the point that although man as such is the sum-total of the universe, it does not mean that any man is the sum-total. He argues that if the word "creation" in the above mentioned divine tradition means man, it can only be the perfect man, because "the man" like "the creation" (with the definite article) must be understood in the "absolute" sense (i.e. the idea of man), and "absolute" turns into "perfect". The most perfect of all perfect ones is evidently Muhammad, the seal of prophets. Therefore, Gisudiraz writes, "I created the creation" really means, "I created Muhammad the seal the Messengers."

An interesting aspect is the analysis by Gisudiraz of the imperfect form of the verb "to know" in the divine tradition—I was a hidden treasure, I loved that I be known....The form "I be known," he writes, should not only be understood in the passive but also in the active voice. The tradition then means also "I created the creation in order to know myself." He further explains what while God was "all-knowing" (*`Alim*) of the things prior to their existence. He became 'all-informed" (*Khabir*) of the things after their existence. This would mean that God's knowledge from being potentially universal before the creation became particular experiential knowledge after the creation. This is the knowledge which Gisudiraz also terms 'direct vision" in the context of mystical experience. These two aspects are explained by the commentator as God's being a gnostic in potentia is "His all-knowingness," while His becoming a gnostic in actua is 'His all-informedness." Gisudiraz himself adduces the image taken from human experience of self-perception through a mirror,

> One cannot be oneself perceive oneself. You have to create a mirror so that your reflection appears in the mirror. So look at your individuality and you will see your own beauty...God is in everything, with everything (but) everything is from Him and subsists through Him. He Himself sees Himself and plays with Himself, not that He engages in something other than Himself.

The above discussion brings us to some important questions like, when Gisudiraz writes, on the one hand, that God is in everything and with everything, then why is everything from and through Him and not Him?, and how is, then, Gisudiraz any different from Ibn 'Arabi? Let me point out to you that Gisudiraz does not mean by the above statements that God exists in everything. Commenting on a saying of Ibn Wasi' (c. 120/737), "I do not see anything but I witness God in it," He states that the above saying means that it is the emanation (*fayd*) of God in everything but not God Himself. Ibn Wasi's utterance, he writes, is the result of his experience through direct vision. God, Gisudiraz says, is transcendental while everything else exists through His emanation. The efforts of both Gisudiraz and Simnani are attempts to save the transcendence of God which, according to them, was lost by Ibn 'Arabi. This will further be clarified in the following discussion of three important technical terms.

Beyond the Beyond (Wara' al-Wara')

The term "beyond the beyond," for Gisudiraz, signifies God in His absolute remoteness. It indicates that God is beyond the comprehension of anyone be it a saint or a prophet. As mentioned above Gisudiraz criticised Ibn 'Arabi for identifying God as absolute existence. He writes that, Ibn 'Arabi pointed out God as being in all the forms and shapes because he was himself not conscious of "beyond the beyond". But this identification Ibn 'Arabi has limited God. On the contrary, Gisudiraz says that God is unidentifiable and the forms and shapes are in reality the manifestations of God's emanation not God. The Essence of God is something which does not have an end. It is an endless line of oceans to infinity. This state of "beyond the beyond" can only be described, he writes, by the saying, "he who knows God, becomes dumb." As a result it is only astonishment. This term indeed is very similar to the idea of *'ama'* or (as translated by Professor Izutsu) abysmal darkness and the concept of the "absolute absolute" which transcends all qualifications and relations that are humanly conceivable.

Emanation (Fayd)

The self-manifestation or theophany (*tajalli*) of God, for Gisudiraz, may be described as "emanation." It is the particular concept which he also calls "divine emanation" that is present with all the entities. He states that this "emanation" is eternal and therefore, he sometimes calls it the "eternal emanation." According to Gisudiraz its relationship to man is like that of a beloved to the lover. It is neither attached to man nor detached, nor is it internal or external to him. Yet it is nearer to man than his own jugular vein or his pupil. It is interesting to note that "emanation" has almost the same relationship with God. This "divine emanation," Gisudiraz states, is also addressed as God or as creator of everything. On the other hand, it is also termed saint (*wali*; a name, incidentally, of God too, in the Qur'an, "Allah is the protecting *wali* of those who believe". The application of the term "emanation" to both the terms God and Saint, the meeting place of both has been defined. Thus divine emanation as "Saint" is the sum-total of the universe taken as that perfect man is whom God recognises His own individuality or the place where God and man unite.

The Perfect Man (Insan-i Kamil)

The term creation in the divine tradition discussed earlier

connotes to the idea of the "perfect man" which according to Gisudiraz is the first creation. The "perfect man" is absolute in the sense that the totality of existences are comprehended by him. It is implied to be the first, and the perfect manifestation of God. It signifies the divine emanation. From one aspect the "perfect man" is totally one with God. It is the manifestation of God's essence, its source being beyond the beyond. This concept is very similar to the "perfect man" that Ibn `Arabi describes for us. He writes that it synthesizes in itself all the existents of the universe and is in a way the absolute itself.

The cosmic process of creation, for Gisudiraz, as it was for Simnani too, centres around the notion of God's act (*fi'l*), rather than the notion of existence of Ibn 'Arabi.

There are five levels on which theophany takes place in the creative process: veiled essence (*dhat*), veiling essence (*dhat*), attributes (*sifat*), acts (*af'al*), and effects (*maf'ulat*). These levels are essentially the same as those of Simnani for whom there are four: essence, attributes, acts, and effects. For Gisudiraz, the level of essence, under the present context, has two aspects: that which is veiled, and, at a lower level, that which veils the former. These aspects have been attributed to the essence for the reason that Gisudiraz has 5 corresponding mystical stages on the Sufi journey; so reminiscent of Najm al-Din al-Razi (d. 654/1256) in his *Mirsad al-'Ibad.* Besides, the "veiled" essence signifies his concept of the beyond the beyond (*wara' al-wara'*): that is to say the transcendental God who is accessible to nobody.

The image which Gisudiraz often quotes to show the significance of the 5 levels of divine self-manifestation is that of an ocean. The restlessness of an ocean is called waves (*mawj*), what rises up from an ocean is called vapours (*bukhar*), when these vapours are condensed in the atmosphere, they are called clouds (*sahab*), when the clouds trickle down they become rain, when the rain flows, it is called stream, and when the stream merges into the ocean it turns into the ocean itself. In fact, he says, "rain is from the ocean and the ocean is from the rain."

This is immediately comparable to the favourite image of Simnani, regarding the act of writing. He gives the example of an individual being (*shakhsuk al-wahid*) corresponding to the level of essence; his quality of writerness (*katibiyah*) corresponds to attributes; his act of writingness (*kitabah*) corresponds to the level of acts;. and the outcome i.e., his letter (*makitub*), corresponds to the level of effects.

By using these images, both of Sufis want to emphasize that even though each level is distinguished from the other, there remains some sort of identity between them, which point Simnani seems to admit frankly, while Gisudiraz clearly implies, when he says that the rain is from the ocean and the ocean from the rain. They also intend to point out that each level precedes the other. In short, the direct cause of effect is the act which precedes it; for example, the direct cause of a flowing stream is the rain, and not the ocean (while in the case of Simnani, the cause of the letter is the act of writing, not the writer). Gisudiraz at the same time wants to clarify that these are various manifestations which are not to be confused with its subject, that is God. They may also denote, as suggested by his commentator, various attributes, multiple names and innumerable acts of God.

For Gisudiraz, there are 5 distinct stages experienced by a Sufi on his spiritual journey. In the ascending order, they are, Law (*shari'at*), Path (*tariqat*), Reality (*haqiqat*), Truth of Reality (*haqq al-haqiqat*), and Reality of Truth (*haqiqat al-Haqq*). Law is explained as the saying of the perfect man, path as the action of the perfect man, Reality as the sight of the perfect man, Truth of Reality as the being of the perfect man, and Reality of Truth as the being of non-being of the perfect man.

Two levels of theophany are distinguished on the two highest stages. Theophany of the attributes and names corresponds to the 4th stage Truth of Reality. On this state, all the attributes and names of God are manifested to the Sufi traveller. By virtue of this manifestation of divine emanation, all the 99 names of God becomes the attribute of the one who experiences it. Gisudiraz's son S. Akbar Husayni, who is commenting on his father's work, writes that the traveller, then, is described by the attribute of "reality of being Muhammad" (*haqiqat-i Muhammadiyat*), a term obviously borrowed from Ibn 'Arabi. The sufi repeats whatever this attribute says, after which the gives in to ecstatic utterances, for the sees himself as God. Both Gisudiraz and his son associate this stage and its theophany to the intoxicated Sufis like Mansur al-Hallaj (d. 309/922), Abu Yazid al-Bastami (d. 261/874) and others. The utterances on this stage, therefore, are said to be, "I am the Truth" and "glory be to me" etc. The implications are that Ibn `Arabi also belonged to this stage.

The second level of theophany is that to the essence itself (*tajalli-i dhat*). It is manifested to the traveller on the 5th and the final stage, Reality of Truth; that is, if he manages to reach this stage, because Gisudiraz feels that the traveller definitely needs a preceptor (*pir*) to guide him on the previous stage where the Sufis usually tend to get lost. The utterances, however, on this final stage are, "He is the Truth" and "Glory be to Allah".

Gisudiraz writes that the significance of this stage is that the Sufi traveller "realizes" that God is really beyond the beyond. "It is like looking for pulp (*maghz*) in an onion," he writes, in an endeavour to save the transcendence of Allah. Here he defines the word *wujud* as consciousness.

Conclusion

In the concluding remarks, let me point out to you that the term *wahdat al-wujud*, which has today been permanently associated with the name Ibn 'Arabi, is not known to have occurred in the Shaykh al-Akbar's own works. As already referred to, the basic idea behind Ibn 'Arabi's whole doctrinal system in his identification of God with absolute Being (*al-Wujud al-Mutlaq*). Kashani further says that either one accepts this identity or he does not, because there is no intermediary solution. This is exactly the idea which the refutations of both Gisudiraz and Simnani are aimed at. The identity had left little or no distinction whatsoever between the Creator and His creation. The Creator-creature bond was depicted as being so strong that it was tantamount to saying that neither can exist without the other.

In a situation like this the Islamic orthodoxy could only pass verdicts of blasphemy or heresy, as the famous Hanbali theologian Ibn Thymiyah (d. 724/1323) did. But a problem created by a sufi could be aptly solved or explained only by another Sufi, because he alone can 'in reality' understand and perceive its nature. This is exactly what Simnani and Gisudiraz did. By re-examining the problem in the light of their own spiritual experiences, they tried to re-establish or save the transcendence of Allah. This does not mean, however, that their system lacked in the realization of any kind of Unity in Being. As a matter of fact, Ibn 'Arabi's spiritual experience has been described by Gisudiraz as pertaining to that stage which is peculiar to the ecstatic Sufis, as already observed. Regarding Simnani Prof. Landolt writes,

> Simnani really tried to work out a different approach which was based on the notion of Act rather than on that of existence, that is to say on a dynamic entity rather than a static one...

The same is true of Gisudiraz. The probabilities of the latter Chishti Sufi's having either read or known Simnani's writings, seem to be remote, as there are no indications to it. Nevertheless, the same mystical tradition as that to Simnani, underlies the spiritual experiences of Gisudiraz; the tradition known as *wahdat al-shuhud* or literally translated as "unity of witnessing," which emphasizes "dynamic becoming," rather than "static being." In this regard, Gisudiraz is, therefore, the link between `Ala' al-Dawlah al-Simnani and Shaykh Ahmad Sirhindi.

REFERENCES

1. Herman Landolt, "Simnani on Wahdat al-Wujud," Collected papers on Islamic philosophy and mysticism, ed. by M. Mohaghegh and H. Landolt, Tehran, 1971.
2. H Corbin, Creative imagination in the Sufism of Ibn 'Arabi. French Trans.by R Manheim, Princeton, 1969.

3. A A Afifi, The mystical philosophy of Muhiyuddin Ibnul Arabi, Cambridge, 1936.
4. S A Q Hussaini, The pantheistic monism of Ibn al-Arabi, Lahore, 1970.
5. F. Meier, "Ala al-Dawlah al-Simanai," Ency. of Islam, n ed., vol. I, Leiden, 1960, pp. 346-47.
6. M Mole, "Les kubrawiyya entre sunnisme et shiisme," Revue des Etudes Islamiques, XXIX (1961) 61-142.
7. S S K Hussaini, Sayyid Muhammad al-Husayni-i Gisudiraz, 721/1321-825/1422: On Sufism, Delhi, 1983.
8. Gisudiraz, Khatimah, ed. S A Husayn, Hyderabad, AH. 1356, pp. 18-19.
9. Ibn Arabi, Fusus al-Hikam, ed. AA Afifi, Cairo, 1946.
10. Gisudiraz, Asmar al-asrar, ed. S A Husayn, Hyderabad, AH.1350.

Revised and edited; originally published in Islamic Culture, Oct. 1985.

3

The Concept of Tauhid

ABDUL JALIL MIA

Describes its connotative and denotative implications in social context.

Since the dawn of intellectual development people have been aspiring after the discovery of a single Reality or Principle or Ideal to explain events and phenomena and life and the universe in a satisfactory way. Right from Thales in the sixth century B.C. down to present age philosophers, by the large, of the world sought refuge in a single Principle or Ideal with a view to explaining things in a logical way. Different philosophers have, however, ascribed different names to this Ideal or Reality. Plato's Idea of Good differs little from that of Hegel's Absolute in their quiddity. The same can be said of 'The Unknowable' of Spencer and the unknown 'Thing-in-Itself' of Kant, the great German advocate of critical philosophy.

It may, however, be added that although in his *Critique of Pure Reason* Kant failed to decipher the nature of the Thing-in-Itself, in his *Critique of Practical Reason* he appears to have substituted it by God to explain moral and other higher values of life; and Spencer also has almost always been looked upon as a worshipper of the Unknowable which he later categorised as the 'mysterious absolute'.

The scientist who is apparently opposed to a philosophy of unity also maintains that the more the events and phenomena can explain a theory or principle the more acceptable it is. Newton's Law of Gravitation has a universal appeal because it explains not only the falling of the apples on the ground but also because it can interpret the relative movement of all material bodies in the heavens and the earth. In the present age of rockets and spaceships the thoughtful scientist speaks of a Supreme Intelligence that lies behind all material bodies and their constituent electrons, ions and other elements. In other words, beyond the atomic world the scientist now senses the presence of one Fundamental Reality which alone can answer unanswered questions of science.

Science is ordinarily understood to be atheistic and a great majority of scientists believe in what is called scientific atheism. However, some scientists like Sir James Jeans and J.S. Haldane initiated a liberal movement in the contemporary scientific world and a good number of scientists today believe in a Universal Spirit. Some of them regard it as a unity behind plurality of the world of atoms and even categorise it, after the Genesis, as God.

Among the spiritual leaders of mankind, who are often enough called prophets as well, we notice a similar tendency. They all call the people to one Ideal. The principal motto of their life has been to proclaim the reality of one and only one Ideal, the Divine. Abraham, Moses, Zoroaster, Jesus, Krishna and Muhammad all called their people to one God and explained every thing with the help of one Universal Ideal. In all sober quarters we thus find an inner tendency to explain all life and Universe in terms of one Ideal or Reality.

The monistic philosophers, no doubt, speak of one reality or the absolute but their absolute is more or less a subtle reality, while speaking of the Idea of Good, Plato takes us to a world quite different from the one we experience and live in. Hegel's Absolute which resolves all theses and anti-theses into syntheses and finally becomes the highest synthesis appears to rank in status with Plato's Idea of Good. Both Plato and Hegel propound such ontological doctrines in which reality is made something abstract. Plato's Idea of Good and Hegel's Absolute are hard metaphysical entities and very few can comprehend them. Not only Plato and Hegel but also other great Philosophers like Aristotle, Kant and Spinoza place before us equally abstract realites like the 'Pure From', the 'Thing-in-Itself' and the 'Substance'. The mortal soul had therefore to choose and select a different path to search out and meet a perfect being capable of explaining things and events in a more satisfactory way. And in a journey different from that of the abstract logical thinker truth was revealed to the minds of many of Moses, Abraham, Zoroaster, Jesus, Muhammad and other brought for their followers better explanations of life and universe.

Man's full awakening to the recognition of a Supreme Power and the troubles through which individuals and races passed before they reached the idea of a Universal Ideal or Reality which regulates, guides and pervades all existence provide matters of great significance. The way through which men made spiritual progress and the track they followed to say good-bye to their idol-gods for the adoration of one Divine God have often been blocked. Now and then many of them broke away from the stream of progress and listened to the whispering of their senses and desires. Masses of mankind fell victims to the craving of their mind and turned back to worship idols, the symbols of their passions. On the hand, the messengers of truth had sounded call to the Divine and always taught men their duties to God and other human beings.

Truth wins the goal and although it takes time to reach the heart of man, the divine penetrated into the soul of the human being sooner or later. And this is why the divine flames kindled by Moses, Abraham, Zoroaster, Jesus and those preceding them had found ways to the heart of man.

Faith which Abraham, Moses, Zoroaster and Jesus preached and acted upon underwent terrible changes in subsequent period of history. The cults of duality, trinity and plurality came into existence and their votaries dividend into contending groups only to add to human sufferings. Man's notions of God and morality debased to such extents that even in the 'House of God' they erected images of tribal, local, regional, and of many other types of gods and goddesses whom they worshipped mainly to create group rivalries and exploit others. Pressed under distorted faiths the children of Adam cried out for deliverance from the misdeeds and cruelty of such faiths and religions. It was in these circumstances that a desert born son of the earth appeared before man with the message of deliverance.

The circumstances in which prophet Muhammad appeared with the message of deliverance have few parallels in man's moral and religious history. Dissatisfied with the prevailing terrifying idolatry which departed greatly from truth and which largely encouraged exploitation and moral debasement, Muhammad absorbed himself in meditation in the cave of Hira for light and guidance, and on sacred night truth was revealed to him. The last Divine Book, *al-Qur'an,* was revealed as the seal of the prophets for calling and guiding man to One God and universal love and brotherhood so as to end all exploitation and torture in the name of religion. The fundamental principle in which his faith is grounded is: There is no deity but Allah.

Muhammad's notion of unqualified unity or Oneness of God was subsequently taken up by Muslim theologians and metaphysicians among whom the Mu'tazilites occupy a unique place. In order to uphold God's unity some Mu'tazilites propounded an extreme view of divine unity and to safeguard that unity they stripped God off all attributes. For, according to them, attribution of a quality to God leads to plurality of reality and as such it weakens divine unity.

The Grand Apostle of *tauhid* or unity of God, Muhammad ibn Abdallah, played a very prominent role in history to fight a great was against the retrogressive disposition of man whose tendency had been to associate partners with the Lord of the universe. With unparallel boldness Muhammad proclaimed the oneness of Allah and discarded every sort of polytheism and sterilised all its germs in the *shahada*: No God but Allah. His historic call was to heal the cavities and to remove the accompanying ills which the germs of polytheism had made in the popular distorted religions.

Truth is eternal. The message brought by the seal of the prophets was not something new. It was delivered before

Muhammad and made perfect with him. The *Qur'an* clearly declared: "This day I have perfected your religion for you, complete my favour upon you, and have chosen for you Islam as a religion.

About the eternal character of religion and prophethood a very unique expression is found in the famous *Gulshan-i raz* of the Persian *sufi* poet Mahmud Shabistari. The poet wrote:

Prophethood began with Adam
And reached its perfection in the Seal of the prophets.

The light and truth which was brought by and revealed to the prophet of Islam was meant to quicken the dead into life and to make the pulse of the humanity beat with unprecedented force. Imbuted with the philosophy of *tauhid* the Arabs built up in a short span of time an empire greater than that of the Romans which they took centuries to accomplish. History is a living evidence of how the waves of this new faith rolled onward fertilising every soil it passed over and assimilating on its way all that it considered good.

We have already mentioned that truth was not confined to a particular age or nation or country. History of the religious philosophy of man discloses that in different ages different prophets came to different peoples with the message of truth and unity of God. Like Islam, Christianity and Judaism and Hinduism as well proclaimed in their purity the same divine unity. The God of Christianity, the Jehova of Judaism and the Vedantic Brahma in Hinduism all stand for the unity of the divine reality. But this unity of divinity was later distorted at the hands of some interested people. And curiously enough, in the name of religion and God tribes and races turned hostile against one another and disfigured the very face of the earth. It was therefore the need of time and history that a great universal teacher came to the distracted humanity, to teach about one God, one creator and about universal love and brotherhood. So came Muhammad with the message that there is no deity but Allah, all men are equal before Allah, and that all men are brethren to one another. This was his great mission and by profession and practice he spared no efforts to fulfil it.

An insight into the philosophy of *tauhid* provides man with that universal Principle or Ideal which he desired long for a satisfactory explanation of life and universe. A question may arise here: Why should there be only one Principle or Reality in the universe? To this question we would like to answer that two equal ultimate beings cannot exist side by side. For if they do so, they must either be similar or dissimilar in nature. This existence of two similar beings alike in all respects does not make satisfactory explanation because they speak of the same reality in their quiddity. On the other hand, two dissimilar principles or beings cannot claim independence and perfection. For either must be then lacking something only to become dependent on the other. And as such they cannot be regarded as ultimate beings.

Besides the above mentioned logical arguments in favour of the unity of divine truth we may also speak of two other arguments, psychological and historical. The psychological one springs out from the very nature of the human mind which feels inclined to be satisfied with only one ultimate principle in its quest for an adequate explanation of the creation. In other words, human mind proceeds from particular facts of experience to the general laws of thought and then to a universal principle of inner experience, that is, man's mind passes from the psychological and scientific stage to the philosophical stage which in turn finds its fullest development in man's religious consciousness. From the historical points of view it is found that all great seers of truth speak of only one ultimate being or God. Thus Abraham, Moses, Christ, Krishna and Muhammad brought message of one God. Again, great philosophers like Plate, Aristotle, Kant, Hegel, Spinoza, al-Farabi, Rumi and many others expounded the theory of one ultimate being.

Divine unity stands for complete oneness of the divine being. It implies that God is fundamentally one and that all plurality is alien to His essence. One may, however, speak of His plurality by way of divine attributes. The varieties in the creation usually calls for such a nature of the ultimate being from which all things and beings derive their existence. Yet God is one and only one in essence. For the attributes of the divine are not outside of his essence.

God the Creator is one and from His unity follow as necessary consequences the unity of creation, the unity of man, and the unity of life and universe. God is the sole Master and Lord of the universe. All human being irrespective of caste, creed and colour are but creations of one God, the Lord of the universe. Thus all human beings belongs to a universal brotherhood. Finally, life is a unity and it admits of no fast and hard dichotomy of the material and the spiritual. A negligence of either baffles the goal, an imbalance between the two mars every attempt for success. And that is why after a long time of torture of the body the greatly emaciated Buddha had to satisfy the normal needs of his flesh in order to achieve the goal of his spirit.

A close study of religions discloses that all great prophets taught about unity, love and universal brotherhood. They taught us about the unity of truth, life, world and creation. The messengers of God preached love and brotherhood instead of hatred and rivalry. They also warned man not to involve in mad race for the acquisition of material riches at the cost of moral and spiritual values. Further, they advised all human beings to develop in them the qualities of simplicity, humility, love, sympathy, and spirituality for the realisation of the goal; the fusion of the human with the divine.

Unity and love, and not division and hostility can assure the establishment of a better society, a happier world. The basic principle of life and society is unity for greater happiness of all mankind and this is the underlying philosophy that has given birth to the international organisations like the United Nations Organisation. The UNO appears to be influenced by the impact of the philosophy of unity and as such it stands for peace, cooperation and co-existence of the member states. Following its ideals other regional and inter-regional organisations have also been established in the present world. All these imply that the philosophy of unity has great impact on man's life and world.

Revised and edited; originally published in Studies in Islam, April 1979.

4

Unity of God in Islam

WAHEEDUDDIN KHAN

It is necessary for the study of Unity of God in Islam to find out the relation between the creation and the creator. In absence of this quest the study will not only be incomplete but also may lead the study to an undesirable direction.

There is one Creator of the world who governs it according to His own laws and designs. Just as the creation is moving in obedience to the will of its Creator the right course for man is to live in accordance with the commands of His Creator. All the prophets and the creation as such teach this lesson.

The *Qur'an* spells out the doubt about the existence of God by posing a question: who separated the earth and the heavens which were once inseparable in (14:10 and 21:30). It is supposed that the radius of the universe is at least ten thousand million light years. The astronomical studies tell us that the universe does not stand on an axle but is spread out all around in the vast space. It means that in the remote past according to astronomers the universe was in one form of a super-atom whose different parts, were united with immense power by the principle of interaction. It is believed that about fifteen billion years ago there was an explosion or a kind of energy release in this primary matter from which different parts of the cosmos were separated in order to make this world possible. Contrary to the nature of atoms their energy began to flow out which makes us believe that there is an independent absolute power which causes this energy release in the expanded form.

> If there had been more than one God there world have been a great confusion, 14:22

This indicated that there is only one God. All the sciences agree on the point that the whole universe is moving under one law. It is because of this uniformity of cosmic law that man began to explore the moon and the mars with the help of space ships. The principle of uniformity of nature, which has its scientific basis, is an evidence for the unity of God.

Practical Importance of Tauhid

The concept of the unity of God in Islam is not an abstract idea. It has intimate relationship with the practical life of man. The character of man should accord with his belief in God; he is responsible to his Creator for his deeds, good and bad, and the reward and punishment there of. Similarly, the belief in the afterlife is the part of parcel of the belief in *tauhid* or unity of God. The present world is the manifestation of unknown reality, while the afterlife is the manifestation of God in direct experience. In the present world *tauhid* is the object of thought and reflection whereas in the afterlife the belief in God will be as clear as daylight. A man who accepts the unity of God, in this life and rejects the notion of divine unity in the afterlife may be counted as a unitarian philosopher, but certainly he is not a believer in the unity of God in the Islamic sense. That God is one is not merely a numerical question but it explains the mystery of known as well as unknown world, past and future. The knowledge of unity of God entails the knowledge of all things. The realisation of this unity of God is possible only when the realisation of unity of mankind and the unit of the world become identical. The concept of the unity of reality negates multiplicity in thought. Ultimately, nothing remains except God in thought. Even Darwin accepted the reality of the Creator God, but he could not find out the relation between man and God.

It is necessary for the study of *tauhid* to find out the relation between man and God. In absence of this quest the study will not only be incomplete but may also lead the seeker after truth to an undesirable direction.

Man and Faith in God

Just as the macrocosm in under God's immediate control, the microcosm should submit to His glory and become one with the nature. This submission under divine control will solve all his problems.

Tauhid is the fountainhead of all goodness, and evil flourishes when *tauhid* does not establish in the world. Man is different from the rest of the universe in the sense that the latter is under direct control of God, while the former is endowed with the freedom of choice—man is free to choose his way, good or bad. It is this freedom of choice that is solely responsible for disorder and disharmony in the human world. On the contrary, the cosmos is in complete order and harmony. By his inclination towards evil, man has proved the doubt of the angels expressed before, God that men who will create confusion in the earth and cause bloodshed (2:30). However, the freedom which man enjoys is not complete freedom. It is limited and has been granted for a definite purpose. It is the freedom for test. (67:2). God sees how man makes the best use of his freedom. The present existence of the world is till it passes through the tests. At the end of this process the owner of this earth will take it back in His direct control and govern in just as He is governing the rest of the universe. At this time the bad coins will be separated from the good ones. i.e., the righteous will live in eternal paradise while the unrighteous will be thrown into the eternal hell-fire. This world is the place where people are selected for the afterlife.

What is the essential characteristic of a man who aims at attaining the life divine? It is not a hidden or mysterious proposition, but is obviously manifest in the spoken language of the *Qur'an* and the silent expression of the nature. To accept the unity of God for life is to accept the cosmic religion which is all around. The cosmic religion is the name for silent obedience of nature to the divine control and command whose characteristics may be summarised as follows:

Complete Submission

The first characteristic of nature is seen in the complete obedience to its Creator. The earth and the sun, stars and planets are all moving in the vast space for millions and millions of years, but there is no difference in their movement for a second. All are performing their duties well without any interruption. Man should exhibit this cosmic character in his life, i.e., he should completely submit to the Will of God and act according to His wishes.

Predictability

Nature behaves in such perfect manner that we can predict its future course. Man should also behave in a manner that one can predict reaction in his life in a given situation.

Harmony

Another quality of the nature is that its different parts combined together function in a harmonious way. The sun and the moon have no rivalry. The stars do not collide with one another. They perform their appointed duties. Man should also act in the manner that his interests should not conflict with the interest of others.

Purposiveness

The movements of the universe are always directed to a good end. If nature is not interrupted by an extraneous force its movements and happenings would always accrue good results. In the same way, the deeds of man should result in goodness and altruism.

Evolutionary Continuity

Nature does not leap into vacuum, rather its process is continuous and evolutionary. Nothing happens all of a sudden, but passes through different stages in slow and continuous way. Man should peep into this act in a planned way.

Uniformity

There is no difference between the external and internal life of the cosmos. The sun is the same in its nature and external behaviour. It shows the ray for man's behaviour; there should be uniformity in man's thought and his deeds. Nature is the true guide of human beings. Whatever is there at the cosmic level is present at the human level also, and just as the revolving stars and the vast milky ways do not conflict, human beings, should not intrude into another's affairs. The tree takes carbon and returns oxygen. The same is expected of man, that he should return good for evil. There is nothing in nature which stands in opposition to its other constituents; everything is playing its role. The process of recycling in nature may be expected in a variety of ways in human behaviour. The silence of the cosmic movement is expected in a man devoted to work and making no noise. Just as nature does not expect any reward for its work, man should act and perform his duty but he should not desire reward for his deeds. Do the trees and rivers take any price for what they give?

Everything in the world reminds us to think what is valuable and what is without value. The most valuable thing for mass is his selfless action, his duty without expectation of reward. But the man who is moved with selfish motive is condemned in the afterlife. Those who deny the truth of *tauhid* are thrown into the eternal fire of hell for which warnings were already given by all the prophets of mankind, the righteous and the believer will enter paradise where they will live forever. There is the promise of God that all those who do good works and obey God shall enter into the Garden of noble life and all those who went against God and proved mischievous will go to hell and live there forever.

(Revised and edited; orignially published in Studies in Islam, April 1979).

5

Unity in Islamic Perspective

S VAHIDUDDIN

Islam means surrender to the God; surrender to this Ultimate being is bound to create a concern for all God's creation. The acknowledgment of God's unity does not remain a passive posture in the Islamic perspective but calls for the cooperation of man in His cause and doing good is indelibly associated with a life of devotion.

Islam means surrender and surrender to the One whose unity it affirms without any compromise, "the Besought of all" and "ever lasting Refuge" (*Qur'an: Sura* 122). But He is not the one among many, he is the One beyond the dichotomy of the One and the many. He has created all that we know and that we know not and all that we know not far exceeds what we know and His creative act knows no cessation and every day He is the novel manifestation (*Qur'an* 55:29). Now we do not know and cannot know what He is in His 'whatness', and in His being as he is in Himself but can take cognisance of Him through His creation, through awareness of oneself in its finitude and insufficiency, in the feeling of absolute dependence and solitariness. But this God according to the *Qur'an* has two sides: He makes himself apparent and manifest through signs (*ayat*), all that is and all that happens are referred back to Him, from Him we come and unto Him we step back but at the same time He has an unmanifested aspect (*batin*). The distinction between the *saguna Brahma* and *nirguna Brahma* is decisive in the Upanishadic thought, though in the Islamic perspective the manifest aspect of God has nothing illusory about it. While God as manifest or *Zahir* is ensrealissimum god as unrevealed stands beyond all categorisation, even beyond the categories of *Sat, Chit* and *Ananda*.

It is in his manifest aspect that He addresses Himself to us and names Himself with the beautiful names (*asma al-husna*), the Master of the world unrevealed and the world made manifest. The gracious, the Merciful, All-holy. All-majesty, All-preserving. All-compeller, The Tremendous, the Creator out of nought, the Mighty, The Fashioner, the Shaper (*Qur'an* 9:22-24) and yet in His supreme transcendence He is anonymous, He has been named through His manifestation, He is beyond what is ascribed to Him. I Am that I am was the answer that was given to Moses when he first enquired of Him and only later that the God of biblical revelation made himself recognisable with reference to his historical involvement as the God of Abraham. This means that God manifests Himself as a person through His names, as one with whom we can communicate and as one with whom we can stand in an I and Thou relationship. It is the divine personal God of revelation which gives a distinctive feature to Christianity, Islam and Judaism and to the religious trends and movements on the Indian soil which developed on the concept of Bhakti and devotion to a personal God when inter-religious cross-currents played a formative role. It is not the God of the philosophers whose thought is confined to itself the unmoved mover and the First cause whose knowledge is restricted to universals but a God in whose knowledge every leaf that falls to the ground is registered, who knows what agitates the human breast and who is reflected in His creation and is involved in history. He sends messengers to warn and guide, He is pleased and displeased, but all His actions and attributes are not subject to human limitations but needs qualified by the acknowledgment of a mystery which is beyond the reach of human understanding. Now I am trying to offer a few comments on the specifically Islamic approach to the Unity of God or *tauhid*, and try to explain what in our understanding of Islam this divine unity or *tauhid* amounts to.

The Prophet of Islam appeared in history in a society which was ridden with a belief in a plurality of divinities and consequent upon this belief man was enslaved by powers which he could not control and his whole life was regulated by norms which were determined and shaped by the belief. Now the prophet of Islam appeared with the zeal of an iconoclast who taught and preached that there is only one supreme and absolute power and his commitment to the one supreme power found expression in the Muslim witness: There is no God but God. He is the one who is really real. In this *kalima* or witness there is first the negation, the negation of the multiplicity of divinities and the affirmation of Allah who has created the world and all that is and to whom ultimately man is destined to return. This means that in the Islamic witness negation precedes affirmation, *la* (no) precedes *illa* (but). The simple affirmation will remain denuded of all contents unless it is determined by *la*. Corresponding to this intention which the Islamic witness embodies is the cry of Allah-u-Akbar which has echoed through centuries of Islamic history as a call before which empires tottered. Allah-u-Akbar or God is greater is not a static statement but a dynamic process. It has most far reaching practical consequences. The greatness of God brings into insignificance any-thing that claims greatness. All that we confront and all that confronts us loses its significance and values the moment it is brought in the dimension of *Allah-u-Akbar*, God is greater. The succinct formula of Islamic *tauhid* indeed embodies the spirit of the ontological argument developed by St. Anselm, God is greater and higher than all that is possible and actual. Whatever exists as a fact, whatever is thought as a possibility which can be realised, whatever one experiences and imagines has to face one who brooks no comparison who is ever greater. What is the One then who is ever greater? Can he be named as One? The *Qur'an* names Him by different names. We need not go into the much discussed question of the relation of the attributes and names, whether the attributes are part of His essence, different from His essence or both different and part of His essence. Indeed God may be attributed with contradictory attributes. He is as much present as absent, present in closest proximity and absent in His otherness (*ghalib*). God's autonomy and self-sufficiency stands by itself and it will be a very vacant concept of *tauhid* to think that this Unity is the negation and rejection of idols only. It is the negation of all ultimacy to anything but God. Hence, it is necessary to distinguish between explicit associationism and implicit associationism. Even if success or the embodiment of any worldly power like State is considered ultimate it violates the Islamic principle of Unity. This means that my I-am ness has no meaning unless it is derived from God who is eminently real and neither I nor the things around me are illusory. The *Qur'an* explicitly declared that God has not created the world in sport or play but in truth, the events in nature, the night that gives rest and the day that gives sight, the rain that quickens nature, and the things of nature which are created in pairs and the marvel or harmony in the adjustment of sexes are signs and signals which transcend their appearance and take us beyond. The conflict of the one and the many which has baffled philosophers poses no problem. The one comprehends the many and still surpasses the many. Nature is not God but God is reflected in nature and in time as it unfolds itself in history in the rise and fall of nations. The ruins which bespeak of ancient glory and the fall of the mighty are all integrated into a world which is planned and conceived by God. And above all man should think of what he is, his roots are in the earth but he has an origin which is divine, the angels were asked to prostrate before him and the disobedience of satan spelled his doom, but the prerogative of man in his metaphysical dimension is not a gift which is to be left uncared for. It is a trust which is to be warily guarded, as man though created in the best of patterns is thrown into the lowest of depths. But this does not mean that man is not free to choose but only that he is capable of swinging between two extremes, he can rise to heights which angels fear to tread but he can also fall to depths which beasts cannot reach. The legend of the fall of Satan as given in the *Qur'an* and his strife with God beautifully illustrates the *Qur'anic* vision of God and man. Any attempt at demythologisation should not miss its metaphysical thrust. Satan really represents the temptations to which man is subject and Adam as the first man is also the first to have sinned and by sinning he proclaimed his freedom. Ironically it is our ability to sin which marks us as free men and with man's capacity to sin God's forgiveness also becomes meaningful and real. The story of Adam and Satan is played on the metahistorical play only to be replayed on the plane of individual experience. Evil does not play in Islam any autonomous role. Satan does not figure as one who questions the sovereignty or as one who pretends to be more than an instrument in bringing about evil and his power is so curtailed that he has to work in a limited frame of activity. Hence the antagonist of Satan is not God but man as the Vicegerent of God whose emergence it was that led to the emergence of Satan. He embodies refusal, the voice of dissent but a dissent which is destructive and motivated. Hence, it is said that Satan shall not have any power on those who have surrendered to God. The Unity of God is not threatened by Satan but it is only man's vicegerency which is menaced by evil and man can not preserve his privilege by his own efforts but by fleeing unto God and taking refuge with God from Satan who tempts man by whispering from within. Being human is not given as a privilege which can always be taken for granted. Hence the *Qur'an* makes reference to the polarity of human existence, its metaphysical status and the risks to which man is exposed in his life on earth. Man as an individual is divided against himself and is all too prone to betray his sacred trust and violate the primordial covenant: success is his who delivers himself from the greed of his soul says the *Qur'an* (59:9).

The concept of Unity in Islam works at three levels, the human level, the cosmic level and the divine level. On the human level the apparent divisions through colour and race, through language and status are considered immaterial. Mankind is divided ethnically and named differently so as to enable men to recognise one another in their specific character. Nay even the division between the believer and the unbeliever is an integral part of the order which is willed by God and any attempt to reduce the multiplicity into a monolithic world order is doomed to failure. Mankind is one, traceable to one source. Corresponding to this Unity on the human plane is the cosmic unity. We are all part of the same cosmos, nature is quickened with life and even of animals it is said that they are nations like us, denoting thereby that even animal life has its own order and purpose and cosmos as a whole is oriented to God. Each part of the cosmos is tuned with the divine purpose and every part of the cosmos has its own invocation in accordance with its assigned place: There is not a thing that hymneth not His praise but ye understand not their praise (*Qur'an* 17:44).

Naturally in the course of time speculations developed on the concept of the Unity. Whereas in the beginning the primitive audience to which the *Qur'an* first addressed itself could only have thought of unity of God in an unsophisticated way. It meant for them that God is one and there are no divinities beside him. This naive way of looking at things holds good for the masses even for today and serves its purpose. The pre-Islamic Arabs were used to worship many Gods and revered each of them in his concrete manifestation as tangible and visible, easily accessible and powerful enough to satisfy their needs, though it is possible that even in primitive idol worship the idea of a supreme being is not absent, a being who works as a kind of an overlord. But the idea of a being whose affirmation itself negates the idea of sub-divine realities who share in his power was foreign to them. Islam naturally does not work in a vacuum, it is heir to a tradition and openly affirms that its revelation is only a continuation of earlier revelation, and that the idea of the unity of God has not evolved from the idea of a plurality of powers but that the idea of plurality of powers had come to dominate only after the idea of one God is forgotten and eclipsed in the consciousness of mankind. Thus according to the Islamic view the idea of unity has not only a metaphysical but a historical priority. It is the deviation from the idea of unity that has given rise to plurality and it is not through the refinement of thought that the idea of the plurality of powers developed into unity. So the Islamic *Kalma* declared there is no God excepting one God who it calls Allah. And it tries to characterise Allah in terms which have human relevance. It is highly significant and interesting to note that of all the attributes of God it is that of Rehma, of graciousness that is made prominent, thought God is attributed in ways in which are equally significant. Hence the placement of these two attributes in the foreground calls for comment. *Rahman* is God in His cosmic mercy and *Rahim* is he in His personal concern. It speaks eloquently of the situation in which man is placed. If the name of God is dinned into our ears from the beginning as *Rahman* and *Rahim* it means that the quality of mercy is that which we most need, on which we can rely and which cannot fails us. Recent trends in philosophical anthropology have laid great imphasis on the helplessness of man. As against animals a human child is born an orphan, unequipped to face the dangers and crises requiring immediate concern and attention. When he grows up he is given to anxiety and dread, born in trouble, (*kabd*) the *Qur'an* says and his freedom becomes a liability and apart from the calamities to which he is exposed through nature he himself contributes to his own self-destruction. Though condemned to death and moving to the inevitable end he still tries to hasten the process. The vicegerent (*khalifa*) of God on earth betrays his trust and justifies the suspicion which angels had nurtured against him as one who will make mischief and create bloodshed. So when man's situation is beset with difficulties which mount with age and when he is made accountable for every act which he wills, when temptations are many, and liability to error and forgetfulness is overwhelming he can only turn to God who is *Rahman* and *Rahim*.

But with the deeper understanding of the *Qur'an* and the refinement of reflection and constant meditation on words of the revelation the concept of unity underwent a radical change. What does unity of God mean? Does the Islamic witness consist of negation of deities other than God and affirmation of a creator who embraces all creation in his knowledge or does it go even farther than this to deny attribution of reality to anything other than God. Now Islamic reflection specially in its mystic dimension tended to understand it in a radically monistic sense. For this way of thought this means that nothing exists other than God. He alone is being and being par excellence. Does it mean then that the multiplicity and plurality to which experience bears witness is nothing but Maya? This view would naturally be exposed to the charge of the denial of transcendence and to make meaningless human struggle and responsibility, and to make nature metaphysically irrelevant. It was against this concept of abstract unity that Hegel raised his voice. It is interesting to note what Hegel says on the Islamic idea of divine unity. He observes that if one would like to see the consciousness of the one not in the undetermined and repetitive monotony but in its most beautiful purity and sublimity one should go to Mohammedans, especially as it finds expression in Jalaluddin Rumi where the Unity of the soul with the One is highlighted as the unity of love, transcending the finite and the commonplace and where the natural and spiritual elements are so transfigured that the evanescent immediacy of the natural and the empirical is both separated and absorbed: (*Hegel Encyclopadie,* S. 482, Leipzig, 1949).

The kind of unity that Islam upholds admits plurality of finite persons, recognises nature as real though its reality is created, attributes to man a privileged place in creation but at the same time recognises God as all in all, comprehending all that is and surpassing all that is. He is reflected in His creation, every piece of His creation however insignificant it may seem is supremely significant in so far as it beckons beyond itself. That God swears by things which to us seems insignificant speaks eloquently for the fact that to Him nothing is insignificant in itself. The *Qur'anic* perspective is beautifully reflected in these verses:

> *Nay I swear by the twilight*
> *and the night and what it envelops*
> *and the moon when it is at the full*
> *Ye shall surely ascend from plane to plane.*

Now when one is committed to unity of God it lends to most far-reaching consequences. If God has created man with a trust and made him vicegerent on earth the division which man has created are robbed of ontological validity. Islamic history in spite of its unfortunate deviation from its original ethos and its all too frequent betrayals of the ideals and values which it cherished in the beginning held fast to the *Qur'anic* vision that the rank with God, whether in this world or in the life to follow, is determined by piety *taqwa*: the most honoured person in the eye of God is one who is most pious (*Qur'an* 49:13). It is self-centredness and arrogance that bedevils man's relations with his fellow beings. The *Qur'anic* version of the biblical legend of the fall of man makes this pride and self-assurance responsible for the fall of Satan. Though Satan did not compromise on the issue of unity he was cursed nevertheless showing thereby that primarily it is through self-effacement that self can mature and humanity can shape itself. Hence the authentic sufism did not consider the annihilation of self (*fana*) as something negative but as the preservation of the self (*baqa*) in life divine.

The acknowledgment of God's unity does not remain a passive posture in the Islamic perspective but calls for the cooperation of man in His cause and doing good is indelibly associated with a life of devotion. The truly devout according to the *Qur'an* are those who "forsake their beds to cry unto the Lord in fear and hope and spend of what we have provided for them" (*Qur'an* 32:17). Surrender to God is bound with one's concern for His creation.

Revised and edited; originally published in Studies in Islam, April 1979.

6

Tauhid—Oneness of God

TAZIMUDDIN SIDDIQUI

Meaning of Tauhid, concepts of accountability, universality, equality, are all discussed in detail.

"Everyone who is seriously involved in the pursuit of science becomes convinced that a spirit is manifest in the laws of the universe, a spirit vastly superior to that of man, and one in the face of which we with our modest powers must feel humble".Einstein

A pertinent question affecting the life of human being is: Has the universe come into existence by itself or some one has created it and if there is a creator, is he one or with him there are other co-creators, finally, what is the relationship between that creator and man? Associationism (*shirk*), atheism (*ilhad*) and monotheism or the concept of unity of God may be the three answers to this question. According to Islam, God is the only one Creator of the Universe and He alone is to be worshipped. This is the Islamic concept of Divine Unity, of God's oneness or His uniqueness.

Meaning of Tauhid

Tauhid is derived from *wahdahu* or *wahid* which means that God is one without a second, without any other co-eternal entity, of complete supremacy, unrivalled, unopposed, unequalled, and unchallenged. He is omnipotent. His authority and sovereignty are not to be questioned. He is ever the same, uncontradicted, internally and externally, absolute in all respects. The concept of *tauhid* excluded all or any king of duality or multiplicity from the divine essence. It is the pure and simple oneness of the transcendental experience. It is not a notion of speculative metaphysics which does not fulfil human hopes and aspiration. The unity of God is the unity of infiniteness. God Himself manifests the nature of *tauhid* in these verses of the Kur'an:

> He is Allah, the one! Allah, the eternally besought of all! He begeth not nor was begotten. And there is none comparable unto Him."

The divine reality of God is always a creative unity in Islam. *Qur'an* is the most formidable exponent of *tauhid*. It strikes at the very roots of ignorance, superstition and blind following and orders its followers to base their lives on knowledge and intellect.

God's two great gifts to man are intellect and emotions. The former enables him to use his mental faculties for discovering the correct path and the latter creates in him an indomitable courage and unsatiated urge to take to this path. A true combination of the two qualities enables him to live a perfect life and this is what *tauhid* desires the man to achieve.

Atheism may satisfy the intellect but not the emotions. By denying the existence of God, an atheist is deprived of a Being whom he could adore and to whose will he could make a complete surrender. Associationism links man with numerous gods. Man cannot worship all of them with equal love and devotion. Thus neither the intellect is satisfied nor the emotions. *Tauhid* means that man should take God as his only Creator, Master, Sustainer, Benefactor, the first and the last resort. It means that man should fear, love and obey God alone, work, live and die for Him, for His approval. Under *tauhid*, the Being discovered with intellect becomes the centre of all emotions and thus there emerges a harmonious relationship between intellect and emotions which provides unshattered peace, both to the head and the heart. To know God one has to know himself. *Tauhid* enables man to know himself, to determine his status in the universe, his relations with fellow-beings, and his responsibilities and rights. With belief in *tauhid* he discovers his latent capabilities, by making a good use of which he may succeed in his life, both in this terrestrial and hereafter.

In religious consciousness and spiritual realisation the true devotee transcends all finite standpoints and understands the one infinite.

Oneness of God

Divine unity stands for complete oneness of the Divine Being, that God is one and all plurality is alien to His essence.

Atheism and materialism leave nothing higher to aspire for their material interests and desires. Divorced from spirituality, the pursuit of material gains and the satisfaction of material desires creates in the pursuer a sense of superiority which if not checked leads to negation of all virtues and to exploitation of man by man. Through *tauhid* one builds an invincible faith that there is no God besides the one Supreme Being, who alone is the true master, the only maker of the destiny, that life or death, loss or gain, respect or disrespect, richness or poverty, authority or subjugation, all are in His control. This faith produces in man the quality of fearlessness acquiring which he refuses to bow before anyone, howsoever mighty, except the one and true God. He feels elated by the Divine Decree that he is the vicegerent of God on earth and as such he has to enforce the Divine Law on earth. He believes that God is Omnipresent and hence whatever he does, good or bad, is watched by Him. This conviction generates in him a tendency to do good and refrain from doing anything not permitted by God. It forces him to be honest in his conduct, fair in his dealings, prompt in the discharge of his obligations, truthful and kind.

Once man begins to believe that he is God's vicegerent on earth, he refuses to forsake the path of truth and righteousness, and the quality of fearlessness, an important corollary of *tauhid,* enables him to hold his ground even in face of the firecest opposition. He realizes his own worth and strives to attain a position that may justify his selection as God's vicegerent.

Accountability to God Under Tauhid

Tauhid reveals to man the reality that he is not free is an absolute sense but is accountable of God, that he has not to be a slave of his worldly ambitions, that he is an humble subject of God and that the purpose of his life is not to gain material benefits through fair or foul means but to live a righteous life doing only that which conforms to God's approbation. *Tauhid* builds the belief that whatever man possesses belongs to God and he is only a custodian, a trustee and ultimately he will have to abandon all his worldly belongings. This belief restrains him from falling a prey to superiority complex, to extravagance, greed, pride, vanity and arrogance. The more he gets the meeker he becomes and bows before God in gratitude. If he is wealthy, he considers his wealth to be a trust for the safeguard and just utilisation for which he has to present before his Master a complete account. If he is a ruler, he considers himself not an uncontrolled despot but a humble servant of God. He is always perplexed lest he may be guilty of any shortcoming in the care of his subjects, in the maintenance of justice and in the enforcement of God's law.

Interpretation of Creation

Creation is an act of God. It is an orderly phenomenon, a purposive cosmos. It is subservient to the purpose of mankind. It is governed by a unitary law, i.e. God. The *Qur'an* says:

> If there were Gods beside Allah, then verily both the heavens and the earth had been disordered. Glorified be Allah, the Lord of the Throne, from all that they ascribe (unto Him).

And again,

> God compelled the sun and the moon to be of service, each runneth unto an appointed term; He ordereth the course, He detaileth the revelations, that happy ye may be certain of the meeting with your Lord.

Just as the universe is under divine control, man is also under His governance, whose sovereignty is reflected in the universe. The *Qur'an* reveals this fact, as under:

> In the creation of the heavens and the earth and (in) the

> difference of night and day are tokens (of His sovereignty) for men of understanding.

Man is the part of this creation. He is made of all the elements of the world, hence he is dependent upon them. The material elements as symbolically enumerated in the *Qur'an* in the form of clay, dust, clot, water, etc., constitute the lower nature of man. His higher nature is the manifestation of the divine spirit in him. Man is not absolutely independent of his material nature, since he is determined by the natural forces; but he is free in his essential nature, i.e., the spirit which comes from God. Man is responsible because he is free in his spirit. God commands to the Prophet with this revelation:

> So set thy purpose (O Muhammad) for religion as a man by nature upright—the nature (framed) of Allah, in which He hath created man.

Man is the most exalted being in the creation of God. Even the pure spiritual beings, the angels, were compelled to prostrate before him. God did not have any doubt in the man is spite of the angels' insistence that he will cause harm and bloodshed on the earth. Thus man is the supreme creation of God who has to fulfil certain obligations to his Creator, the Supreme Being; the discharge of obligations manifesting his obedience to this Supreme Being and thus acknowledging His oneness.

God, the Creator, is one and from His unity follow, as a necessary consequence, the unity of Creation, the unity of man, the unity of life and universe. Thus all human beings belong to one universal brother-hood. Further, life is a unity and it admits of no dichotomy of the material and spiritual. A negligence of either or an imbalance between the two is fraught with grave dangers and is not approved by God. Normal human needs have to be satisfied in order to attain the goal of spirit.

Universality of Tauhid

The belief in *tauhid* is not a kind of faith in an abstract idea or notion, an abstruse metaphysical entity, but a living faith in the reality which is all-preserving, the Creator out of nought, the Mighty, the Fashioner, the Shaper and yet in His supreme transcendence He is anonymous, He is beyond what is ascribed to Him. However, it is the living personal God of revelation which was the basis of all religions. It is the belief which does not engage in promotion of ritualistic activities and ceremonial behaviour, but exhorts man to worship the true reality, described in Arabic language as *Allah* and to embrace all His messages conveyed by scriptures and prophets. *Tauhid* teaches man to believe in such kind of world order in which, as the *Qur'an* says:

> Mankind were one community; and Allah sent (unto them) Prophets as bearers of good tidings and as warners, and revealed therewith the Scripture with the truth that it might judge between mankind concerning that wherein they differed.

The belief in the universality of Divine unity is an integral part of Islamic faith. Besides Islam, it is a distinct feature of all religious consciousness as the *Qur'an* has described:

> There is not a nation but a warner hath passed among them. . . And for every nation there is a messenger. And when there cometh (the Day of Judgment) it will be judged between them fairly, and they will not be wronged.

And again the *Qur'an* revealing to the Prophet says:

> And messengers we have mentioned unto thee before and messengers we have not mentioned unto thee.

Moreover, the message has not been made universal by a single set of idioms of one language. The beauty of the message of God has been manifested in all the languages of mankind. The *Qur'an* reveals it as:

> And we never sent a messenger save with the language of his folk, that he might make the (message) clear for them.

The prophet of Islam belonged to Arabia, and his first addressees were the Arabic knowing people. Hence the *Qur'an* was revealed in Arabic:

> Lo! We have revealed it, a Lecture in Arabic, that you may understand.

In an address to newly converted Muslims at Medina God revealed these facts of great international understanding:

> Say (O Muslims): We believe in Allah and that which is revealed unto us and that which was revealed unto Abraham, and Ishmael, and Issac and Jacob, and the tribes, and that which Moses and Jesus received, and that which the prophets received from their Lord. We make no distinction between any of them, and unto Him we have surrendered.

In the primitive religions of China and Japan, Taoism and Shintoism, there was a strong religious belief "that at the basis of all created and manifested existence in an underlying unitary, spiritual Reality, the absolute spiritual source of all things." In Taoism, *Tao* means a Way or a Road, and *Tao Teaching* means a First and all-embracing principle whereby all things are produced. It is the unchanging unity underlying the shifting plurality of phenomena. It is self-caused. It is formless and yet complete; it is nameless and yet it is called Tao. We do not know when the Chinese people began to believe in Tao Teaching as the unitary principle of life and existence. Similarly, Hinduism is not all pluralistic polytheism. Since the very early times, the idea of *Ekam Sat* was prevalent in the Hindu Society, an idea which in the days of *Upanishads* was vigorously advocated by the seers. Christianity and Judaism are unquestionably accepted as monotheistic religions.

Tauhid enables its follower to build a character based on piety, truthfulness, observance of promise or fulfilment of agreement, honesty, trustworthiness, justice, kindness and sense of responsibility. With such character an individual as well as a society is bound to succeed, both materially and spiritually and bring about a universal brotherhood.

Tauhid explains that God has no caste, community or race. All human beings are His subjects. His is universal law and whosoever shall disobey His commands shall merit punishment and none can intercede in the matter of punishment. The doctrine of *tauhid* emphasizes in no uncertain terms that it is not enough to worship God, but to do what He has commanded to do and to refrain from doing what He has forbidden to do, is equally necessary. To follow the Divine Law he has to discharge the obligations cast on him in the following *Qur'anic* words:

> God commands justice, the doing of good, and liberality to kith and kin, and He forbids all shameful deeds and injustice, and rebellion:

By acting according to this Divine Law and by having a resolute faith in the Divine Will man cultivates the quality of looking for sustenance and succour to God alone. For him his Lord is enough. Such faith saves him from frustration in failure, and from disappointment and loss of courage even in gravest situations. Hopefully he travels avoiding pitfalls, taking the hazards of journey in his strides and strives against heavy odds to reach his destination, to attain his goal and justify his vicegerency on earth.

Idea of Equality

It is from the concept of *tauhid* that we can deduce the existence of a harmonious world order, the purposive cosmos, the equality of sex and race, the equal freedom in socio-economic spheres and religious tolerance. *Tauhid* is not only a religious faith, or one's own concern to God as ultimate source of salvation or protection in the world and in the hereafter, but it is also the very principle of social equality. The entire mankind was one community. Later on, God Himself made the variety of nations, not to conflict and clash with each other, but to "know one another... The noblest in the sight of Allah, being the best in conduct." The Prophet of Islam said to his followers: "The creation is an God's family; ... therefore, the most beloved unto God is the person who doth good to God's family. God is not merciful to him who is not so to mankind." The Prophet was a man of action. For his actions *tauhid* was the theoretical base. He would tell his followers that they would not attain the ultimate end of life, i.e., paradise, until they had faith; and they would not complete their faith till they loved on another." And again: "A perfect Muslim is he from whose tongue and hands mankind is safe." His prescription of prayer is the great reminder to the rich and the poor alike that there is no distinction between man and man on account of their socio-economic status; that greatness is determined by the realisation of righteousness and good conduct. This consciousness of aiming at righteousness is the greatest doctrine of equality for it is perpetual.

What kind of equality one could find in the text of *tauhid* about the status of woman in the man-dominated society? The status of woman, half the population of mankind, is an interesting chapter in the Book of *Tauhid.* The idea of equality of woman is based on the sound spiritual and psychological considerations. The *Qur'an* does not make any distinction between men and women:

> O mankind! Be careful of your duty to your Lord Who created you from a single soul and from it created its mate and from them twain hath spread abroad a multitude of men and women.

It is this theoretical background on which the practice implications are based. Woman enjoys a right of livelihood as much as man enjoys; she is entitled to get the share of inheritance on the principle of equality that man and woman have the same source of existence.

This equality has been established by the following command of God:

> Unto the men (of a family) belongeth a share of that which parents and near kindred leave, and unto the women a share of that which parents and near kindred leave.

Apart from economic equality, women were chosen for divine inspiration as well as God Himself says: "We inspired the mother of Moses." Similarly, Mary was chosen by God and made pure.

According to the Islamic doctrine of *tauhid*, there is only one religion, the religion of God, but they (mankind) have broken their religion among them into sects, each sect rejoicing in its tenets.

Many religion flowed from one religion. None has a right to be a judge of another's religious faith. There is no compulsion in matters of religions. Even in a dialogue with the disbelievers one can end argument or controversy by uttering the divine words that "unto you your religion, and unto me my religion."

Revised and edited; originally published in Studies in Islam, April 1979.

7

Tauhid and 'Adl: A Discussion

HAKIM ABDUL HAMEED

Tauhid as the guiding principle of life, unity of religions, `adl or justice and human society, adl and its relation with social, economic and other aspects - including medical- are covered

Tauhid as the Guiding Principle of Human Life

The problem of the one and the many has always haunted philosophical consciousness. A human being is confronted primarily with multiplicity and the world appears to him in its infinite hues. Even mankind appears divided in racial, nations, ethnic and tribal groupings. One man cannot understand the language of another, and one nation appears incentive to the sufferings and travails of another. On the religious plane, man's loyalty was claimed by any number of gods and deities. Now the question arises whether this apparent multiplicity is ultimate and final, or behind the conflict of the many there is an underlying unity. The unity that must prevail is often eclipsed and misunderstood. What appears as multiplicity is considered real and the idea of unity and oneness is held to be illusory and deceptive. The Muslims are supposed to be upholders of the underlying unity behind the phenomenal multiplicity. However, this multiplicity is not considered 'Maya' but the status of the many is recognized though it is firmly believed that the phenomenal multiplicity is not ultimate. The conviction and faith in this ultimate unity is what is called *tauhid* in the language of Islam. It must be admitted that the Muslims themselves have not taken the ideas of *tauhid* very seriously though it is impossible to think of Islam without it. It need not be interpreted exclusively in religious terms. Without denying the fact that the idea primarily is a religious one, it must be emphasised at the outset that the idea has tremendous social, political and even scientific implications.

Islam appeared in this world as an effective protest against idolatry and succeeded in its mission to such an extent that the justification of idolatry in its necked form will not be attempted by any school of thought, be it religious or secular. It is however necessary to understand what is meant by idolatry. It is recognition of forces multiple in character that claim loyalty and allegiance as ultimate in their own right. According to the article on 'Monotheism' in the new *Encyclopaedia Britannica* many scholars hold that monotheism is a higher form of religion. But *tauhid* is not a higher form of religion as such it is in fact the only form of religion which answers to man's deepest craving and aspiration. The distinguished historian, Arnold Toynbee, raised the question why power over nature was only possible after scientific revolution of the present, and offered the reply himself by saying that it was possible only because the greatest obstacle in its way was the worship of the forces of nature in their phenomenal representation. We know that the primitive man was given to animism the belief that every manifestation of nature was animated by a spirit which animates it. The Greeks considered their rivers and valleys their forests and woods peopled by invisible spirits. These were all the dominates ideas of animistic belief and superstitions which enslaved men for centuries. The belief of associationism converted the powers of nature into all powerful deities. The associationist considered these forces as demanding his worship and hence there was no question of his control over the nature. Only when the belief in *tauhid* in the ultimate character of Divine oneness, dawned upon him that man began to consider these powers as subservient to him and succeeded in gaining control over them. It is significant to note that *tauhid* is not considered by the Prophet as an exclusive asset of Islam but held to be the heritage which belongs to mankind as a whole and a lost principle which needs to be restored. It has brought it not only in relation to the prophets of Israel but even acknowledged the presence of a divine warner in every nation. *Tauhid* thus, assumes a universal significance to which every nation can lay a claim.

There is no denying the fact that idea of *tauhid* is intimately associated with a universal perspective. It is the denial of parochial and regional loyalties which warp the vision of man, and make way for particularism which is the denial of a humanistic ideology based on a vision of the oneness of the universe. There cannot be any cosmopolitanism worth its name which is ready to accommodate tribal and national loyalties and which allows them to override humanistic considerations.

As the idea of oneness is based on theistic foundation in Islam, a question may well arise: is it not a fact that a commitment to a belief in the Unknown and a claim to the apprehension of unknown realities is not an impediment to the progress of man? In our own days every form of religion which holds the belief in a transcendental reality is regarded as an opiate to the masses. It is believed that religion as a system of beliefs which assume a transcendental reality cripples human activity and makes man dream of a world which does not exist. Religion then, according to this view, serves as an escape from reality. But the rise and growth of Islam itself is a sufficient answer to this charge and belies its fundamental assumption. Islam appeared in the world as an active and dynamic force. Its belief in an invisible and unknown God instead of making its followers inactive and indolent turned them into the torchbearers of culture and civilization in many countries of the world. It is however true that the dynamism of early Muslims soon lost its momentum and Muslims became in course of time lethargic and inactive. Islam cannot by any means be held responsible for this sorry state of affairs. It had nothing to do with their vision of *tauhid* and their belief in the invisible sovereign of the world but it was the result of causes which have their origin in social, historical and geographical conditions which at least party determine the rise and growth of nations. Unfortunately, Muslims failed to bring their belief in *tauhid* in tune with the scientific and practical tendencies and realities of their times. The beliefs in *tauhid* has, according to the *Qur'an* a collective reference. The *Qur'anic* revelation is oriented towards human collectivity and considers *tauhid* as the only authentic foundation of it. It makes collectivity possible as without the unifying idea of *tauhid* collectivity is apt to degenerate into numerical aggregation. Mankind needed for its global activity a universal nucleus and this was provided by the idea of *tauhid*. It is true that we find the principle of collectivity at work everywhere in the world both at the level of brutes and at the level of men, but so far as animals are concerned the principle of collectivity has only a limited application but man being a social animal, he cannot survive without a collective urge to unite and to live in peace and harmony. It is the basis of the formation of state. Hobbes and Rousseau made the idea of social contract responsible for the formation of the State. But the idea of a social contract is only a philosophical construction, it does not take into account the metaphysical urge which impels men to come together for super-individual ends. Islam with its insistence on the idea of *tauhid* has given to mankind a principle which does not resort to fictitious constructions to provide for man the solid foundation for his collective existence. There is no denying the fact that religions in their different manifestations have implicit in them what appeared in Islam as an explicit and effective reality. The idea of *tauhid* assumed a more definite form when it was given a teleological direction. Now it was shown that all that is in the world subserves potentially and actually men's vital needs. But all the world is brought into his power and is tuned to his needs only because, man is made for God, has a God-oriented dimension, he is in fact as the *Qur'an* says the vicegerent of God on earth.

The history of Islamic thought clearly shows that in spite of the magnificent efforts of the Muslim Scholastics, Mutazilites and Ashrites, and in spite of their dialectical subtleties, the pure Islamic idea of unity, with all its transcendence has been left vague and undefined. Of course among them were such great souls for whom the question of *tauhid* was a question of life and death and they did not hesitate to combat the incursion of *shirk* be it in the form of mediation or in the form of unification with God and any other form or association which allowed for identity was strongly rejected so as to preserve the Islamic concept of unity in all its purity and authenticity.

The idea of the unity of religion and of human rights cannot be considered only as a modern phenomenon. It is not only the urge to seek unity behind diversity that inspired mankind in the past. It was the United States of America and even before that the revolutionary slogans of French revolution which reminded mankind of the values and ideals for which it has to fight. But in spite of all agitation for human rights and for the unity of man, in spite of all that has been said for the equality of man and for his liberty on the basis of this equality, these ideals have yet to find their realisation on the stage of modern history. Most unfortunately these ideals themselves have lulled men into sleep and they have served as slogans to be fought for on international platforms but without any effective endorsement by the nations which have assumed a decisive role in international affairs. These principles have of course manifested themselves from time to time in concrete form but whether we think of the League of Nations of the past or whether of the U.N.O. today it is yet a long way before these ideals can be decisively implemented in face of any critical situation. This sorry state of affairs can be traced to the lack of response which the belief in the oneness has received intellectually, politically and emotionally. To uphold this belief--which promises to usher in a great social revolution—to re-interpret it in the context of the present situation unraveling its wide ramifications and applying it as a yardstick in the various spheres of human life, is the duty of everyone having a sincere desire to promote the cause of human welfare. There are verities which can be made intelligible only today. Now that man is no more allowed to deviate from the path of belief in one underlined reality the conviction can be easily conveyed to one and all that peace of mind and inner spiritual tranquillity may only be reached through an unconditional commitment to a belief in unity. Human rights cannot be preserved except on the basis of a full consciousness of oneness. If the idea of the unity or religion can ever be found acceptable it will be only on the basis of human faith in oneness. The foundation of human rights can only be laid on a categorical faith in unit because unity of mankind is a necessary assumption of human equality or human right. Unfortunately Muslim apologetic has allowed itself to be diverted into secondary issues and has not assigned the priority which Islam has given to unity. Islam is not a religion which is lost in futile speculations or in hair-splitting subtleties. Nor it is a religion which intoxicates man by holding before him the vision of supernatural realities. Its main concern is human existence, its problems and travails, its affections and sufferings. The way one lives in this world in relation to fellow human beings in peace and harmony is the primary concern of Islam. It is a pity however that this main concern is often eclipsed by problems which have long their relevance.

The idea of the unity of religions about which we hear so much can only be based on the common denominator which is the consciousness of all pervasive unity. Once the idea of oneness becomes not only the theoretical commitment but is converted into action, the possibility of the idea of unity of mankind becomes a reality. To the man who is given to a complete acceptance of oneness as the guiding principle of life and action its political implication will soon become apparent. Unfortunately, the majority of mankind has not responded positively to the idea of oneness. The time will soon come when the belief in oneness will prove decisive for the development of mankind, and it will necessarily lead to values which have been eclipsed by man's attachments to all kinds of particularities and divisions. Whatever may be the reaction and response of others, a heavy responsibility devolves on Muslims. They will be doing great service to mankind if they could make a belief, to which they have been devoted from the beginning, prevail all over the world at all levels.

It is high time to develop a well thought out and systematic scheme for exhaustive studies of the belief in *tauhid* in its varied manifestation. I hereby venture to offer a tentative programme of studies, subject, of course, to modifications and alteration. An in-depth study of different dimensions is called for.

The metaphysical dimension : The meaning of oneness—Quantitative oneness and Qualitative oneness — Unity and Multiplicity—Abstract Unity and Concrete Unity — Permanence and Change.

Psychological dimension : Self and its conditions. Is self a Necessary Assumption of psychic process ? — Change and Identity — The problem of individuality — Unity in the changing patterns of human behaviour.

Sociological dimension : Individual and society — Diversity and Unity in Society — Does social unity exclude social diversity ? — The idea of integration on the basis of *tauhid.*

Religious dimension : The clarification of the idea of tauhid on the basis of the *Qur'an* and *Hadith.* The *Quranic* vision of the unity of mankind on the basis of the Oneness of God — The Systematic interpretation of the *Quranic* ideas — Innovation and its implications— Different theological perspectives — Associations (*shrik*).

The mystic approach to *tauhid* — Unity of God—*Wahdat al-wujud.* Unity of Being, and *Wahdat al-shuhud.* Testimonial Unity.

Muslim scholastic approach to tauhid: 'Asharites and Mutazilites— The relation of Attributes to Divine Attributes — The negation of Attributes necessary for the affirmation of Divine Unity.

Classical philosophers and their concepts of *tauhid,* al-Kindi, al-Farabi, Ibn Sina, Ibn Rushd, Shahab al-Din Suhrawardi Maqtul Sadr al-Din Shirazi and others.

The idea of Unity in Indian thought — the *Upanishads* and *Bhagvad Gita* — The monistic Trends — Vedantic schools.

The idea of *tauhid* in Chinese and ancient Iranian thought—The idea of *tauhid* in Western thought—Pre-Socratic views—the idea of *tauhid* in classical Greek thought—the problem of one and many.

The idea of *tauhid* in contemporary philosophical and religious thought. The idea of *tauhid* in religious and theological movements of Islam, reformation of the idea of *tauhid* with full consideration of recent developments in science and philosophy, especially in physics and life sciences.

It goes without saying that only when the idea of oneness is made effective in the life of the individuals as in that of nations, the divisive forces which are threatening the future of mankind can be countered with success. Hence the relevance of this project in the present context of the world situation is all too apparent.

'Adl and Human Society

A few years ago I had expressed my views on *'adl* in the following manner :

> The negligent attitude of Muslims towards *'adl* which should have been the base and pivot of their social and economic life, stress on which has been laid in scores of Quranic verses and which was scrupulously followed by the great Prophet of Islam (may benediction and peace be on him) in every single activity of his life, is that great tragedy of Islamic history. The principle of *tauhid* revolutionized the world of belief and left tangible result. The principle of *'adl* could create in human society and economics a revolution far greater than that brought about by *tauhid* in the realm of creed and could have salvaged both of them from that waywardness which is tormenting the modern man : provided the Muslim should have practised this revolutionary principle in their life and set an example for others. To practise this principle is a far cry. They did not even think in an organized manner over the utility of *'adl* nor could they enunciate those fundamental rules with the help of which it could be adopted for actual practice in life.

These and many other similar doctrines are awaiting their practical demonstration in the proposed departments and colleges of the Indian Institute of Islamic Studies, New Delhi. During the past few months I myself have been able to collect vast material on *'adl* and I have to find time for studying and analysing this material.

After a long gap, I now got an opportunity to go through the material I had been able to collect on *'adl* and its research. The Material contains : papers not only on *'adl* but also on philological research of such connected words as *qist, wazan, nazm, mizan, asl, zulm wa tashattut* etc., a systematic arrangement of *suras* and verses of the *Qura'n* and *handith* which deal with these words. Then there are papers dealing with different meanings of *'adl* and its derivatives, clarifying and distinguishing them with the help of relevant texts of the Qur'an and its five Persian and Urdu translations, the translators being Sa'di, Shah Waliallah, Shah Rafi al-Din, Shah "Abd al-Qadir and Maulana Ashraf Ali Thanwi. The *hadiths* on add contained in *Sahih Bukhari, Muatta* of Imam Malik, *Muslim, Abu Da ud* and *Nasai* etc., have been collected at one place. The collection also includes the photostat copies of relevant material from different encyclopaedias as well as books of law and philosophy dealing with *adl* and justice, besides some personal notings and writings.

In the past three or four years I could not get time to attend to this subject and consequently there could not be any significant advance. However, this efflux of time has only reinforced my views on *adl* and its principles which are reflected by the extracts given earlier. Now the reality that the primary cause of man's troubles is the separation of religion from his temporal life is unfolding itself with greater vividity. When one observes the division between spirit and matter on one hand and between mass and energy on the other has been eliminated by the new discoveries of science, he feels convinced that the detachment of science from religion can also not last longer, that the necessity of enunciating principles of *adl* will become all the more apparent and ultimately the doors of research for application of these principle to the human society shall open.

It is evident from the above brief statement that what *adl* connotes literally, can be described in plain word as 'equipoise' or 'moderation' which does not let its follower incline excessively in one direction. A follower of *adl* has to adopt the middle course, the golden mean, in every state of his life, be it social or economic, spiritual or terrestrial and whether he is in grief or in exultation, asleep or awake, moving or motionless and in it alone he sees and procures both the worldly and celestial bliss.

In my collection I got a note written by me some time on this elucidation and scope of *adl* and the method of its application. To clarify the purpose further. I give below a few extracts of that note:

> The controversy regarding the exact status of spirit and matter and other associated issues and the resultant schism between spiritualism, and materialism, religion and science, inwardness and outwardness, time and space has divided mankind into two warring groups, and this strife or conflict is continuing unabatedly with frequent disastrous effects. This conflict has spared no phase of human life. The whole panorama of human civilization and the social, economic, moral, religious and civic orders, which it produced, all are subject to this conflict and its off-shoots : there is restlessness in individual, family and corporate life. Man stands deprived of an integrated, un divided and unified life. The cherished dream of achieving human equality and brotherhood remains a mere dream. Our good Earth, in spite of our pious wishes, could not become a real paradise and the dejected man had to concentrate all his thoughts on some other paradise in the hereafter. There have been endless discussions on the merits and demerits of this conflict. Some hold that this conflict alone is the moving force behind human evolution and growth of civilization, that struggle for existence, is the external law of nature and this law is operative in every walk of life, rather in everything in and beyond this world. Whereas there are others who have laid down limits for the 'evolution' and 'conflict' and while acknowledging the importance of the law of 'struggle of existence' they are of the view that an integrated and unified human life is essential.
>
> Religious leaders, moralists and philosophers have often recognized the necessity of 'integration' in human life and

tried to surface up the causes of its absence. They did not confine themselves to the diagnosis of the disease but also offered formulas to treat it. These formulas suppressed the symptoms of the disease, even gave temporary relief and occasionally the signs of recovery were also noticeable, but the disease was never completely eradicated and whenever it found favourable conditions it re-emerged.

The East has often cursed science and extolled its own spiritual superiority. However, even this spirituality of the East could not turn this world into a paradise. The West is performing miracles in science and has fulfilled man's material and physical requirements to an extent that it has left little room for hankering after greater comforts of life. Even this earthly paradise of the West has failed to give to man real relief and peace of mind. The moving pictures of misery and restlessness and the living samples of internal disquit are there to be seen even by the superficial observer and the discerning observer can hear the restlessness in the heartbeats of philosophers and scientists.

This unending controversy of spirit and matter and the consequential conflict between the spiritualists and materialists pushed the world and its people at times to spiritualism and at times to materialism. This imbalance is continuing and there seems to be no way for deliverance. The fact is that spirit and matter have got their respective values recognized by all at different times. A materialist in the event of one single calamity befalling him begins to turn his attention to the spirit and its creator. Similarly, a spiritualist, who is accustomed to condemn the materialist, gets ready to give up his spiritualism when he is confronted with penury. Is not there a way to get rid of this controversy of spirit and matter and its deleterious effects? Has not the time come to close this controversy, cut off the whole chain of imbalances generated by it and recognize the existence of both and instead of wasting human energy on futile research as to their nature and other characteristics, utilize the same in research on establishing the true relationship between the two ? The idea for such research is not new. Already it has been propagated, though with tepidity. Arts and sciences are unwittingly moving towards this position. Arts are entering into sciences and *vice versa*, and there are indications that ultimately they may merge in one another. Material bases for psychology and allied disciplines are being sought for. Similarly, efforts are on to discover *nafs* and spirit in different fields of physical knowledge. So far medicine is concerned, the psychosomatic viewpoint is gaining ground. As a matter of fact, medicine is such a unifying entity that it combines within itself arts and sciences, spirit and matter. It is, indeed, a distinctive embodiment of synthesis.

On integration or synthesis I had made some observations at the Annual Session of the All-India Unani Tibbi Conference held at Simla in June 1963 under the chairmanship of Dr. Zakir Husain, the then Vice-President of India. Below I reproduce some of them :

> We have received great enlightenment from the pioneers of our medicine. While discussing the respective roles of art and science in medicine, they always adopted the course of moderation. With the knowledge they had, they tried to demarcate boundaries for art and science in medicine. From the very beginning experimentation (observation) and philosophy have held an important position in medicine. Synthesis has to do practically with the principles and practices of an art or science. It requires free scope of action and for this purpose unwarranted prejudices have necessarily to be avoided. Aggressive attack on a principle is exceedingly harmful while the artificial atmosphere of emotional policy is unfavourable to it. It is in no way the purpose of synthesis that an unpalatable hotch-potch of different principles and practices be cooked; for the integration of different principles and practices it is necessary in the first place to take stock of their details carefully, then find such a principle as may from to some extent a common factor in all of them and serve as a nucleus upon which different principles and practices may condense at the right place and in right proportion. Synthesis

cannot be created by any mechanical or artificial means; it necessarily requires logical processes. With it can associate freely different, even some contradictory, principles. In brief, synthesis is the widest generalization of a law embracing individual laws and their application. A synthesiser strives to arrive at the actual and final aim of the different principles and practices, then classifies every phase of action of those principles and laws and removes their limitations and incompatibilities and in this way can succeed in passing over the stage of integration impartially.

In the synthesis of medicine, as in other arts and sciences, stock should, in the same way, be taken of the principles and practices of the differnt systems of treatment and their details. There are basic principles in every regular system of medicine which characterize that system. Hence it is evident that the intergration of two or more systems of medicine requires much care, capacity and impartiality. It is difficult to determine any particular period or set of circumstances for the integration. In the presence of honesty and industry any difficult task can b accomplished at all times and under all circumstances. However, if integration were to be accepted as a good deed, then a good deed shouid be done even under adverse circumstances, because sometimes it so happens that the basis of the whole problem suffers such a fundamental change that circumstances have no more the same influence on it. In connexion with the integration of the medical systems it should be borne in mind that it is possible that in future quite a new system of medicine may come into existence. The achievements of physics have changed the old concept of matter. Formerly, matter and energy were considered not interconvertible, now matter has been transformed into energy. No limits can be assigned to the progress of science considering its present rate of advancement . Possibly the question of matter and consciousness (life) may also be solved in future and the basic conceptions of philosophy may suffer changes, thus altering the system of medicine.

It is good luck of mankind that now even highest scientific researches are favouring the elimination of any division or distinction between spirit and matter, time and space, mass and energy. Science may or may not inform us about the origin of spirit and matter but it is now admitted that these are two faces of one and the same thing and as stated earlier spirit can be transformed into matter and matter into spirit. The nature of a material object is not permanent by itself but depends upon its movement which rises or falls according to velocity. Sometime a material object moves in a straight line and some time it advances like the spreading waves of water. Modern physics has also changed the old concept of time and space. No longer they are considered to be two permanent entities. They are taken as interdependent. Neither time is a part of space nor space of time but both of them are parts of a third whole called 'Space-time Continuum' which is a four dimensional vector. This important discovery of modern physics has revolutionalized old concepts and has facilitated the coming into existence of the paradise on earth which man had relentlessly been searching for.

Arts and sciences, as well as religion and sciences are bound to be influenced by the integration of time and space and mass and energy and the determination of laws and rules of *adl* appears to be imminent.

The above quotation is a bit lengthy but it sheds sufficient light on the application of *adl* to man and different stages and stations of his life. It is also helps in determining the meaning of *adl.* It now getting clearer that *adl* is positive in every type of life, be it human, animal or vegetative. It is positive *vis-a-vis* certain negative principles e.g. non-violence, non-cooperation, non-intervention, non-interference, non-involvement etc., and this positive character of *adl* can be seen in action in people who follow it.

Being a physician, I can explain such terms as *adl, ta'dil, mu tadil* only in relation to medicine and health. In this connexion I reproduce below an article of mine which has a complete discussion on *adl* in medicine. Towards the end of the article a programme of research is on *adl* in medicine. The extent of the programme shows what intensive research is necessary for the exact determination of the scope of *adl* in relation to medicine. The application of the principle of *adl* in social, economic and other aspects of human life requires a much more detailed study.

Attemperament in Medicine

Every system of medicine is based on a definte concept of man. But the concept of man which is prevalent at any given time may undergo changes with the changing situation in science. It is at the same time important to note that what we think of man is also closely related to what one thinks of reality as a whole. The primitive man, for example though of reality or rather felt it in a way which is different from ours. Man was not isolated from nature. Nor was there any division of the world into the living and non-living. Again, for primitive man the living and the non-living world was equally inhabited by personal forces. The modern man is much obsessed by division. On the one side there is the inorganic world subject to its own laws; on the other side, there is the organic world which seems to have its own characteristics. Of course, the mechanistic view of reality does not consider the division of the non-living and living as fundamental and considers life as the more complex manifestation of the same processes as we find on the non-living layer of reality. But all that is living is not conscious and all that is conscious is not self -conscious. Hence, we may imagine that reality is constituted of different layers, the non-living, the living the conscious and the self-conscious. Only when we have to do with the self-conscious level that we encounter persons or individuals. Persons are self -conscious centres of experience and in our experience we are only aware of persons as human beings. Every human being as a self-conscious individual includes all the lower levels of reality. We are only aware of persons as human embodies. If somebody asks us about disembodied persons or disincarnate spirits we can only admit our ignorance. Now human beings are embodied minds. Materialists will of course insist that minds are unobservable through the senses and what cannot be 'verified' through the sense does not exist. On the contrary, the spiritualists will insist with equal vehemence that bodies have no existence independent of mind and will try to seek support in the recent development of physics. Now it is a moot question in physics whether matter has more a character of particles or waves or both are equally valid aspects of reality. What we are trying to show is that in medicine we cannot afford to take any extremist posture. Naive experience as experience is much more valuable in practical respects than metaphysical construction. Our experience then shows us reality at different levels and we must accept them as they are without trying to reduce the one into the other. The body for the medical man is as much an immediate datum of experience as the mind. But the body in which the medical man is interested is not the 'dead body' but a living body and when the living body is considered in the human context it has an invariable reference to a conscious centre of experience. Man then with whom we have to do in medical Practice is a living body with conscious experience. It is a great error to think that the primitive experience of man is of no avail. First of all the primitive mind did not consider man in isolation from nature however naive his way of thinking or of feeling might have been otherwise. His thought was really a form of feeling as a pre-logical and a pre-conceptual grasp of reality. Now the ancient systems of medicine also do not consider man in isolation from nature. The view that man as microcosm mirrors nature as macrocosm has found its echo even in modern thought when a philosopher, as modern and subtle as Leibniz thought every monad reflects the world from its own stand-point. This means that Leibnez moved even one step further and thought that not only man mirrored nature but that every particle of the world reflected the whole of the world from its own angle and that every unit of the world is imbued with consciousness, however dim and faint that consciousness may be.

Now to understand the spirit of the Greco-Arab medicine, it is necessary to know its conceptual framework and overcome the difficulties of the medical jargon in which the terms are conveyed. At times they may appear rather unfamiliar to the modern mind. The idea of *arkan* (elements) and *akhlat* (humours) does not, however, present any insuperable difficulties as they were the ideas with which the masters of Greek medicine worked. The views that there are four humours has a long history. Dr. Rudolf E. Siegel writes:

> The concept of the number four has to be attributed to Pythagoras (530 B.C.) and his school. The founder of the Silicean medical tradition, Alcmaeon (beginning of 5th century B.C.) spoke of innumerable qualities as basis of health. His successors Empedocles and Philistion and also Philolaos (later part of 5th century B.C.) restricted the number of elements and qualities of four. The doctrine that a perfect combination of the basic qualities leads to their equal mixture (*Krasis* from *erannymi, mix*) as a guarantee of health, had persisted since this remote time and remained a dominant medical concept for centuries.

The main problem here lies with concept of *mizaj* (temperament and unless we are clear what it is all about we are bound to get ourselves involved in endless confusion. While the modern concept of temperament is strictly psychosomatic, the Arab physicians applied it on a universal scale. Everything, no matter whether it is a fluid or a human organ or a drug or an article of food has its own *mizaj* and it was the primary concern of the physician to know the *mizaj* or temperament of things. Nay they went so far as to hold that *mizaj* is universal in its application and that it transcends the limitation of the earthy sphere. Their notion of health and disease was moulded on this conceptual pattern. But the modern concept of temperament does not fully coincide with the concept of *mizaj* as it was understood by the Arab physicians. In this regard Dr. O.C. Gruner's observations are very instructive:

> The word 'temperament' is not exactly satisfactory. The Arabic word *mizaj* contains the idea of 'mixture'. So the medieval translators used the words *commixtio* or *complexio* which carry the idea of mixing or blending, or weaving. But neither word fits in with modern usage. The word 'constitution is more meaningful to the lay person, as referring to the

> make- up of the physical body; 'temperament', the idea of the mental body or make-up. The word 'constitution' carries the idea of something stationary, unchanging. One has, therefore, to use the word temperament in psychological sense; in a medical sense it should imply a blend of humours as in the *Canon*. There is a pattern of humours, since all four are present in every individual. But whether the temperament is hot, or cold, or dry, or moist is determined by the proportions of the four elements. This is one advantage to restoring the doctrine of the elements to their original position—they are the common denominator between temperament, humours, mental make-up, faculties and emotional character of a person.

Temperament, indeed, occupies a very important place in the Greco-Arab medicine and forms the basis of pathology, diagnosis and treatment in this medical system. It has been defined in our classics in the following way:

It is the pattern resulting from the interaction of the opposing qualities of elements. The elements divide themselves into minute particle to secure intimate contact with one another. When the qualities of these particles act and react on one another there emerges a new pattern of qualities which is uniformly distributed throughout the elements.

While a majority of the physicians subscribed to this definition they expressed differnt opinions on the reciprocal action of the elements. However, there is unanimity of view that three things are essential in respect of an element. These are (1) Matter (2) Form (3) State. The question as to what contribution three made in the formation of a compound or in the determination of its temperament led to unending philosophical discussions.

Four *arkan* (element), four *arkhlat* (humours) and the resultant four main *mizaj* (temperaments) and their various classes consititute the basis of Greco-Arab medicine. According to the philosophy of Greco-Arab medicine the scope of *mizaj* (temperament) is all extensive. Arab Physicians do not confine it to the terrestrial sphere but ascribe a cosmic significance to it.

Before explaining what is meant by 'attemperament' in Greco-Arab medicine it is necessary to mention the general classes of human temperament as given in the old medical texts. These are:

I. Balanced (equable or normal) temperament with the following varieties:

A. In relation to beings other than man

- (i) the equability of temperament seen in man as compared with other creatures;
- (ii) that which is found in different human beings;
- (iii) that which is taken in relation to external factors, such as race, climate, atmosphere;
- (iv) one taken in comparison with the temperament of extremes of climate.

B. In relation to individual himself

- (i) as compared with another person;
- (ii) as compared with the states of one and the same person;
- (iii) as compared, one member with another;
- (iv) as compared with the state of one and the same member, at different times.

II. Imbalanced (inequable, abnormal) temperament. It may be simple or compound with the following varieties:

A. Varieties of simple imbalanced temperament

- (i) hot, those in which there is more heat that there should be;
- (ii) cold, those in which there is more cold that there should be;
- (iii) dry, those in which there is more dryness then there should be;
- (iv) moist, those in which there is more moistness than there

should be.

B. Varieties of compound imbalanced temperament

(i) hot and dry, those that are at the same time hotter and drier then should be;
(ii) hot and moist those that are at the same time hotter and moister, than they should be;
(iii) cold and dry those that are at the same time colder and drier than they should be;
(iv) cold and moist those that are all the same time colder and moister than they should be.

In the discussion on the role of temperament in the maintenance of human health and eradication of disease words *tadil* (attemperament) and *tawazun* (balance) have been used very frequently. The range of meaning in the use of these words is not determined with precision. Sometimes they are used as synonyms. However, it would be safe to conclude that *tadil* has a constitutional use and *tawazun* a diagnostic and therapeutic one. Here we are concerned with *tadil* as understood in our medicine.

The root of *tadil* is the Arabic word *adl* whose derivatives abound in Arabic dictionaries and is so rich in shades of meaning that no word of any other language can adequately convey what the word actually means.

The word 'attemperament' as used in Greco-Arab medicine does not mean equating or balancing of elements or faculties or states. The reason is simple. The existence of a really attempered object which embodies exactly equated elements or faculties or states is far from possible. The element cannot coalesce with one another and this is because of their innate powers and attractions. All the existing compounds are intempered as there is excess of earthy elements in them and by virtue of this characteristic they are forced to mutual association.

When some compound is found composed of contrary elements

(hot, cold, moist and dry elements) the attempering shall always be virtual. It will not be real or actual. According to physicians no compound is found to exist which contains antagonistic elements in equal parts. It is clear that the compound which can be found on the terrestrial sphere will be intempered because as it is natural, earthy elements will here dominate.

Now it seems very odd that according to the above definition every compound in this world appears to be attempered whereas it is only human species as such which can truly lay claim to attemperament. The reason in not far to seek. As Shifa al-Mulk Hakim Abd al-Latif has observed:

> That while true attempering is not found in the human, yet the admixture of his elements is nearer to the truly attempered admixture than that of other species and compounds and that his proximity to attempering is probably in this sense that because all actions and re-actions of human beings, as the noblest of creatures are carried out more moderately than those of other species and creatures ; hence it was assumed that the admixture of his elements should also be proximate to equipoise. Then this equipoise of the human species in comparison with other ones is named species' specific equipoise. But if the individuals and members of the human species were to be taken into account the equipoise of each individual appears different. As long as that individual maintains his equipoise his health is assured and when it is disturbed his health suffers.

Now it clearly follows that equipoise is a relative condition acquired by one species of individual with reference to other species or individuals. Similarly, the climate of a country is considered attempered where the hours of day and night as well as the heat of the day and the cool of the night are equal and such tracts are called temperate. In the same manner the word 'attempered' is applied to drugs and diet, but here a quite different meaning is adopted, namely, an attempered medicine is that which when administered to a healthy and normal person does not produce any extra symptom.

An attempered medicine is intrinsically an intempered one and its effects are so weak that after the reaction of the human body they are nullified and the human body is not affected by them.

However, it is not necessary to subscribe to the view given above. On the contrary it may well be contested that to be attempered all elements need not be equal and even if it were assumed there may be cases in which some elements, by force of their attraction, can retain other elements within their orbit of influence as it is hinted at by Avicenna in his book *Kitab al-shifa*. Now in the very idea of *mizaj* as blending or mixture of elements there is involved the idea of integration or balance. Health denotes the miantenance of balance between different elements. Naturally the balance can never reach an ideal point. There always underlies a tension and the balance is always relative. Once the balance is disturbed disease or dis-ease ensues. Gruner observes:

> The idea of balance can be applied to a variety of phenomena in health and disease, both of body and mind. Lack of balance brings sickness and may be precursor of death. For instance, modern text books record atony, hypertonicity, hyperacidity, hypotonicity, excessive trichosis, and the modern hormone-imbalance, mental imbalance. One can speak of dynamic balance and static balance.

Some modern physicians and psychiatrists instead of talking of imbalance, speak of 'disorganization' even though they do not subscribe to the Arab medical theory or *mizaj*. Even for them the person is a unity in multiplicity and the disease brings when 'disorganization' sets in. " The more severe the illness, the more altered is integration and the more effort must be devoted to prevention of dissolution."

A careful analysis of *i'tidal* will provide an important clue to the understanding of *tadil* as a crucial medical term. *Adl* is equivalent to justice but justice connotes balance. Plato did not consider justice and individual's virtue but the virtue of the state. It holds the balance between the other cardinal virtues and does not allow any to dominate the other. Applied in the medical context it will mean that health is the maintenance of equipoise in different functions of the organism and disease is the condition in which the balance shifts in one direction at the expense of another. Sometimes in disease the balance is disturbed in such a way that the restoration becomes impossible. Non-restorability of balance signals death. The organism is held in constant tension by the tendency of different functions to become autonomous. As organism is unity in multiplicity, any functional dissociation tends to dissolve the unity and the more the unity is disturbed the more severe will be the nature of the disease and more difficult will it be to restore the original unity which characterizes the state of health. What is called recovery of health is just the process of the restoration of balance. Through the process of *tadil* the balanced state of the organism is maintained, a state in which each organ is guaranteed freedom in its sphere of action and at the same time its functional autonomy is not allowed to over-reach itself. In fact the above discussion on 'temperament' and 'attemperament' may help in determining (1) the generalized principles; (2) objective of medicine; (3) bases of treatment ; and (4) laws of treatment. These issues have been dealt with elaborately in the volume *philosophy of Medicine and Science—Problems and Presoectives* the recent publication of the Department of Philosophy of Medicine and Science of the Institute of History of Medicine and Medical Research, New Delhi. The volume contains a chapter on 'Elements' also. While dealing with this subject I have suggested that first we should know all those elements which man has. If according to the ancient philosophical tradition, man belongs to the macrocosm then the only logical inference can be that he should posses all the known elements. Accordingly, I have invited the medical man and scientists to conduct necessary research on the subject for which the following may serve as guidelines:

I. The definition of element from the medical point of view.

II. Determination of the number of elements and classification therefore, from the medical point of view

(a) general principles of classification of elements;

(b) number and distribution of elements in space or atmosphere;
(c) number and distribution of elements in the ocean;
(d) number and distribution of elements in the earth and its crust;
(e) number and distribution of elements in
 (i) mineral or inorganic kingdom;
 (ii) vegetable kingdom;
 (iii) animal kingdom;
 (iv) human kingdom.

III. Human body and elements

(a) number, quantity and proportion of elements in the human body;
(b) number, quantity and proportion of elements in:
 i. different sexes;
 ii. different ages;
 iii. different individuals;
 iv. different races, nations and geographical region;
 v. different seasons;
(c) Reasons for specific human content of elements in number, quantity and proportion;
(d) Distinction among humans due to difference of number, quantity and proportion of elements;
(e) Connection and relation between 'human elements' and other elements;
(f) Relation between humans and plants with respect to number, quantity and proportion of elements;
(g) Relation between humans and inorganic-bodies with respect to number, quantity and proportion of elements;
(h) If human body is really a microcosm as considered by some Philosophers then should all the elements be present in it which are contained in the macrocosm?

IV. Will this idea not hold scientifically that attention should be paid in health, disease and treatment to the quantity, number and quality of elements of the human body?

With the help of this type of research only it would be possible to determine medically the place of man in the universe and this world so that may be able to determine the true scope of medicine itself.

REFERENCES

1. Galen's System of philosophy of medicine.
2. O C Gruner's Commentary on the 'zCanon of medicine' Hamdard Medical Digest, July-Sept. 1967, 14-16.
3. Hakim Abd al-Latif, I'tidal-i tibbi, unpublished Urdu Ms.
4. Gruner, Philosophy of medicine and science - problems and perspectives, New Delhi, 1973, p. 121.
5. Keslie A Osborn, Psychiatry and medicine.

Revised and edited; originally published in Studies in Islam, July 1978.

8

The Unity of God

KHAIR-UL-NISA SARAWAK

> As there are seven ways of interpreting the Koran, if the verses can have seven different meanings, are'nt there also seven ways to comprehend God?.

Humanity evolves slowly, but continually in accordance with unbreakable laws following what we call the Path of God.Let us examine the idea which guided the evolution of the human spirit (man) on his way to progress. This idea which finally transformed the world had far-reaching consequences. It is the conception of a spiritual God and the notion of His Unity. This conception is more than a dogma as dogmas belong to theology only. It is the divine and eternal Truth.

A careful study of the origin and evolution of spiritual monotheism shows that this conception was due to Divine revelation more than the result of reason, intellect or religious feeling, and had no mystical or imaginative basis. God Himself spoke through His Prophets.

God desired the Truth to be revealed to the mortals because monotheism as a seed, growing among them, started the era of powerful moral and social transformations. It was important to lay down the idea of Divine Unity as the basis of all religious doctrines, which since a certain epoch have led humanity and consecrated already accomplished progress. To be fertile this idea has to reach the whole of mankind. The difficulty of this task becomes obvious when one considers that humanity is not a homogeneous unity, but rather a conglomeration of more or less ancient and evolved elements, and that every new idea has to fight its way through the inertia of the masses, their ignorance and their fanaticism.

A new conception seldom had to face so many difficulties and vicissitudes as this superior conception of God. Thanks to the evident protection of God and the heroism of its defenders only, could this conception resist every attack and live throughout the history of mankind.

We see in history how this conception was at times obliged to give way to the polytheistic cult, and seemingly disappeared, but in reality it was preciously preserved by an elite. It came forth again with renewed vigour as if its temporary suppression had given a new impulse to this high ideal. This persistency is the characteristic of conceptions which are just and in accordance with the Diving Will. Erroneous ideas do not last and false conceptions easily show their frailness. As all human work their time is limited and they are soon forgotten.

Only the ideas placed obviously under the Divine protection progress with the help of God and are eternal. They progress victoriously and stand all attempts of deformation and dissimulation and are accepted because of their evidence and simplicity. Time, the great judge of all things does not affect them; on the contrary, it is over time that they triumph. Such is the case of the spiritual conception of the Unity of God. This revelation was the intervention of God through His Prophets in the destiny of humanity.

The difference which existed between the teaching of these inspired men is only a difference of Time, and not a difference of direction or sense. It was the same Divine influence which spoke through them at different stages of human evolution. This Divine protection granted to the idea of monotheism is sufficient to make us realise its importance.

We will give a short sketch of the path followed by this revelation, of which today Islam is the foremost representative.

In the first stages of humanity, men fascinated by the marvels of creation and realising their weakness, filled the world with divinities to whom they attributed their own appearance, passions and faults.

We know enough of the religious evolution of mankind to avoid the description of pagan cults which we can still find among certain tribes. We know the progression which leads from the vulgar fetichism to the more complex mythologies, all of them attempting to explain the mysteries of creation, or symbolising some metaphysical theory.

We need not mention the cult of idols, as this was simply the worship of a Divinity in visual form. The longing for miracles, tales and extaneous manifestations of the Divinity is a characteristic of childhood of man and races.

For a long time man thought that sacrifice was the only way to attract the favour of the Gods or to appease their anger. To obtain the indifference of these blind Gods was considered a great achievement because the culprits and the innocent were equally punished by them. Subconsciously man felt the influence of God in their life, but this idea was still very dormant. Man could conceive a superior power only by means of senses and imagination.

How was it possible to differentiate the good and evil, when man lived without any moral aim or spiritual ideal and had no rules except those of social and civil life. He had no conception of the kindness of God and no moral ideas as we understand them today.

One can hardly conceive today what life was liked in this society, where men were easy prey to their instincts and appetites and had no other law but that of force, and they submitted to gods only because they were exposed to their cruel vengeance. The gods themselves were not always all powerful and had man only known the means they would have been attacked as minor deities in ritualistic simulations.

It is obvious that under these circumstances humanity could only progress slowly. Worshiping several gods, men only realised some of the Divine manifestations and adored parts of God but not Himself. They could not therefore realise the Divine Laws, the foremost being hidden from their knowledge. Divine Laws are eternal and it was not because they ignored them that men were freed from submission. God was sometimes severe to men when the limits of His kindness were exceeded,but His mercy never failed in enlightening the most evolved spirits and helping those who, with their whole hearts looked for God.

Humanity had to pass through this first stage of evolution on its way to progress. The moral and physical laws having both the same basis and their origin in God it became possible to deduct one, knowing the other.

During the course of centuries, wise men, specialised in the study of nature, did not miss this analogy and its transcendent consequences, seeing in the harmony of creation an indication of the Unity of God. A philosopher cannot admit several superior facts which lead to the negation of the marvellous unity of the Divine Will, whilst the study of nature is proving the reverse.

God never specially favoured any race or epoch, all men are equal in His presence. Highly evolved spirits and great souls can be found anywhere at any time. Their work,thoughts and observations are outliving them, and finally unite in a perpetual chain of truth which is called Tradition. Slowly and simultaneously among the elite in different places the monotheistic idea started to germinate. It started under the influence of Tradition of races which already had disappeared and was brought back to this elite by far eastern or African philosophers.

The high priests of Egypt possessing a vast knowledge among their numerous divinities, the superior trinity, and foresaw the existence of one non-created God, the Creator.

The Chaldeans who discovered the great laws in the study

of planets, saw behind their idols, one God with three aspects.

We know the pure fraternity which reigns among men who attain level of knowledge and wisdom, and therefore, are above the interest, hatred and rivalities which divide nations and races. It becomes understandable that through wars and migrations of races of a different origin the fusion of tradition and knowledge took place.

Historical observation shows that the invasions and migrations which infused the antique Egyptian civilisation with the races of Asiatic descent with old traditions, had to pass through Palestine and Sinai, which forms a natural corridor between the two continents. It is then equally understandable the God chose to appear in this meeting-place of races and Traditions. He selected Abraham as being the best among the evolved races, inspired him and made him his messenger of earth.

In the time of Abraham, the monotheistic idea existed vaguely and more by intuition than by anything else. God the Creator was felt behind and above the idols, and historical proofs, such as prayers, incartations and sculptures show that if God was mentioned. He was unrepresented everywhere. It was unnecessary to make idols of Hirn as the notion of Him belonged only to the Priests and was unfelt by the masses. This is the origin of monotheism and the seed of the spiritual conception of God forthcoming from the notion of God the Creator. Man at this time was not far off the superior conception of God but it was still an object of uncertainty, being misunderstood by the masses who were still strongly attached to their idols. A divine confirmation was necessary to present this idea and give it the required impulse. God then intervened in the destiny of Men, speaking to Abraham at the right moment to reassure his followers and confirm the truth. These men deserved the knowledge having foreseen it. Abraham publicly proclaimed the idea of One Eternal God, Creator of everything, and thus, fought the ancient cults. Isaac and Jacob and the descendants of Abraham followed his example and today the divine truth confined in the races descending from Abraham, who are the monotheistic races.

But Abraham's monotheism inherited in practice many sides of the cults, he overthrew.

Men could not suddenly evolve towards the full understanding of Abraham's revelation, which appealed only to a minority. The Holy Scripture shows that at this time if man accepted the idea of Divine Unity and forsook their idols, they could only then realise the idea of a spiritual God. The Bible and the Koran mention that God spoke to Abraham and that he replied and argued. This Tradition of a direct revelation of God to man admits human attributes of God, although he remained invisible but intervened by human means. His manifestations were material and touched men directly.

Since Abraham, the monotheistic idea is precise enough to lead to a new conception of Divine justice, which is expressed in the dialogue of God and Abraham about the ten good men in Sodome.

Man realised that God was just, and in opposition to their ancestors were no more afraid of the idols who had terrorised man by their bloodthirsty fancies, and the just man had no more dread of God, when he avoided disobeying or displeasing Him.

This idea of Divine justice leads in its turn to the idea of fault and punishment, and men realised that they could avoid the anger of God, not by means of sacrifice, but buy carrying out His Divine Will. This is the first notion of distinction between good and evil, based on a superior moral, and giving the rules one has to follow, first not to displease God, and secondly to obey His Will.

The tribes of Israel during their migrations and dispersion, kept upright as an inheritance from Patriarchs, not only the oldest traditions concerning the beginning of everything and the first steps of humanity, but also and especially the monotheism with the ideas which derived from it. These treasures risked to be lost and it was necessary to fertilise this truth, to exact, elaborate and codify the rules of life in conformity with the Divine Will, to convert them into laws and to impose them.

To materialise the moral and social consequences of the monotheism of Abraham, God inspired Moses the moral basis he gave to humanity which still lives in every soul. It is unnecessary to speak about the personality of Moses and his life, let us only follow the idea of the Unity of God.

The genius of Moses materalised the union of a people with such a peculiar character that it would always remain outside, without fusing with every other race. This race with Moses'impulse, kept his teachings unspoilt and transmitted them with their old traditions to the next generation .This same race was the first to be organised in the name of One God, and its social laws were divine, whilst the supreme power was subordinated to God only. We find the same form of organisation much later in the time of the last Prophet and the first Caliphs. Such a society was the fruit of monotheism. Moses gave it a legislation, based upon the commandments he received from God at Sinai. These laws were inseparable from the idea of One God, and could not be understood or applied without the comprehension of the divine unity.

Time confirmed this great truth:one can say today that all morals are derived from the Commandments God gave to the Hebrews, the moral code of humanity is one with human conscience, and is the expression of the Divine Will.

Moses cleared the conception of God of the last vestige of idolatry and it is interesting to think of God appearing to Moses bearing the Law engraved by Himself. This corresponds to the monotheistic idea of Abraham: the direct correspondence of God to man and the attribution of human faculties to God. Such was the idea that man had of God at the time of the first Pentateuch; later on we find the pure idea of Moses, and the invisible, immaterial, eternal and omnipresent God.

The history of Israel shows that Moses' teaching did not reach the masses, and it was not for about another thousand years that he overcame the false cults. God granted his protection to the truth He revealed to men, Truth which had to be victoriously spread over the whole of humanity. Man tried in vain to return to foreign cults; they always found some Nabis faithful to God to remind them of Moses' teaching and foretell the chastisement God would send upon them if they forsook Him.

Ezra then appeared, followed by Nehemias. Again we see the sign of Divine favour when Ezra was allowed by the Bobylonian King to return to Jerusalem and we have enough proof to state that the whole evolution of monotheism was placed under the sign of the protection of God. It was through Ezra's teaching that Moses' words were brought to the masses and with it the everlasting idea of One God. We find for the first time the idea of Divine mercy added to Divine justice. Ezra shows us God, being not only just but kind, patient and merciful. He is no more the implacable God we have seem before, but a God of kindness who punishes in sorrow and-redeems generously with joy.

Higher moral consequences derived from a true conception of God which at first belonging only to a few, gradually conquered every nation. God then intervened once more and inspired Jesus.

Abraham was the Prophet of Divine Unity Moses the Prophet of Divine Law and Justice, Jesus became the Prophet of Charity and Love. As far as monotheism was concerned, Jesus only confirmed what had been taught before by Moses and the Prophet of Israel, the existence of one eternal and Almighty God.

This conception was at this time well-known among the Jews. Last link of a chain passing from Abraham to the Doctors of the Second Temple, Jesus, proclaimed in the name of God the most glorious principles derived from the conception of One God.

His teaching was specially moralising but what made the grandeur of Jesus was the fact that he became the origin of the diffusion of Divine truth throughout a large part of the world.

We now follow the path by which monotheism passed the frontiers of the Jewish people, and later we will see this idea in other branches of Abraham's descendants, namely, the branch of

Ishmail which merits a special study.

The first favourable events to the expansion of monotheism was the dispersion of Jews, after the destruction of the Temple of Jerusalem. Leaving their fatherland to Rome, the Jews took with them into exile the spiritual treasures they derived from the Prophets of God and thus, became the guardians and deposit of pure monotheism.

They brought the Pagan world of those days, together with their tradition the cult of One God. Reassembled together on a limited territory they could perish and disappear under an invasion of barbars. Dispersed, they became unseizable and whatever happened the flame of the great truth of which they were the guardians could not be extinguished. The part played by the Jews in the history of monotheism is therefore passive. We heard of the existence of several Jewish colonies which made some proselytes but their number was so small that they never could dominate the local cults.

The great movement which started to spread monotheism began with Jesus : it was Christianity.

Jesus left some of his disciples who gathered round Peter and devoted themselves to the love and glory of their master whose memory and teaching they religiously kept. One must consider that Jesus represented the highest doctrine ever known by man, and that this doctrine was Jewish. His disciples followed strictly at first the Jewish orthodoxy which was always respected by Jesus as he declared that he came to fulfil the Law. The first Christians, the Ebionites were Jews, and they lived on friendly terms with the rest of the community until they proclaimed Jesus to be grater than Moses and insisted on his resurrection and taught that he was the Messiah promised by the Prophets. There was nothing in this new idea against Monotheism,but when Peter started to speak in the name of Jesus, instead of God, his sect, which had numerous followers was condemned by the Jewish community as immoderate in matters of orthodoxy.

Such was the beginning of the Christian deviation, which unaffecting the Unity of God, proved useful for the progress of humanity.

If one follows the progress of the Christian deviation, one sees that if the doctrine itself was altered, the moral and traditional basis remained immutable: it was still the same idea of One Spiritual God that spread out and triumphed. The Christian doctrine adapted itself to the need of the time and local conditions, but the truth remained the same and progressed under a different form. Jesus gave to those who were disinherited the highest verities known only to the superior classes he popularised them and they penetrated the whole of humanity.

The disciples of Jesus materialised his thoughts and followed his words: "Go, and preach to every Nation."

It is through Ebionism, (a Jewish heresy out of which Christianity spread) that the work of the Prophets started to conquer the polytheistic world, and through them the idea of one Spiritual God was preached.

During the struggle of Peter with the hellenising Jews (a shadow on the pure monotheism or a resistance of paganism) Saul of Tarse started to preach and while aiming exclusively at the conversion of foreigners, had the genius of adapting his teaching to the state of mind of those, whom he wanted to touch. If we consider the exterior form only, we are far from Judaism but the teaching and morals of Moses and Jesus, reached, thanks to him, many remote points, and converted many followers.

A new discussion took place between Peter and Saul, who became Paul, one disapproving the ideas of the other. Hundreds of years after the death of both Apostles, the situation was not cleared and later when the Jewish nation was definitely destroyed and Judaism persecuted by the Roman Empire, Paul's teaching was tolerated and triumphed for the same reasons by which it had been rejected by the strict Jews. A kind of union was then made between the followers of the first Judeo-Christian doctrine and the followers of Paul, aiming at a conciliation and a common defence of their interests.

This conciliation is really the beginning of Christianity which had no other links with Judaism, but the traditional and moral basis, reposing in the Unity of God on one side and on the other Mooses' Commandments, confirmed by the Sermon on the Mount.

With time, the Christian doctrine went further and further away from its origin, following the system of adaptation and absorption of ancient cults and philosophies until it became trinitarian.

Those who are interested in the study of the trinitarian side of Christianity can find some information in my book "From Rome to Mecca," Chap.IX. The limited space of this article does not allow us to investigate this question thoroughly. In this respect I could say quite a lot, not about the dogma itself but about its consequences in the evolution of humanity as it is not wise to take a brusque decision in such a delicate question. The dogma itself does not affect the Unity of God, it can be conceived philosophically but remains today perfectly obscure from its followers, who, loosing the monotheistic point of view, imagine three gods mingling together, the Verbe, the Spirit and God the Infinite Principle.

This equivoque has made worse by the use of images. It would be a mistake to state positively that the modern Christianity is polytheistic or idolatrous but one can say without making as error that its followers have, to a certain extent, lost the just and pure conception of God. The Church will reply by saying that this doctrine allows her to touch every brain and that she gained in universality what has been lost in precision and every person can find in the doctrine an appropriate answer to their spiritual needs.

This reply would be justified, only if the Church encouraged the personal researches instead of ordering a blind belief. As a result, the true conception of God lost the force it had at the beginning of the Christian Era.

But if one considers impartially the results which have been acquired with time, one realises why God allowed this deviation of Christianity to take place.

As we have seen, monotheism having attained its full development by the virtue of the Prophets and the right conception of God, had to reach the whole of humanity.

It is possible to divide humanity into two branches, common in their origin but yet totally different. Some elements of the branch, we will call occidental, such as the Greeks, reached a high degree of culture. Though their philosophers preached very elevated doctrines they felt it difficult to free themselves from matter. For this reason they remained more intellectual than spiritual as they lacked the Divine teaching and were untouched by the Prophets. On the other hand, other nations remained in a primitive condition. It is clear, if one takes into consideration the ethnical differences and social and climatic influences, that the great truth taught in the pure form of monotheism would never have entered among these races. It was necessary to compromise with the ancient cults and adapt the form to the brains with different reactions : more realistic than speculative and more active than physical. Thus was sown the seed of Christianity. It is possible of course to accuse the Christian teaching of hiding and deforming the Truth but judging by the practical results, one had to admit that pagan nations, once having adopted Christianity made an enormous progress in the spiritual evolution and in the knowledge of Divine Verity. The descent of Sem, seems throughout history to have been granted the divine favour, being the race among which flourished the great verities and out of which Prophets were born.

The race of Isaac and Jacob followed the course of evolution, whilst Christianity overthrew idolatrous cults. Let us see how the idea of Divine Unity, the other branch of Sem developed in the East and how it reached its idolatrous neighbours. Were these people condemned to stick to the cult of false gods? No. The kindness of God does not allow us to face such an eventuality. The only distinction God makes among men is their degree of evolution in the path of Divine Laws. Every individual participates in different personal ways to the harmony of the whole big to every people a revelation which had to lead towards evolution and progress in the most favourable form. This was the miracle that happened through the Prophets, first among the races issued from Abraham, then among those of Isaac, Jacob and Joseph and finally among those of Ishmail.

Ishmail, was the beloved son of Abraham, who inherited his qualities, was just and submitted to God. He was banished because of his birth and had to leave the land of the Hebrews, settled in Arabia where he brought with him the teaching of Abraham and the belief of One God. There he met some old Arab tribes descended from Eber by Hoctan, lived with them and converted them to monotheism. Thus the sacred truth once proclaimed by Abraham was not only confined to the Hebrews but the whole of Abraham's posterity became the People of God.

About a thousand years before the construction of the Temple of Jerusalem by Solomon and Hiram, Ishmail, with Abraham's help had built the Kaaba, to the glory of God near the miraculous spring, and Mecca became the center of tribes which followed the God of Abraham, some of which settled in the neighbourhood.

After the death of Ishmail during an indefinite time, Abraham's religion remained the religion of the majority of Arabs, but like the Jews they fell back to idolatry. One knows the legend of Asaf and Naila who profaned the Kaaba and were for this crime converted into statues. The statues were placed on hills and finally worshipped. This is the trace of some ancient cult, where people adored the two principles: the sun and the moon, the day and night, cults which were imported into Arabia by foreigners with the legend of Mithra and Astarte.

The sixth century was the epoch when Christianity was codified and when the deviation was sealed. Long before this time the bitter struggles between the different schools forced some Christians to emigrate and many came to Arabia and Egypt. They belonged to what the Church calls the Nestorian heresy. Having settled in Arabia they professed their cult and probably had schools where they discussed the various theories of Christianity. The Arabs were specifically nomads, and often got in touch with their neighbours which, to a certain extent explains that they took up the cult of their divinities and idols. The Koran mentions the statues of Hobal, the idols of Manah, Uzza and Lat and one can find in some regions, in accordance with nations with which the Arabs were in contact the cult of stones, the cult of fire, planets, magic or obscene rites.

Abraham's monotheism did not disappear among the tribes of Ishmail, among the elite, hidden from the crowd it was secretly perpetuated. The Arabs frequently got in touch with Jews, and the same above-mentioned influence contributed to keep up a communication with the people who remained the most loyal to Abraham's monotheism. It is true that Arabs took from the Jews the cult of the Hights and Asheras, but at the same time they learnt the deeds and names of the great Jewish Kings and Prophets.

By means of caravans, the Arabs touched every nation of the Mediterranean, and their philosophers at the time of religious effervescence which followed the death of Jesus, learnt not only the pure Truth from the Prophets but also the different shades of Christianity and Greek philosophy. The dispersion of the Jews as well as the religious quarrels, forced a great amount of Jews, and Christian to emigrate to Arabia and Africa and form small colonies. Saul of Tarse spent the three first years of his apostolate among the tribes of Hauran and if one adds to these influences the military expeditions which crossed the Arabic land, one realises the religious confusion which reigned among the people, who had known but forgotten Abraham's revelation.

When the Jewish mission came to an end and they were dispersed and persecuted, Christianity became definitely settled and threatened by its power to become fatal to the work of the Prophets, of which it was only a vain reflection, God intervened yet again in the destiny of men. We then see not a slow evolution as it had been in the case of the Jews nor the use of artifices as the

Christian did, but the sudden appearance of the Prophet of God. With him like a thunder-bolt and with the help of God, monotheism suddenly spread out over the sixth part of the world.

Once more the descendants of Abraham had been favoured by God, and it was among Semits in the tribe of Ishmail that He selected His last Prophet.

The last Prophet—Glorified be his name—was really inspired by God. His life, his actions, and his words aim at one point: to teach and to broadcast monotheism. He was the Prophet of Divine Unity and through him God desired to confirm and regenerate the Truth he had already given to humanity. The teaching of the Prophet is a combination the most sublime Truth, the last expression of the preceding revelations which God desired to be confirmed and established so that they could be well anchored in the soul of men.

The centuries that the Arabs spent in idolatry are like an eclipse, period of immobility. The race started to live only when it came back to the belief of its remote ancestors. When the Prophet accomplished his mission, he spoke of Abraham's God, thus coming back to the oldest and just conception of God, the basis of monotheism. It was the religion of Abraham, enriched by the spiritual acquisitions of the past centuries, as well as by the revelations of other Prophets, that he preached and gave to his followers.

The Koran says: "You know the Scriptures why do you argue about Abraham. The Pentateuch and the Gospel came after his time. Don't you know this? Abraham was not Christian nor Jew, he was a true believer and submitted to God."

The idea which is exalted in the Koran is the Unity of God, therefore, the social and moral rules of the Koran are only its consequences. The belief in one God, invisible and almighty, leads to the disappearance of superstition, it gives the possibility of a clear understanding of evil and good. The idea of Diving mercy and justice, brings forth the understanding of brotherhood and equality among men, of their mutual love, and of their reconciliation in a common ideal.

God desired that the teaching He gave to His last Prophet should not be limited to one race only, He desired that in every respect it should be synthesis. God as He is understood by the Prophet is not exclusively an Islamic God, He is the God of every man and universe, appearing in a form which is comprehensible to every race and is not limited by time.

"Your God is the God of every man, there is no other God."

If philosophically Islam contains the truth of both Judaism and Christianity, in practice Islam unites the depth of Hebruism to the faculty of the expansion of Catholicism. Thanks to the Prophet, the eternal Truth becomes clearer and more positive than in all other doctrines. The Prophet does not use anything supernatural or mysterious. The reality is easy to find among the flourished style of the Koran, the tales of which, when they are not reproducing some Biblical stories are symbols hardly veiled and obvious for those who can see with open eyes. The sincerity of the Prophet is seen in his confirmation of a natural spiritual indirect revelation. Through the legends which say that fragments of the Koran, written in Heaven, reached the Prophet through Gabriel, it is easy to see in it the only form of revelation: the indirect revelation by inspiration of the truth written in the universe itself. This is very superior form compared to the direct supernatural revelation which we find at the childhood of monotheism.

The Prophet formally recognised the Koran to be the indirect work of God and when he spoke of Gabriel, the messenger of God, one must not consider it as an anthropomorphic entity but as a reality of extra-human order.

One can assert that monotheism taught by the last Prophet reached its perfection and certainly is the best suited to the spiritual conditions of our epoch, having been beforehand adapted to the aspirations of man, in a more perfect degree of cyclic evolution of humanity. For this reason the teaching of the Prophet is as fresh and alive today as it was at the beginning of the Hegira and therefore appears in the sense we investigate, to be the latest manifestation of Divine Will, to spread all over the world the knowledge and belief in One God.

It is likely that in this respect the limit of human possibilities of comprehension has been reached.

It is indeed vain to aim at the knowledge of the Unknowable and there in no evolved brain which does not realise that because of the difference in human and divine nature, the exact knowledge of God is beyond our poser. We can know His Laws and to a certain extent His Will and what counts more than the vain attempts to define God, is the submission to His Will, and the realisation of His universality and almightiness in the effects we can judge, rather than in the causes which are inaccessible to us. What is the use of theological subtilities, if humanity is not better? Every doctrine, even if it is not religious, which can lead man in the direction of Divine Will is blessed by God because of its aim.

We can even say, that such a doctrine requires the forcible recognition of the unity of God, and that in this case because of its origin will be related to the teaching of the Prophet.

Thanks to its universality and expansiveness which finds echoes everywhere, Islam is designed to spread out widely and will find in every land and place affinities and sympathizer of doctrines which are "muslim,' though their followers never realised it.

It is not only Islam that progresses, it is monotheism, the Koran being its expression. Both being the same it does not matter which comes first and how many fervent "muslims" are there in the world who would be surprised if one called them so, especially in the West?

God of Mohammed is the God of Tradition which one is entitled to comment upon as one thinks best, but the basis of which remains immovable throughout all the vissicitudes of humanity. This is the infinite Principle of even atheistic philosophers who change the name, not being able to replace the divine reality by a human formula. It is God that appears in the laboratories of science, the same God who made Islam the less opposed religion to modern discoveries.

A positive even materialistic brain without a preconceived idea can find in the teaching of Islam a superior spiritual direction. It is based upon the only conception of God which stood upright for thousands of years, the only one; which has been proved experimentally right, if one is allowed to apply this term to religion.

To conclude this article, may I propose to those who can reason the following suggestion. If one admits that there are seven ways of interpreting the Koran, if the verses can have seven different meanings, in accordance to the "plan" one chooses, are'nt there also seven ways to comprehend God? and if one sees in the evolution of humanity like a symbolical snake the last interpretation joins the first, is this not a proof that there is but One God? and is this not a proof of the bright future and universality of this Book which contains such immense treasures.

Revised and edited; originally published in Islamic Culture, July 1936.

9

God's Oneness

T. B. IRVING

Islam is a monotheistic and unitarian religion. It is the belief in Oneness of God which brings in social unity despite the diversities in the human beings of different races, and different geographical inhabitants.

Islam is based on the concept of divine Unity, and all of its principles lead back ultimately to this central thought. This idea has been worked out clearly in the short chapter called *Sincerity* (Sura 112) in the Qur'an:

Say: God is Unique !
God, the Source (for everything) !
He has not fathered anything
nor is He fathered:
and there is nothing
comparable to Him !

This concept is strictly monotheistic and unitarian. A Muslim's attitude towards the Deity springs from the fact that everything in the universe praises Him, or in other words, fulfil the purpose for which it was created. The shadows of everything on earth move from right to left, thus bowing down before God (16:48). The Prophet likewise turned to all the points in the sky during his search for God, before he was finally told to settle on Mecca as his Direction for prayer.

God is thus the Factor which unites the universe out of its diversity. We are asked: "Do not hearts feel tranquil whenever God is mentioned?" (13 : *28*). Though His face is to be found everywhere [2 (xiv. b)] man still "finds God within himself" (24 :'*39*). Islam, Muslim and the greeting of "Peace"! are all words which are based on this root concept of *salam* in Arabic. The great hymn on God's unity [27(v)] emphasizes this fact. Yet Muhammad 'Ali states about God's role as the *Ghani* or 'Self-Sufficient' on p. xiv of his introduction to the Qur'an: "If the whole world is engaged in praying to Him, it does not add one whit to His transcendental glory, and if the whole world disbelieves in Him and is ungrateful to Him, it does not detract from His dignity in the least."

A Muslim's profession of faith comes from the twin statement: "Your God is One God" found in (2 : *163*), and "Muhammad is God's messenger" in 48 :*29*. God as well as His attributes are defined [in 42(ii)], and the sense of infinity is stressed in the "Words of the Lord" which appear at the end of The Cave [18 (xii)] and in *Luqman:*

If all the trees on earth were pens
and the sea were replenished later
with seven others seas,
God's words would not be exhausted;
God is so Almighty, Wise ! (31 :27)

Those who are anxious from awe of God feel like the Danish and Spanish thinkers Kierkegaard and Unamuno (23 :*58*). There is evidence for God's existence following the great hymn on light [24(vi): "There is nothing like Him!" (42 :*11*); He is Incomparable, and in the sublime verse called "The Seat", neither slumbers nor sleeps (2 : *255*). God possesses everything [27 (v)], controlling it all right down to each mustard seed or atom [21 (ii)]. God is Just [53 (ii)] for He knows everything, or in other words is all Knowing or Aware, as this is somethings translated (6 : *59*). The passage full of poetic which ends *Luqman* explain thus:

God has knowledge of the Hour.
He sends down showers and knows

whatever lies in wombs. No soul
knows what it will earn tomorrow,
nor does any soul know
in what land it will die.
Yet God is so Aware, Informed !

God's bounties or favours are mentioned at length in *The Mercy-giving* (Sura 55), a prose poem with another recurring refrain: "Which of your Lord's signs will you both reject?." "Among His signs are..." makes another introductory refrain to a long passage [30 (iii)].

Parallel with this attempt to understand Who and What God is, we struggle with the concept of the Unseen or Absent —*al-Ghaib*. This is what other religions call a mystery. Mention of it first occurs in 2: *3*, when we are told about those "who believe in the Unseen." In the final verse of *The Apartments* (49 :*18*), we are told that God knows the Unseen and that this belongs only to Him, since it lies beyond our imagination: "No one in heaven or earth knows the Unseen except God." Those who "dread their Lord although Unseen" take Him on faith; to know God *bil-Ghaib* 'in the Unseen or while Unseen' means to believe in God even though we do not visualize Him with our eyes. God's attributes occur in the "Key's to the Unseen", one of the great poetic passages embedded in the Qur'an which merits being read on its own:

He holds the keys to the Unseen;
only He knows them ! He knows
everything on land and at sea ;
no leaf drops down unless He knows it,
nor any seed in the darkness of the earth,
nor any tends shoot nor any dry (stalk)
unless it is in a plain book.
He is the one Who gathers you in at night.
He knows what you have inflicted by day;
then He will revive you in it

so a stated period may be fulfilled.
Then your return will be unto Him;
when He will announce to you
everything you have been doing.
He is the Irresistible,
High above His servants !
He sends forth guardians over you
so that whenever death comes for one of you,
Our messengers will gather him up.
They will not neglect their duty;
then they will be sent back to God;
their real Sponsor. Is not judgment His?
He is the swiftest Reckoner ! 6 : 59—62, Livestock.

This is only part of Islam which requires a step beyond scientific knowledge and involves intuitive acceptance of divine truth. Moses initiated the Sufic vision when he was allowed to view the mountain instead of seeing God directly [7(xvii.b)]. When we are cautioned against guessing about the Unseen in the story of *The Cave* [18(iii). b)], this means that allegorical matters must not be taken too literally; if we cannot understand the message, we are not to probe too deeply because this may lead to disbelief: "You who believe, do not ask about things which would trouble you if they were shown to you... A folk before you asked about them; then became disbelievers because of it" [5(xiv)]. Solomon is the hero of another such allegory [2(xii. d)], especially when his dead body held authority till his staff was eaten away be worm, because the sprites under him could not interpret the Unseen (34 :*14*). There is much philosophy of history involved in Noah's mission as well: "Those are news of the Unseen which We reveal to you. Neither you nor your folk knew of them before this" [11(iv)]. In the tale of *Joseph*, we are told that the Prophet could not have known this previously: "Such are some of the news from the Unseen We reveal to you" (12 : *102*). We are likewise given some information about the Unseen in the case of Mary.

Although this concept involves mystery, mysteries are not the property of any priesthood since any Muslim can sit down and think things out for himself. However, since God does not require any intercessor in order to be reached, this idea does not please many Christians, who believe they need a mediator. Intercession or mediation is controlled entirely by God, although those who take on such patrons or sponsors instead of Him may claim: "We do not serve them except to bring us closer to God in homage" (39 : *3* & *44*). One thus feels that Christians do not fully believe or trust in God, and this makes their system faulty (17 : *110*). Jesus himself declares against the concept of the trinity, and states that he was only one of God's servants [19(*ii*)].

A sinner's burden must be carried by the one responsible for committing the deed. It likewise follows that God has no son, because the concept of the Mercy-giving is so all-embracing that God does-not need any intercessor in order for us to reach Him, nor for any man to be associated in his worship. God's care embraces all the world for He made it and takes care of it; his personal care lies as close to us as our jugular vein [50(ii).b)]. God's guidance is important and we must accept it from Him because it is not thrust upon us willy nilly, but we are given free choice in the matter:

Have We not granted him two eyes,
a tongue and two lips,
and shown him both highroads?
Yet he does not tackle the Obstacle !
What will make you realize
What the Obstacle is? 90 : 8-12, The Countryside.

Islam is thus a practical faith with few secrets. The only real mystery is what God Himself knows, and He should be praised for this, and His decisions accepted. True knowledge consists in the conquest of the Unseen by man so that the relationship between the various parts of the universe can be appreciated. Fear of the Unknown leads to superstition, and this tendency should be avoided.

On the other hand, the idea of the Oneness of God and of experience produced that fusion of styles which has distinguished Islam from Spain to Indonesia. It is interesting to trace how Islam worked out this problem of divine Unity, because it led to the triumphs of Islamic culture and philosophy; abstract intelligence produced a spiritual is intellectually satisfying, and its rational basis has not been stressed enough.

The worship of God in His Oneness is undermined by three shortcomings which I shall call: outright *denial or rejection* of God; *association* or letting any other person or thing share in His worship; and *arrogation* or actively trying to associate oneself with Him, especially so as to tyrannize over others through such arrogated powers. This can mean either civil or religious tyranny.

Let us take up these points one by one.

1. The word *kufr* in Arabic means the denial of God, or disbelief in Him. It is the simplest fault to describe and control, although there are degrees in the form of such rejection.

Disbelievers are described in the passage. 2 : *6-20* while we meet believers in 49 : 15 and hear of the sincere worship of God at the beginning of *Throngs* (Sura 39) and in "These serve me and do not associate anything with Me" [24 (vii)]. Rejection of God, within the Arabic concept, includes ingratitude for His favours. Grateful likewise implies more than merely thanking God, since "anyone who is grateful, is grateful merely for his own sake" (31: *12*). "The worst animal for God are those who disbelieve" (8 :*56*); and "Anyone who disbelieves is responsible for his own disbelief" (35 : *39*).

Atheism is a modern European term for such disbelief, while infidel is a medieval word for the person who does so. An agnostic would be a *jahil* or 'know-nothing' in religious matters, but this refers generally to the Arabs who lived before Islam. The Kaffirs of South Africa were so-called by the Arab traders who met them, and the term was picked up by the Portuguese and Dutch who rounded Cape of Good Hope later on.

Apostasy means rejecting God after one has once expressed belief in Him, and apostates or backsliders are those "who die while unjust to their own souls." Some believers ask too many questions instead of accepting things on faith, and thus become backsliders [5(xiv.a)]. Similarly we should not give in to wheedlers who only want us to compromise (68 : *7-9*).

2. Association or *shrik*, as this is called in Arabic, is the easiest failing to fall into. It involves associating others with god and then worshipping them: "There are some people who adopt rivals along with God whom they love just as they should love God." "Have they any association in heaven ?" we are asked — "have your associates any explanation for creation?" A refrain from *The Ants* (Sura) 27 yields another constant message: "Exalted is He above what they associate (with Him)!"

The chapter called *Poets* concerns Abraham's quest for the Ultimate power in the universe [26(v)]; that prophet therefore informs us: "I have been forbidden to serve the ones you call on instead of God" (40:*66*). Association thus means letting anything or anyone come in between you and your pure worship of God, and implies that you do not have absolute confidence in the Deity. Philosophically this attitude is sound since *shrik* means that other gods besides God would have ruined the earth, because each would have wanted to have his own way with things [21 (ii)].

On Judgment Day, associates will leave their worshippers in the lurch and associators themselves will be asked: "Where are the associates you gave Me?" These partners in worship will not help their worshippers at all [18 (vii. end)] and deny they have ever been worshipped, explaining how such action is unworthy of anyone [10(iii)]. Worship becomes mere show when it is directed at anything except God. The Queen of Sheba, for instance, could not think straight because her bondage to her false gods hindered her.

Associating is condemned first in the Islamic "Do Not's" which are given in 6(xix) and 17(ii-iv), as well as *Luqman,* where this ancient sage advises his son that "association is such a serious wrong"! [31(ii.a)]. This moral legislation begins in such each instance with injunction against associating others with God: "Do not set up any other god lest you sit back discharged, forsaken;" so it is in fact the principal or cardinal sin so far as God is concerned: "God does not forgive anyone for associating things with Him, while He does forgive anyone He wants for anything besides that" [4(vii.g)].

Partnership might be another term for association, since this means ascribing a partner to God which He does not need. Polytheism is another restricted name often given this sin which has been preferred by Westerners outside of Islam who do not want to include their own saints' worship within this prohibition. However, associating others in your worship of God is not polytheism, nor is it idolatry. Association is broader than idolatry and should be fought on a modern basis; our false gods are no longer idols, but moods like laziness in approaching God, taking one's passion [25(iv.c)] or a "whim to be his god" [45(iii.a)], deputing worship to priests or ministers, even within Islam, or wearing a rabbit's foot to ward off bad luck. It is an active rather than a passive failing, however, as we find in the passage: "Most of them do not believe in God unless they associate (others with Him)" (12 : *106*). The common excuse is that "we do not serve them except to bring us closer to God in homage" [39(i.a)], even though it is obvious that such an object of worship is something "that neither harms nor benefits them" (10 : *18*).

Saints worship is another false approach which is feudal in concept since its exploitation becomes a property or vested interest which can be controlled by people interested in profiting from it. Mortmain or tying up large blocks of property in the hands of a church or its clergy is still another by-product of association [6(xvi.a)] which has led to serious political and economical difficulties in France and Mexico recently, and Egypt and India in ancient times. At the beginning of Livestock (Sura 6), we are told that dualism or the Persian error consider the prevalence of evil to be unavoidable; while pure monotheism views God Alone as the ultimate Goal and true Reality. The Christian view is a triple error, especially when its saints and clergy are included. In some sects this has led to the worship of Jesus's mother, since once you lose full confidence in God, and feel the need of a mediator between you and Him, you will soon be needing still another mediator or even a mediatrix; "they only call on females instead of Him", says the Qur'an. Jesus himself rejected godhood for God has not needed to have any son or associate, nor do we need any such partner as we approach Him in prayer or otherwise. However, Christians are considered to be closer to Islam than are the Jews [5(xi)]. It is clear too that anyone with a revealed religion worships essentially the same God: "Our God and your God is one" [29(v.b)].

What should we do not about association and associators? We are told to "shun associators...who place another god alongside God" [15(vi)]; do not agree with them if they are so blind. This passage is very personal as it consoles Muhammad for being persecuted for his beliefs in Mecca. Since associators do not contemplate Divinity clearly, however, they are not fit to visit mosques, for without proper contemplation or study, they will not visit them for worship but merely for the purpose of sightseeing and probably while they are unclean or impure [9(iii)].

3. Arrogating the privileges that accompany divine worship of oneself or a class is the third cardinal sin of Islam. *Al-taghut* or 'the arrogant ones' are mentioned in 5 (ix.a). An arrogant person is someone who usurps some position in order to benefit from it selfishly: the inmates of the garden, for instance, were arrogant because they tried to do without God [68(i.c)].

Arrogation might be further as meaning that anything tries to exceed its function. In the very first call to the Prophet, he was told: "Indeed man is so arrogant!" (96 : *6*); while when we hear how "his sight was not arrogant," this means that the Prophet's vision was not carried away [53(i.d)]. Even "the water was arrogant" or rose too high (69 : *11*), and we are cautioned in our business transactions: " So you may not be arrogant (or skimp) in weighing" [55(i.b)]. Pride is a corollary failing. Man, despite all of his latent faculties, is quarrelsome, unjust, impatient and ungrateful. His possibilities of integration and disintegration are anticipated in the line about how the soul had injected "both its debauchery and its heedfulness" (91:8).

Those who study the Book and then want "people to worship them instead of God", as well as other arrogant leaders are mentioned in several places, and we are warned how some people are such "arrogant folk." On these *al-taghut,* see: "Whoever of them should say: 'I am a god instead of Him' [39(ii.b)]. Pharaoh was arrogant because he wanted to be worshipped, as when he declares : "Councilmen, 'I have not known of any god for you except myself!" He thus becomes the personification of tyranny, just as Haman is the corrupt and fawning minister and Qur'an the overweaning man of wealth. Christian recall the divine worship which the Roman emperors arrogated to themselves and which led to much persecution when the former resisted it. Egypt, Rome and Spain are the great examples of civil and religious arrogance.

We are also reminded of those who make a living out of trying to disprove the Qur'an when we are asked: "Are you making (the fact) that you rejected it into your means of substenance?" [56(iii.b)]; while people who study yet do not earn the message into practice are "like a donkey carrying tomes" [62(i.c)]. All these may take the form of a hierarchy when we are cautioned: "Nor shall any of us take lords instead of God." During collective prayer, it stands to reason that someone must act as leader, but no one person nor any class should arrogate such leadership to itself nor himself. The danger of ceremonialism creeping in is shown in 22 : *37*; this is what the stricter Protestants call "popery". Monasticism is treated in the chapter called *Iron:* "Monkhood they invented!" [57(vi)]. This passage on the Christians and Jews is not a bitter rejection however, especially because many monks are God-fearing people.

Those who lead other men astray, like priests and politicians are pictured as "grouping along in their arrogance" [10(ii.a)]; they can bear no one else's burden, although they will nonetheless be held responsible for this misleading, as a personal sin committed by themselves alone. We may make them afraid, but it only increases great arrogance in them [17(*vi.d*)], while their dupes will complain that they have been imposed on by being led astray from God to worship other things. Intercession nevertheless, as we have already mentioned, clearly belongs to God alone [39(*v*)]. Man's soulmate will plead: "I did not act arrogantly towards him" [50(*ii.c*)] during the final Judgment. Abraham did not follow in his own father's ways, and likewise we must reject the faith of our fathers if this is wrong [21(*v*)].

Natural religion based on sincere worship is discussed in 30:*30*. In the section on God's Oneness, we mentioned how fear of the Unknown leads to superstition, and that this tendency must be controlled. True knowledge means man's intellectual conquest of the Unseen so that the relationship between the various parts of the universe can be understood. A deeply rooted social fear hinders us today from solving the entanglements of contemporary civilization, and this combined with an ingrained curse of laziness which keeps us from thinking things out clearly, leads to a modern form of superstition that relies on the deification of science as cure-all as potent as any witch-doctor's brew ever was in primitive times. This might be considered as our modern *tughyan* or arrogation.

Revised and edited; originally published in Studies in Islam, Jan. 1964.

10

Jami's Concept of God in the 'Lawa'ih'

R.S. BHATNAGAR

An essay on the book, Lawa`ih (=Flashes of light), by Jami, discusses God as a unique existing being. His sufi inclination allowed him to dwell on the mystical side of the religious literature.

Nur Al-Din 'Abd Al-Rahman Jami (A.D. 1492) was an inspired sufi poet who was well versed in theology and sufism. He elaborated his concept of the Real in the *Lawa'ih* (*Flashes of Light*) which had a great impact upon the later development of sufism and Muslim theology.

In the *Lawa'ih* Jami regards only One God in existence who is a perfect Unity in Himself. "If thou regardest theyself, it is He whom thou art regarding; if thou speakest of thyself, it is He of whom thou art speaking. The relative has become the Absolute, and 'I am the Truth' is equivalent to 'He is the Truth.' "When I say 'me', it is 'Thee' I mean to name." Hence, the objects of the universe are nothing in themselves since nothing exists except God. They can be regarded as the mirrors to illuminate the One Divine Being. "The various grades of created things are theatres of His revealed beauty, and all things that exist are mirrors of His perfections." All these reflections or the manifestations belong to God Himself or His Essence. His Essence and Existence are one. The Divine Attributes like knowledge, power and will might appear to us as distinct from each other and different in their meanings but in reality they are identical with Him. The qualities and the names merely qualify the One Existent Being. "There are not in Him many existences, but only one sole existence, and His various names and attributes are merely His modes and aspects." As regards the problem of God's immanence and transcendence, Jami believes that the pure immanence or the pure transcendence implies the limitation of Godhead. God is transcendent because everything is from Him and He is immanent in everything, for everything is identical with Him. "The essence of the `Truth' most glorious and most exalted is nothing but Being. His Being is not subject to defect or diminution. He is untouched by change or variation, and is exempt from plurality and multiplicity; He transcends all manifestations, and in unknowable and invisible. "Every 'how' and 'why' have made their appearance through Him; but in Himself He transcends every 'how' and 'why'. God is transcendent as well as immanent.

All the things of the universe are unreal apart from God. They are superficial or fictitious because God is the only Eternal Truth. "Everything other than the `Truth' is subject to decay and annihilation. It substance is a mental figment with no objective existence, and its form is a merely imaginary entity." There is only One Unity in Existence (*wahdatu'l-wujud*).

From the stage of the *wahdatu'l-wujud* Jami passes on to the pantheistic stage of *hama ust* (all is God) like Ibn al-'Arabi. The One Real Being may be viewed from two sides—its unity and its display in the form of plurality. Jami explains it in a passage: "Thus unique Substance, viewed as absolute and void of all phenomena, all limitations, and all multiplicity, is the 'Truth.' On the other hand, viewed in His aspect of multiplicity and plurality, under which he displays Himself when clothed with phenomena, He is the whole created universe. Therefore the universe is the outward visible expression of the 'Truth,' and 'Truth' is the inner unseen reality of the universe. The universe before it was evolved to outward view was identical with the 'Truth'; and the 'Truth' after this evolution is identical with the universe. Nay, more, in reality there is but One Real Being; His posteriority, are all merely His relations and His aspects. 'It is He who is the first and the last, the exterior and the interior.'" Thus God is in everything and everything is in God.

"Being's the essence of the Lord of all,

All things exist in Him and He in all;
This is the meaning of the Gnostic phrase,
'All things are comprehended in All.' "

There is perfect unity between God and the universe. "It is the 'Truth' who is Himself at once the lover and the beloved, the seeker and the sought. He is loved and sought in His character of the 'One who is all'; and He is lover and seeker when viewed as the sum of all particulars and plurality." In other words, everything is God.

God reveals Himself in a number of ways. In His first manifestation He manifests Himself to Himself. In Himself He reveals Himself with the attributes of Knowledge, Light, Existence and Presence. The attribute of Knowledge includes both the features of 'knowing' and 'being known,' Light is meant for both the qualities of 'manifesting' and 'being manifest,' Existence contains the characteristics of creating or 'causing to exist' and 'being existent' and Presence signifies the qualities of 'beholding' and 'beheld.'

In the scheme of the emanations the first emanation of God is pure 'Unity,' which is unconditioned as well as conditioned by the qualities. When the 'Unity' is unconditioned by any quality or its aspect, it is 'Absolute' *(wahid)* and when it is regarded as a Reality conditioned by modes or qualities, it can be called 'Single' *(ahad)*. The second emanation is the Universal Soul *(martaba-i Jama')* appearing in the forms of the rational soul, the animal soul and the vegetative soul. The Universal Soul contains the attributes of life, knowledge and will. The different forms of the one Real Being with these attributes may be called Divine Substances. Outwardly, these Divine Substances are the so-called sensible and empirical objects. There are some other modes also which simply qualify the one Real Being. They can be named 'Mundane Substances' like 'difference,' 'property', 'accident,' 'genus' and 'species.' Hence the one Real Being assumes the forms of both the Divine Substances and the Mundane Substances in the state of the 'Unity of the Whole'.

The end or the final cause of the series of emanations consists in the realisation of the perfection of Divine Names in two ways —*Jala'* and *Istijla'*. *Jala'* signifies the outward expression of the Divine Names of the One Real Being and *Istijla'* implies the inward manifestation of the Names of the One. *Jala'* is the visible display and *Istijla'* is the invisible revelation of God to Himself. In *Istijla'* "the perfection of the Divine Essence is the manifestation of the One Real Being to Himself, for Himself, without relation to anything beside Himself." In this way the One Existent Being transcends even the existence of the various beings appearing in the form of the manifestations belonging ultimately to it. "In the external world there is only One Real Being, who, by clothing Himself with different modes and attributes, appears to be endowed with multiplicity and plurality to those who are confined in the narrow prison of the `stages', and whose view is limited to visible properties and results."

The One Existent Being is not a Unity in the sense of the 'synthesis' or the 'collection' of the separate unity. The relation of plurality of objects to the Unity of the One Being is not that of the part of the whole but that of the effect proceeding logically from its cause. "When one says that the 'Truth' most glorious comprehends all beings, the meaning is that He comprehends them as a cause comprehends its effects, not that He is a whole containing them as His parts, or a vase containing things within it." Moreover, the Real Being is independent of His outward appearances. He is a Perfect and Infinite Being and as such He is not limited by anything. He is not affected by His manifestations like the purity of light which is not affected if the light illuminates the clean as well as unclean. Though the Real is apart from everything, yet its various modes or the outward forms require the Real because it is their essence "The Absolute does not exist without the relative, and the relative is not formulated without the Absolute; but the relative stands in need of the Absolute, while the Absolute has no need of the relative."

Jami followed Neoplatonic theory of the Degrees of Perfection in his mystical cosmology. Creation for Plotinus means manifestation of Reality is *Nous*, World Soul and Matter. As the Light goes ahead, the spirituality falls in various degrees. Jami also holds that a particular emanation possesses a particular degree of spiritual perfection. The word Allah, for example, cannot be used for the emanation at the place of the sensible things. The first degree of God's perfection consists in His transcending Himself. "In the first degree He is unmanifested and unconditioned, and exempt from all limitation or relation." Here He is beyond all categories and attributed. He is beyond human thinking and He transcends all the ways of description. "His first characteristic is the lack of all characteristics, and the last result of the attempt to know Him is stupefaction." The second degree of perfection lies in the emanation of God's 'active,' 'necessary,' 'divine', 'passive,' contingent' and 'mundane' aspects. This is the stage of the First Emanation (*ta'ayyun-i awwal*) or the Universal Reason (*'aql-i kull*). It is like the *nous* of Plotinus. The third degree of spiritual perfection consists in His active and efficient phases. It is the 'Unity of the Whole Aggregate.' It can be called the Second Emanation or Divinity (*Ilahiyat*). The fourth degree of His perfection is contained in the detailed expression of the Second Emanation. It is exposed in various named forms. This is the plane of the Third Emanation or Necessary Being (*wujud*). The fifth degree of spirituality lies in 'passivity' or the quality of receiving impressions. This is again a 'Unity of the Whole Aggregate.' It is the Fourth Emanation or 'Mundane Existence' and 'Contingency.' The sixth degree of perfection consists in the detailed manifestation of the Fourth Emanation. It is the stage of the Fifth Emanation or the Sensible World (*alam*). The last two Emanations are the outward aspects of the intelligible world belonging to contingency.

All the degrees of spiritual perfection belong to Unity of Existence or One Being. The One Reality or the Perfect Unity appears in different forms assuming the various degree of spirituality. "In reality there is but One Sole Being, who is interfused in all these degrees and hierarchies which are only the details of the Unity (*wahidiyat*). 'Very Being' in these degrees is identical with them, just as these degrees when they were in the Very Being were identical therewith."

All the emanations of the Real possessing the degrees of spiritual perfection and belonging to One Existent Being can be viewed from two sides—subjective and objective. A subjective emanation means the self-manifestation of the Absolute to Himself or the self-consciousness of the Divine Being. It has an inward character. This can be named 'Most Sacred Emanation' (*fayd-i aqdas*). The objective emanation consist in the manifestation of the Absolute in an outward form. It can be regarded 'Sacred Emanation' (*favd-i muqaddas*). The distinction between the two forms of revelation is only a matter of approach. The objective manifestation of the Real merely means external exposition of that which was revealed inwardly within the Absolute. Thus, that which is intelligible to us does belong to the Absolute.

Jami recognised the theory of dynamic pantheism. No Divine manifestation is static. The Reality comes out of itself at every moment. Every revelation is absolutely new indicating the self-annihilation of everything. God "reveals Himself at every breath in a fresh revelation, and that He never repeats the same revelation; that is to say, He never reveals Himself during two consecutive moments under the guise of the same phenomena and modes, but every moment presents fresh phenomena and modes."

Since God is the only Existent Being, man as such is non-existent and unreal. He is a nonentity apart from God. The existence of man logically implies the existence of God in a particular aspect. The human qualities are the Divine Attributes in the manifested form. Hence, there cannot be any qualitative distinction between the two kinds of qualities. The human qualities are related to the Divine Attributed like a part of the whole which appears from the whole and does not remain separate from its origin. The attributes of man, like intelligence and wisdom, "are attributes of Deity which have descended from the zenith of the Universal and Absolute to the nadir of the particular and relative. They have descended to the end that thou mayest direct thy course from the part towards the Whole, and from the relative deduce the Absolute, and not imagine the part to be distinct from the whole, nor be so engrossed with what is merely relative as to cut thyself off from the Absolute."

The Sufi experiences the Truth (*al-Haqq*) through his contemplation on the Existent Being or the Perfect Unity, the Absolute. According to Jami, God has granted a heart to man so that he may identify himself with Him. Nothing except God should become the object of his devotion. "Distraction or disunion consists in dividing the heart by attaching it to diverse objects. Union consists in forsaking all else and being wholly engrossed in the contemplation of the One Unique Being." The heart of the true mystic remains free from all thoughts except the thought of God. His real state of the annihilation of self means complete annihilation of all the human qualities including the quality of his awareness concerning self-annihilation. "Self annihilation consists in this, that through the overpowering influence of the Very Being upon the inner man there remains no consciousness of aught beside Him. Annihilation of annihilation consists in this, that there remains no consciousness even of that unconsciousness. It is evident that annihilation of annihilation is involved in annihilation."

Since all the manifestations belong to the Absolute or His Essence, the imperfection in the universe is visible due to the lack of the knowledge of the Real (*ma'rifah*). "Being, qua Being is pure good." The evil must come from `non-being, meaning thereby that our ignorance or the non-mystical knowledge about the Truth is the sole cause of evil.

Revised and edited; originally published in Islamic Culture Jan. 1982.

11

Muslims' on Christian and Traditional African Concepts of the Godhead

E. DADA ADELOWO

Discusses Muslim concept of monotheism, and reaction to the Godhead concept. Analyses the sources of theological differences, as perceived by Muslims, between Islamic and both the Christian and the traditional views of the nature of the Godhead. The finale expected is a greater understanding and tolerance among the various groups in Africa and elsewhere.

Every religion that has its foundation in a scripture is *the* religion and *a* religion. It is the religion in so far as it contains a medium of attaining the Truth; and so far as it underlines a particular aspect of the Truth in consonance with the spiritual and psychological needs of the audience. Thus every religion *qua* religion has, ultimately, two cardinal elements which constitute its basis and foundation: a doctrine, which distinguished between the Absolute and the relative, between the absolutely Real and its opposite, between that which has absolute Value and its opposite, and, at the same time, a method of concentrating upon the Real, of attaching oneself to the Absolute, Reality, the Wholly Other and the Living, according to the Will of Heaven and in tune with the purpose and meaning of human existence.

These two elements, the doctrine and the method, the means of distinguishing between what is Real and what is apparently real, and attaching oneself to the Real, exist in every orthodox and integral religion and are, in fact, the essence of every religion. No religion, be it Islam or Christianity, Hinduism or Buddhism can exist without a doctrine as to what is absolute and what is relative. Only the doctrinal language differs from one tradition to another. Nor can any religion be without a method of concentrating on the Real and Living, although the means again differ in different traditional claimes.

Every religion *qua* religion claims a transcendental origin. Thus every religion *qua* religion believes in a transcendent Reality that stands above the world. Thus we see the need for a critical and lucid interpretation of the Muslim concept of the nature of the Godhead *vis-a-vis* the concept of the Godhead in Christianity and African traditional religion.

The Muslim concept of the Godhead is the first aspect of the Islamic Articles of Faith. It is so important that one is not considered a Muslim until one accepts the Truth.

In short, it is the basis of Islam. This paper is an attempt to analyse the Truth and present the analysis both to Muslim and non-Muslims for proper understanding the further appraisal.

The concept of the Godhead occupies a significant place in the history of religions in the world. In one of the last addresses given by the well-known theologian, Paul Tillich, ten days before his death, he said that if he were to have the time to write a new systematic theology, it would be oriented towards the history of religions and in *dialogue* with them. The relevance of the foregoing is seen in the age-old theological differences and dialogues operating between Muslims and both the Christians and the traditional Africans on the question of the nature of the Godhead. This paper is intended to throw more light on the viewpoints of the various religious groups on the nature of the Godhead and eventually to help to resolve the theological differences between Muslims and non-Muslims with regard to the nature of the Godhead.

The Muslim Concept of Monotheism

Tauhid is an Arabic word which, in the literal sense, means 'The making one'. In the context of Islamic theology, it is used to express the Unity or Oneness of the Godhead. It is the concept of *monotheism* in Islam. In this context, it is absolute monotheism and not otherwise. With regard to this aspect of theology, Muslims generally cannot afford to sacrifice dignity for depravity. They maintain the doctrine even to the point of death. They are very rigid concerning the issue since it is regarded as the fundamental basis of Islam.

In Arabic the affirmation of *tauhid* reads thus: *La ilaa illa llah* meaning. "There is no god but Allah".

The sum-total of the concept of *tauhid* in Islam is that only the Supreme Being is recognised in ritual and no other being. It is monotheism *per se* and not a diffused one. In the belief of Muslims, the existence and maintenance of everything in the world are attributed to Allah, the only God, the sole object of all worship. There is no other god but He alone. For Prophet Muhammad, the essential element of genuine belief was an uncompromising monotheism. At the inchoative stage of Islam in its birth place Arabia, Muhammad rejected, outright, the pretension that the goddesses, *Al-Manat, Al-Uzza* and *Al-Lal*, were 'daughters of *Allah'*, as later on he rejected the worship of Jesus and Mary as 'Lords' and reproached the Jews for referring to their teachers as *rabbi*, 'my lord'. The doctrine of the 'unity' or 'oneness' of the Godhead so occupied the mind of Muhammad that at the inception of Islam in Mecca, he spent up to twenty days practising iconoclasm. The Ka'ba and the private houses were cleansed of idols. Troops were sent to destroy *Manat* at Mushallal (between Mecca and Yathrib), *Uzza* at Nakhla and a host of others. True belief, in the Muslim context, demands *ikhlas*, the submission of one's whole and untainted allegiance to Allah; Islam condemns anyone who associated any partner with Allah. Belief in the partnership of other gods with His is branded as associationism, or *shirk*. So also is the worship of any other creature (*abd*) apart from Allah. *Shirk* is regarded as the greatest of all sins, hence unforgivable.

Just as in the earthly domain the worst crime is that of

treason, as it cuts at the very fabric of the State, so in the spiritual realm, the unforgivable or monstrous sin is that of contumacious treason against Allah by putting up Allah's creatures in invidious rivalry against Him. This is nothing short of revolt against the essence and source of spiritual life. This is what Plato regards as "the lie in the soul".

It is important to analyse here the various circumstances that might surround the commission of *shirk*. *Shirk* committed willingly is tantamount to 'cultic syncretism'. Cultic syncretism is an odious phenomenon in Islam. One who commits this sin is regarded as an apostate, or an infidel (*kafir*). *Tauhid* guides religious life, designs the social pattern and gives life to the moral code. The principle name of God in Islam is Allah. This is a word which denotes a "Being who exists necessarily by Himself, comprising all the attributes of perfection".

The importance of *tauhid* as the basis of Islam in further corroborated by the fact that it is a recurrent expression in the Holy Quran.

This submission is not confined to the domain of Sunnism. Except with regard to details, it embraces the Islamic world in so far as the basis of our submission is the Holy Quran, the Word of the one God, for the totality of Muslims in the world.

Muslim Reaction to the Christian Concept of the Nature of the Godhead

The question of the Trinity has been a major bone of contention between the Muslims and the Christians from the beginning. In the foregoing, we have analysed the Muslim concept of monotheism. Now let us examine the Christian concept of the Godhead before we come to examine the reaction of the Muslims to this concept and why they have reacted in certain ways of forms in the history of interaction between Muslims and Christians in the contemporary world with its multiplicity of religions.

The word Trinity is not found in the Bible, and, though used by Tertullian in the last decade of the second century, it did not find a place formally in the theology of the church till the fourth century. It is, however, the distinctive and comprehensive doctrine of the Christian Faith and 'gathers up into the seam of a single grand generalisation with respect to the being and activity of God all the major aspects of Christian truth' (Loury). Theology seeks to define the subsistence of God by stating that God is one in His essential being, but that the divine essence exists in *three modes or forms,* each constituting a Person, yet in such a way that the divine essence is wholly in each person.

The Concept of Trinity in the Old Testament

Though the doctrine is not developed in the Old testament, it is implicit in the divine self-disclosure from the very beginning. But in accordance with the historical character of the divine revolution, it is presented at first only in a very rudimentary form. This is found not only in isolated passages but interwoven in the entire organism of the Old Testament revelation. The earlier foreshadowing is contained in the narrative of the creation, where *Elohim* seen to create by means of the Word and Spirit. Here, we are for the first time introduced to Word presented as a personal creative power, and to the Spirit as the bringer of life and order to the creation. Thus there is revealed at an early stage a threefold centre of activity. God as Creator thought out the universe, expressed the thought in a Word, and made His spirit its animating principle, thus indicating that the universe was not to have a separate existence apart from God or opposed to Him.

The threefold source revealed in creation became still more evident in the unfolding or redemption. The revelation of redemption was entrusted to the messenger of Yahweh, sometimes referred to as the Angel of the covenant. It is God who revealed Himself objectively through the Angel-messenger and subjectively in and through the Spirit, the Dispenser of all Blessings and gifts within the sphere of redemption.

The Concept of Trinity in the Inter-testamental Period

In this period, there was a definite, if vague and shadowy, preparation for the full revelation of the Trinity to be given in the

New Testament. The transcendence and remoteness of God in Jewish thought made men look for a *mediator*. Philo, under an apprehension of the absolute metaphysical contrast between God and the world, conceived of mediating entities who are assumed to mediate between God and the creation. This was recognised by many to be the office of the Messiah, but there was a strong proclivity to ascribe the same remoteness and transcendence to the heavenly Messiah. It was felt, however, that when the Messiah came to earth, the holy Spirit also, which had left the prophetic scene since Malachi, would return in prophetic power. Though three persons were vaguely thought of, the subject of their relationship was scarcely touched on and was left in complete obscurity.

The Concept of Trinity in the New Testament

Preparatory to the coming of Christ, the Holy Spirit came into the consciousness of God-fearing men to a degree unknown since the close of Malachi's history. John the Baptist, more especially, was conscious of the presence and calling of the Spirit, and it is probable that his preaching had a trinitarian reference: he called for repentance towards God and faith in the coming of Messiah, and he spoke of a baptism of the Holy Spirit, of which his baptism with water was a symbol. The agency of the Spirit in the incarnation is disclosed to Mary together with the intimation that the son born to her would be called the son of the Highest, and that "the Lord God (would) give unto him the throne of his father David". Thus the Father and the spirit were disclosed as operating in the incarnation of the son. Compare also the incident of baptism in the Jordan. In the case, three persons can be distinguished: the Son being baptised, the Father speaking from heaven, and the Spirit descending in the objective symbol of a dove.

The fellowship of the Father and Spirit appears in the work of redemption as revealed by Christ, the Father sending the son to undertake the work and the Father as well as the son sending the Spirit to apply the salvation which Christ wrought.

Thus it became evident why the God of the covenant was revealed as triune, since salvation was seen to rest upon each of the persons in the Godhead. Christ's trinitarian teaching received its most clear and concise expression in the baptismal formula: baptism in the name of the Father, and of the Son and of the Holy Ghost.

The outpouring of the Spirit at Pentecost brought the personality of the Holy Spirit into greater prominence and at the same time shed new light from the Spirit upon the Son. The apostolic conception of the Holy Ghost and of His relation to the Father and the Son is clear from Acts. Paul, in explaining the phenomenon of *Pentecost*, represents it as the activity of the Trinity. 'This Jesus... being by the right hand of God exalted, and having received of the Father the promise of the Holy Ghost, he hath shed forth this, which ye now see and hear". The Trinity in Christian experience is seen in the context of the saving grace of the Son, as that which gives access to the love of the Father and the communion of the Spirit.

Formulation

As already indicated, Scripture does not give us a fully formulated doctrine of the Trinity, but it contains all the elements out of which theology has constructed the doctrine. The teaching of Jesus bears testimony to the true personality of each of distinctions within the Godhead and also sheds light upon the relations existing among the three. It was left to theology to formulate from this a doctrine of the Trinity.

In most formulations, it is stated that God is one in His essential being, but that in this being there are three persons, yet not so as to form separate and distinct individuals. They are three modes or forms in which the divine essence exists. 'Person' is, however, an imperfect expression of the truth in as much as the term denoted to us a separate rational and moral individual. But in the being of God, there are not three individuals, but only three personal self-distinctions within the one divine essence. In this connection, when Christians say God is a Unity, they mean that, though God is in Himself a three-fold centre of life, His life is not split into three. He is one in essence, in personality and in will. When they say that God is a Trinity in Unity they mean that there is Unity in diversity, and that diversity manifests itself in Person, in characteristics, and in operations. The Father as the fount of deity is First. He is said to originate. The Son eternally begotten of the Father, is Second: he is said to reveal. The Spirit eternally proceeding that creation is from the Father, through the Son, by the Holy Spirit.

Implications of the Doctrine

The implications of the doctrine are vitally important not only for theology but for Christian experience and life. As to the Godhead, it reveals that God is the truly loving one. It removes Him far from any conception of stagnation or mere passivity. God in Trinity is fullness of life, living in eternal relationships and in never ceasing fellowship. This again makes intelligible the revelation and self-communication of God. As God can, in an absolute sense, communicate Himself inwards in an act of self-relevation among the three persons, so He is able, in a relative sense, to impart Himself outward in relevation and communication to His creation. As to the universe, the doctrine of the Trinity gives both unity and diversity, making the universe into a cosmos. Since all things hang on the will of God, there can be no dualism at the heart of the universe.

Moreover, the fellowship that constitutes the Trinity is the basis of fellowship within the human family, within the home, within society, and more especially within the Church, where the Holy Spirit is the Agent and Medium of fellowship.

Muslim Reaction

Muslim reaction to the Christian concept of Trinity can be analysed under the following points: over-emphasis of the ontological aspect of God, contact with the Nestorian and Monophysite Christian in the early days of Islam, the absence in Islam of the doctrine of co-eternity, the absence of the theory of adoptionism, the Muslim concept of sin, forgiveness and salvation or redemption, the absence of the concept of *incarnation*, the Jewish reaction to Jesus and reserve about his divinity, and finally the undefined concept of the Holy Ghost and the Angel Gabriel in the Quran.

Muslims lay emphasis on the ontological aspect of the Godhead while at the same time they posit that, despite this, God is highly functional or operative in the universe. Their belief as contained in their credal statement *la ilaha illa'llah* borders almost on impersonality, but at the same time they hold that Islam is a theistic religion with Allah as both transcendent and immanent. Allah's ninety-nine attributes are a testimony in this connection. Moreover in the Quran we have the following statement. Lord of the two Easts and the two Wests, Lord of the Dawn; God in heaven and God on earth; Lord of the mystery of heaven and earth and a host of others. The Muslim stand is that there is no need for a split in essence before He could accomplish his activities on earth. To them He is both one in essence and in function, for one of His attributes is omnipotence. Thus they oppose the Christians who are of the opinion that there is the need for diversity in unity for the purpose of proper functionalism in order to avoid passivity or impersonality. For Christians, the emphasis of Muslims on absolute or undivided unity with regard to God's essence is tantamount to creating a gap of a vacuum between God and his creation. The situation is resolved if we admit that both Muslim and Christians speak about God in anthropomorphic terms which, in fact, imply the immanence of God. In Sufism total absorption into the Deity is the method adopted to get rid of the element of impersonality apparently involved in the Muslim thought of the Godhead.

Related to the foregoing is the question of baptismal formulae. The question of baptismal formularies does not exist in Islam. The mere declaration of the *kalimatu shahada* is sufficient to make one a Muslim, whereas in Christianity the baptism involves the diversity in Unity, known as the Trinity. Here again we see the initiation rites in the two religions over against each other.

The negative attitude on the part of the Muslim could also be attributed to their contact with the Nestorian and Monophysite Christians, in the early days of Islam, who held the view that the Trinity comprised God, Mary and Jesus when, as a matter of fact, Mary gave birth to Jesus.

Next is the question of co-eternity. Here Saint John's Gospel throws light. In John we have the following: "In the beginning was the Word, and the Word was with God, and the Word was God. He was in the beginning with God." In the book of Genesis we have the following: ".... and the Spirit of God moved over the face of the waters. This concept is totally absent in the Quran, nor is it raised in the Hadith. The basis of Islam is contained in the expression *la ilaha illa Allah*, meaning there is no god but Allah. Thus, on the basis of this belief, the Christian doctrine of co-eternity involving the Christness of Jesus is rejected.

Moreover, Muslims do not understand the difference between what is known as the Christness of Jesus, which in fact has a reference to the divine aspect of Jesus, and the "Jesusness" of Christ which, in fact, is a reference to the human aspect of Jesus. All they find in the Quran is the "Jesusness" of Christ. Thus they, in addition to their non-toleration of the theory of adoptionism, reject Christ as the son of God. They accept a relationship that is biological and not otherwise. This they corroborate with the following expressions as contained in the Quran.

Associated with the foregoing is the fatherhood of God. God the Father in Christianity is abhorrent of Muslims because it is understood in the sense of physical generation. They maintain the thesis that to say God is a father, He must have a wife. And since it is stated in the Quran that He has neither consorts nor daughters He could not be said to have offspring. They fail to appreciate the Christian metaphorical sense that God is the father of all men, who stand to Him in the relation of children since, according to Muslims, such a notion is tantamount to plurality rather than singularity. Whereas, the Christians speak thus to underline the fact of the immanence of the transcendent God in the theophanic world.

The Muslim's uncompromising attitude with regard to the Christian triune Godhead is seen in their concept of sin, forgiveness of sins, salvation or redemption, and the absence of the concept of incarnation as well as of intermediaries between man and God. In Islam, sin is divided into two: *kabira* "great", and *saghira* "little sins". *Kabira* sins are those great sin such as associating a partner with God (*shirk*) for which, if a Muslim does not repent, he will be sent to the purgatorial hell reserved for sinful Muslims, while *saghira* are those venial sins which are inherent in our fallen nature. The question of original sin perpetuated by Adam which god the incarnate came to dissipate through his blood or vicarious death does not exist in Islam. For Muslim, Adam, the first prophet, and his wife, Eve, did sin and were cast down from paradise (*al-janna*)... Adam fell on the side of Ceylon, or Sarabdib and Eve near Jiddah (the port of Makkah) in Arabia; and after a separation of two hundred years, Adam was, on his repentance, conducted by the Angel Gabriel to a mountain near Makkah, where he found and knew his wife, the mountain being then named 'Arafat, and the afterwards retired to Ceylon. Thus the Muslims could not understand the history of redemption in Christianity in which Jesus, the second Adam, came to dissipate the sin perpetuated by the first Adam. Next is the question of salvation. In Christianity, incarnation is necessary for the purpose of salvation of redemption. The blood of Jesus crucified is necessary to effect salvation. Thus God became man, God and Incarnate, to identify Himself with the sinful world so that He might conquer sin in the flesh. Whereas in Islam, salvation (*najat*) is not generally used in Muslim works of divinity, although the Sunni Muslims claim the title of *Najiya*, "those who are being saved".

The word *maghfira*, "forgiveness", is frequently used in the Quran to express what Christians understand by "Salvation", also *Islam, Imam*, and *Din*, are words which express the idea of a state of salvation.

According to Islam, a man obtains salvation by a recital of the *kalima*, or creed, but if he be an evildoer, he will suffer the pains of a purgatorial fire until his sins are atoned for; while he who has not accepted the Muslim creed will endure the pain of everlasting punishment (Hell). It is on the basis of this belief that the Muslims fail to recognise and appreciate the redemptive or salvific act of Jesus in history, and the Quran denies the crucifixion in the words: "They did not kill him and they did not crucify him, but one was made to resemble him." However, inspite of the denial of crucification, there are some passages which speak of the death of Jesus, who is said to have spoken of "the day that I die and the day what I am raised to life".

Moreover, the Muslim negative to the divinity or the Christness of Jesus, a metaphysical issue indeed which Muslims find difficult to comprehend, could be attributed to the supra-emphasis which the Bible itself properly lays on the "Jesusness" of Christ or the human aspect of Christ— He was born of woman (Virgin Mary), historically descended from Israel (son of David), developed from childhood to manhood, was eating and drinking, was hungry and had the practical experience of sleep. He had human feelings such as wrath, sorrow, anxiety, indignation, tiredness, fatigue, and he was troubled. He suffered and died. Furthermore, Muslims corroborate their viewpoint by the fact that the Jews, Jesus' kith and kin, opposed the idea that He was the son of God. As a matter of fact, they did not understand Jesus' mission, since the Messiah of their dream was in contradistinction to Jesus' Messiahship. They wanted somebody who would free them from the oppression of the Romans. The temptation of Jesus, as recorded by the synoptics, is a testimony to the expectation. The temptation of Jesus was symbolic of the type of Messiah they were expecting. They thought Jesus to be one who followed Moses (who gave the Jews manna in the wildness during the exodus and who led them to the wilderness across the Red Sea during the Egyptian oppression), a wonder worker who could drive their enemies, the Romans, to their knees, and David, (a renowned warrior and king in the history of Israel) come back to life. Jesus' "Membership" was a disappointment to the Jewish expectation. No wonder that they opposed Jesus and his ministry vehemently throughout Jesus' ministry even up to the time he died.

The Muslims viewpoint is further buttressed by Jesus' reserve about the title 'Son of God'. More often than not, he referred to himself as the 'son of man', and this is nothing but the "Jesusness" or human aspect of Christ. Admittedly, he was bound to say this, quite often, and at least for the sake of the redemptive work in the sinful world which he had come to accomplish on earth.

However, it is interesting to note that despite the negative attitude of Muslims to the "Christness" or divinity of Jesus, there is unanimity of opinion among some Muslims that Jesus was a man whose behaviour made a tremendous impression. He is called in the Quran, a righeous prophet.

The Christian concept of God the Holy Ghost is another bone of contention between Muslims and Christians. For Christians, *ruhu'llah* is the 'holy Spirit' or 'Holy Ghost' of God. It is that which descended on the Apostles on the Day of Pentecost as promised by Jesus. As said earlier, this has been operative right from the beginning of creation. It forms a component part of the Christian Trinity. Muslims' reaction to the Holy Ghost as one of Three is negative. They go to the extent of postulating that *ruhu'llah* does not signify the Holy Ghost in Christianity and that what we have in Saint John's Gosptel (Chapter Fourteen, verse 17) the 'Spirit of truth', is not the same as the 'Holy Ghost' as contained in the synoptics but a reference to the advent of the Prophet of Islam, Muhammad. This thesis may be difficult to accept since John, writing in the age of philosophy, might interpret the 'Holy Ghost' of the synoptics to mean 'Spirit of truth' or 'Spirit of enlightenment'. The implications of the words 'Christ' in the synoptics and the 'Word' in Saint John's Gospel are pertinent here. Furthermore, one might, giving the benefit of doubt, say that the viewpoint of Muslims in this regard is more of conjecture than reality. It is patent that, the word 'Muhammad' does not occur in any portion of the Bible while the Quran talks a good deal about Jesus since Christianity appeared in the world long before Islam. Here, the more probable is the *a posteriori* side of the issue and not *a priori*.

The more likely interpretation of that passage in John is that Jesus meant the Comforter (Greek *paraklete*). This, except by later extension, was with particular reference to the twelve disciples of Jesus.

The Holy Spirit is mentioned three times in the Quran. First in the *Suratu'n-Nahl* it is mentioned as the inspiring agent of the Quran. It is mentioned twice in the *Suratu'l-Baqarah* as the divine power which aided Jesus.

The Jalalain, al-Baidawi, and the Muslim commentators in general maintain the thesis that this Holy Spirit was the Angel Gabriel, who sanctified Jesus and constantly aided him. It is also believed that it was the Holy Spirit that brought the Quran down from heaven and revealed it to Muhammad.

Muslims regard it an incongruous, on the basis of the submission above, that the same 'Holy Spirit' should be given the title 'God'. The attitude might be due to the fact that in the thought of Muslim theologians there is no clear-cut separation of personalities and functions between the Holy Spirit and the Angel Gabriel. No wonder that the issue perpetrated some sort of misunderstanding between the two religious groups.

Regarding this issue, the Bible and the Quran are almost at opposite poles. There appears to be in the thought of Muslim theologians, based mostly on Quranic evidence, a synthesis of personalities and functions, whereas in christianity there is a clear-cut distinction of personalities and functions. In Christianity, the Holy spirit is one to the Three and not the one that is referred to as the Angel Gabriel, who is just a messenger of God, a point that is also contained in the Quran. If we would learn to call people what they call themselves, on the basis of the truth revealed to them, the gate of misunderstanding or apparent misunderstanding between the two religious groups would henceforth remain shut.

Muslim Reaction to the Traditional African Concept of the Nature of the Godhead

Scholars of African Traditional Religion agree that God is admittedly real to the Africans. Moreover, it is their thesis that divinities, constituting the pantheon, exist in the religion.

Idowu, a renowned scholar of African traditional religion

admits the fact that a pantheon implies pluralism, though he uses 'diffused monotheism' instead of the word 'polytheism' since, according to him, the divinities do not have absolute existence and that the African world is under a unitary theocratic government.

Regarding the relationship between Deity and the divinities Idowu opines that from the paint of view of the theology of African traditional religion, it will be erroneous to maintain the thesis that the divinities were created. According to him, it will be correct to say that they were brought into being, or that they came into being in the nature of things with regard to the divine ordering of the universe. Orisa-nla (arch divinity among the Yoruba) is definitely a derivation partaking of the very nature and metaphysical attributes of Olodumaro. Hence he is often known as Deity's son or deputy, vested with the power and authority of royal sonship. And this is why, according to Idowu, it has been possible in Bahia to syncretise his cult with Christianity and identify him as Jesus Christ.

Olokun (Benin) is known as the son of Osanobwa. All Akan divinities are called sons of Onyame. According to Idowu, the divinities are derivatives from Deity. Since this idea does not tally with the Muslim concept of the Godhead as contained in their expression *la ilaha illa 'illah,* they feel apathetic to the concept and brand it *shirk* instead of monotheism *perse*. Their stand is to maintain the being of Allah intact as one who is unique, incomparable, and at the same time functional in the theocratic world.

Moreover, Idowu says, the divinities were brought into being as functionaries in the theocratic government of the universe. They are ministers with different portfolios. Idowu says, according to Dahomey belief, the whole set-up makes this clear. Yoruba traditional religion is another meet example. Then he goes on to say that the correct interpretation of the position of the divinities is that they constitute a half-way house which is not meant to be the permanent resting place for man's soul and that technically, the divinities are only means to an end and not ends in themselves. When Idowu is saying here is that the divinities serve as intermediaries between man and God. Whereas in Islam, the question of intermediaries does not arise. As said earlier in this paper, Muhammad is not regarded as an intermediary between Allah and man but a prophet (*nabi*) and a messenger (*rasul*) and no more. A Muslim can have a direct contact with Allah apathetic towards the African concept of God and gods.

Moreover, the negative attitude of the Muslims to the African concept of the Godhead might be that, though Africans regard God as the *prius* of all on earth and in heaven at the same time they regard the divinities as ends in themselves in some cases. They pray to them, offer them sacrifice and hold periodical sacrifice in their honour. In some cases, the question about God has become highly obliterated.

The question of pluralism is not in tune with the Islamic concept of *tauhid.* African Muslims are advised to focus their attention on God and not on the traditional deities. Moreover, during prayers, Prophet Muhammad should be praised instead of the traditional gods. The pre-Islamic period is regarded as a "*period of ignorance*" (*jahiliyya*) while that of Islam is regarded as that of "*enlightenment*" when Allah and Allah alone, who has neither partner nor associate, should be worshipped. The argument in this context is that, if there is only One God who does not require anything besides praises and fear of Him, there is absolutely no need to offer sacrifice to the various divinities, neither is there any need to have secret societies in which some sacrificial practices incompatible with the will of Allah are indulged in. The epitome of all this is that "all honour and glory" should be given to Allah, the One who is.

Concluding Remarks

This paper makes it clear that in Islam, the doctrine of the Unity of God is unique (*al-tauhid wahid*). Islam seeks to accomplish this in the world of multiplicity of religions, doctrines and beliefs by its uncompromising emphasis upon Divine Unity. According to the Islamic perspective, God did not send different truths, but different expressions and forms of the same fundamental and indivisible Truth of Unity.

I have, therefore, x-rayed the sources of theological differences, as perceived by Muslims, between the Islamic and both the Christian and the traditional views of the nature of the Godhead.

In Islam, there is no equivocation that it is *rigid* monotheism. No wonder that they find it difficult to comprehend the theological standpoint of Christian theologians concerning the triune Godhead, and the idea of 'diffused monotheism' emerging from *theologia Africana*. However,this difficulty on the part of the Muslim, should not be viewed as being insurmountable since in Africa, for example, these differences have not led to, and hopefully will never lead to social and political acrimony. In Africa, religious co-fraternity or what may be termed religious peaceful co-existence is a phenomenon which should be treasured.

I hope that the spirit of the this paper is one which would generate greater religious understanding and tolerance among the various religious groups not only in Africa but in the world at large.

Revised and edited; originally published in Islamic Quarterly.

12

Devil's Delusion (Part I)

D.S. MARGOLIOUTH

Devil deludes everyone, but deludes in different ways. Does the devil delude a sufi too? Ibn Jauzi presents opposite view.

Account of the way wherein the devil Deludes Ascetics and Devotees

An ordinary man may hear the condemnation of the world in the Glorious Qur'an and the Tradition, and hold that salvation lies in abandoning it, not knowing what the world which is condemned is. The devil will delude him, saying : You cannot be saved in the next world except by abandoning this and such a man will go off headlong to the mountains, where he will be away from the congregation and the company and from knowledge, becoming like a wild beast, imagining that this is genuine asceticism. How could it be otherwise when he has heard that one person wandered away and another took to devotion on a mountain, though he may have had a family which went to ruin, or a mother who wept over his departure, and may not be acquainted with the rules of prayer, or have inflicted injuries on others which he has not made good. The devil can only succeed in deluding such a man by reason of his ignorance, to which is due his complacency with the amount which he knows. Had he had the good fortune to associate with a jurist who understood the realities, such jurist would have shown him that the world is not condemned on its own account—how indeed can condemnation fall on a fight of God and an institution which is necessary for the continuance of the human species, and a means of aiding him to procure knowledge by furnishing him with food, drink, clothing and a sanctuary wherein he can pray? What is condemned is the taking of things from illicit sources or handling them extravagantly, not according to need, and disposing of them capriciously, not as the code permits. Such jurist would have shown him too that going out to lonely mountains is forbidden; for the Prophet forbade spending the night alone; and that his venturing to abandon company and congregation is loss not gain; and that distance from knowledge and the learned strengthens the power of ignorance. Further that desertion of father and mother in such a case is unfilial, and unfilial conduct is a capital offence. Those who have been reported to have gone out to a mountain may well have been person who had neither families nor parents, and went out in company to some place to practise devotion; those whose condition admits of no sound explanation yet do this are in error whoever they may be. One of the ancient said : We went out to a mountain to practise devotion, then Sufyan al-Thauri came and brought us back.

Among the delusions which he practises on the ascetics is his diverting them from learning while occupying themselves with asceticism. They thereby take the worse in exchange for the better; for the profit of the ascetic does not go beyond his own threshold, whereas that of the savant does go beyond. Many a devotee has been brought back to the right path.

He further deludes them by making them fancy that asceticism means abstension from lawful things. Some of them therefore will not go beyond barley bread; some will not taste fruit; some reduce their food to such an extent that the body dries up, torture themselves by wearing wool, and abstaining from cold water. This was not the way of the Prophet nor of his Companions nor their followers. They hungered indeed when they found no food, but ate when they found it. The Prophet ate meat and liked it, and poultry and liked it; he also liked sweets, and enjoyed the taste of water, which he preferred stale, holding that flowing water injured the stomach and did not slake the thirst.

A certain man said: I cannot eat date and almond paste, since I cannot be adequately grateful for it. Al-Hasan said : The man is a fool; can he be adequately grateful for cold water?

Sufyan al-Thauri when he travelled used to take with him as provision roast meat and almond and honey paste.

A man ought to know that his soul is his mount, which he must treat gently in order that it may bring him to his destination. So he had better take what benefits it and eschew what harms it, such as satiety and excessive gratification of desires. For this injures both body and religion.

Further, people differ in nature, so when the Bedouin wear wool and restrict themselves to milk as a drink, we do not blame them, the mounts of their bodies can endure this. Similarly when the inhabitants of the Black Country wear wool and eat unleavened bread, we do not blame them either nor do we speak of them as having burdened themselves, since such is their custom; only when the body is fastidious, being accustomed to delicacies, we forbid its owner to make it endure what will harm it. If such a man is ascetically inclined and prefers to abstain from desirable things either because what is lawful does not admit of luxury, or because delicious food involves frequent meals with much sleep and idleness, such a person should know what it will injure him to give up and what he can give up without injury, and so take as much as is good for his health without causing himself pain. Some people suppose that plain bread is sufficient for the maintenance of the body; even if this were so, restriction thereto would be injurious, inasmuch as the humours of the body require the sour and the sweet, the hot and the cold, the astringent and the aperient. There is implanted in nature an inclination towards what suits it, and sometimes it inclines to the sour but at others to the sweet, and for this there are reasons, e.g., paucity of phlegm which is indispensable for its maintenance, whence there is a desire for milk, or there may be an excess of yellow bile so that it has an inclination for sourness; one who restrains it from following its natural craving for what benefits it injures it, unless indeed he restrain it from surfeit and greed and what may have dangerous consequences, for such will ruin it. Mere abstinence is an error; you should know this and take no notice of the sayings of al-Harith al-Muhasibi and Abu Talib al-Mekki concerning exiguity of food and combating the soul by abstinence from what is lawful for it. It is better to follow the Legislator and his Companions. Ibn 'Aqil used to say : How extraordinary it is that pious people should harbour caprices to be followed or newfangled monasticism, trailing the skirts of licentiousness in love and sport, or neglecting their duties, deserting their families, and retiring to the corners of mosques! Why cannot they serve God reasonably and legitimately?

One of the delusions which he casts upon them is making them fancy that asceticism means contentment with a minimum of food and clothing. Contenting themselves therewith, in their hearts they aspire to leadership and seek for honour, so that you may see them looking out for visits from princes, and to be honoured as the poor are not; when they meet people they assume a devout attitude as though they had just been experiencing a vision. Such a man often refuses money for fear it should be said that he has changed his mind about asceticism whereas they open the door widely to worldly advancement in the matter of receiving visits and having their hands kissed—worldly, since leadership is the summit of worldly ambition.

The commonest delusion which the devil casts on devotees and ascetics is secret hypocrisy. Manifest hypocrisy, such as display of emaciation, paleness of face, and matted hair, does not come within this form of delusion. The same is the case with hypocritical praying and alms giving, for such acts are not hidden. We are referring to secret hypocrisy; the Prophet said : Acts are by their intentions. When the purpose of an act is not God's approval, it is not accepted. Malik b. Dinar said : Tell the person who is not sincere not to trouble himself.

You should know that the Believer in his conduct is thinking of God only, but he is liable to secret hypocrisy through delusion, and from this escape is hard. There is a Tradition going back uninterruptedly to Yasar according to which he said : Yusuf b. Asbat said to me : Learn to distinguish sound conduct from unsound; it took me twenty-two years to learn. There is a tradition going back uninterruptedly to Ibrahim al-Hanzali according to which he said: I heard Baqiyyah b. al-Walid say that he had heard Ibrahim b. Adham say: I learned the meaning of knowledge from a monk named Sam'aqn, whose cell I entered. I asked him how long he had been in his cell.—Seventy years, he replied.—What, I asked, is your food?—He said : What makes you ask that, Hanefite?—I said : I should like to know.—One chick-pea a night was his reply.—What emotion, I asked, does it stir in your heart so that this chick-pea can suffice you?—He asked me whether I saw the people in front of him.—I replied that I did.—They, he said, come to me one day in each year, deck my cell, make circuit of it, and pay me honour in this way. Whenever I feel weary of my devotions I remind myself of that hour; and I can endure the strain of a year for the glory of an hour; endure therefore, Henefite, the strain of an hour for the glory of eternity.—This furnished my heart with copious knowledge. He then asked whether he should add more?—I bade him do so.—He told me to descend from the cell, which I did, and then he let down to me a bucket containing twenty chick-peas. He bade me enter the monastery, as the people had seen what he had let down to me.—When I entered it, the Christians. collected and said : Hanefite, what did the old man let down to you?—Some of his food, I replied.—What, they said, will you do with it? We have the better night to it. Ask your price. —Twenty dinars, I said. —They gave me the money.—I went back to the old man, who said : You have made a mistake. Had you asked for twenty thousand, they would have given them to you. This is the glory of one whom you do not worship; think what will come of the glory of Him Whom you do worship; Hanefite. Turn you face to your Lord!

I would observe that for fear of hypocrisy the saints have concealed their doings, giving them the appearance of the country. Ibn Sirin used to laugh during the day and weep during the night. Ayyub al-Sakhtiyani used to wear a robe with a somewhat lengthy skirt; when Ibn Adham was ill, food fit for the healthy was to be found set before him. There is a Tradition going back to 'Abdallah b. al-Mubarak after Bakkar b. 'Abdallah according to which the letter heard Wahb b. Munabbih say: There was a certain man, one of the best of his time, whom people used to visit and honour. One day they gathered round him and he said: We have left the world, abandoning family and goods for fear of impiety, yet I am afraid that more impiety has befallen us in this condition than befalls the wealthy in their wealth. I find we like people to render us services; if we make a purchase, to get easy terms on account of our piety: if we met, to be greeted and made much of on account of our piety.—This speech was noised abroad till it reached the king, who marvelled threat and rode out to salute the man and gaze upon him. When the man saw him, he was told that it was the king who had come to salute him.—What is he going to do? asked the man.—It is on account of your sermon, they said:—He asked his attendant whether he had any food, and was told that there was some of the fruit whereon he ordinarily breakfasted. He ordered that this should be brought on a mat and set before him. He began to eat, though it was his practice to fast during the day and eat nothing. The king approached him and saluted him. He replied in a low voice and proceeded to eat. The king asked where the man of whom he had heard was, and was told that they said.—There is no good in him, said the king, who turned away.—The man said : Praise be to God Who has caused you to depart by this expedient.

According to another report Wahb said that when the king came forward the man made large mouthfuls of the vegetables, dipped them in oil, and began to eat voraciously. The king said to him : How are you, whoever you may be?—The man said : Like other people.—The king then turned away the rein of his mount, saying : There is no good in *him.* The man said : Praise be to God Who has sent him away from me with censure.

There is a Tradition going back to 'Ata according to which he said: al-Walid b. 'Abd al-Malik wanted to appoint Yazid b. Marthad to an office and when Yazid heard this, he put on a fur with the skin on his back and the wool outside; in his hand he took a loaf of bread, and some Arack, and started out without cloak, hood, sandals, or shoes. He ate as he walked in the street. Al-Walid was told that Yazid had lost his reason, and was informed of his proceedings. So he let him alone.

There are ascetics who practise asceticism both outwardly and inwardly, yet such a man, being aware that his friends or his wife will certainly talk about his abandoning the world, will find this easy to endure as the monk whose encounter with Ibrahim b. Adham have recorded it. If such a man were sincere in his asceticism he would eat with his family such quantity as would win no reputation for sanctity and cause talk about him to stop. Dawud b. Abi Hind fasted twenty years without letting his family know. He would take his food, go out into the street and give it away. So the people in the street thought that he had eaten at home, whereas his household thought he ate in the street. Such were people then!

There are besides ascetics whose sustenance is retreat in a mosque or monastery or on a mountain, and whose pleasure consists in people knowing of their isolation. Such a man may plead in defence of his retirement that he is afraid of seeing something of which he disapproves if he came out. He has, however, various ends in view; among them pride and contempt of other people, fear lest they should not pay him sufficient attention; preservation of his dignity and leadership, which would be impaired by mixing with people, whereas he is anxious that his credit and reputation should remain intact. At times indeed his object is the concealment of his faults and failings, and general ignorance, which might be seen; and he desires to be visited and not have to pay visits, and takes delight in princes coming to him, and commoners crowding at his door and kissing his hand. So he neglects visitation of the sick, and attendance at funerals, and his friends say : Excuse the shaikh, this is his custom (he had better not have had a custom which violates the code). Should such a person be in want of food and have no-one with him to buy it, he would endure hunger so that he might not have to go out to buy it himself, and so lose dignity by walking among the populace. If he were to go out and buy what he wanted, his reputation would be at an end! His inner purpose is maintenance of his dignity. Yet the Prophet used to go out into the street, buy what he needed, and carry it himself. Abu Bakr used to carry clothes on his shoulder and sell and boy. There is a Tradition going back to Muhammad b. al-Qasim who stated that it was reported on the authority of 'Abdallah b. Hanzalah how 'Abdallah b. Salam was seen walking with a bundle of firewood on his head. People said to him : What induces you to do this, when God has enriched you? He said : I wanted to keep off pride thereby, for I heard the Prophet say : He in whose heart their is an atom's weight of pride shall not enter paradise.

I would observe that the practice which I have mentioned of going out to buy what is required and similar sacrifices of dignity were customary with the ancients; the practice has changed like conditions and fashions in dress. I should not advise a learned man in our time to go out to buy what he wants, since such a proceeding would eclipse the light of learning in the eyes of the ignorant, who are bound to respect it. Regard for their sentiments in this mater would not degenerate into hypocrisy, and employment of such measures as will enforce respect is not to be forbidden. Not every proceeding whereby men of old time avoided changing people's sentiments can be practised in our time. Al-Auza'i said : We used to laugh and make merry, but when we find that people follow our example I do not think this proper for us. It is reported how one day the friends of Ibrahim b. Adham were making merry, when a man knocked at the door and bade them be quiet and dignified. They said to him : You would teach us hypocrisy.—He said: I do not wish god to be disobeyed through you.

This man, I would observe, was afraid of what the ignorant would say, viz., see what these ascetics are doing!—For the populace cannot endure such conduct on the part of professed devotees.

Among these people there are those of whom if one were asked to do soft raiment, he would decline, for fear of loss of dignity; he would rather expire than be seen eating. He would restrain himself from smiling, not to speak of laughing. The devil makes him fancy that this is for the improvement of his character; in reality it is hypocrisy, a means of maintaining his prestige. So too you may see him with bowed head, showing the signs of grief. When he is by himself, there is no knowing what he would look like.

The man of old time used to keep off anything which would bring them into notice; they would flee from any place in which they might be pointed at. There is a Tradition traced to 'Abdallah b. Khafif, according to which Yusuf b. Asbat said : I started on foot from Manbij and reached Missisah (Mopusuestia) with my wallet on my neck. Then one man rose up from his booth and saluted me, and another, so I threw down my wallet and entered the mosque, where I made a prayer of two inclinations. People surrounded me, and one man gazed on my face. So I said to myself : How long will my heart endure this? —So I took up my wallet, and returned sweating and tried to Manbij, and for two years my heart did not return to me.

There are ascetics who wear tattered garments and do not stitch them neither adjust their turbans nor comb their beards, to let people see that they know nothing of mundane matters. This is a form of hypocrisy; for if the man be sincere in his neglect of externals, as when Dawud al-Ta'i was asked why he did not comb his beard, he replied "I have other things to think of"—he should know that he is off the high road; for this was not the procedure of the Prophet or of his Companions. He combed his hair, looked in the mirror, used ointment and perfume, though more occupied with the next world than any other creature. Abu Bakr and 'Umar used to dye their hair with henna and phyllirea; yet they were the most scrupulous and most ascetic of the Companions. No attention should be paid to one who claims rank which surpasses the Sunnah and the practice of the chief men.

There are ascetics who maintain continual silence and isolate themselves from the society of their families, whom they annoy by their unamiability and excessive moroseness, forgetting the saying of the Prophet "You have a duty to your family." The Prophet used to be of good humour, play with children and talk to his wives, run races with 'A'ishah, and do other amiable things. This devotee who makes his wife into a widow and his children orphans by his unamiability and isolation, supposing that different conduct will distract him from the next world, is so ignorant as not to know that cheerfulness with one's family is an aid to the next world. In both the *Sahih* there is a Tradition that the Prophet said to Jabir : Why not marry a virgin so that you could play together — Such an ascetic often neglects his conjugal duty, and so violates an ordinance for an improper act of supererogation.

There are ascetics who are pleased with their conduct and if anyone were to tell them they were the pillars of the earth, would regard it as the truth. Some of them watch for the occurrence of miracles in their honour, and such fancies that if he were to come to water he could walk upon it. If occasion comes for him to pray and he is not answered, he feels indignation, as though he were a hireling demanding payment for his work. Had he been favoured with intelligence he would have known that he is a bonded servant who earns no thanks for his labour. Had he considered how he had been divinely guided to his work, he would have seen cause for gratitude and been afraid of falling short therein. His fear of such shortcoming might well have kept him from thinking about his work, as Rabi'ah said : I ask God's forgiveness for the want of veracity in my speech.—She was asked whether she had performed any act which she thought would be accepted of her. She said : If there be any, it is my fear of its rejection.

One of the delusions which the devil practises on certain ascetics whom he approaches through their ignorance is their acting according to their own imaginings without attending to what the jurist says. Ibn 'Aqil said : Abu Ishaq al-Kharraz was a saintly man, and the first person who taught me the Book of God. It was his practice to abstain from speech in the month of Ramadan, only utterring phrases from the Qur'an when occasion demanded speech. Thus for the admission of visitors he would say (v. 26) *Enter unto them the gate,* and to his son at the evening of the fast (ii. 58) *of its greens and its cucumbers* as an order to buy vegetables.

I said to him : This is a thing which you believe to be a pious act, whereas it is a sin.—This grieved him, and I went on to say: This Glorious Qur'an was revealed for the explanation of the ordinances of the Code, and should not be used for mundane purposes. You might as well wrap your soap in leaves of the Sacred Volume, or make of it a pillow for your head.—He cut me and would not listen to the argument.

At times (I observe) an ignorant ascetic hears something from the laity and gives a legal opinion according to it. I was told by the jurist Abu Hakim Ibrahim b. Dinar how a man had asked him for an opinion on the following question : If a woman after a third divorce gives birth to a male child, can she lawfully be taken back by her husband? I answered No, he said. There was present with me al-Sharif al-Dhhali, a man renowned for his asceticism, and highly esteemed by the populace. He said to me : On the contrary, she may be taken back.—I said : No-one has taken that view.—He said : I assure you I have given this opinion from here to Basrah.

So see the effect which ignorance has on those who suffer from it, and how there is added thereto the maintenance of dignity for fear lest the ascetic be regarded as an ignorant man. Men of old time used to disapprove of an ascetic giving legal opinions even though he possessed much learning, on the ground that he did not possess all the qualifications for doing so. What then would they say if they were to see the devotees of our time giving wrong opinions out of their imaginations? There is a Tradition going back to Isma'il b. Shabbah according to which he said : I entered the presence of Ahmad b. Hanbal, when Ahmad b. Harb had arrived from Meccah. Ahmad asked me : Who is this man of Khurasar who has arrived?—I proceed to tell him about the man's asceticism and integrity. He said : A man who professes what he does ought not to meddle with legal opinions.

Among the delusions which he practises on ascetics is their

contempt for and vituperation of the learned. They assert that the object to be aimed at is action; not knowing that knowledge is the action of the heart. If they understood the rank of the learned in memorizing the Code, and that it is the rank of prophets, they would regard themselves as dumb brutes by the side of correct speakers and blind by the side of the seeing. The learned are the guides of the path, with the rest of mankind behind them, and one of them, if he be fit, can walk alone. In the two *Sahih* there is a Tradition of Sahl b. Sa'd that the Prophet said : By Allah that he should guide any man by you is better for you than ruddy camels.

Among the faults which they find with the learned is that the latter allow themselves certain liberty in things permitted, to gain strength therewith for the prosecution of study; and similarly they find fault with one who amasses wealth. Had they understood the meaning of the word "permitted" they would have known that no blame attaches to the person who do not are better than those who do. Would it be proper for one who prays the whole night to find fault with one who performs the obligatory prayer and then goes to sleep? There is a Tradition going back to Muhyammad b. Ja'far al-Khaulani according to which he said : The following was told me by Abdu 'Abdallah al-Khawwas who was a companion of Hatim al Asamm : We entered Rayy with Hatim al-Balkhi who was accompanied by three hundred and twenty followers and was on his way to the pilgrimage. They all wore wool, with tunics of the same material, not one of them bringing wallet or food. We stopped at the house of a devout trader, who entertained us. The next morning he said to Hatim : Abu 'Abd al-Rahman, do you need anything? For I wish to visit one of our jurists who is ill.—Hatim said : If there is a sick jurist among you, visiting such a person is highly meritorious, and indeed to gaze upon a jurist is a pious act. I will come with you.—Now the sick man was Muhammad b. Muqatil, qadi of Rayy. The trader bade him come with him. They came to the door of the sick man's house, and there was a door-keeper. Hatim kept thinking and saying : O Lord, is the house of a learned man of this style!—Permission was then given them to enter, and they found it to be a spacious mansion with fine furniture, hangings, carpets and curtains. Hatim kept thinking and staring till they entered the room wherein Muhammad b. Maqatil was, and there they found him lying on a soft, handsome couch, with a flyflap at his head, and men standing. The trader from Rayy sat down, but Hatim remained standing; Muhammad b. Muqatil with a gesture bade him take a seat.—Hatim said : I will not sit down.—Ibn Muqatil asked him whether he wanted anything. He said Yes.—What is it? asked Ibn Muqatil. He said : I wish to ask you a question.—Ask me, he said.—Hatim said : Rise and sit up that I may ask you about it.—Hatim ordered his servants to prop him up. Then Hatim said : Whence did you procure this knowledge of yours? He replied : By instruction from trustworthy persons who had it from others who were trustworthy who had it from the founders of the Science.—From whom, asked Hatim, did they obtain it?—From the epigoni, he answered. —And from whom did the epigoni obtain it? —From the Companions of the Prophet, he replied.—And whence did the Prophet procure it? He asked.—From Gabriel, who had it from God Almighty, he replied.—Then Hatim said: In the matter conveyed by Gabriel from God Almighty to the Prophet, by the Prophet to his Companions, by his Companions to the epigony, by the epigoni to the founders, by the founders to trustworthy persons, and by those trustworthy persons to you, have you heard that the finer a man's house, the softer his bedding, and the more copious his decoration in this world, the higher will be his rank with God?—He said: No.—Then what, he asked, have you heard?—He said: I have heard that the man who is averse to mundane things, has his affections fixed on the next world, loves the poor, and makes preparation for the future life, is of higher rank with, and nearer to, God.—Hatim said: And whom have *you* taken for your model? The Prophet, his Companions, the epigoni who followed, the saints who trod in their footsteps?—or Pharaoh and Nimrod? They were the first to build with gypsum and brick. O ye that are learned in mischief! The ignorant man who is passionately attached to the world will say: This man of learning lives in this style; shall I not do the like?

Hatim departed from his presence; Muhammad b. Muqatil's

illness became worse. The people of Rayy heard what had passed between Hatim and Ibn Muqatil, and told Hatim that Muhammad b. 'Ubaid al-Tanafisi in Qazwin was yet more luxurious than Ibn Muqatil. So Hatim went to him, entered his house, and found a number of people with him to whom he was discoursing. Hatim said to him: God have mercy on you, I am a foreigner who has come to learn from you the elements of my religion, and the preliminaries of prayer: how should I wash for prayer?—Muhammad b. 'Ubaid said: Most certainly; slave, bring a vessel with water.—One was brought, Muhammad b. 'Ubaid squatted down, washed himself three times, and said: This is why you should wash.—Hatim said: Please wait till I wash in your presence, in order to enforce my point.—So al-Tanafisi rose, and Hatim squatted down in his place and began to wash. He washed his face three times, but when he got to his arm he washed that four times. Al-Tanafisi said: You have been too lavish.—Hatim asked wherein? He said: Washing your arm four times.—Hatim said: Good heavens! I have been too lavish with a handful of water, and have you not been too lavish in all this that I see?—Al-Tanafisi understood that Hatim's intention was to rebuke him, entered his house, and did not appear in public for forty days.

Hatim departed for the Hijaz. When he got to Medinah he wanted to dispute with the savants of that city. Entering it, he said: Ye people, what city is this?—They said: The City of God's Prophet.—Where, he asked, is the palace of God's Prophet that I may go and offer there a prayer of a couple of inclinations?—They said: The Prophet of God had no palace, he had only a low hut.—Where then, he proceeded to ask, are the palaces of his family, his Companions, and his wives?—They said: They had no palaces, but only low huts.—Then, said he, this is Pharaoh's city!—They reviled him (says the narrator) and brought him to the governor, saying: This foreigner calls this Pharaoh's city.—The governor asked him why he had said that.—He replied: Prince, do not be hasty with me. I am a stranger, and entering this city asked what city it was. They said: The city of God's Prophet. I then asked for the palace of God's Prophet and the palaces of his Companions. They told me that they had had only low huts. Now I have heard God Almighty say: (xxxiii. 21) *Ye have had in God's Prophet a good model;* now whom have you taken for your model? God's Prophet, or Pharaoh?

Here I would observe: Woe to the learned from the ignorant ascetic who is satisfied with his knowledge and thinks obligatory that which is supererogatory. For that which he disapproves is permitted, and that which is permitted has the assent of the Code; the Code would not assent to an act and then remonstrate on its account. Such ignorance is disgraceful. Had Hatim said to them: Might you not have moderated your style of living so as to give an example to others, it would have been more fitting. What too would the man have said had he heard that 'Abd al-Rahman b. 'Auf, al-Zubair b. al'Awwam, 'Abdallah b. Mas'ud, and many more of the Companions left huge fortunes? Tamim al-Dari gave a thousand dirhams for a cloak in which he used to keep vigil.

It is the duty of the ascetic to learn to the learned, and if he has not learned, he had better keep silence. There is a Tradition traced to Malik b. Dinar according to which he said: Satan plays with the Readers as boys with nuts. The same Tradition is traced to Habib al-Farisi.

"Readers", I would observe, here mean ascetics; it is an old and well-known name for them. God is the Guide to what is correct, and to Him is recourse and return.

Section X.—Account of the Way Wherein he Deludes the Sufis Among the Ascetics

The Sufis belong to the ascetic group, and we devote a fresh section to them, although we have described the manner wherein the devil confuses the ascetics, because the Sufis are distinguished from other ascetics by certain qualities and states and bear certain badges. Sufism is a system which commences with general asceticism, whose adherents afterwards permitted themselves music and dancing. They have won the favour of seekers of the next world from among the multitude by reason of the asceticism which they exhibit; and by seekers after this world owing to the comfort and amusement which they find these persons enjoy. It is necessary to dispel the delusions which the devil introduces into their system, and this can only be done by revealing the system with its branches, and explaining it methods.

In the time of the Prophet men took their appellations from Belief and Islam, calling themselves Believer and Muslim. Then there came into use the names Ascetic and Devotee; then there arose persons who attached themselves to asceticism and devotion, separated themselves from the world and gave themselves up to devoutness, adopting therein a system of their own and conforming themselves to a certain character. They supposed that the first person to isolate himself for the worship of God in His holy house was a man called Sufah, whose name was al-Ghauth b. Murr; so they named themselves Sufis after him, as they resembled him in separating themselves to serve God.

I was told by Muhammad b. Nasir after Abu Ishaq Ibrahim b. Sa'id al-Habbal that the following had been said by Abu Muhammad 'Abu al-Ghani b. Sa'id the Hafiz: I asked, he said, Walid b. al-Qasim from what did the Sufis take their name?—He replied: There was certain people in the days of paganism called Sufah, who separated themselves for the worship of God and inhabited the Ka'bah; those who imitate them are the Sufis. 'Abd al-Ghani added: the people known as Sufah were the children of al-Ghauth b. Murr, brother's son to Tamim b. Murr. According to a Tradition going back to al-zubair b. Bakkar he said: The conducting of the pilgrims from 'Arafah was committed to al-Ghauth b. Murr b. Tabikhah and continued among his descendants who were called Sufah. When the time arrived from such conducting the arabs said, Conduct, Sufah!—Al-Zubair added: Abu 'Ubaidah asserted that the name Sufah or Sufan was given to anyone who was in charge of any business connected with the House, not being one of its chief officials, or who looked after any part of the ceremonial. Zubair also said: I was told by Abu'l-Hasan al-Athram after Hisham b. Muhammad b. al-Sa'ib al-Kalbi that according to this last al-Ghauth b. Murr was called Sufah because his mother, finding that all her children died, vowed that if he lived she would attach a piece of wool to his head and make him bound to the Ka'bah. She carried this out, and in consequence he and his descendants were called Sufah. Al-Zubair further states that he was told by Ibrahim b. al-Mundhiri after 'Abd al-'Aziz b. Imran that this last had been told by 'Aqqal b. Shabbah that the mother of Tamim b. Murr having given birth to a number of girls promised Allah that if she bore a boy she would make him a slave of the House. She gave birth to al-Ghauth b. Murr. and when she attached him to the House he felt the heat. Passing by him when he had fallen down and was in a state of collapse she said: This boy of mine is no better than a piece of wool, whence he was called Sufah. Sufah had charge of conducting the pilgrims from 'Arafah to Mina and from Mina to Meccah. This right continued with the descendants of Sufah till it was taken by 'Udwan, who also held it till it was taken by Quraish.

Some people, I would observe, take the views that Sufism is traceable to the "people of the Suffah? (the bench in the Prophet's Mosque). Their reason for this opinion was that they found the people of the Suffah agree with our description of Sufah in devotion to God and the practice of poverty; for these were poor people who came to the Prophet, having neither families nor possessions, and a bench was built for them in the Prophet's mosque, whence they were called People of the Bench. There is a Tradition traced to al-Hasan as having said: A bench was built for the weak Muslims, and the other Muslims used to bring them any charity they could. The Prophet would come to them and say, Peace be upon you, ye people of the Bench; to which they would reply, And on thee, O Prophet of God!—He would ask them how they were and they would reply, Well, O Prophet of God.

There is a Tradition traced to Nu'aim b. al-Mujammir after his father after Abu Dharr, according to which the last of these said: I was one of the people of the Bench, and when evening came, we used to present ourselves at the Prophet's door, who would order each of us to go off with some man, until only ten or fewer of the people of the Bench remained; the Prophet would sacrifice his own supper to us, and when we had supped would bid us go and sleep in the mosque.

These people, I would observe, only sat in the mosque of necessity and only fed on charity out of necessity. When God bestowed victory on the Muslims they could dispense with this state and went away. Moreover the derivation of Sufi from Suffah is erroneous, since the form would have been Suffi. There is an opinion that the name is derive from *Sufanah,* which is a soft and stumpy vegetable; the people according to this were called from it because they were satisfied with the herbs of the field. This also is erroneous, because the form should have been *Sufani.* Others derive it from the *sufah* of the nape of the neck, i.e. certain hairs which grow on the back of it; the idea being that the Sufi turns away from creatures and swerves towards God. Other derive it from the word for wool, which is admissible; only the first derivation is the correct one.

The name came into use before the year 200, and when the first of these people proclaimed it, they talked about it, expressing its import in various ways; whereof the gist is that according to them Sufism means disciplining of the soul, and resistance to nature by restraining it from vices and impelling it to virtues such as asceticism, gentleness, patience, sincerity, veracity, etc., such as earn praise in this world and reward in the next. There is a tradition going back to al-Tusi according to which he said: I heard Abu Bakr b. al-Muthaqif say: I ask Junaid b. Muhammad about Sufism, and he replied: It is departure from all evil qualities and entrance into all noble qualities.—There is a Tradition going back to 'abd al-Wahid b. Bakr according to which he said: I heard Muhammad b. Khafif say: Ruwaim said: All mankind are seated on semblances, save this sect which is seated on realities. All mankind demand of themselves the externals of the Code, whereas these people demand of themselves the reality of chastity, and constancy in veracity.

I would observe that the first Sufis carried this out; the devil however deluded them in certain ways, and yet further deluded their successors. As a century elapsed his hopes for the next century increased, and he deluded them still further, and obtained complete control over the later generations.

He started deluding them by diverting them from knowledge, making them suppose that the object to be aimed at is action. When he had extinguished the lamp of knowledge which they had, they floundered in darkness. He persuaded some that the purpose of their system was complete abandonment of the world; hence they discarded what was good for their bodies; compared wealth to scorpions, forgetting that it was ordained for useful purposes; imposed all sorts of penances on themselves, so that some of them would never lie down. The aims of these people were indeed good, only they were off the right path. Some of them through want of knowledge used to act according to fabricated Traditions of which they got hold, not knowing them to be fabrications.

Then came persons who discoursed to them about hunger, poverty, suggestions and insinuations and composed works on the subject like al-Harith al-Muhasibi. Others arose who systematized Sufism, and gave it certain distinguishing characteristics, such as the patched garment, music, erotic sentiment, dancing, clapping of the hands: they further distinguished themselves by excessive purity and cleanliness. Then the process continued, and their shaikhs made continual inventions, and discoursed of their imaginations. So the gulf between them and the learned widened, nay, they came to regard their own system as the most complete knowledge, which they called "the inner knowledge", whereas they made knowledge of the code "the outer knowledge." Some of them were led by hunger into false fancies, professing to be enamoured with God and to rave about Him: imagining Him to be an individual of beautiful form, about whom they raved. These were something between unbelievers and innovators; and then the paths of some branched out, and their beliefs were corrupted. Some of them adopted the doctrine of incarnation, others of union; and the devil continued to encompass them with various heresies so that they even made for themselves laws. There arose Abu 'Abd al-Rahman al-Sulami who composed for them a Book of *Sunan,* and collected for them *The Realities of Interpretation,* in which he mentioned extraordinary ways that they have of interpreting the Qur'an according to their fancies without finding support for them in any scientific principles, but merely accommodating it to their doctrines. Strange indeed that they should be so scrupulous in the matter of food and take such liberties with the Qur'an! The following was told us by Abu Mansur 'Abd al-Rahman al-Qazzaz after Abu Bakr al-Khatib. At last said he had been told by Muhammad b. Yusuf al-Qattan al-Naisaburi that Abu 'Abd al-Rahman al-Sulami was untrustworthy, only having heard a little from al-Asamm; yet, when al-Hakam Abu 'Abdallah b. al-Bay` died, he taught on the authority of al-Asamm the history of Yahya b. Mu'in and many things besides. He was also in the habit of fabricating Traditions for the Sufis.

Further Abu Nasr al-Sarraj composed a book to which he gave the title *Flashes of Sufism* wherein he set forth wrong beliefs and vicious utterances, of which we shall presently produce some specimens, if God will. Abu Talib al-Makki composed for them *The Provision of the Hearts* wherein he set forth false Traditions, continuous fastings for days and nights supported by no authority, with other fictions and erroneous doctrines. He frequently employs the phrase *One of those favoured with revelations says,* which is meaningless, and recounts on the authority of Sufis that God appears in this world to His saints.

I was told by Abu Mansur al-Qazzaz after Abu Bakr al-Khatib that Abu Tahir Muhammad b. 'Ali al-'Allaf said: Abu Talib al-Makki came to Basrah after the death of 'Abu'l-Hasan b. Salim and professed to be one of his followers. Then he went to Baghdad, where people gathered to the room in which he preached, and his speech was confused; he was remembered to have said *There is naught more injurious to the creature than the Creator.* He was charged with heresy and shunned and spoke no more in public after that Al-Khatib added: Abu Talib al-Makki composed a book which he called *The Provision of the Hearts,* in the language of the Sufis, wherein he sets forth many things which are to be disapproved, and abominable concerning the attributes.

Then (I would observe) came Abu Nu'aim al-Isfahani, who composed for them a book called *The Ornament,* in which he sets forth very disgraceful things within the bounds of Sufism, and is not ashamed to mention among Sufis Abu Bakr, 'Umar, 'Uthman, 'ali, and the chief Companions, about whom he records marvellous things. Among them too he mentions Suraih the qadi, al-Hasan al-Basri, Sufyan al-Thauri, and Ahmad b. Hanbal. Likewise al-sulami in his *Classes of Sufis* mentions al-Fudail, Ibrahim b. Adham, and Ma'ruf al-Karkhi, whom he makes out to have been Sufis by pointing out that they were ascetics.

Sufism is a well-known system, which goes beyond asceticism; the difference between the two is indicated by the fact that no-one has ever found fault with asceticism, whereas Sufism, has been censured as will presently be recorded. A treatise called *The Epistle* was composed for them by 'Abd al-Karim b. Hawazin al-Qushairi, wherein he gives marvellous accounts of *extinction, persistence, contraction, expansion, time, state, emotion, existence, combination, separation, sobriety, intoxication, taste, drink, erasure, confirmation, revelation, conversation, unveiling, perceptions, arisings, flashings, fashioning, empowering, the code, the reality,* etc., al baseless illusions, with yet more marvellous comments. Then there arose Muhammad b. Tahir al-Maqdisi, who composed for them *The Quintessence of Sufism,* wherein he recounted things which a man of sense would be ashamed to mention. We shall give such specimens as it will be suitable to mention in their places, if God will.

Our shaikh abu'l-Fadl b. Nasir the Hafiz used to say: Ibn Tahir held the doctrine of Licence, and wrote a book dealing with the lawfulness of gazing on beardless lads, into which he introduced a story of Yahya b. Mu'in, who said: I saw a pretty girl in Egypt, God be gracious to her!—People said to him: What, do you invoke a blessing on her!—He said: God be gracious to her and every one who is beautiful—Our shaikh Ibn Nasir added: Ibn Tahir is not a person to be employed as evidence.—Then arose Abu Hamid al-Ghazzali, who composed for them the work *Revival* according to their system which he filled with fictitious Traditions, not knowing them to be fictions; he also discoursed on Unveiling, and transgressed the rules of jurisprudence. He asserts that what is meant by the stars, sun, and moon, which were seen by Abraham (vi. 76-78) were lights which veiled God Almighty, and not the objects known. This is a comment in the style of the Esoterists. In his work called *Clear Account of States* he asserts that the Sufis in their waking hours witness the angels and the souls of the prophets, hear their voices, and acquire information from them; then their "state" ascends from witnessing forms to stages too grand for language.

I would observe that the cause which led these people to compose these things was their ignorance of the laws, of Islam, and of Tradition, and the attraction which they felt for parts of the system which they approved; their approval being due to their conviction of the merit asceticism, and to their regarding no condition as in form than that of these people, and no language as more affecting than theirs. Then the biographies of the men of old display a sort of roughness. Further these people enjoy popular favour to a high degree because their system is outwardly one of cleanness and devotion, and involves quiet and music, and which people naturally favour. Besides, the original Sufis used to keep away from kings and princes, which made people friendly.

Now the bulk of the works composed for them are based on no authority, being merely fancies which one has learned from another, and which they have compiled and called esoteric science. There is a Tradition going back to Abu Ya'qub Ishaq b. Hayyah according to which he said: I heard Ahmad b. Hanbal say on the subject of "suggestions" and "occurrences" that neither the Companions nor the Epigoni talked of them.

At the beginning of this book we have recorded a similar Tradition traced to Dhu'l-Nun, and one traced to Ahmad b. Hanbal to the effect that, having heard the language of al-Harith al-Muhasibi he told one of his followers that he thought he had better not associate with them. There is a Tradition going back to Sa'id b. 'Amr al-Barda'i according to which he said: I was in the presence of Abu Zur'ah when he was asked about al-Harith al-Muhasibi and his books, and he warned the questioner against them. These books, he said, are innovations and misleading; go to the Tradition, wherein you will find what will enable you to dispense with these books.—He was told that these books contained warning. He said: Who so does not find warning in the Book of God will not find it in these books. Have you ever heard that Malik b. Anas, Sufyan al-Thauri, al-Auza'i, and the early authorities composed such works on Occurrences and Suggestions, etc.? These are people who oppose the men of knowledge, citing to us at one time al-Harith al-Muhasibi, at another 'Abd al-Rahim - Dabili, at another Hatim al-Asamm, at another Shaqiq.—He went on to say: How ready people are to innovate!

We have been told by Muhammad b. 'Abd al-Baqi after Abu Muhammad Rizq Allah b. 'Abd al-Wahhab al-Tamimi after 'Abd al-Rahim al-Sulami a Tradition according to which the last of these said: The first person who discoursed in our town on the order of States and the stages of sainthood was Dhu'l-Nun al-Misri.—His statement was disapproved by 'Abd-allah b. 'Abd al-Hakam who was a leading man in Egypt and a follower of Malik's system. Accordingly al-Sulami was shunned by the savants of Egypt when it had got abroad that he had invented a science about which the men of old had not spoken. They went so far as to charge him with atheism.—Al-Sulami says that Abu Sulaiman al-Darani was expelled from Damascus, it being said that he asserted that he saw the angels, and that they talked to him. Some persons attested that Ahmad b. Abi'l-Hawari regarded the saints as superior to the prophets, and had to flee from Damascus to Meccah. The people of Bistam so strongly disapproved of the sayings of Abu Yazid al-Bistami, who was reported to al-Husain b. 'Isa to have gone so far as to say that he had had an Ascent just as the Prophet had had an Ascent, that they expelled him from Bistam. He remained in Meccah for two years, then returned to Jurjan, where he remained till the death of al-Husain b. 'Isa, when he returned to Bistam. Al-Sulami says: A certain man reported that Sahl b. 'Abdallah al-Tustari declared that the angels, the Jinn, and the demons visited him and that he discoursed to them. This was disapproved by the populace, who went so far as to attribute evil acts to him, so that he fled to Basrah, where he died. He also states that al-Harith al-Muhasibi talked about some theological matters, including the Attributes, and was shunned by Ahmad b. Hanbal, in consequence of which he went into hiding till he died.

Abu Bakr al-Khallal also states in his work *The Sunnah* that Ahmad b. Hanbal bade people beware of al-Harith to the utmost of their ability. Al-Harith, he asserted, is the root of trouble;—with reference to the results of *their learning* the theology of Jahm. One person and another associated with al-Harith and he perverted them to the opinion of Jahm. He has always been the resort of the metaphysicians. Harith is like a lion on the watch; look out for the day when he will spring on people!

Now the first Sufis used to acknowledge that reliance was to be placed on the book and the Sunnah, only owing to their ignorance the devil was able to delude them. There is a Tradition going back to Ja'far al-Khuldi according to which he said: I heard Junaid say that he had heard Abu Sulaiman al-Darani say: Often I am impressed for days by some point that the people (the ascetics) make, only I do not accept it without two trustworthy witnesses, the Book and the Sunnah. There is a Tradition going back to Taifur al-bistami according to which he said: I heard Musa b. 'Isa say that his father had told him that Abu Yazid said: If you see a man endowed with such miraculous powers that he can elevate himself into the air, do not be deceived by him, but first see how you find him in the matter of enjoining and forbidding, and observance of the rules. According to another Tradition the father of this Musa said: I heard Abu Yazid al-Bistami say: Whosoever neglects the reading of the Qur'an, mortification of the flesh, attendance at public worship, attendance at funerals, and visitation of the sick, and professes to be a Sufi is a heretic. A Tradition which goes back to 'Abd al-Hamid al-Hubli (?) records that he said: I heard Sari say: Whosoever professes esoteric knowledge which contradicts a manifest rule commits an error. Junaid is reported to have said: This doctrine of ours is limited by the foundations, the Book and the Sunnah. And again: Our science depends on the Book and the Sunnah. No-one is to be imitated who has not memorized the Qur'an, written Tradition, and studied Law. And again: We have not taken Sufism from people's talk but from hunger, abandonment of the world, and parting from what is familiar and admired; for Sufism has its name from purity of dealing with God Almighty, and its basis is self-knowledge in this world, as Harithah says: I got to know myself in this world, kept awake at night, and thirsted during the day. There is a Tradition that Abu Bakr al-Shaqqaq said: Whosoever violates the rules of enjoining and forbidding in externals forfeits internal communication of the heart. Al-Husain al-Nuri said: Have nothing to do with anyone who claims that he has in his dealings with God a state which takes him outside the bounds of knowledge of the Code. Suspect the religion of one whom you see claiming a state for which there is no evidence and which is unattested by any clear text that can be remembered. Al-Jurairi is recorded to have said: Our whole system can be comprised in one article, viz., that you should compel your heart to watchfulness, while knowledge governs your external conduct. Abu Ja'far is recorded to have said: Reckon no man in the register of men who does not weigh his words, deeds, and states by the Book and the Sunnah, and is not suspicious of his thoughts.

If these be ascertained sayings of their leading men, then some of them too have committed errors owing to their want of knowledge; if such sayings be genuinely theirs, then the refutation falls on them, since there can be no respect of persons in dealing with the truth; if the sayings are not theirs, then let us be on our guard against similar sayings and similar doctrine from whomsoever it proceeds. As for those who do not belong to these people but only imitate them, their errors are numerous; we will record some of those which have come to our knowledge; God knows that our purpose in exposing such errors is only to keep the Code pure, and anxiety to see that it is not corrupted. We are not concerned with the personality of the speaker; we are only discharging the obligation which knowledge imposes. The learned have always exposed each other's errors, their purpose therein being to bring the truth to light, not to show up the failing of the delinquent. No attention need be paid to the question of some ignorant person: How can such an ascetic who brings luck be refuted?—For obedience is due to the content of the Code, not to individuals. A man may be a saint, deserving Paradise, and yet commit errors; his station does not exclude their exposure.

You should know that one who looks at the honour paid to an individual and does not look at his procedure and what is to be inferred from it is like one who looks at the miracles performed by Christ without studying his person, and so claims divinity for him; had he studied his person, seeing how he was sustained by food, he would not give him what he does not deserve. We have been told by Isma'il b. Ahmad al-Samarqandi with a chain of authorities going back to Yahya b. Sa'id that the latter said: I asked Shu'bah, Sufyan b. 'Uyamah, and Malik b. Anas whether a man who had not memorized the Qur'an was suspect in Tradition. They all said: His case is clear. The Imam Ahmad b. Hanbal would praise a man excessively and then mention a series of mistakes which he had committed. He would say: An excellent man, were it not that he has a certain failing. Of Sari al-Saqati he said: He is the shaikh who is renowned for his taste in food.—Presently he was told that Sari had said that when God created the letters, the B prostrated itself. He then said: Keep the people away from him!

Enumeration of the False Doctrines Which are Recorded of a Number of Them

Abu 'Abdallah al-Ramli narrates that Abu Hamzah discoursed in the mosque of Tarsus and was favourably received. One day when he was discoursing a raven croaked on the roof of the mosque. Abu Hamzah cried out "I obey thee" twice. He was charged with heresy and supposed to be a believer in Immanence. His horse was sold at the gate of the mosque by auction, as the heretic's horse. There is a Tradition going back to Abu Bakr al-Farghani according to which he said: Abu Hamzah was generally supposed to be a believer in Immanence, because when he heard any sound he used to say I obey thee! Abu 'Ali however stated that Abu Hamzah only supposed the sound to be a summons from

God to arouse him to devotion. Abu 'Ali al-Rudhbari said that Abu Hamzah was generally supposed to be a believer in Immanence because when he heard a sound like the whistling of the wind, the rush of water, the singing of birds, he would cry out I obey thee! twice. This was the reason for the charge. Al-Sarraj says: I have been told that Abu Hamzah entered the dwelling of al-Harith al-Muhasibi once when a sheep bleated; Abu Hamzah groaned and said: I obey thee, my Lord!—Al-Harith al-Muhasibi was angry, took up a knife, and said: If you do not repent of your practice, I will cut your throat.—Abu Hamzah replied: If you cannot listen decently to this practice of mine, why do you eat bran mingled with ashes?

Al-Sarraj proceeds: Some men of learning disapproved and attributed to infidelity certain phrases which they found in *The Book of Mystery* composed by Abu Sa'id Ahmad b. 'Isa al-Kharraz, among them the saying: *A servant obedient in what was permitted to him, for which God should be glorified,* and *God sanctify his soul.* Likewise infidelity and atheism were attributed to Abu'l-abbas Ahmad b. 'Ata. many a time too Junaid with all his learning was arrested and his infidelity and atheism attested. Al-Sarraj further asserts that it was reported that Abu Bakrah Muhammad b. Musa al-Farghani al-Wasiti said: Whoso makes mention of *God* fabricates, and whoso endures is audacious: beware lest thou find a means of glancing at God.—He was asked: May I not then pray for them?—He said: Pray for them without solemnity, and let the prayer have no importance in thy heart.

Al-Sarraj proceeds: I have been told that a number of the believers in Immanence maintain that God Almighty has chosen certain bodies to abide in with the concepts of Lordship, having removed from them the concepts of humanity. Some of them maintain this by looking at the evidences of God's power which win admiration. Some of them say: He abides in those things which win admiration.

He proceeds: I have also been informed that certain Syrians claim vision with the heart in this world similar to vision with the eyes in the next. Further that Ghulam al-Khalil testified that he had heard Abu'l-Husain al-Nuri say: I am enamoured of God and He is enamoured of me—al-Nuri said: I hear God say (v. 59) *He loves them and they love Him,* and "to be enamoured of " is no more than "to love." So, said Abu Ya'la the quadi, God in the opinion of the believers in Immanence can be enamoured.

I would observe that this is a case of ignorance from three aspects. One in regard to the name; for "to be enamoured" according to authorities on the language is only applied to the marriageable. The second is that the attributes of God are known by communication, whence we know that He loves, but we may not say He is enamoured, and He is loved, not enamoured of. Just as it is said that He knows, but not that He cognizes. The third—whence has the man the right to say that God loves him? This is a claim without evidence. The Prophet said: A man who says he is in Paradise is really in Hell.

It is recorded that Abu 'Abd al-Rahman said: It is related that 'Amr al-Makki said: I used to walk with al-Husain b. Mansur in some of the streets of Meccah, while I recited the Qur'an; hearing my recitation he said: I could myself say the like of that. I left him in consequence.—Muhammad b. Yahya al-Razi is recorded to have said: I heard 'Amr b. 'Uthman cursing al-Hallaj and saying: Were I able, I should kill him with my own hand.—I said: How has he angered the shaikh?—He replied: I recited a text of God's Book and he said I could say or compose and utter the like of this.

There is a Tradition going back to Abu'l-Qasim al-Razi according to which he said: Abu Bakr b. Mimshad related as follows : There was a man present with us in Dinawar with a sack from which he would not part night or day; the sack was examined and there was found therein a letter of al-Hallaj addressed from the Merciful the Clement to so-and-so son of So-and-so. It was sent to Baghdad, and Hallaj was summoned and shown it. He admitted that it was his script and that the letter had been written by him. They said: You used to claim prophethood and now you claim divinity.—He said : I do not claim divinity; only this is the essence of the mystic state according to us. Is the writer but God, while the hand therein is an instrument? He said Yes, Ibn 'Ata,' Abu Muhammad al-Jurairi, and Abu Bakr al-Shibli. The second and the third are in hiding, so if there be anyone, it will be Ibn 'Ata.' Al-Jurairi was produced and asked; he said: The man who says that is an Unbeliever, and should be put to death. Shibli was asked and said : He who says that should be stooped.—Ibn 'Ata' was asked about al-Hallaj's assertion and adhered to it; this was the cause of his execution.

There is a Tradition going back to Ibn Bakuyah according to which he said : I heard 'Isa b. Bardal narrate when Abu 'Abdallah bin Khafif was asked about the sense of the following verses :

> Praise be to him whose manhood here displays
> The secret of His Godhead's piercing rays;
> Plainly Himself He manifested then
> As on who eats and drinks like other men.
> So that His creatures glancing at His sheen
> Their dazzled vision with their eyelids screen,

he said, The curse of God be on their author. 'Isa b. Furak said they were the verses of al-Husain b. Mansur. He added : If this be his belief, then he is an infidel; only the verses may be falsely attributed to him.

There is a tradition going back to the qadi 'Ali b. al-Muhassin after Abu'l-Qasim Isma'il b. Muhammad b. Zanji after his father according to which the daughter of al-Samarri being brought before the vizier Hamid and asked by him about Hallaj said : My father brought me to him, and he said : I marry you to my son Sulaiman, who resides in Nasabur. If any act on his part displeases you, fast for the rest of the day, at the end of it mount the roof, stand on the ashes, and breakfast off them and coarse salt. Then turn your face in my direction, tell me what displeases you, and I will hear and see. One night, she said, I was asleep on the roof and felt him approaching me. I woke up in a fright at his procedure. He said : I have only come to wake you up for prayer.—When we had descended his daughter told me to prostrate myself before him. I asked her whether prostration should be performed to anyone but God.—He heard what I said and said : Yes, there is a god in heaven and a god on earth.

I observe that the doctors of the time agreed that the life of al-Hallaj was forfeit. The first who gave his opinion to that effect was the qadi Abu 'Umar; the others agreed. Only Abu'l-Abbas Suraij kept silence on the subject, alleging that he did not know what al-Hallaj said. Consensus is an infallible guide. There is a Tradition traced to Abu'l-Qasim Yusuf b. Ya'qub al-Nu'mani according to which he said: The Prophet said : God guarantees you against general agreement in error. There is also one going back to Abu'l-Qasim Yusuf b. Ya'qub al Nu'mani according to which he said : I heard my father say that he had heard the jurist of Ispahan Abu Bakr Muhammad b. Dawud say : If what God revealed to His Prophet be true, then what al-Hallaj says is false. He was vehemently opposed to him.

A number of the Sufis take the part of al-Hallaj out of ignorance and carelessness about the consensus of the jurists. There is a Tradition traced to Muhammad b. al-Husain al-Nisaburi according to which he said : I heard Ibrahim b. Muhammad al-Nasrabadi say : If there was ever a monotheist after the prophets and the saints, it was al-Hallaj. The same view, I may say, is taken by most of the story-tellers and Sufis of our time, being due in all cases to ignorance of the Code, and unacquaintance with Tradition. I have myself composed a work on the life of al-Hallaj in which I have set forth his tricks and deceptions with what has been said about him by the learned. God aid us in suppressing the ignorant!

There is a Tradition going back to the Hafiz Abu Nu'aim according to which he said : I heard 'Umar al-Banna al-Baghdadi in Meccah narrating how, when there was the trouble of Ghulam al-Khalil and the ascription of atheism to the Sufis, the Caliph ordered their arrest. Al-Nuri was taken with a number of others, they were brought before the Caliph and he ordered them to be decapitated. Al-Nuri pressed forward to the executioner for decapitation. Why this haste? asked the executioner. He said : I prefer that my comrades should live for this short space rather than I.—The matter was brought before the Caliph, who referred it to the qadi of qadis Isma'il b. Ishaq who ordered their release. There is further a Tradition going back to Abu'l-'Abbas Ahmad b. 'Ata' according to which he said: Ghulam al-Khalil used to bring charges against the Sufis in Baghdad to the Caliph, saying there are atheists here. There were arrested Abu'l-Husain al-Nuri, Abu Hamzah the Sufi, Abu Bakr al-Daqqaq, and a number of their companions. Al-Junaid b. Muhammad alleged in his defence that he followed the juridical system of Abu Thaur. The others were brought before the Caliph who ordered their decapitation. Abu'l-Husain al-Nuri hastened to be first. The executioner asked why he hurried in front of his fellows and felt no fear. He said : I prefer that my comrades should live for this short period. The Caliph referred their case to the qadi and they were released.

One of the causes which led to this affair was al-Nuri's saying: I am enamoured of God and He is enamoured of me. This was testified against him. Then al-Nuri pressed forward to the executioner to be killed, assisting in his own death—which also is an error.

There is a Tradition going back to Ibn Bakuyah according to which he said : I heard Abu 'Amr, disciple of al-Raqqi, say: I heard al-Raqqi say : We had a guest-house; there came to us a poor man clad in a couple of rags, whose patronymic was Abu Sulaiman. He requested entertainment, and I bade my son take him to the house. He stayed with us nine days, eating once in three days. I asked him to stay one more, but he said "entertainment is for three days." So I asked him not to withhold news about himself. He was away for twelve years and then returned. I asked him whence he came, and he said : I saw a shaikh called Abu Shu'aib al-Muqaffa who was afflicted; so I stayed with him for a year to minister to him, when it occurred to me to ask him what had been the cause of his affliction. When I approached him, before I had asked he anticipated me, saying; Why ask about what is no concern of your? So I restrained myself till three years were completed; when the fourth had begun he said I suppose you must.—I said, If you please.—Then he said : while I was praying one night there appeared a light from the niche; I said; Avaunt, accursed one! My Almighty Lord has no need to appear to His creatures. Three times I said this; then It said : Wouldst thou that I take thee now that we should reward thee for what has passed, or try thee with affliction whereby we shall rise thee *in excelsis?* — I chose the trial, and my eyes, feet, and hands fell away.—So (said the narrator) I stayed and ministered to him for full twelve years. One day he bade me approach him, which I did. I heard his members say to each other Come out, and they did all come out in front of him, while he gave praise and glory, after which he died.

I would observe that this narrative suggests that the man saw God Almighty, and was punished because he refused to believe it. We have already mentioned that some say that God is seen in this world. Abu'l-Qasim 'Abdallah b. Ahmad al-Balkhi in his book *Discourses* states that certain anthro-promorphists record that they allow that God may be seen with the eyes in this world, and do not reject the idea that He may be someone who meets them in the street. Further that some besides allow that he may be embraced,touched, and held in contact. They profess to visit Him and receive His visits, and are called in Iraq Esoterists, or followers of hallucinations or fancies.

This I may observe, is more than atrocious. We implore God's protection from abandonment by Him.

Revised and edited; originally published in Islamic Culture, in a series of articles in 1930s & 1940s.

13

Devil's Delusion (Part II)

D. S. MARGOLIOUTH

Devil deludes everyone, but deludes in different ways. Can the devil delude a sufi too? Ibn al-Jauzi presents opposite view.

Account of the Way Wherein the Devil Deludes the Sufis When They Return from a Journey

I would observe: It is part of these people's system that a returning traveller who enters a monastery in which there are several persons should not salute them till after he enters the lavatory; when he has washed he comes and say a prayer of two inclinations, then salutes the Shaikh, and then the company. This is an innovation of the later Sufis which violates the code, since the Islamic jurists are agreed that, according to the Sunnah, one who arrives among people would salute them, whether he be in a state of legal purity or not: unless indeed they have taken over the practice from children, who when asked why they do not salute, say they have not washed their faces; or possibly children have taught these innovators the practice. We have been told by Ibn al-Hussain a tradition going back to Abu Hurairah according to which the latter said: The Prophet said: Let the younger salute the older, him who walks him who sits, the small company the large; this is cited in both *Sahih.*

Another of their practices is to massage one who arrives from a journey in the evening. We have been informed by Abu Zur'ah Tahir b. Muhammad after his father that the latter said: (*Section dealing with the Sunnah concerning the massaging of one who arrives from a journey on the first night owing to his fatigue)*, alleging the tradition of 'Umar, who said: I went to see the Prophet and found an Abyssinian slave massaging his back. I said: what is the matter with thee, O Prophet of God?—He replied: My camel flung me on some rough ground.

I would observe: Consider, my brethren, the legal acumen of the person who adduces this argument. He should have said: (*Section dealing with the Sunnah concerning the massaging of one who has been thrown by a camel*) then the Sunnah should be massaging of the back, not of the foot; and how could he know that the Prophet had been on a journey and that he was massaged on the first night? Further he makes a Sunnah of the fact that the Prophet casually had his back massaged on account of a pain in it. Surely it would have been better to suppress this subtle attempt at a juristic inference than to record it.

Another practice of theirs is arranging a party for one who arrives, as 'Ibn Tahir says: *Section dealing with their employing the guitar for an arrival*, alleging the tradition of 'A'ishah according to which once, when the Prophet went on a journey, a Qurashite damsel vowed that if God brought him back she would play a tambour in 'A'ishah's house. When the Prophet returned, he said to her. If you have vowed, then play the tambour.

I would observe that we have already shown that the tambour is allowed. Since the woman vowed the performance of a legal act, the Prophet bade her perform it. How can this be alleged in defence of singing and dancing when a traveller arrives?

Account of the Mode Wherein the Devil Deludes Them When a Death Occurs

In this matter he practises two forms of delusion. The first is that they say there must be no weeping over one who perishes, and one who does so strays from the path of the people of knowledge. Ibn 'Uqail says: This is a pretence which goes beyond the code, is foolish talk, and alien to custom and nature. Indeed it is an interference with the proper proportion of the humours, and should be treated with those drugs which restore the true proportion. God narrates of a holy prophet (XII, 84): *And his eyes were whitened with the sorrow that he was suppressing and Ah, woe is me for Joseph.* The Prophet Muhammad also wept over the death of his son, saying, "The eye weeps," and "Oh, what grief!" Fatimah said: "Oh what grief to my father," and he found no faults with her. 'Umar heard Mutammim bewailing his brother and repeating:

> Jadhimah's two companions we two seemed!
> Those twain will never part—so people deemed.

'Umar said: Would that I were a poet, so that I could bewail my brother Zaid.—Mutammim said: If my brother had died like yours. I should not lament him. Malik (Mutammim's brother) had died in unbelief, whereas Zaid had died a martyr's death. 'Umar said: No one has ever consoled me for my brother's death as you have done.—Further, camels for all the coarseness of their livers, yearn after their familiar drinking-places and persons and pigeons desire their "home". Anyone, whom affliction befalls must of necessity supplicate, and one who is unmoved by joys and delights, and unaffected by disgrace is nearer a lifeless object than a human being. The Prophet made it clear that it was a defect to diverge from the path of nature: to one who said to him, "I have not kissed one of my children" (he had ten) the Prophet replied: Is it under my control that God had taken affection out of your heart?—When he departed from Mecca he kept turning towards it. One who demands what is not ordained and what is unnatural is ignorant and makes an ignorant demand. The Code is satisfied with our refraining from beating our cheeks and rending our garments; it finds no fault with flowing tears or grieving hearts.

The second delusion is their making a party, which they call a bridal feast, when anyone dies; at this they sing, dance, and play saying: Let us rejoice for the dead man's entry unto his Lord. This is a delusion from three aspects. One is that there is indeed an ordinance that food should be got for the dead man's family, since they are too much occupied with their trouble to prepare it for themselves; there is no Sunnah to the effect that the dead man's family should provide it and entertain other people therewith. The basis for the practice of getting food for a dead man's sake is a tradition told us by Abu'l-Fath al-Karukhi and going back to 'Abdullah b. Ja'far who said: When the news of Ja'fars death arrived, the Prophet said: Prepare food for the family of Ja'far, for there has come to them what will distract them. At-Tirmidhi calls this a good, sound tradition.

The second is that they rejoice for the dead man, saying that he has entered unto his Lord. Now there is no ground for such rejoicing, since we cannot be certain that he has been pardoned, neither is there anything to assure us that we may not be rejoicing for one who is undergoing punishment.

'Umar b. Dharr when his son died said: Sorrowing of thee keeps me from sorrowing over thee.— We have been told by 'abd al-Awwal a tradition going back to Umm al-'Ala who said: When 'Uthman b. Maz'un died, the Prophet came to visit us, I then said: May God preserve you in Mercy, O, Abas Saib, I witness that god certainly entertained you (the dead). The Prophet, peace be on him, said to her, Who told you that God had entertained him?

The third is that they dance and play when this party is made and in this way they deviate from correct behaviour which prefers abandonment of such manners on these occasions. Again, if the dead man has been pardoned, then the dance and playing would not have been expressions of their thankfulness, and if the dead had been tortured, where would be the effect of mourning?

Account of the Way wherein the Devil Deludes the People in the Matter of Burying Books and Throwing Them Into the Water

I would observe: Some of them had indulged in compiling books. The devil deluded them and said that the aim of life is nothing but work, so they buried their books. It is stated that Ahmed ibn 'Ali al-Hawari threw his books into the sea and said. The best of guides am I; and after reaching (one's destination) to engage guides is impossible. And Ahmad ibn 'Ali al-Hawari continued the search of the Hadith for thirty years. When he acquired the maximum learning, he carried his books to the sea and threw them in; and he said, O, my learning, I treat you like this not because I insult you, not do I belittle your status, but because I sought you to lead me to God, and when I have been led to God I am no more in need of you.

We have been informed by Abu Bakr ibn Habib in a tradition going back to ibn Bakawayh that he heard Abu'l-Hasan, the slave of Shawana in Basgah saying that the latter heard Abu al-Hasan ibn Salim say that Abu 'abdullah Muhammad ibn 'Abdullah the Hafiz said: Ahmad ibn Muhammad ibn Isma'il Abu Hasan al-Khallal was a man of good understanding, patient in his search for tradition; but he also practised Sufism, and would abandon tradition for a time and then resume the writing of it. I have been told that the flung into the Tigris a quantity of his original dictation. His first lessons were from Abu'l 'Abbas al-Asamm and men of his period and he wrote down a great deal.

We have been told by Zahir b. Tahir a tradition going back on Abu Tahir al-Junabidhi according to which the latter said: Musa b. Harun used to read to us, and when he had finished with a volume he would fling his manuscripts into the Tigris, saying, "I have delivered it."

Account of the Way wherein the Devil Deludes the Sufis in the Matter of Abandoning the Pursuit of Knowledge

We have been told by Muhammad b. Nasir a tradition going back to Abu Nasr at-Tusi according to which the latter said: I heard a number of the Shaikhs of Rayy say: Abu 'Abdallah al-Muqri, inherited from his father 50,000 dinars besides estates and furniture, but gave it all away, expending on the poor—I (said Abu Nasr) asked Abu 'Abdallah about this, and his reply was: In my early youth I donned pilgrim attire and departed to Meccah alone, having left myself nothing to which I could return. The effort which it cost me to relinquish my books and the knowledge and tradition which I had amassed was more painful to me than the journey to Meccah, the vexations of travel, and relinquishing my property.

We have been told by Abu Mansur al-Qazzaz a tradition going back to Abu'l-'Abbas b. al-Husain al-Baghdadi, according to which the latter said: I heard ash-Shibli say: I know a man who did not enter this business till he had expended all his property and sunk in the Tigris seventy cases of books all written in his own script, he having memorised and read with a number of chains of authorities which he mentioned. He was referring to himself.

I would observe that it has already been stated how knowledge is light, and how the devil persuades a man to extinguish the light in order that he, the devil, may get the man into his power in the darkness, there being no darkness like ignorance. The devil, fearing that these people might go back to reading their books, whence they might obtain insight into his wiles, persuaded them to bury or destroy them. It is indeed a wicked and illicit action, involving ignorance of the purpose of books.

The explanation of this knowledge is the Qur'an and the Sunnah; the Code, being aware that memorizing these is difficult, has enjoined the writing of the Scripture and of the Tradition. With regard to the Qur'an, when a text was revealed to the Prophet, he summoned a scribe to put it down; it was written at that time on palm-branches, stones, and shoulder-bones. Afterwards the Qur'an was collected into the form of a book by Abu Bakr, with the view of preserving it for his own use; presently copies were made thence by 'Uthman b. 'Affan, and the other Companions. All this was done to prevent anything missing from the Qur'an. With regard to the Sunnah: at the commencement of Islam the Prophet restricted people of the Qur'an, saying: Write nothing you hear from me except the Qur'an. Only when Traditions multiplied, and he saw people's inaccuracy, he gave permission for them to be written down. It is recorded that Abu Hurairah complained to the Prophet of the weakness of his memory, when the Prophet bade him spread out his cloak. He did so; the Prophet proceeded to talk to him, and then bade him gather the cloak to his body. "There after", said Abu Hurairah, "I forgot nothing that the Prophet said to me." There is also a tradition that the Prophet said: Get your right hand to help your memory—meaning by writing. Further,

'Abdullah b. 'Amr reported that the Prophet said: Fetter knowledge—I (said 'Abdullah) asked what fettering it meant. He replied: Writing it down. Rafi' b. Khudaij also reported: We said: O Apostle of God, we hear things from thee, may we write them down. Write (he replied), there is no objection.

We know, too, I would observe, that the Companions registered the Prophet's utterances, movements, and actions, and that the Code was compiled from various persons' records. The Prophet also said: Communicate what I say, and may God illuminate anyone who, having heard a saying of mine, memorizes it and reports it as he heard it. Now reporting a saying it is heard can scarcely be effected without writing, since the memory is deceptive. When Ahmad b. Hanbal produced a tradition, he was asked to recite it to his audience; but he would say, Nay rather, from the book.—'Ali b. al-Madini said: I was commanded by my master Ahmad b. Hanbal to communicate no tradition except from a book.

When the Companions had reported the Sunnah, and the Epigone received it from them, and the Traditionalists went on their travels, traversing East and West to procure a sentence from here and a sentence from there, ascertaining what was genuine and what was fictitious, labelling some transmitters as trustworthy and others as untrustworthy, revising the Sunnahs and compiling them, if the result were obliterated, all their labour would be wasted, neither would the rule of God be known when a case arose. The Code prescribes no such practice; had any other before us a chain of transmitters going back to the people Prophet? This is an privilege of this community.

We have been told that the Imam Ahmad b. Hanbal, who had traversed East and West in search of tradition, once asked his son what he had written down from a certain traditionalist. His son replied that on the Feast-day the Prophet used to go out by one route the return by another. "Good gracious," exclaimed Ahmad, "a Sunnah of the Prophet which had never reached me!"—Such then was the language of a man who had collected so much; what must be the case of one who wrote nothing down, or washed out anything he did write? Tell me, pray, if writings are washed out or buried, on what will reliance be placed when judgments have to be given and emergencies arise? On so-and-so the Ascetic or so-and-so the Sufi, or whatever may occur to them? We ask God's protection from error after guidance.

I would further observe: The content of the writings which they bury must be either true or false, or truth mingled with falsehood. If the content be false, they are not to be blamed for burying them. If truth is indistinguishably mingled with falsehood, destruction of such writings is excusable; for people have written down matter dictated by the trust-worthy and the mendacious; the matter getting mixed, they have buried what they have written. This is how we are to interpret the story of Sufyan ath-Thauri burying his books. If, however, the content be true and the Code, their destruction cannot on any ground be lawful, seeing that they register knowledge and property. so one who proposes to destroy them should be asked what his object is. If he replies that they distract him from his devotions, three rejoinders may be given. Had you understood, you would know that being occupied with learning is the sincerest of all devotions. The spiritual awakening which you have obtained does not last long and I can see that after its loss you are ashamed of what you have done: and you should know that hearts cannot retain their purity; they are defiled and often require purgation, for instance, by reading books. Yusuf ibn Asbat buried his books and afterwards he could not refrain from saying Hadith. Thus, he mentioned apostolic Traditions on recollection and made mistakes. The third is that we appreciate your spiritual awakening and accept that it will last and that you are in no more need of these books; but why did you not give it away to those students who have not obtained your place in learning, or to those who wish to be benefitted by them. However, destruction of books is not permissible. Al-Marwazi said that Ahmad ibn Hanbi was asked about a person who wished that his books should be buried. Ibn Hanbal said that no wonder if he buried his knowledge. Al-Marwazi also said that Ahmad ibn Hanbal used to say that 'I see no reason in burying the books.'

Account of the Way wherein the Devil Deludes the Sufis in their Views on Knowledge

You should know that these people, having neglected study, and in accordance with their doctrines restricted themselves to ascetic practice, have not restrained themselves from talking about the different branches of knowledge, giving utterance to their fancies, and committing gross errors. At times they talk of Qur'an-interpretation, at others of Tradition, of jurisprudence, etc., subordinating these subjects to the implications of their particular form of knowledge. But God, to whom by glory, does not leave any age without persons to maintain His Code, refute the fabricators, and expose errors.

Some Specimens of what they say about the Qur'an

We have been told by Abu Mansur Abd ar-Rahman b. Muhammad al-Qazzaz after Abu Bakr Ahmad b. 'Ali b. Thabit how the latter had been told by Abu'l-Qasim 'Abd al-Wahid b. Muhammad b. 'Uthman al-Bajali thát he had heard Ja'far b. Muhammad al-Khuldi say: I was in the presence of our Shaikh al-Junaid when he was asked by Ibn Kaisan about the word of God (LXXXVII, 6) We *shall make thee read and thou shall not forget*; Junaid said "thou shall not forget to act thereby." To a further question about the words (VII, 168) *and they have studied what is therein* Junaid replied that it meant "they neglected to act thereby." Ibn Kaisan said: May God not break thy mouthpiece!

I would observe: as for his gloss "thou shalt not forget," it is groundless and clearly erroneous; for he interprets the text as a prohibition, whereas it is a statement, "thou art not about to forget." Had it been a prohibition, the verb would have been in the jussive mood. Hence, this gloss is contrary to the consensus of scholars. The same is the case with the other text *and they have studied what is therein*, where the verb *darasu* comes from the infinitive *dars*, meaning to read, as in III, 73, not from *durus*, which means to be destroyed.

We have been told by Muhammad b. 'Abd al-Baqi a tradition

going back to Ahmad b. Muhammad b. Miqsam, according to which the latter said: I was present when Abu Bakr ash-Shibli was asked the meaning of the text (L, 36) *Verily there is therein a reminder to him that hath a heart,* and replied "to him whose heart is God."

We have been told by 'Umar b. Zafar a tradition going back to Muhammad b. Jarir according to which the latter said: I heard Abu'l-'Abbas b. 'Ata, when asked the sense of the text (XX, 41) *And we delivered thee from distress and tried thee severely,* reply 'We saved thee from distress about thy people and tempted thee with Ourselves away from all else." This, I would observe, is an outrage on God's Book, and to ascribe being tempted with the love of Him to His interlocutor, and to make love of Him tempt, is atrocious.

We have been told by Abu Mansur al-Qazzaz a tradition going back to Abu Bakr Muhammad b. 'Abdallah ar-Razi, according to which the latter said: I heard Abu'l-'Abbas b. 'Ata say in explanation of the text (LVI, 88) *And if he is of those brought nigh, then comfort and abundance and a Garden of delight,* "the comfort is gazing on God's face; the abundance is listening to His speech; and the Garden of delight is not being screened therein from God." This, I would observe, is a fanciful utterance opposed to the sayings of the commentators. And indeed Abu 'Abd ar-Rahman al-Sulami compiled out of their comments on the Qur'an (most of them illicit prattle) some two volumes to which he gave the title "Truths of Interpretation." He quotes from them with reference to *The Opening of the Book* the assertion: "It is only so-called as consisting in the first discourses which We have addressed to you. If you put this into practice, well and good; otherwise you will forfeit the choice sayings which follow."

I would observe that this is quite wrong, since the commentators are agreed that the "Opening" was not the first Surah revealed. Then *Amen* uttered by a man means according to him "directing ourselves towards Thee"; which also is quite wrong, since the word does not come from the group *Amm* for if it did, it would be *Ammim.*

On the text (II, 79) *and if they come to you captive* he says: According to Abu 'Uthman "drowned in sins"; according to Al-Wasiti "drowned in the sight of their acts'; according to Junaid "bound in the affairs of this world"; *ye would ransom them* unto the breaking off of these ties. I would observe that the text is a remonstrance, the sense being "if you capture them, you take ransom for them, whereas if you fight with them, you slaughter them": and these people interpret it as a eulogy!

Muhammad b. 'Ali glossed (II, 222) *God saveth the repentant* "from their repentance." An-Nuri glossed (II, 246) *God grasps* and expands" i.e., He grasps thee with *Him* and expands thee to *Him.* And he glossed (III, 91) *"and whose enters it shall be safe"* i.e., from the suggestions of his mind and the insinuations of Satan." This is exceedingly bad, since the text, though worked as a statement, has the sense of a command, the full force being "grant safety to any one who enters the sanctuary." These people interpret it as a statement, but they cannot make their interpretation correct, since many of men who enter the sanctuary is not safe from suggestion and insinuations.

He also states that Abu Turab explained the text (IV, 35) *If ye avoid the capital offences which ye have been forbidden* of false pretences. Further that Sahl explained *the near neighbour* (of IV, 40) as "the heart", *the distant neighbour* as the soul, and *the son of the road* as the limbs. He also quotes Abu Bakr al-Warraq for the comment on (XII, 24) *she desired him and he desired her* "both desires were hers; Joseph did not desire her." This, I must observe, contradicts the plain statement of the Qur'an. The words (XII, 31) *this is not a human being* according to Muhammad b. 'Ali mean "this is not a suitable person to invite to intimacy." Az-Zinjani asserted that the thunder is angels' cries and the lightning the sighing of their hearts, and the rain their tears. He (the author cited) further states that al-Husain commented on (XIII, 42) *and God's is the plotting altogether* thus: "there is no more conspicuous plotting therein than that of the Deity with His servants, when he causes them to fancy that there is a path to Him somehow, or that the created can be coupled with the uncreated."

I would observe that anyone who considers the meaning of this will know that it is pure infidelity, since it indicates that it (God's plotting) is a sort of frivollous sport. This Husain meant is, however, al-Hallaj, whom such a comment suits. And on (XV, 72) *la 'amruka* he comments "i.e., by peopling thy inner self with beholding Us."

And indeed the whole book is composed of similar stuff; it was my idea to reproduce much of it, but I decided that it would be a waste of time to write out what was either infidelity or erroneous or non-sensical. It is all in the "esoteric style" which we have been describing, and if anyone wants a general idea of its contents, this is a specimen; if any one wants more, let him look at the book itself.

Abu Nasr as-Sarraj mentions in the *Luma* that the Sufis elicit certain ideas from the Qur'an such as from (XII, 108, *I summon unto God in perspicacity,* of which al-Wasiti asserts the sense to be "I do not see myself," and ash-Shibli says in explanation of XVII, 17, "Wert thou to survey all that is beside Us, thou wouldst turn away therefrom, fleeing unto Us." I would observe that this is not admissible, since the Divine Speaker only meant the Seven Sleepers. Thus as-Sarraj calls these comments "elicitations" in his book!

Abu Hamid at-Tusi in his Chapter *Censure of Wealth* comments thus on the text (XIV, 38) *preserve me and my sons from worshipping idols*: "He means gold and silver, since the prophetic rank is too exalted to admit of the fear that they might worship gods and idols; so by their worship he must mean love of them and being deceived by them." This, I may observe, is not said by any of the commentators. And indeed Shu'aib says (VII, 87) *And it is not for us to return to it unless God our Lord so will*; and it is common knowledge that inclination to polytheism is excluded in the case of prophet by their infallibility, not because it is impossible. Further, Abraham in the former text couples with himself persons who might conceivable become polytheists and unbelievers and so may well-introduce himself among them saying *preserve me and my sons;* it is well-known that the Arabs are his sons, and most of them were idolatrous.

We have been told by 'Abd al-Haqq b. 'Abd al-Khaliq a tradition going back to Abu Hafs b. Shahin according to which the latter said: Certain of the Sufis have said unlawful things about the Qur'an itself, e.g. on the text (III, 187) *Verily in the creation of the heavens and the earth and the alternation of night and day there are signs to those that have brains* glossing "signs to Me," thus attaching to God what He attached to "those that have brains," which is altering the Qur'an; and on (XXI, 81) *And to Solomon the wind,* "and Solomon to Me."

We have been told by Ahmad b. 'ali b. Khalaf after Abu 'Abd ar-Rahman as-Sulami that Abu Hamzah al-Khurasani said: Some people will be stopped in Paradise, being told (LXIX, 24) *Eat and drink in comfort for that which ye sent before you in past days*; God diverting them from Himself by food and drink. No plot could surpass this, and no woe could be more terrible.

I would observe: Consider, God guide you, this folly, and the designation of God's bounty as a plot! According to this person's doctrine the blessed prophets do not eat or drink, but are exclusively occupied with God. What audacity to use such evil words! Is it permissible to attribute "plotting" to God in the ordinary meaning of term? "Plotting" and "deception" as applied to the Deity men only that He repays those who plot and deceive. I am truly amazed that these persons, who are so scrupulous about a morsel or an expression, indulge in such licence in the interpretation of the Qur'an.

We have been told by 'Ali b. 'Ubaidallah, Ahmad b. al-Hasan, and 'Abd ar-Rahman b. Muhammad a tradition going back to Jundub according to which the latter said: The Prophet said: Who so speaks about the Qur'an according to his own notion errors even if he speak aright.

We have been told by Hibat Allah b. Muhammad a tradition going back to Sa'id b. Jubair after Ibn 'Abbas, according to which the prophet said: Whoso speaks about the Qur'an according to his own notion had better prepare for himself a place in Hell.

There has also been related to us a story about some of them, dealing with the "plotting," which shocks me to report, only by doing so I am calling attention to the atrocity of these ignorant people's fancies. We have been told by Abd Bakr b. Habib a tradition going back to Abu 'Abdallah b. Khafif according to which the latter said : I heard Ruwaim say: One night is Syria there was an assembly of Shaikhs, who said: We have never experienced so agreeable a night, so come let us discuss some question so that our night may not be wasted. They said: Let us talk about Love, since that is the people's mamstay. Each proceeded to speak according to his view. Among them was 'Amr b. 'Uthman al-Makki, who had to go out to court of the house. It was a moonlit night, and he found a slip of parchment with writing on it, which he took and brought to the others. Friends, he said, you may keep still, for here is your reply. Look at the contents of this message. It was found to contain the words: A plotter, a plotter, and you all profess to love Him. They parted, some of them putting on pilgrim attire, and only met at the Feast.

I would observe that this is an improbable story, and Ibn Khafif is untrustworthy. If it is true, then Satan must have thrown down that parchment, though these people falsely supposed it to be a message from God. We have explained that the meaning of plotting as ascribed to God is repaying for plotting. To apply the term to Him generally is worse than ignorance and worse than folly.

We have been told by Ibn Zafar a tradition going back to al-Khuldi, according to which the latter said: I heard Ruwaim say: God has hidden certain things in others: He has hidden His plotting in His knowledge; His deception in His kindness; His punishments in the category of His miracles.

This is confusion and audacity of the same sort as before.

We have been told by Muhammad b. Nasir a tradition going back to al-Hasan b. 'Alawaihi according to which the latter said: Abu Yazid went to visit a brother of his, and when he got to river Oxus, the banks of the river came together for him. He said: O Lord, what is this secret plot? By Thy might, I have not served Thee for this! So he turned back and did not cross. I also, said al-Sahlaki, heard the aforementioned and did not cross. I also, said as-Sahlaki, heard the aforementioned Muhammad b. Ahmad relate how Abu Yazid said: Whoso knows God becomes a janitor to Paradise, and Paradise becomes a misfortune to him.

It is, I would observe, terrible audacity to attribute plotting to God, and to make of Paradise, which is the ultimate desire, a misfortune. If it be a misfortune to "those who know", what must it be like to others! The source of all this is ignorance and misunderstanding.

We have been told by Ibn Habib a tradition going back to Ahmad b. al-'Abbas al-Muhallabi according to which the latter said : I heard Taifur (Abu Yazid) say: Those who know, when they visit the Deity in the next world, are of two classes: one, who visit Him when and where they will; another, who visit Him once, and never again. How so? he was asked. He replied: When those who know see Him for the first time, He makes for them a market, wherein is no buying or selling, only forms of men and women; any one of them who enters that market never again visits the Deity. Abu Yazid further said: He deceives thee with the market in this world, and with the market in the next world; so thou art always a slave of the market.

I would observe that calling Paradise a deception and a cause of exclusion from the Deity is gross ignorance. The "market" will be appointed for them as a reward, not as a deception; if permission be accorded then to take what is in the market, and they are afterwards punished by being forbidden to visit, the reward will have become a punishment. And whence does he learn that whoso selects anything out of the market will not visit the Deity again nor ever see Him? We implore God's protection from this confusion, this arbitrary assertion, and making statements about mysteries known only to a prophet.

Whence, indeed, does he know them, and what becomes of such sayings as that of Abu Hurairah, the transmitter of traditions, to Sai'd b. al-Musayyib: May God brings us together in the market of Paradise! Do you suppose that he desired to be punished with distance from the Deity? Nay, it is these people who are distant from knowledge, and whose satisfaction with their vain fancies has involved them in this confusion. A man ought to know that thoughts and imaginings are the fruits of his knowledge, so that if a man knows, his thoughts will be sound, being the fruits of knowledge, whereas if he be ignorant the fruits of his ignorance will be uniformly erroneous.

I saw in the handwriting of Ibn 'Uqail: "Abu Yazid, passing by a Jewish graveyard, said: What are these that Thou shouldst punish them? A handful of bones, whose doom has overtaken them! Forgive them!"

I would observe that this is a display of ignorance. The expression "a handful of bones" is one of contempt for the human being, for a Believer too when he dies becomes a handful of bones. "Whose doom has overtaken them" the same was Pharaoh's case. The prayer "Forgive them" display ignorance of the code: the Deity has stated that association of others with Himself will not be forgiven to one who dies in unbelief (IV, 51). If this person's intercession would be accepted, then that of Abraham for his father would have been accepted (LX, 4), and that of the Prophet Muhammad for his mother. God protect us from ignorance!

We have been told by Abu'l-Waqt 'Abd al-Awwal b. 'Isa a tradition going back to Abu Nasr as-Sarraj, to the effect that Ibn

Salim used to say: Abu Yazid, passing by a Jewish graveyard, said "Excusable," and passing by a Muslim graveyard said "Dupes." Of this as-Sarraj offers the following explanation. Probably, the ways, considering the damnation which had been predestined for them from eternity without any action of their own, and how God had made His wrath their portion, he said "They are excusable."

I would observe that as-Sarraj's explanation is improper, since it would involve that neither Pharaoh nor anyone else was to be punished.

Now some specimens of what they say about tradition and other matters. We have been told by Abu Mansur al-Qazzaz a tradition going back to 'Abdallah son of Ahmad b. Hanbal, according to which the latter said: Abu Turab an-Nakhshabi came to my father, who began saying, So-and-so is weak, So-and-so is trustworthy: Abu Turab said, Shaikh, do not malign the learned. Turning to him, my father said: Nay, this is counsel, not slander.

We have been told by Yahya b. 'Ali al-Mudabbir a tradition going back to Muhammad b. al-Fadl al-'Abbasi, according to which the latter said: We were with 'Abd ar-Rahman b. Abi Hatim, who was reading out to his *Book of Discrediting and Approving*, and said: I shall reveal the characters of the learned, showing which of them is trustworthy, and which untrustworthy. Yusuf b. al-Husain said to him: I am ashamed of you, Abu Muhammad; how many of these people a century or two centuries ago have come to rest in Paradise, while you, here on earth, malign their names! 'Abd ar-Rahman burst into tears, and said: Abu Ya'qub, had I heard this saying before I composed this book, I should never have composed it.

I would observe: God forgive Ibn Hatim! Had he been a jurist, he would have replied to him as Ahmad b. Hanbal replied to Abu Turab: Were it not for "discrediting and approving," how would the genuine be distinguished from the spurious? Further, the fact of these people being in Paradise does not prevent our mentioning them with their appropriate descriptions; to call this maligning is improper language. Besides, if a man does not know the principles of "discrediting and approving," how can his words give a certificate of veracity? Yusuf had better occupied himself with the wonders narrated of him than with this sort of talk.

We have been told by Abu Bakr b. Habib a tradition going back to Abu'l 'Abbas b. 'Ata, according to which the latter said: Whoso knows God refrains from bringing his needs before Him, knowing that God is the One who knows about his affairs.

This, I would observe, bars the door against petition and prayer, and is a display of ignorance.

We have been told by Muhammad b. 'Abd al-Malik b. Khairun a tradition said to have been read to Muhammad b. al-Hasan al-Ahwazi as follows : I heard Abu Bakr Dulaf the Sufi (or, he may have said ash-Shabli) say, when asked by a lad why he said "God" instead of saying "There is no god but God"; I am ashamed of putting something positive after a negation. The lad said he wanted a stronger plea than that. Ash-Shibli replied: I am afraid of being taken while uttering the negation and never getting to the affirmation.

I would observe: Consider this subtlety! The Prophet used to enjoin the utterance of "There is no god but God," and encourage it. In both *Sahih* it is recorded that he used to say at the termination of each regular prayer, "There is no god but God only; He hath no associate," and when he rose up for the nightly prayer, "There is no god but Thou;" and he mentioned the great reward earned by one who utters "There is no god but God." Consider then this defiance of the Code, and choice of something which the Prophet did not choose!

We have been told by Muhammad b. 'Abd al-Baqi a tradition going back to 'Abdallah b. 'Ali as-Sarraj according to which the latter said: I have been informed how Abu'l-Husain an-Nuri was charged with saying, when he heard a Mu'adhdhin calling to prayer, "May some deadly poison penetrate him," and when he heard a dog bark, "I wait upon Thy service and upon aiding Thy cause"; being asked about this, he replied: I resent this Mu'adhdhin's mentioning God negligently, taking pay for doing so, whereas otherwise he would not have called to prayer, and for this reason I cursed him; whilst the dog makes mention of God without hypocrisy. For God says (XXII, 46) *Nought is there but chants His praise.*

I would observe: Consider, my friends (God keep us all from error!) this juristic subtlety, and elicitation of the true path?

We have been told by Abu Bakr b. Habib a tradition going back to Abu Ya'qub al-Kharrat, according to which the latter had been told as follows by an-Nuri: Seeing a man take hold to his own beard I said to him: Remove your hand from God's beard! The matter was brought to the notice of the Caliph, search was made for me, and I was arrested. When I appeared before the Caliph, he said to me: I have been told that when a dog barked you said "I wait upon Thy service and upon aiding Thy cause," but that when the Mu'adhdhin uttered the call to prayer you said "May he be poisoned." Yes, I said, God says *Nought is there but chants His praise,* so I said "I said upon Thy service," because the dog had made mention of God. As for the Mu'adhdhin, he being steeped in sin and negligent of God makes mention of Him. The Caliph proceeded to ask about my saying to the man: Remove your hand from God's beard. I said: True, is not the man, his beard, and everything both in this world and in the next God's?

I would observe: It is ignorance which has plunged these people into this confusion. What led the man to fancy that an attribute of possession is a personal attribute?

We have been told by Ibn Habib a tradition going back to Ahmad b. Muhammad b. 'Abd al-'Aziz according to which the latter said: I heard ash-Shibli say when asked about knowledge: I tell you, one who say Allah knows not Allah; by Allah had they known Him they would not have said it.

The transmitter of the above (Ibn Bakuyah) proceeds: And I heard Abu'l-Qasim Ahmad b. Yusuf al-Baradani say: I heard ash-Shibli say one day to a man who to his question as to his name replied, Adam: Wretch, do you know that Adam did? He sold his Lord for a mouthful. Further, he used to say: Praise to Him who has given me the excuse of melancholia.

The same transmitter proceeds: And I heard Bakran b. Ahmad al-Jili say: Ash-Shibli had a companion, who informed him that he wished to repent. Ash-Shibli said to him: Sell your property, pay your debts, and divorce your wife. The man did so. Then he said to him: Make orphans of your children by causing them to despair of having any connexion with you. The man agreed. Then he produced some scraps which he had collected, and bade the man throw them before the poor and eat with them.

We have been told by Abu'l-Muzaffar 'Abd al-Mun'im b. 'Abd al-Karim that his father had informed him as follows: I heard, he said, one of the "poor" say: I heard Abu'l-Hasan al-Harraqani say, "There is not god but God" from the interior of the heart, "Muhammad is God's apostle" without thinking.

We have been told by Abu Bakr b. Habib a tradition going back to Ahmad b. Muhammad al-Halfa'i according to which the latter said: Ash-Shibli, seeing a young lad in the public bath without a bathing dress, said to him: My lad, cover your nakedness. The lad replied: Be quiet, foolish man. If you are upon the truth, you will witness nothing but the truth; if you are upon the false, you will witness nothing but the false. For the truth is occupied with truth, and falsehood with falsehood.

We have been told by Abu Bakr Muhammad b. Abi Tahir a tradition going back to 'Ali b. al-Muhassin al-Tanukhi, which he had from his father. I was told, he said, the following by Abu'l Qasim 'Abd ar-Rahim b. Ja'far as-Sirafi the jurist. I was present, he said, in Shiraz, at the court of the Qadi of the place, Abu sa'd Bishr b. al-Hasan ad-Dawudi, when there came before him a Sufi man, and a Sufi woman, Now sufism is there very rampant, he observed; it is said that the men and women who follow that system are in thousands. The woman demanded the help of the Qadi against her husband, and when they presented themselves she said to him: Qadi, this husband of mine wants to divorce me, which he has no right to do; will you please stop him? The Qadi Abu Sa'd, who disapproved of the Sufi systems, showed surprise, then said to her: How do you mean that he has no right to do this? She said: Because when he married me his intent on me was stable, and now he states that this intent has ceased from me, whereas my intent on him is stable and has not ceased. He must wait till intent has ceased from him even as his intent has ceased from me. Abu Sa'd said to me: What do you think of this jurisprudence? He then reconciled the parties and they went away without divorce.

Abu Hamid at-Tusi in his "Revival" states that one of them said: "Lordship contains a mystery by the revelation of which prophethood would be annulled; prophethood contains a mystery by the divulging of which knowledge would be annulled; and those who know God possess a mystery whereby, if they were to disclose it, the commandments would be annulled."

I would observe: Consider, my brethren, this offensive nonsense, and the allegation that the letter of the Code contradicts its inner meaning.

Abu Hamid says: A young son of one of the Sufis was lost, and it was suggested to the father to ask God to restore him. The Sufi answered: Resistance on my part to God's decree would be more painful to me than the loss of my child.

I would observe: I have long wondered how Abu Hamid can relate these utterances with approval and consent, though he was aware that prayer and petition are not resistance.

Ahmad al-Ghazzali says: A Jew presented himself to the Sufi Abu Sa'id b. Abi'l Khair saying: I wish to become a Muslim at thy hand. Do not wish it, said Abu Sa'id. The people gathered together saying: Shaikh, do you forbid him to accept Islam? Abu Sa'id then said to the man: You wish this decidedly? The man said: I do. Abu Sa'id said: You give up yourself and your possessions? The man said: I do. This, said Abu Sa'id, is what I mean by *Islam* (abandonment); now convey him to the Shaikh Abu Hamid, to learn the "no, no" of the hypocrites, meaning the formula "There is no god but God."

I would observe that the impropriety of this language is too obvious for censure; it is indeed most atrocious.

A story of discouraging conversion to Islam similar to this was told us by Abu Mansur al-Qazzaz on the authority of Abu Bakr b. Thabit who had it one the authority of various member of the Masargis family. Al-Hasan and al-Husain (he says) were brothers, sons of 'Isa b. Masargis, who rode with him, and whose beauty and equipment struck people with amazement. Having agreed to adopt Islam they went to call on Hafs b. 'Abd ar-Rahman in order to accept it at his hand. He said to them: You are among the most distinguished of the Christians. Now 'Abdallah b. al-Mubarak has gone on pilgrimage this year, and if you were to accept Islam at his hand this would win you more honour among the Muslims, and increase your dignity and importance, since he is admittedly Shaikh on the East and the West. So they departed, but al-Husain fell ill and died as a Christian before the arrival of Ibn al-Mubarak; on his arrival al-Hasan accepted Islam.

I would observe that this disaster was brought on by sheer ignorance, and the amount of the man's knowledge may be gauged thereby. Had he known anything at all, he would have told them to accept Islam at once, since that may not be delayed on moment. Still the fact that Abu Sa'id said to the Jew what he did is more extraordinary, since the latter wanted to accept it.

Abu Nasr as-Sarraj in his book *Lum'a* (traits of the Sufis) says Sahl b. 'Abdallah used to say to any of his friends who was ailing: When you want to complain say *Auh*, which is one of the names of God, and will comfort the Believer; do not say *Aukh*, for that is one of Satan's names.

These then are specimens of these people's language and juristic attainments; they indicate how little they know, how they misunderstand, and how frequently they err. Now I have heard Abu 'Abdallah al-Husain b. 'Ali al-Muqri recite a tradition going back to Muhammad son of Muhammad b. Idris ash-Shafi'i, according to which he had heard his father say: I associated with the Sufis for ten years, and got nothing from them but these two maxims: Time is a sword; and the best protection is incapacity.

Revised and edited; originally published in Islamic Culture as a series in 1930s and 1940s.

14

Devil's Delusion (Part III)

D.S. MARGOLIOUTH

Science, the Belief in the existence of God, and the Holy Qur'an

"Is there any doubt about Allah, who has made such wonderful heavenly bodies and such a wonderful earth?"

Has belief in the existence of God not become a vain and an empty thing in the light of what we call modern progress? Or, in other words, has not the belief in the existence of God been proved to be vain, through the scientific advancement of the human race? Or again, is it not a fact that both theism and idealism as opposed to materialism are but remains of the old superstitions? Or is it not a fact that science has shown to all those who are capable of seeing things, as they are and exist, that blind forces which are quite unaware of bad and good, always control the world and the course of events in the world? It is these questions which are being asked on all hands. How far is it possible to answer them? These are questions to be found not only among the educated, but among the masses as well. People assert that the natural sciences, which afford us an objective picture of the reality in life, have so far definitely removed the phantastic world of belief and superstition that even metaphysical speculation has also been pushed into the background; which speculation, they say, conceals within itself nothing more than the seeds of religion and its faint and faded traces. Men like Haeckel have preached this unwise wisdom, and they really believe that the whole world thinks and ought to think in the way they think.

I admit that the belief in the gods—human-like gods—that haunt the lucid interspace of world and world, as Tennyson puts it, and exert their influence on the earthly world, is disappearing; nay, is all but dead, and will never come to life again. Islam, which was also the religion of the prophets before Muhammad, came to establish Divine Unity. Abraham, Moses, Jesus, Muhammad (peace be upon them), were raised up and sent to preach the Unity of the godhead. The Holy Qur'an says in Chap. vi 3: "And He is Allah in the Heavens and in the Earth." These words contain a clear reference to the ultimate triumph of the doctrine of Unity. The whole Qur'an is directed against polytheism, which, it roundly declares, is against the nature of man and is repulsive thereto. One who has but a modicum of understanding and uses it can never believe in the doctrine of Polytheism. A monotheism which looks upon god as a Being existing with other beings or deities, and believes Him to be a Being that has no connection with this world, representing Him as a foreign and a strange Existence, is not materially different from polytheism. This kind of monotheism is to be met with in Christianity, which in its origin was a purely monotheistic religion; but owing to the loss of the original book, by reason of interpolations, people forgot the real teachings of Jesus Christ. If one were to preach and insist on the monotheism of Christianity, then it would be difficult to contradict those who believe that knowledge and learning lead us to atheism. Atheism is not a philosophy in itself—it is a beginning to philosophy; for it is not a positive theory; it is through and through a negation of a theory, of a view which maintains that there is one Being that exists in, out, over, under, everywhere in the world, that looks after the universe just like a watchmaker, who, after having constructed a watch, sees that it remains in good working order. Denial of such a theory is not tantamount to a theory. Let us examine the positive theory—theory of the existence of the Supreme Being. Let us examine whether there is any reality in it; whether there is any reason to believe in it and take it to be true. But there are people—and they are the atheists—who say there is no necessity for going into the details of this theory. They say that the world is nothing more than a heaping up of innumerable small bodies, which, from eternity, existing quite independently of one another, have come together in the empty space and undergone a reciprocal action and have adopted those groupings which are shown to us, which are manifested to us by reality. The atheists, those who deny the existence of a Supreme Being, take the existence of this universe of ours for granted; as something which came into existence, out of chaos into cosmos, by itself. You will find many of them who hold this view; but it is noteworthy that those who do so are generally young men who have just come out of school, and have divested themselves of views acquired in school and have picked up instead here and there some knowledge from popular book dealing with natural sciences. You will never come across these views among men who are profound independent thinkers. You will never find the view that this world of ours in something which should be taken for granted and self-understood, and is composed of small bodies quite independent of each other and which have come into contact without the will or the control of a Supreme Being, prevalent amongst the learned and the thoughtful. Neither Plato nor Aristotle, neither Spinoza nor Leibniz, neither Hume nor Kant, neither Schopenhauer nor Hegel, neither Lotze nor Fechner, neither Mill nor Spencer, could ever afford to convince themselves of the sufficiency of this theory. I would substantiate my argument by referring the reader to the few verses at the end of the *Mathnawi-Rumuz-i-Bekhudi* of Dr. Iqbal, the philosopher-poet of India, wherein he admits that he fell a victim to scepticism but could never find satisfaction of mind in it and could never convince himself of its sufficiency.

The conception of a world without God, without a Supreme Being, is quite possible so long as one remains a superficial observer. The moment one tries to comprehend the nature of this universe of ours, it appears to one quite wonderful, amazingly wonderful and quite rare. That is why Believers who believe in Allah, after having used their power of intellect and understanding, are the stronger in love for Allah. How beautiful are the words of verse 165 in chap, ii. : "And there are some among men, who take for themselves objects of worship besides Allah, whom they love as they love

Allah—*and those who believe are stronger in love for Allah."* Similarly in chap. xiii., verse 16, the Qur'an, while advancing arguments for the existence of God, says : "Are the blind and the seeing alike?"—which points out in explicit terms that it is only the people who are mentally blind that can afford to set up associates with Allah and deny His existence. The atheists believe that the world consists of innumerable, absolutely independent atoms which are, in nature and existence, quite independent of each other, every atom of which is there for its own self and exists without reference to the other atoms. Well and good; but the question arises : How does it come to pass that all of them—I mean all those atoms—do really have regard for one another?—so much regard, indeed, that, according to the physicists, every atom, every element has to determine its course and its conduct with a due regard to the other elements; that the conduct of each atom is fixed through the collectivity, the totality of all the remaining atoms. An atheist says : "That is quite true; it means nothing more than the principle, or rather assertion, of a common reciprocal action, which means nothing more than the collectivity of all the physical processes which go to make a single, big, great, in-itself-connected and coherent process." But the doubt arises, is it not a great boldness on the part of the atheists to adopt such an attitude? It is not really amazing, on their part, that they should shelve the whole question in such an airy and simple manner? Should not one rather expect that every atom, just as it is absolutely independent, goes its way too absolutely independent and does not care a bit for the other atoms. Or should not one expect that the atoms would be compelled by laws to have consideration, to make allowances for one another and to accommodate themselves to one another according to certain laws? Everyone who believes that atoms are independent should also believe that they are independent in their movement. But we find that they are not independent; they have regard for one another. Then is it not more reasonable to believe that they are controlled by law? It is better, and more in the fitness of things, to believe them to be under certain laws which they have to obey than to take them to be absolutely independent of one another, and to believe them to have come into contact with one another by chance. It is still more amazing and astonishing to find that all the atoms, all the beings which, according to the atheist, have come into reality without having regard to one another, show such homogeneousness and congeniality in their essence, in their conduct, in their beings that it can be expressed and couched in general formula. If one were to believe in the atheists and accept their views, then it would be more probable to expect rather an endless diversity in their being and in their conduct. And further, how singular is all that which proceeds from the atoms which the atheists hold to be independent and quite careless of one another, and not controlled by a Supreme Being. Again, how singular is all that which results from the atoms: cosmic systems, organic bodies, beings which feel and think. How astonishing that through a simple change in the arrangement of those very small particles, of which the world is supposed to be made, are formed such wonderful models. It must appear extremely astonishing and unexpected to the atomist who has not seen the world as it exists and is, but only the original chaos of the moving atoms; the world, as it is, must appear strange to the atomist if he, on his through investigation and examination of all the arrangements and combinations, were to find, all of a sudden, a being with feelings, ideas and conceptions coming to meet him. He shakes the atoms a thousand-fold and brings them into a medley and confusion, and all of a sudden he finds a body standing before him, a body which bursts out in sounds, which yields a poem, a continuity of ideas, a philosophy and sometimes even perhaps an inspired illuminating atomic philosophy. I am not sure whether he would, even then, take this as self-understood and as a matter of fact, whether he would, even then, take these atoms, which think on and about their own selves, these atoms which say to themselves: "Yes, we atoms, if we only come into the proper and congenial grouping, can do many things, more than pushing and pressing, which functions are the only functions which are believed by an atomist to be inherent in us." I am not sure whether he would not say that there is hidden in the atoms more than he believed or thought—expansion and movement. I do not know whether he would not feel obliged to say in the end: "Although the theory of atoms seemed to be promising in the beginning, yet the question of reality cannot be solved through it." He will say that if pushing and pressing are the only functions of the atoms, then they do not solve the mystery of the world; but that, on the other hand, it seems unavoidable to believe that they possess inwardness and spirituality, continuity and an inward unity in their origin and their essence. It is worthy of note that the biologists, who thought to find the explanation of the life of the living beings of this world and their functions in mechanical principles, have now begun to realize that the processes of life cannot, positively, be traced back to pressure and pushing, physics and chemistry.

Now it is thought, considerations like these, which bring us round to believe that everything which seems to our superficial eyes to be independent in its essence is, in reality, dependent and a part of the one Great Reality; that the world or the reality is, in reality, an absolute homogeneous coherent entity.

Bacon has said somewhere, the deeper one tries to peep into Nature, the deeper one drinks at the fountain of philosophy which in the first place seems to lead one to atheism, the more overawed, the greater the reverence one gets for God. For we should and must admit that although we have made such a great progress, yet we are still very far off from solving the problem of this life, and the problem of all life. The more we try to fathom its depth, the more we find it to be mysterious and wonderful. The depth becomes all the more abysmal always, the more inexhaustible, the greater the manifoldness and the exuberance of the forms of the universe. Imagine for a moment how simple and understandable was the world in the days of Aristotle, in the days of Thomas the Apostle, as compared with to-day. Imagine into what an abyss of the unimaginable the science of astronomy and physics have thrown us—the billions of moles and years and movements with which they calculate are things which make our heads whirl and become dizzy. The truth is that we pretend to know so much of our universe, yet we know so little. The more we know, the more we realize that we are "picking pebbles on the shores of knowledge." And really the feelings of awe, reverence, grip us. The deeper we go into the mysteries of the universe, the more the feelings of respect and veneration—*never the feelings of pride and arrogance*—are created in us. Newton and Kant had the same feelings of respect and awe for Nature. It was in this world of respect and awe that the Holy Prophet Muhammad lived. The Qur'an draws our attention to the grandeur and glory of Nature over and over again. And it is to the manifestations of Divine Power in Nature bearing testimony to the existence of God, of a Supreme Being who is beneficent, kind, merciful, who listens to His pious men and answers to their calls, that the Holy Qur'an repeatedly invites our attention. The whole of the Qur'an is filled with the description of natural beauties and natural phenomena. I will quote *in extenso* the translations of a few sections from the Holy Qur'an which have been picked up at random.

Islamic Review

Have you not considered (the work of) *your* Lord, how He extends the shade? And if He had pleased He would certainly have made it stationary; then, We have made the sun *an indication* of it:

Then we take it to Ourselves, taking little by little.

And He it is Who made the night a covering for you, and the sleep a rest, and He made the day to rise up again.

And He it is Who sends the winds as good news before His mercy; and We send down pure water from the cloud,

That We may give life thereby to a dead land and give it for drink, out of what We have created, to cattle and many people.

And certainly We have repeated this to them that they may be mindful, but the greater number of men do not consent to aught except denying.

And if We had pleased We would certainly have raised a warner in every town.

So do not follow the unbelievers, and strive against them a mighty striving with it.

And He it is Who has *made* the two seas *to flow freely,* the one sweet that subdues thirst by its sweetness, and the other salt that burns by its saltness; and between the two He has made a barrier and inviolable obstruction.

And He it is Who has created man from the water, then He has made for him blood-relationship and marriage-relationship, and *your* Lord is powerful.

And they serve besides Allah that which neither profits them nor causes them harm; and the unbeliever is an aider against his Lord.

And We have not sent *you* but as a giver of good news and as a warner.

Say : I do not ask you aught in return except that he, who will may take the way to his Lord.

And rely on the Everliving Who dies not, and celebrate His praise; and sufficient is He as being aware of the faults of His servants,

Who created the heavens and the earth and what is between them in six periods, and He is firm in power; the Beneficent God: so ask respecting *it* one aware.

And when it is said to them : Make obeisance to the Beneficent God, they say : And what is the God of beneficence? Shall we make obeisance to what *you bid* us? and it adds to their aversion.

Science and the Holy Qur'an

And one of His signs is that He created you from dust, then lo! you are mortals (who) scatter.

And one of His signs is that He created mates for you from yourselves that you may find quiet of mind in *them, and He put between you love and compassion; most surely there are signs in this for a people who reflect.*

And one of His signs is the creation of the heavens and the earth and the diversity of your tongues and colours; most surely there are signs in this for the learned.

And one of His signs is your sleeping and your seeking of His grace by night and (by) day; most surely there are signs in this for a people who would hear.

And one of His signs is that He shows you the lighting for fear and for hope, and sends down water from the cloud, then gives life therewith to the earth after its death; most surely there are signs in this for a people who understand.

And one of His signs is that the heaven and the earth subsist by His command, then when He calls you with a (single) call from out the earth, lo! you come forth.

And His is whosoever is in the heavens and the earth: all are obedient to Him :

And He it is Who originates the creation, then reproduces, it, and it is easy to Him; and His *is the most exalted state* in the heavens and the earth, and He is the Mighty, the Wise.

Allah is He Who made for you the night that you may rest therein and the day to see; most surely Allah is Gracious to men, but most men do not give thanks.

That is Allah, your Lord, the Creator of every thing; there is no God but He; whence are you then turned away?

Thus were turned away those who denied the communications of Allah.

Allah is He Who made the earth a resting-place for you and the *heaven a structure,* and He formed you, then made goodly your forms, and He provided you with goodly things; that is Allah, your Lord; blessed then is Allah, the Lord of the worlds.

He is the Living, there is no god but He, therefore call on Him, being sincere to Him in obedience; (all) praise is due to Allah, the Lord of the worlds.

Say : I am forbidden to serve those whom you call upon besides Allah when clear arguments have come to me from my Lord, and I am commanded that I should submit to the Lord of the worlds.

He it is Who created you from dust, then from a small life germ, then from a clot, then He brings you forth as a child, then that you may attain your maturity, then that you may be old—and of you there are some who are caused to die before—and that you may reach an appointed term, and that you may understand.

He it is Who gives life and brings death, so when He decrees an affair, He only says to it, Be, and it is.

Have you considered the *life-germ?*

Is it your create it or are We the creators?

Dealing with the Way wherein the Devil Deludes Savants in Different Departments of Knowledge

You are to know that the devil intrudes on people with his delusion by different paths, one of them manifest, only by encouraging the man's passion he gets the better of him, so that he blinds him to what he knows : another path is obscure, and so is concealed from many of the learned. We shall point out various forms of his delusion, those which we mention serving as a guide to those which we neglect; since to exhaust the methods would take too long. God will keep us from error.

Account of the Way Wherein he Deludes the Readers of the Qur'an

One is a man's occupying himself with the uncanonical Readings and procuring them, wasting most of his life in collecting them, booking them, and teaching them to people. This will divert him from learning precepts and duties. You will often find the Imam of a mosque undertake to teach the reading of the Qur'an, when he does not know what vitiates prayer; and often the desire to be first makes him out of sheer ignorance give as a reply to a legal question the first thing which occurs to him, though it be unlawful in the system of law which he follows. Had such people reflected, they would have known that what is wanted is to know the Qur'an by heart, to get the pronunciation of it correct, then to understand it, then to act according to it, then to proceed to what will reform the soul and purify the character, then to study some important topics of the code. It is gross stupidity to waste time in what is not of chief importance. Al-Hasan al-Basri said : The Qur'an was revealed that men should act according to it.—Such a case is when one of them reads in his sanctuary according to an uncanonical text rejecting the traditional vulgate. Now the learned are sure that prayer is not valid with uncanonical readings, the purpose of using them being to display out-of-the-way knowledge in order to win people's praise, so that they will flock to him while he holds that he is studying the Qur'an. Some of them combine Readings saying *malik, malik, mallak* which is not permissible, since it takes the Qur'an out of its order. Some combine prostrations, utterances of the creed, and repeat the formula "God is greater," to which practice also there is objection. They also have started lighting numerous fires for their completions of the reading of the Qur'an, thus combining waste of substance with imitation of the Mazdians, and providing an occasion for the assembling of women and men at night with mischievous results. The devil persuades them that therein is the glorification of Islam. This is a serious delusion, Since a code is glorified by practising what it enjoins. To this category belongs the case of those who allow themselves to claim that they have studied with persons with whom they had not studied, though they may have received a licence from them. Such a person will say falsely "I was informed by so-an-so," regarding this as a light matter, since he is recording Readings, which he supposes to be a virtuous act, forgetting that this is a falsehood to which the liars' penalty attaches. To it also belongs the case of the competent teacher of Reading who studies with two or three teachers, talks with any visitor while his mind cannot contain all these things, and then declares in writing that he has read with so-and-so according to the Reading of so-and-so. Now some scrupulous persons used to maintain that two or three should come together and study with one. To it further belongs the case of Readers who vie with each other in the amount that they can get through. I have seen shaikhs among them who hold meetings and put forward an individual who on a long day gets through the whole Qur'an three times. If he fails, he is censured, and praised if he succeeds. The populace gather for such an occasion, and admire the man as they would a runner. The devil persuades them that heavenly reward is earned by much reading. It is however one of his delusions, since reading ought to be for God, not to win admiration. Further it ought to be slow, since God says (xvii. 107) *That thou mayest read it unto the people slowly* and (lxxiii. 4) *And chant the Qur'an chanting.* To this category also belongs the case of a number of Readers who have invented musical reading, which had indeed previously been used to a moderate extent. Ahmad b. Hanbal and others disapproved of it, but not al-Shaf'i. We were informed by Muhammad b. Nasir in a Tradition going back to al-Rabi' b. Sulaiman that al-Shaf'i said : There is no objection to listening to camel-drivers' music or Bedouin intonation, nor to reading the Qur'an with chant and modulation of the voice.

My own opinion is that Shaf'i merely referred to contemporary practice, in which slight modulation was practised, whereas in the present day it is done according to the rules of vocal music; and the more closely it approaches singing, the more is it to be disapproved. If the Qur'an is removed from its original structure, it is forbidden.

To the same category belongs the case of Readers who permit themselves certain sins, such as maligning their rivals, or even some greater offence, in the belief that their knowing the Qur'an by heart will avert punishment from them, and alleging the saying of the Prophet: *If the Qur'an were placed in a skin it would not burn.* This is one of the devil's delusions, since the punishment of one who knows is greater than that of one who does not know; greater knowledge strengthens the case against him. Then there is another sin in the Reader not respecting what he has committed to memory. God says *What, is one who knows like one who knows not?* And concerning the Prophet's wives He says (xxxiii. 30) *And whoever of you doeth manifest foulness, her punishment shall be doubled twice.* We were informed by Ahmad b. Ahmad al-Mutawakkili in a Tradition going back to Ma'ruf al-Karkhi that Bakr b. Khunais said : Verily in Gehenna there is a ravine against which Gehenna implores aid seven times in the day; and in that ravine there is a pit against which both Gehenna and the ravine implore aid seven times in the day, and in the pit there is a snake against which Gehenna, the ravine, and the pit, implore aid seven times in the day; its operation commences with evil-doers who know the Qur'an by heart. They will say : O Lord, is it to commence with us before the idolaters? And there will be said to them: One who knows is not like one who knows not.

Let us confine ourselves to this specimen in what concerns the Readers.

Account of the Way Wherein the Devil Deludes the Traditionalists

To this category belongs the case of people who have spent their lives in hearing Tradition, travelling in pursuit of it, collecting numerous avenues, and looking for authoritative chains and unfamiliar texts. They are of two classes. One class aims at preserving the code by ascertaining which Traditions are sound as opposed to the accused, and they deserve gratitude for their endeavour, only the devil deludes them by distracting them through this from the duty, which is incumbent on every individual, of ascertaining what his obligations are, striving to discharge them, using Tradition as a source of law. If it be said that many of our ancestors did the like, such as Yahya b. Mu'in, Ibn al-Madini, al-Bukhari, and Muslim, the reply is that these persons combined knowledge of important matters of religion and the laws concerning them with their search for Tradition. They were helped herein by the shortness of the chains and the small quantity of Tradition, so that they had time for both these things. In our time the avenues are lengthy and the works dealing with the subject vast, wherein only the avenues are different.

It is scarcely possible for any one to combine both these things; you will find a Traditionalist write, hear, and collect books for fifty years without knowing their contents; supposing that any accident occurs during prayer he will stand in need of one of the young law-students who come to him to hear Tradition. These give a handle to the assailants of the Traditionalists, who call them book-laden animals, who do not know what they are carrying. If one of them is fortunate enough to look into his Tradition, very likely he will act according to an abrogated Tradition, or will understand his Tradition in the sense wherein the vulgar understand it, and act accordingly , although that was not what the Tradition meant. Thus we have been told that a certain Traditionalist recorded that the Prophet had forbidden a man receiving the water of another man's plantation. Several of the audience said: It has been our practice if we had more water than we wanted in our gardens to send it on to our neighbours: we ask God's pardon for having done so. Neither the reader nor the hearer understood or perceived that the reference was to *coitus cum feminis captivis praegnantibus.* Al-Khattabi says : One of our shaikhs used to recite a Tradition that the Prophet had forbidden *(halq)* cutting the hair before prayer, on Friday, and informed me that for forty years he had never cut his hair before prayer. I said to him : The word is *halaq* (circles), the objection being to people gathering for study and discussion; what the Prophet commanded was that a man should occupy his mind with prayer and listen to the sermon. The man said to me: You have indeed relieved me, and he was a pious man. Ibn Sa'id was of high rank among Traditionalists, only having had little intercourse with jurists he could not understand how to answer a legal question. We were told by Abu Mansur al-Bazzar in a Tradition going back to the jurist Abu Bakr al-Abhari that he said: I was with Yahya b. Muhammad b. Sa'id when a woman came to him and said : Shaikh, what say you of a well into which a chicken has fallen and died; is its water clean or unclean?—Yahya said: Tell me, how came the chicken to fall into the well?—She said : It was not covered.—He said : Why did you not cover it so that nothing could fall into it?—Al-Abhari said : I said My friend, if the water has changed, it is unclean, otherwise it is clean.

Ibn Shahin composed many works on Tradition, the smallest of them one volume and the largest a commentary in 1000 volumes; yet he knew nothing about law. Some of them ventured to give legal opinions that were erroneous for fear of being thought ignorant. Some became laughing-stocks in consequence of their opinions. One of them was asked a question about the division of an inheritance, and wrote in reply let it be divided in accordance with the ordinances of God. We were informed by Muhammad b. Abi Mansur in a Tradition going back to Ibrahim al-Harbi that he said : I was told that a woman came to 'Ali b. Dawud while he was repeating Traditions, having in front of him some thousand persons. She said to him: I have sworn to give my wrapper in alms.—He said : How much did you pay for it?—She replied : Twenty-two dirhems.—He said : Then go and fast twenty-two days.--When she had left, he began to lament saying : Alas, we made a mistake. We ordered her to perform the atonement for a repudiation.

Now, I would observe, consider these two disgraces, that of ignorance and that of venturing to give a legal opinion with such a muddle. And know that the majority of the Traditionalists take what concerns the attributes of the Creator in its literal and material sense, thus adopting anthropomorphist doctrine; because they have not associated with jurists so as to learn how to interpret the ambiguous texts in accordance with the ascertained law. In our time we have seen such a person amass books and hear much, without understanding what he has procured. Some of them do not know the Qur'an by heart, or know the rules of prayer. These people suppose that they are occupying themselves with what is enjoined on the community as a whole, instead of what is enjoined on the individuals. Now to prefer the unimportant to the important is a delusion of the devil.

The second section consists of persons who have heard much Tradition, only their purpose was not sound. By collecting the "avenues" they did not want to ascertain what was genuine and what not, what they wanted were Traditions of high antiquity, and such as were little known, and they would go round the countries in order that one of them might say I met so-and-so, and I have chains of authorities which no one else has, and I have Traditions which are known to no one but me. A student of Tradition came to us in Baghdad, and he would take a teacher and set him down in al-Raqqah—a garden on the bank of the Tigris—and read with him; he would then say in his collections "I was informed by so-and-so son of so-and-so in al-Raqqah," leading men to suppose that it was the Raqqah in the direction of Syria, and to think that he had undertaken arduous journeys in search of Tradition. Or he would set him down between the Nahr 'Isa and the Euphrates and say "I was informed by so-and-so Beyond the River," to make people suppose that he had crossed the Oxus in search of Tradition. Or he would say "I was informed by so-and-so on my second or my third journey," that people might know the amount of trouble which he had taken in pursuit of Tradition. He won no blessing, as he died while still a student.

All this, I may observe, is far removed from sincerity; their object is leadership and vainglory. And this is why they follow after the rare and strange Traditions. It often happens that one of them gets hold of a note-book containing the Traditions which some fellow-Muslim has heard, and conceals the fact in order to monopolize the transmission; and he may die without ever having transmitted the contents, so that both these persons will lose their reward. Often too it happens that one of them travels to a teacher whose name can begin with either a Q or a K, in order to write that fact in his copy and nothing more.

To the delusion which the devil practises on the Traditionalists belongs their fault-finding with one another, to satisfy private grudges, which they carry out in the style of the "discrediting and crediting" which was practised by the earlier representatives of this discipline, whose object was the protection of the code. God indeed knows best what people's intentions are; but the proof that the intentions of these people are base lies in the fact that they say nothing about the persons from whom they themselves have received. The ancients did not act thus; 'Ali b. al-Madini used to report from his father, who was untrustworthy, but he would add "and the reports of this shaikh are such as they are." We were informed by Abu Bakr b. Habib al-'Amiri in a Tradition going back to Yusuf b. al-Hussain that he said : I asked Harith al-Muhasibi about backbiting, and he said : Beware of it, for it is the worst of acquisitions. What think you of a thing which will rob you of your merits in order to give satisfaction to your opponents? How will you be able to satisfy one whom you hate in this world when he is your opponent on the Day of Judgment? Either he will take some of your merits or you will take some of his demerits, since there will be no dinars nor dirhems there. Beware of it therefore and learn its source. Backbiting by the vulgar and the ignorant springs from the desire to gratify anger, ill-will, envy, and suspicion, qualities that are manifest, not concealed. Backbiting by the learned springs from self-deception, the man thinking that he is displaying sincere care for others, and from interpretation of a report which is untrustworthy, and which, were it trustworthy, would not assist backbiting. The report is the saying attributed to him (the Prophet?). Do you dislike recording it? Record it stating the objections to it, that people may be on their guard against it. If this report were preserved and correct, it would not involve the open defamation of a brother Muslims except when you are asked about him. If, e.g., a man comes and asks your advice saying I want to marry my daughter to so-and-so, and you know the man to be an innovator or not to be trusted with a Muslim woman, you should dissuade the parent as courteously as possible. Or if another comes and says to you I want to deposit a sum of money with so-and-so, and the man is not fit to be trusted with a deposit, you should dissuade the proposing depositor as courteously as possible. Or if a man says to you I want to pray behind so-and-so or make him my authority for some branch of knowledge, you should also dissuade as courteously as possible but not gratify resentment by backbiting.

In the case of Qur'an-readers and devotees it springs from self-conceit. A man reveals his brother's defect, and then plumes himself on praying for him secretly. He makes free with his Muslim brother's flesh, and then glorifies himself by praying for him.

In the case of high officials such as are called *Ustadh* it springs from the desire to make a show of kindliness. The man will say : Poor fellow, he is afflicted with such and such a failing, how trying! God protect us from such abandonment! The man plumes himself on his display of kindliness towards his brother, and then on praying for him in the presence of his brother, and then on praying for him in the presence of his fellows, he will say : I have only revealed that to you in order that you may offer many prayers for him.—We ask God's protection from backbiting whether indirect or direct. Beware of it, for the Qur'an has declared it to be odious. God says (xliv. 12) *Would one of you like to devour the flesh of his dead brother? Nay, ye abhor it.* Many a saying of the Prophet to the same purport is reported.

Among the ways wherein the devil deludes the Traditionalists is the reporting of spurious Traditions without stating that they are spurious. This is a crime against the code, and their purpose is to advertise their Traditions and the quantity of their information. The Prophet said : Whosoever reports a Tradition as from me, while holding it to be false, is a liar.—To this category belongs their falsification of authorities, when one of them says "X from Y" or "Said X on the authority of Y" suggesting that he had heard from him a Tradition, in whose chain of authorities a link is missing, whereas he did not hear it; and this is reprehensible, because it is giving the broken chain the authority of the complete chain. Some of them report on the authority of a "weak" transmitter or a liar, either not naming him or giving him a name that is not his, or calling him by his *kunyah* or after some ancestor in order that he may not be recognized. This is a crime against the code, because it bases a rule on what is no proper basis for it. As for the case in which the transmitter cited is a trustworthy person, and his relation to in ancestor or merely his *kunyah* is given so that it may not seem that the same person is cited too frequently, or the case in which the transmitter is on a level with the reporter of the Tradition and the latter is ashamed to mention the former, though such prócedure is to be disapproved and far removed from correctness, still it is venial on condition that the transmitter is trustworthy—may God guide us!

Account of the Way Wherein the Devil Deludes the Jurists

In olden times the jurists were the students of the Qur'an and the Tradition, but the practice constantly declined till the later generation said It suffices us to know the legal texts of the Qur'an and to rely on the celebrated works on Tradition such as the *Sunan* of Abu Dawud, etc. Presently they neglected this also, and a jurist would allege a verse of which he did not know the meaning, or a Tradition which for all he knew might be genuine or spurious. Many a time too he would rely on an analogy which was opposed to a genuine Tradition, being unaware of this, owing to his having paid little attention to the subject of transmission. Now jurisprudence is extracting from the Book and the Sunnah: and how can a man extract from a thing with which he is not acquainted? It is reprehensible to make a rule depend on a Tradition of which the soundness or unsoundness is not ascertained. Such knowledge was at one time hard to procure and a man needed to travel far and undergo much fatigue in order to obtain it; then books were composed, *Sunan* established, and the sound distinguished from the unsound. Only the later generations have been too completely overcome by idleness to read the literature of Tradition; so much so that I have seen a great jurist say in a work of his concerning words occurring in the collections of sound Tradition "the Prophet cannot have said this," and I have seen him say when arguing about a certain question "our proof is the report of certain persons that the Prophet said" something, his reply to the citation of a sound Tradition by his opponent being "that Tradition is unknown." All this is crime against Islam.

To the delusions which the devil inflicts on the jurists belongs their reliance on their acquisition of eristic (the science of disputation), claiming that they are searching for the correct ascertainment of the evidence for a rule, and the elicitation of minute points of law, and the grounds for doctrines. If their claim were just, they would occupy themselves with all the questions, whereas they confine themselves to great questions, whereon they can dilate, so that the disputant may gain repute with the public in the process of discussion. One of them concerns himself with arranging his disputation and inquiring into contradictions, with the object of gaining glory and defeating rivals. Often he is unacquainted with the rule dealing with a small question, which however involves general disaster.

Account of the Way in Which he Deludes them into Introducing into their Disputation of the Talk of the Philosophers, and into Relying on their Inventions

To this category belongs their preferring analogy to the Tradition which furnishes evidence on the question at issue in order to get greater scope for their discussion. If any one of them adduces a Tradition as evidence, he falls into disrepute, although propriety would demand that the adduction of Tradition should have the preference. To this category also belongs their making discussion their chiefs occupation, unmingled with what is calculated to soften the heart, such as reciting the Qur'an, listening to Tradition and the biography of the Prophet and his Companions. It is well-known that the heart is not rendered humble by repeated removal of impurity and dirty water; what it needs is reminding and exhortation that it may set itself to earn the next world. Disputed questions may indeed belong to jurisprudence, but they do not furnish every requisite. Those who have not penetrated the mysteries of the ancients and the character of those systems they have adopted cannot tread their path. It should be understood that human nature is predatory and if left alone with its contemporaries it steals from their characteristics and becomes like them; whereas if it study the lives of the ancients it emulates them, and models itself on their character. One of the ancients said : A narrative which softens my heart is more agreeable to me than a hundred judgments of Shuraih.— He only said this because the softening of the heart is what is wanted, and there are causes which produce it.

To the same category belongs their confining themselves to disputation while neglecting to memorize the system and the other studies connected with the code. You will see a consulting jurist asked about a text of the Qur'an or a Tradition and ignorant of it. This is imposture: pride has no place for deficiency! Further, discussion was introduced for the purpose of bringing the truth to light; and the aim of our ancestors was to help people by showing what was fight. They would proceed from argument to argument and if some matter escaped one of them, the other would call his attention to it, their purpose being to make clear what was right. Hence if one of these old jurists based a judgment by analogy on an established rule for a reason which he surmised, and he was asked What is the evidence that the judgment in the case of the established rule is based on the reason assigned, he would say : This is what appears to me; if something preferable appears to you, then state it, for the opponent cannot compel me to state it.—He is right in saying that he is not bound to do so, only where it is a case of giving sincere advice and bringing the truth to light, he is so bound.

To the same category belongs the case wherein it is made clear to one of them that the truth lies with his opponent, but for all that he does not recant, being oppressed by the thought that his opponent is shown to be in the right. Indeed often-times he will try hard to confute that opponent while aware that the right is on his side. This is indeed outrageous, since the whole object of disputation is to arrive at the truth. Shaf'i said: Whenever a person with whom I have disputed has declined to accept a sound argument, I have despised him, whereas if he has accepted it, I have respected him; nor have I ever, when disputing with any one, cared which was the winning side : if it were my opponent's, I would go over to him.

Further their desire to achieve supremacy by discussion arouses the ambition which is latent in their souls, and if any one sees in his discourse some weakness which will enable the opponent to vanquish him, he proceeds to commit himself to preposterous propositions, and if he finds the opponent openly claim the advantage over him, and give way to the passion of pride, he will counter that with abuse, so that the disputation turns into a brawl.

To the same category belongs the licence which they allow themselves when the opponent is not present, on the pretence of reporting a discussion : one of them will say "I talked with so-and-so, and he said nothing." With this plea he uses language which will enable him to gratify himself at the expense of the opponent's honour.

Further the devil has deluded them into thinking that Jurisprudence by itself is the science of the code, with no other, so that if a Traditionalist is mentioned to them, they say : Oh, that man does not understand, forgetting that Tradition is the source. If some saying is cited to them calculated to soften the heart, they say Oh, that is what preachers say.

To the same category belongs their venturing to give legal opinions without having reached the rank which would justify their doing so; frequently improvising they give opinions which contradict the texts; it would be better if they were to take their time over difficult questions. I was told by Isma'il b. Ahmad al-Samarqandi in a Tradition going back to 'Abd al-Rahman b. Abi Laila that the latter said: I have been contemporary with a hundred and twenty of the Prophet's Companions, and when one of them was asked concerning a question he would refer it to another and he to another and this other to a third till it came back to the first. 'Ata b. al-Sa'ib is reported to have said : I also heard 'Abd al-Rahman b. Abi Laila say : In this mosque I have come across a hundred and twenty Helpers who are Companions of the Prophet, not one of whom would repeat a Tradition but wished that his brother had repeated it instead of him, or would be asked about a question but would wish that his brother would deliver an opinion in his stead.

We have been told that Ibrahim al-Nakha'i being asked about a question said : could you find not any one to ask except me?— It is related that Malik b. Anas said : I have never given a legal opinion without having first asked seventy shaikhs whether they approved of my giving it and their assenting. He was asked: And suppose they had forbidden you?—Had they done so, he replied, I would have refrained. A man said to Ahmad b. Hanbal : I have sworn and I do not know how I have sworn.—He said : Would that when you knew how you had sworn I knew how to give you an opinion.

This (I observed) was the style of our ancestors owing to their fear of God and their reverence for Him. One who studies their careers will be enlightened.

One of the ways wherein the devil deludes the jurists is their association with princes and Sultans, their flattering them, and declining to find fault with them though they are able to do so. Often they give them permission to do what they have no right to permit, in order to acquire some temporal advantage; thereby mischief comes in three directions: first, the prince says "were I not in the right, the jurist would have found fault with me; Surely I must be in the right, since he is maintained by my property. Secondly, the ordinary man says "There is nothing the matter with this prince or his wealth or his acts, since this particular jurist remains with him." Thirdly, the jurist, who ruins his religion thereby.

The devil has deluded them concerning their appearing before the Sultan, so that one of them says : We only appear before him in order to intercede for a Muslim. This delusion is cleared away by the observation that had any one else gone to the Sultan to intercede, this would not have pleased the jurist, who might very well have attacked such an individual for monopolizing the Sultan's attention. The devil further deludes him on the matter of taking the Sultan's money, saying "You have a right to it." Now it is well-known that if that money comes from an illegal source, the man has no right to take any of it, and if it is from a doubtful source, the better course is to abstain from it; if however it comes from a lawful source, it is permissible for the jurist to take such amount as religion allows, not such as can be expended in the maintenance of a luxurious establishment. Now often the populace imitate what they see the jurist do, and regard as lawful what is not so.

The devil also deludes men of learning, who keep away from the Sultan in order to practise devotion; he persuads them to malign those scholars who do present themselves to the Sultan, thereby rendering them victims of two vices, maligning others, and self-praise. In general it may be said that appearance at the courts is a serious danger, for whereas the intention at the commencement may be good, it changes with the bestowal of honours and fights, or through covetousness; so the man cannot keep himself from flattering the Sultan, and abstaining from finding fault with him. Sufyan al-Thauri said : I am not afraid of their humiliating me; I am only afraid of their doing me honour, so that my heart will incline to them.

The learned men of antiquity used to keep away from princes, owing to their manifest wrongdoing; so the princes used to send for them, needing them to give legal opinions and to undertake governments; so there sprang up a class of men who were very desirous of worldly prosperity, studied the sciences which are of use to princes, and brought their knowledge to them in order to gain worldly advantage. The proof that they had the princes in view in their studies lies in the fact that at one time the princes like to hear the arguments about the principles of religion, and people produced the science of metaphysical theology; then some of the former showed a taste for legal discussion, and the people took up with eristic; then some of the former showed a liking for homilies, and many a student took up with this pursuit. And when the mass of the populace had a liking for anecdotes, the anecdote-mongers became numerous, and the number of jurists declined.

Among the ways wherein the devil deludes the jurists is this : one of them may live upon a trust fund belonging to a school built for students, and stay there for years without studying, being satisfied with what he already knows, or indeed he may have come to the end of his study, so as to have no share in the endowment, which was meant for persons still learning, unless indeed such an individual may be a reciter or teacher, and so continually employed.

To this category there belongs what is reported of some among the younger law-students, viz., that they allow themselves licence in forbidden things, some of them wearing silk and ornaments of gold, at the cost of the school in which they protract their stay, and whose endowment they employ for other inquities as well;

the reasons for their licentiousness vary, some of them having no sound belief in the basis of religion, and studying law to acquire respectability or to get a share in the endowment, or to gain eminence or to dispute; whereas others are sound in belie, but are overcome by passion and concupiscence, having nothing to divert them therefrom, since the mere practice of arguing and disputing encourages conceit and pride, inasmuch as a man can only keep himself straight by ascetic exercise and perusal of the lives of the ancients—practices from which most of them are far removed, all that they do being calculated to encourage natural pride, so that passion is unrestrained. Some of them are deluded by the devil with the thought that they are savants, jurists, and muftis, and that learning exempts its possessors from ill consequences : it does nothing of the kind, for the man's knowledge in such a case convicts him, and doubles his punishment, as we have stated in the case of the Readers.

Al-Hasan al-Basri said : He only is a jurist who fears God Almighty. Ibn Aqil said : I saw a jurist of Khorasan wearing silk and gold rings, and said to him : What is this?—He said : Gifts of the Sultan and vexation of the enemies.—I said : On the contrary, the triumph of the enemies over you, if you are a Muslim, since the devil is your enemy, and if he has got you to wear what angers the code, you have let him triumph over you. Is the prohibition of the Merciful satisfied with the Sultan's gifts, wretched man? The Sultan has robed you, but you have been stripped of your faith. Better would it have been that the Sultan should make you strip people of the robe of wickedness and clothe you with the robe of piety. May God cast disgrace upon you inasmuch as you have made light of His commandment! Would that you had said : These are natural vanities! As it is, your condemnation is complete, since your contumacy proves that you are inwardly rotten.

One of his ways of deluding them is that he persuades them to despise preachers and forbid their visits, saying : Who are these people—story-tellers! The devil's purpose is to prevent the jurists from being present where the heart will be humbled and softened. The story-tellers are not to be censured because of this name, since

God says (xii. 3) *We shall tell thee the best of stories* and (vii. 175) *And tell thou the stories.* The story-tellers are only to be censured because they are given to dilate without introducing any useful knowledge, and most of them mix things up in their narrations, or insist on absurdities. But when the stories are true, and edifying, the story-teller is worthy of praise. Ahmad b. Hanbal used to say : How much men need a truthful story-teller!

Account of the Way Wherein he Deludes Preachers and Story-tellers

In old times the preachers were scholars and jurists; 'Abdallah b. 'Umar used to attend the meetings of 'Ubaid b. 'Umair, and 'Umar b. 'Abd al-Aziz used to attend the meetings of a story-teller. Later on the profession became degraded, and was taken up by ignorant men, so that discreet persons kept away from their company, which was sought by the vulgar and women. These persons spent no time in acquiring knowledge, but concentrated on anecdotes and what suited the taste of the ignorant. Various innovations were introduced into this profession.

We have mentioned their failings in the *Book of Story-tellers and Narrators,* but will also give some account of them here. One is that some of them invent Traditions calculated to encourage or to warn, being deluded by the devil and supposing that their purpose is to urge men to virtue and deter them from vice. This, however, is an insult to the Code, since such conduct on their part implies that it is defective, needing a supplement. Further they forget the saying of the Prophet *Whoso intentionally lies about me had better secure his place in Hell.* To this category also belongs their looking out for what will tickle people's minds and gratify their hearts, so that they vary their style accordingly, and you will find them reciting delightful erotic songs; the devil deludes them into thinking that the purpose of such is to point to the love of God, whereas the majority of their audience are common people, whose interior is filled with the love of passion; so the story-teller is misled, and by his procedure there is also misled the man who displays more emotion and humility than he actually feels. A larger audience necessitates additional simulation, and the soul will concede more tears and more humility: if one of them is feigning, he has forfeited the next world: and the man who is genuine cannot keep his sincerity free from an admixture of hypocrisy. Some of them make the motions with which the intonation of tunes is accompanied, and the intonations which they produce in our time resemble singing, and so come closer to what is forbidden than to what is merely disapproved. The Reader chants and the story-teller recites erotic verses, clapping his hands and beating with his feet, so that the performance resembles a drunken bout, and it causes mental agitation and exhilaration, with shouting by men and women, and rending of garments by reason of the passions hidden in the mind. Then they go away saying. It was an agreeable meeting, "agreeable" referring to something illicit. Some of those who practise the conduct that has been explained recite dirges over the dead, describing the afflictions which they endure, and telling of travelling and those who have met death in a strange land: causing the women to weep so that the place comes to be like a wailing room: but it would have been more fitting to speak of resignation to the loss of the departed, not what make people despair. Some of them talk of the subtleties of asceticism and the love of God: and the devil deludes them with the suggestion "you are of those to whom this epithet applies, since you would not have been able to describe it all had you not known what you describe and walked the path." The removal of this delusion is the fact that a description is a case of knowledge, whereas walking is not knowledge. Some of them talk of catastrophies and illegal "intoxication", quoting amatory verses, with the object of increasing the applause of the company though the subject be improper. Many of them utter flowers of speech with no underlying meaning; most of their talk in the present day is of Moses and the mountain, and Zulaikha and Joseph; they scarcely ever mention the divine ordinances, or forbid sin. When, then, is the adulterer or usurer likely to repent, or a woman to recognize her husband's rights and those of her relations? Alas, these people have abandoned the code, and that is why their wares find so good a market; for truth is heavy, and falsehood light. Some of them urge people to asceticism and vigils, without explaining to the populace the purpose of these proceedings; in consequence one of them may repent and retire to a hermitage, or to the mountain, leaving his family without provision. Some of them talk of hope and desire, with no admixture of what will induce fear and caution, only emboldening people thereby to commit sin, and enforcing this by their own taste for worldly things such as fine horses, and splendid attire; so their words and actions corrupt men's hearts.

The preacher indeed may be sincere and well-meaning, only some of them get imbued with ambition as time goes on, and what to be revered; the sign of this is that if another preacher comes to take such a man's place or assist him with the congregation the former preacher dislikes it; whereas, were he in earnest, he would have no objection to being helped with the morals of the congregation.

Some story-tellers mix the men and the women at their meetings, and you may see the women uttering many cries, out of emotion, as the story-tellers suppose, who find no fault with these cries, hoping to win all their hearts. In out time the story-tellers act in a way which has no connection with delusion, since it is an evident way of making the stories a source of livelihood, and of getting gifts from tyrannical princes, or obtaining the like from the gatherers of unlawful imposts, and earning money by them in the provinces. Some of them go to the cemeteries where they dilate on affliction and parting with friends, drawing tears from the women, but not exhorting them to take warning.

The devil even deludes the conscientious preacher, saying to him: You are not the person to preach, *that* should be done by one who is wide awake: urging the man to silence and retirement. This is one of the devil's suggestions, who thereby prevents good being done, as he goes on to say: You take delight in what you recount, and find solace therein; hypocrisy may well enter into your discourse, so that the path of isolation is safer. Satan's object thereby is to block the way of good. There is a Tradition on the authority of Thabit that al-Hasan was at a meeting, and said to al-'Ala: Speak.— Al-'Ala said: We shall be weakening your authority; he proceeded to recount the troubles connected with speaking and its consequences.—I, said Thabit, was pleased; then al-Hasan spoke, while we were in this state of mind, and said: Satan would like you to accept his doctrine, so that no one would enjoin right or forbid wrong.

Account of the Way Wherein he Deludes Philologists and Scholars

He has deluded the majority of them, distracting them by the study of grammar and the dictionary from those important matters which are obligatory on the individual, such as knowledge of their religious duties, and from more appropriate studies such as moral science and the reformation of the heart, and more excellent studies, such as the interpretation of the Qur'an, Tradition, and Law. They give up all their time to studies which are not wanted on their own account but for something else; for when a man understands the word, he ought to proceed to act accordingly, since that is the purpose of the former. You will find one of these people scarcely knowing more than a little of the lore of the code or of jurisprudence, and paying no attention to the purification of his mind and the reformation of his heart. And withal they are exceedingly proud and have been persuaded by the devil that they are the savants of Islam, because grammar and lexicography are Islamic sciences, and by them the meaning of the glorious Qur'an is ascertained. This indeed cannot be denied; only the knowledge of the amount of grammar necessary for the correction of the tongue, and of lexicography for the interpretation of the Qur'an and the Tradition, is easily acquired and indeed incumbent; anything more is superfluous and unnecessary, and it is a mistake to expend time in acquiring this unimportant superfluity while neglecting what is important; and preferring it to what is more profitable and more excellent, such as Jurisprudence and Tradition, is wasteful. If life were long enough for the acquisition of all knowledge, it would be all right; but since life is short, it is proper to give the preference to the more important and the more excellent.

The author proceeds to give examples of fetwas given where the ruling should distinguish two senses of the same word, which would call for different rulings. They are not fit for translation.

Being chiefly occupied with pagan poetry, nature finding no restraint to its instincts from the perusal of Traditions and the biographies of the saints of old, it carries them away to the abyss of passion, and the floodgates of frivolity are opened. Rarely will you see one of them troubling himself about piety, or scrupulous about food: the grammarian is a courtier, and will eat the rulers' forbidden food, as indeed Abu 'Ali al-Farisi enjoyed the protection of 'Adud al-daulah, and others; through want of understanding they fancy that to be lawful which is not so, as happened to Abu Ishaq Ibrahim b. al-Sari al-Zajjaj. I was, he said, tutor to al-Qasim son of 'Ubaidallah, and I said to him: If you attain to your father's rank and are invested with the vizierate, what will you do for me?—What *would* you like? he asked.—I said: I should like you to give me twenty thousand dinars.—This was the summit of my ambition, and only a few years elapsed before he was invested with the vizierate while I was still in his employ. I had become his messmate and felt tempted to remind him of his promise, but I was afraid of him; on the third day of his vizierate he said to me: Abu Ishaq, I have not seen you reminding me of the vow.—I said: I relied on the good faith of the vizier, who needs no reminding of a vow which he made with regard to a meritorious servant.—He said: It is Mu'tadid; were it not for him it would not be difficult for me to pay you this sum straight off; only I am afraid that he would talk to me about it, so kindly take it in instalments.—I said certainly.—Then he said: You are to sit and receive people's petitions on important matters, and be quick with them, never failing to ask me for something about which you are addressed, whether it be right or wrong, until the sum of the vow has come into your hands.—I did this, and used every day to present papers to him, which he would sign, sometimes asking me how much had been promised me for getting it through, when I would tell him, and he would say You have been cheated; this is worth so much, so make the man pay more.—I would then go back to the people, and haggle with them till they had raised their offers to the amount which he had fixed. So in a short time I had amassed

20,000 dinars and more.—After a month he asked me whether I had amassed the amount which he had vowed; I said No, and I went on presenting the papers, and once a month or so he would ask me the same question, and I would say No for fear of the income coming to an end. This went on till I had amassed the double of the amount, and one day when he asked me I was ashamed of continuing to lie, and replied: By the good luck of the vizier that sum has been amassed.—He said: You have relieved me, by Allah, for I have been in anxiety till you got it.—He then took his inkhorn and wrote an order on his treasurer for three thousand dinars as a bonus. I took this and then ceased presenting documents to him, not knowing what view he would take of my conduct. The next day I went to him and sat in my usual place, when he signed to me to bring what I had got, meaning to demand the petitions as usual. I said: I have taken no paper from any one, since the vow has been fulfilled, and I did not know what view the vizier would take.—He said: Good heavens, do you suppose I would deprive you of a business that has become your practice, about which people know and which has won for you their respect and made them come to your door morning and evening? The cause of the stoppage will not be known and people will suppose that it is due to a weakening of your influence with me, or a change in your position. So present the petitions as usual, and take your fees without reckoning.—I kissed his hand, and next morning brought him the petitions, and kept on bringing him something everyday till he died, having an established position with him.

I would observe that here we may see the effort of ignorance of the law. Had this great grammarian and philologist known that this procedure of his was illegal, he would not have narrated it with such pride. The presentation of complaints is obligatory, and it is unlawful to take bribes for doing this, or any other of the public business which the vizier committed to him. And this shows the superiority of jurisprudence to other studies.

Account of the Way Wherein he Deludes the Poets

He deludes them into thinking that they are men of learning

and possessors of sagacity which distinguishes them from their follows, and that He who favoured them with this sagacity is likely to pardon their failings. Hence you find them "philandering in every valley" of falsehood, slander, satire, vilification and confession of atrocities. The mildest of their methods is to eulogize a man, who fearing that the poet may satirize him, will pay him, out of fear or shame before the company. All this is a sort of blackmail; and you may see many a poet and man of letters wearing silk without scruple, and lying beyond measure in his eulogies; narrating love-feasts and wine-bout, " I with other men of letters made a party and die thus and thus." Such procedure is far removed from "learning"; that is "reverence" towards God shown by practising piety.

And most of these poets and men of letters when in strained circumstances repine, disbelieve, and start finding fault with destiny, as in the following utterance

> Although my ambition may soar to the skies,
> My luck, buried deep underground, cannot rise;
> Full many a buffet from fate must I bear;
> How mischievous , fate, how unkind, how unfair!

These people forget that their own misconduct is what causes their distress; they suppose themselves to be worthy of favours, and to deserve immunity from trial, having paid no attention to their duty of obeying the enactments of the code. Their sagacity therefore is a fault in this negligence.

Account of the Way Wherein the Devil Deludes the Most Accomplished Scholars

Certain ambitious people have acquired all the sciences connected with the code, Qur'an, Tradition, Jurisprudence, Philology, etc., and then been privily deluded by the devil making them "think more highly of themselves than they ought to think" in consequence of their attainments and the services they have rendered to their fellows. Some of them he puffs up with the thought of the length of time they have devoted to study, and recommends indulgence to them, saying "How long in this labour to last? Give your limbs some rest from these arduous occupations, and indulge your soul in its desires: if some lapse occurs, your knowledge will avert the punishment," dilating on the superiority of the learned. If the man accepts this, and yields to the delusion, he is lost; if he is helped by God, he should reply: The answer to you is threefold: one is that the superiority of the learned lies in their acting according to their knowledge; it would have no sense unless it were to be practised. If I do not act in accordance with it, I am like one who does not understand its purport, and might be compared to a man who amasses food, but does not eat, so that his hunger is not thereby allayed. A second mode of reply is to confront him with texts which censure him who does not put his knowledge into practice, such as the Prophet's saying *The man who will be punished most severely is a savant whom God has not profited by his knowledge,* and his narrative of a man who shall be thrown into hell-fire and his bowels gush out, and who will say "I used to enjoin right and not do it, and forbid wrong and commit it." And a third is to recount to him the punishment of those who perished, having known but not acted by their knowledge, such as the devil and Balaam. And sufficient censure of the person who knows but does not act is to be found in the words of God (lxii. 5) *the like of an ass that carries books.*

The devil has deluded some of those who are sound in both knowledge and practice in another way: he persuades them to be conceited of their knowledge, jealous of rivals, and to play the hypocrite in order to gain supremacy. Sometimes he makes them think that this is something which is their due; sometimes he encourages their desire for it, which they do not abandon though knowing it to be sinful. The remedy for this in the case of those who are helped by God is to think carefully about the guilt of conceit, jealousy, and hypocrisy, and assure the mind that knowledge will not avert the mischief of these acquirements. On the contrary their punishment will be doubled, there being a double reason for it. One who studies the biographies of those ancients who both knew and practised will despise himself and feel no pride. Whoso knows God will be no hypocrite, and whoso knows God will be no hypocrite, and whoso observes how fate works as His will demands will feel no jealousy.

The devil approaches these people with a curious fallacy. There is nothing wrong, he says, in your seeking elevation, since you are the representatives of the Code, and your object is merely to glorify religion and suppress innovations. Your giving free rein to your tongues concerning those who are envious of you is indignation on behalf of the code, since those persons censure its supporters: and what you suppose to be hypocrisy is nothing of the kind, since whosoever among you humbles himself and makes show of weeping will be imitated by people, just as they imitate a physician who practises cautery on himself more than one who merely prescribes it.

This delusion can be thus dispelled. If some other member of their class were to claim superiority over another and take a higher place in the assembly, or were to be slandered by an envious person, this savant would not feel as indignant as he would in his own case even if the victim were a representative of the code, so that it would be known that his anger was not on his own account but on that of the code. As for hypocrisy, that is inexcusable in all cases, and is unsuitable as a means of conversion. Ayyub al-Sakhtiyani used to sweat when he repeated a Tradition but would wipe his face, and say: what a bad cold I have! Further "acts are to be judged by the unintentions," and critics have sharp eyes. Now many a man who will not himself slander Muslims will rejoice in his heart when they are slandered in his presence, incurring threefold guilt thereby: first by his rejoicing; since this was what caused the slanderer to commit the offence; secondly by his taking pleasure in the maligning of Muslims; and thirdly by not remonstrating.

The devil has yet further deluded these experts, who stay up all night and labour all day in the composition of learned worker, by making them suppose that the object is the propagation of the faith. Their secret object is the propagation of their own fame, increase of reputation, supremacy and the attraction of students form all regions to the writer.

The delusion can be thus dispelled. If one of these students were to desert the writer for someone more learned then he, this would annoy the former; and this is no characteristic of a sincere teacher, for the sincere teacher should be like a physician, who treats patients for God Almighty's sake, and rejoices if a patient be cured by some other physician. We mentioned up above the Tradition of ibn Abi Laila, which we will repeat here with a different chain of authorities going back to 'Abd al-Rahman his son. He said: I have been contemporary with a hundred and twenty of the Prophet's Companions, of the Helpers, and there was not one of them but if asked about any matter would have wished that one of his brethren would have answered for him; and likewise with the reporting of Traditions.

Now the experts at times escape the delusions of the devil which are known among them, and such as he conceals; to such a man the devil says: Never have I met you like! How will you know my coming in and my going out!-If the man accept this, he is ruined by his conceit; if he declines to accept it, he escapes. Al-Sari al-Saqati said: Were a man to enter a garden containing all the trees created by God, with all the birds created by God perched on them, and every bird to address him in his language, saying "Peace upon thee, O saint of God," and he were to acquiesce, he would be a prisoner in their hands.—God is the guide, there is no God but He!

Dealing With the Way Wherein the Devil Deludes Governors and Sovereigns

He deludes them in numerous ways of which we shall mention the chief categories. The first is making them suppose that God loves them, and were it not for that, He would not have given such a man His office or made him His deputy over His servants. This delusion is to be dispelled by the consideration that if they are His deputies in reality, they had better judge in accordance with His code, and follow His pleasure. In that case

He will love them for their obedience. As for the titles king and sovereign, they have been given by God to many whom He hates, as indeed he has bestowed worldly on many on whom He would not look; to a number of such persons He has given authority over saintly and pious men, whom they have murdered and to whom they have done violence. Such a gift, however, is not for their benefit, but for their disadvantage; this being a case of the text (iii. 172) *We only give them respite that they may increase in guilt.* The second is his telling them that government requires awe, so that they become too proud to seek knowledge and make assessor of the learned, so as to act be their advice and be instructed in religion. Now it is well known that a man's nature borrows from the qualities of his associates, and when men mix with those whose preference is for worldly prosperity and who are ignorant of the code, their natures will borrow these people's qualities in addition to what they already possess of the like, and this leads to ruin.—The third is his making them afraid of enemies, and bidding them screen themselves securely so that complainants can have no access to them, and official appointed to remedy injustices can neglect his duties. Abu Maryam al-Asadi* has reported the following Tradition of the Prophet: Whenever, he said, a man whom God has put in charge of Muslim business screens himself from attending to their wants God will screen Himself from attending to that man's wants, needs, or distress.—The fourth is getting them to put in office unsuitable, ignorant, and ungodly persons. The injuries which these officials inflict on people cause their curses to fall on the sovereign. Further the devil gives them illicit profits out of illegal sales and the infliction of punishment on innocent individuals. They suppose that they can free themselves from responsibility with God for what they have put on the neck of the deputy. They are mistaken. If the minister of Alms appoints rogues to distribute them, and they cheat, he has to make their defalcation good.—The fifth is his persuading them to act arbitrarily, amputating hands which the law does not permit to be amputated, and executing persons who ought not to be executed. He makes them fancy that this is politic; the underlying idea being that the sacred code is imperfect, and requires supplementing, so that we are to supplement it according to our own views.

This is indeed the worst of delusions; for the code is divine polity, and it is absurd to suppose that there can occur in God's polity any flaw which it needs human polity to remedy. God says (vi. 38) *We have neglected nothing in the book and* (xiii. 41) *there is none that can rebut His judgment.* Hence one who claims to be politic claim that there is some flaw in the code. We have been told how 'Adud al-daulah was attached to a slave-girl, and finding that she occupied his mind, he ordered that she should be drowned lest she divert her mind from managing his realm. This is sheer madness, since it is unlawful to put a Muslim to death save for a crime. His belief that such an act was lawful, only thought it advantageous, then there is no advantage in what is contrary to the code.

The sixth is his persuading them to be lavish with money, supposing it to be under their control.—This delusion can be dispelled by the observation that such control is withdrawn from a man who is extravagant with his own property: how much more must this be the case with one who is hired to look after other people's property! Only such amount of the money is his as is in proportion to his work; he has no right to squander. Ibn 'Aqil said: it is recorded that Hammad the Reciter repeated some verses to al-Walid b. Yazid, who gave him 50,000 dirhems and two slave-girls; this, he observes, is recorded by way of praise, but it is in fact a serious charge; for it means squandering the treasure of the Muslims. The devil further persuades some to withhold from the deserving their due, and this is as bad as squandering.

The seventh is to suggest to them that they may indulge in offences, deluding them with the idea that their protection of the roads and making the country safe will avert punishment from them. The reply to this is to tell them that they have been put in authority for the purpose of guarding the country and making the roads safe, and these are duties incumbent upon them; the offences wherein they indulge are illicit and their discharge of their duty will not avert punishment.

The eighth is to delude most of them with the consideration that such a one has discharged his duty inasmuch as things are superficially right; whereas if he were to scrutinize he would find that there was much disorder. It is recorded of al-Qasim b. Talhah b. Muhammad that he said: I observed how the vizier 'Ali b. 'Isa set a salaried official over the Melon House, his business being to go round the dealers in grapes; if a man bought a basket of grapes suitable for wine, he was to throw salt over them, that it might not be possible for the man to make them into wine. Further, he says: I have witnessed sovereigns forbidding astrologers to sit in the streets so that the practice of acting by the stars might not spread. I have also known the army to be without a single beardless boy with tresses until Bachkam the foreigner appeared.

The ninth is to persuade them to procure money and extort it by violent scourging, confiscating all the possessions of the dishonest officials and making them swear *that there is nothing more.* We have been told how 'Umar b. 'Abd al-'Aziz received a letter from a retainer to the effect that certain persons had embezzled the money of Allah, and infliction of torture; and the Caliph wrote him: *I prefer that they should meet Allah with their dishonesty to my meeting Him with their blood.*

The tenth is to suggest to them to give alms after plundering, telling them that a dirhem given in alms wipes away the guilt of ten obtained by plundering. This is absurd, for the guilt of the robbery endures, whereas the dirhem given in alms will not be accepted from a lawful source it will not avert the guilt of robbery, since the gift to a poor man will not invalidate the other man's right.

The eleventh is to encourage them while persisting in their inequities to visit saintly men and implore their prayers, and make them think that this will lighten their guilt. This good act will not cancel the other bad act; Mani' said: A trader passed by a tithe-collector, and an embargo was put on his vessel. The trader went to Malik b. Dinar and informed him about this. Malik arose and went with him to the tithe-collector. When the people saw Malik, they said to him: O Abu Yahya, why did you not send some to us about your business? He said: My business is that you should release this man's vessel.—They said: We have done so.—Now they had an urn into which they put the dirhems which collected from the traders. They asked Malik to pray for them. He said: You had better tell the urn to pray for you; How can I pray for you when a thousand others are calling down curses upon you? Do you suppose one man's prayer will be answered, and those of a thousand receive no answer?

The twelfth is in the case of officials who are in the service of a superior, and do wrong when they are commanded to do it, for the devil to delude them with the idea that the guilt falls not on them but on their superior. This is false, since such a person aids in wrongdoing and whosoever assists transgression is himself a transgressor. For the Prophet cursed ten persons in the matter of wine, and cursed the taker of usury, the man who lets him take it, and those who witness the act.

To this category belongs collecting taxes for a superior who it has known, will squander and embezzle. For this too is a case of giving help in wrongdoing. It is recorded that Ja'far b. Sulaiman said: I heard Malik b. Dinar say: It is sufficient dishonesty for a man to be the trusted agent of one who is dishonest. It is God who guides up to the truth.

Account of the Way Wherein the Devil Deludes Devotees in their Devotions

You should know that the widest doorway whereby the devil enters is ignorance. He can get at the ignorant with impunity; at the learned only with difficulty. The devil has deluded many devotees by reason of their lack of knowledge, since most of them are occupied with their devotion and have acquired no profound knowledge. Rabi' b. Kuthaim said: Study jurisprudence, and then become an anchorite.

His first delusion is the idea that devotion is superior to knowledge, whereas knowledge is more excellent than works of supererogation. He puts into their minds that the object of learning is work, and the only work which they know is what is done with the limbs of the body, being unaware that work is the work of the heart, and that the work of the heart is superior to the work of the limbs. Mutarrif b. 'Abd-allah said: excellence in knowledge is better than excellence in devoutness: Yusuf b. Asbat said: one chapter of knowledge learned is better than seventy raids. Al-Mu'afa b. 'Imran said: The writing out of a single Tradition is to my mind preferable to a whole night spent in prayer.

Now I observe that these people having suffered this delusion, causing them to prefer acts of devotion with their limbs to knowledge, the devil was enabled to delude them in various forms of devotion.

Account of his Delusions in the Matter of Ablution

There are some whom be deludes in the matter of intention, and you will see such a person say "the filth has been removed," after which he will say "prayer is permissible," and then after that he will say "I will remove the filth." Now the source of this delusion is ignorance of the code; for intention is in the heart not in the utterance, and there is no need to take the trouble of uttering, and further there is no sense in repeating the utterance. There are some whom he deludes by examination of the water used for ablution, saying to such a person How do you know that it is clean? Making all sorts of improbable suggestion about it. He ought to be satisfied with the decision of the code that purity is the essence of water, and an essential quality is not to be rejected for a possibility. Some are deluded into using a quantity of water, to which there are four objection; waste of water: frittering away invaluable life over what is neither necessary nor commendable; encroaching on the law, since such a person is not satisfied with the small amount of water which satisfies the law; entering on a course forbidden by the law, by exceeding the three *washing of the hands*. Often-times such a person takes so long over his ablution that he misses the prayer time or its commencement, which is of prime importance, or misses public prayer.

Account of the Way Wherein he Deludes them in the Call to Prayer

A case of this is intoning the Call; Malik b. Anas and other men of learning disapproved of this practice exceedingly, because it removes the Call from being a reverential performance to resemble singing. Another case of it is their mixing the Call to the morning prayer with exhortations, praises, and homilies, inserting it in between. Learned men have disapproved of all addition to the Call. We have seen people mount the minaret at night and exhort or preach. Some read Surahs of the Qur'an in a loud voice, interfering with people's sleep, and confusing the reading of those who keep vigil. All these practices are reprehensible.

Account of the Way Wherein he Confuses them in Prayer

A case of this is his deluding them in the matter of the clothes with which they cover themselves; you will see one of them wash a clean garment a number of times, and wash it after a Muslim his touched it. Some of them wash their garments in the Tigris, thinking that washing them at home is insufficient. Some of them plunge the garment into the well, as do the Jews; the Prophet's Companions did not do these things: indeed they prayed in Persian clothes, when they conquered the country, and made use of the Persian mats and wearing apparel. Some of the misguided sprinkle water over the garment and wash the whole of it, which sometimes makes them late for public worship. Some of them neglect public worship because of a little rain, which they fear may drip on their clothes.

Let not any one suppose that I object to cleanliness and decency; only excess which is beyond the limits of the code and involves waste of time is what I forbid.

Another case is his deluding them in the matter of intention in prayer. One of them says: I will make such and such a prayer, and presently repeat this, thinking that he has lessened his intention, whereas intention is not lessened by his dissatisfaction with the wording. One of them says *Allahu Akbar,* then cancels it, and when the Imam makes an inclination, this deluded person says the words and makes inclination simultaneously; I should like to know what has produced the intention at the latter rather than at the former time, unless it be that the devil wishes the man to miss the advantage. There are deluded people who swear "By Allah I will not say *Allahu Akbar* except this time"; and some who swear with the sanction of loss of property and divorce. All these are delusions of the devil. The code is liberal, easy, and free from these affilictions. Neither the Prophet nor his Companions practised anything of the sort. We have been told that Abu Hazim once entered the mosque when the devil suggested to him that he was about to pray without ablution. He said : You are not as careful of my interests as that!

The illusion is thus to be dispelled. Let it be said to the victim of it: If what you want is to produce the intention, such intention is already present, since you are about to perform a religious obligation, and that is an intention and the seat of intention is the heart, not the utterance, so the utterance is unnecessary. Further you have uttered it in a sound state, so why repeat it? Do you suppose that you have lost the memory of what you have said? That indeed would be unsoundness.

A certain shaikh told me a strange story about Ibn 'Aqil. He was met by a man who said : I wash a member of my body and say that I have not washed it; and I utter *Allahu Akbar,* and say that I have not uttered it.—Ibn 'Aqil said to him: Omit to pray as it is not incumbent on you.—Some people said to Ibn 'Aqil : How can you say this?—He said to them; The Prophet said "The pen is withdrawn from a madman till he recover." A man who utters *Allahu Akbar,* and then says he has not uttered it is not sane, and prayer is not incumbent on the insane.

I would observe that you are to know that the cause of such delusion about intention in prayer is mental disease and ignorance of the code. It is certain that a man would be thought to be of unsound mind if when he rose up in honour of a learned visitor he were to say "I am going to stand up as a mark of respect to the visit of this scholar on account of his learning", coming forward to greet him, because the man must have had the notion in his mind from the time when he saw the scholar. Similarly a man's rising to pray in order to perform his religious obligation is a notion which takes shape in his mind in a single moment which takes no time; time is only taken by the stringing of these words, which are not obligatory; the delusion is mere ignorance. Further the deluded person forces himself to produce in his mind the ideas of purity, performance, and obligation, all at once in separate utterances which he reads—and this is impossible. Were he to undertake the like in the matter of rising up before the scholar he could not do it. The man who knows this knows intention. Further it is permissible to prefix it with a brief interval to the utterance *Allahu Akbar* provided the man does not cancel it; why then take such trouble to attach it to that utterance, since, if the man make it and does not cancel it, he has practically attached it to that utterance? Musawwir is reported to have said: Ma'n b. 'Abd al-Rahman showed me a document which he swore was in the script of his father, containing the words: 'Abdallah said; "By him than whom there is no other God I have never seen any one more vehement against the prolix than the Prophet, nor any one after him more afraid on their account than Abu Bakr; and I think 'Umar was more afraid on their account than any one in the world."

There are some deluded persons who after making sincere intention and uttering *Allahu Akbar* are careless about the rest of the prayer as though that utterance were the sole purpose of the ceremony. This delusion may be dispelled by the thought that the purpose of that utterance is to enter into worship. How then may worship be neglected when it is the dwelling, the man contenting himself with taking care to guard the door?

Certain deluded persons are satisfied with uttering the formula *Allahu Akbar* behind the Imam when the inclination is not quite complete, and then start afresh and utter the formula of "taking refuge" after which the Imam makes the inclination. This too is a delusion; for the fresh start and the formula of taking refuge are enactments of the Sunnah, whereas that which he neglects, viz., the recitation of the Fatihah, is according to a number of learned men obligatory; when an enactment of the Sunnah should not be preferred to it.

I may observe that in my youth I used to pray behind our master the jurist al-Dinawari, who once saw me do this; he said to me: My boy, the jurists differ as to the obligation of reciting the Fatihah behind an Imam, but they do not differ about the starting formula being a Sunnah; so pay attention to what is obligatory and omit the Sunnahs.

The devil has further deluded various people who have neglected many Sunnahs owing to fancies which have occurred to them. Some would keep back from the front row, such a man saying that his intention was proximity of heart; someone would not let one hand down on the other in prayer, saying "I am unwilling to make a display of humility which is not in my heart". These two proceedings have been told us of certain saints. It must have been due to want of knowledge; in the *Sahih* of Muslim there is a Tradition that according to Abu Hurairah the prophet said: If men only knew the value of the Call to prayer and the front row, and found no other way to get into it, they would draw lots for it. And among the Traditions of Abu Hurairah found only in Muslim there is this: The best row is the front, and the worst is the back. As for putting one hand on the other, this is a Sunnah. Abu Dawud in his *Sunan* records that Ibn Zubair said: Placing hand upon hand is of the Sunnah. Also that Ibn Mas'ud used to pray putting his left hand on his right, but the Prophet seeing him do this placed the right hand on the left.

I will state my objection to the man who says he meant nearness of heart and will not put one hand on the other, however great a man he may be. It is the code which objects, not we; someone said to Ahmad b. Hanbal that Ibn al-Mubarak said so and so: Ahmad replied that Ibn al-Mubarak had not descended from heaven. Someone quoted to him Ibrahim b. Adham, and he said: You have brought me evidences of the Way; what you should produce is the Original. This ought not to be neglected for the saying of someone for whom there is personal respect. For the code is greater, and mistaken interpretation may become current.—It is, however, possible that he had not heard the Tradition.

The devil has further deluded certain persons in the pronunciation of the letters in their prayers. You may see a man saying the word *al-hamd* (praise) twice; such repetition is a transgression of the proper practice in prayer. Sometimes he deludes people in the doubling of a consonant, or in the pronunciation of the word *maghdub* (in the phrase "against whom there is anger"); I have known people to pronounce it *maghsub* owing to the stress which they put on the *dad*; what is wanted is the correct pronunciation of the letter, nothing more. The devil gets them away from correctness by an increase of effort, and distracts them from understanding what they recite by over-attention to the letters. All this is his delusion. It is recorded that Sa'id b. 'Abd al-Rahman reported that Abu'l 'Amya had been told by Sahl b. Abi Umamah as follows. He and his son visited Anas b. Malik when he was performing an abbreviated prayer like that of a traveller, and said to him: God have mercy on you, do you regard this as the prescribed prayer? Is it the prophet's prayer or an additional act of worship?—He said: It is the Prophet's prayer; any mistake I may have made is unintentional. The Prophet used to say: Do not make things difficult for yourselves lest God make them difficult for you. This happened to certain people, of whom the relics are in the cells and the monasteries. *Monkery which they invented, and which We had not prescribed for them* (lvii. 27).—Among the Traditions of 'Uthman b. al-`As found only in Muslim there is the following: I said to the prophet "Truly the devil comes between me and my prayer and confuses my recitation". The Prophet said: "That is a demon called Khanzab. When you perceive him, ask God's protection from him three times, and spit on your left". I did so, and God removed him from me.

The devil has further deluded a number of ignorant devotees into thinking that devotion consists merely in standing and squatting. They are sedulous in these performances, knowing no better. I have noticed how a number of people say the *salam* when the Imam says it, although they have not finished reciting the obligatory confession of faith; that obligation cannot be borne vicariously by the Imam. He has deluded others into prolonging the prayer and increasing the recitation while neglecting what the Sunnah has prescribed in the prayer, and perpetrating what is disapproved therein. I once visited a devotee who was uttering a non-obligatory prayer in he daytime, and reciting aloud. I said to him: The Sunnahs ought not to be neglected because you stay awake at night, so when sleep overcomes you, sleep, for your soul has certain rights over you. Buraidah is recorded to have said: The Prophet said: If a man recites aloud in the daytime, fling dung at him.

The devil has deluded a number of devotees into praying much in the night, some of them staying up and praying at midday than in performing the prescribed devotions; only such a person may fall asleep a little before dawn, and so miss the prescribed prayer. Or he may get up and make ready for it but miss the assembly, or feel lazy in the morning and unable to earn for his family. I saw a devout shaikh named Hussain al-Qazwini walking for much of the day in the Mosque of al-Mansur. I asked him why he walked, and he said it was in order not to fall asleep. I said: This is ignorance of what is demanded by the code and the reason. As for the code—the prophet said "Your soul has certain rights over you" so go to sleep. He used also to say: Go gently, for if any one treats this religion with violence, it will overcome him.—It is recorded that Anas b. Malik said: The Prophet entered the Mosque one day and noticed a rope stretched between two pillars. He asked what is this? He was told that it was for Zainab; she was praying, and could take hold of it when she felt lazy or faint. He bade them loosen it; and he said: Let any one of you pray when he feels vigorous, and if he feel weak or faint, let him squat. 'A'ishah is recorded to have said: The Prophet said: If one of you dozes, let him lie down till his sleep passes from him; for if he were to pray while dozing, he might start asking for forgiveness and revile himself.

I may observe that this is a genuine Tradition, recorded by Bukhari and Muslim, whereas the previous one is found only in Muslim.

As for the intelligence: since sleep renovotes the powers which are tired out by wakefulness, if a man keeps it off at the time when he needs it, it affects both his body and his mind; so we ask God to protect us from ignorance. If any one say: You have reported to us that a number of the ancients used to stay awake all night: the reply is that those persons gradually acquired the capacity to do so, and could be sure of attending public prayer at dawn. Further they used to get help from a siesta and from paucity of food. Hence they could do this without harm. In addition we have no record that the prophet ever kept awake for a whole night, taking no sleep therein; and his is the practice which should be followed.

The devil has deluded several of those who keep vigil into talking about it in the daytime. Such a man will say: A certain *muedhdhin* uttered the Call to prayer at such and such an hour, in order that people may know that he was awake at the time. The least objection to this, supposing it to be free from hypocrisy, is that is removes the action from the sphere of secrecy to that of publicity, and so reduces the divine reward.

He has deluded others who isolate themselves in the mosques for prayer and devotion, and are known to do so, so that people gather round them and follow their lead in prayer, and they become famous. This is a temptation of the devil, whereby the soul is enured to devotion, knowing that this will spread abroad and earn eulogy. Zaid b. Thabit is recorded to have stated that the Prophet said: A man's best prayer is one offered in his own house, except the prescribed prayers.

I may observe that this Tradition is to be found in both

Sahih. 'Amir b. 'Abd Qais used to dislike being seen praying, and would offer no additional prayers in the mosque; yet he prayed a thousand inclinations every day. If any one visited Ibn Abi Laila while he was praying, he would lie down.

Some devotees have been deluded into weeping while people are around them. Such a fit may overtake a man, and he be unable to suppress it. A man who displays it when he can conceal it lays himself open to the charge of hypocrisy. It is recorded on the authority of 'Asim, that when Abu Wa'il prayed at home, he used to sob violently; only he would not do the like in any one's presence, though the whole world were offered him. Ayyub al-Sakhtiyani used to rise up when he was overcome by a fit of weeping.

A number of devotees also have been deluded into praying night and day while taking no trouble to reform secret faults nor about food. Attention to such matters would be their duty rather than suprenumerary prayers.

Account of the Way Wherein he Deludes them Over the Reading of the Qur'an

A number of people have been deluded into frequent recitation of the Qur'an which they gabble without modulation of the voice and without pauses; this practice is not commendable. It is indeed recorded that some of the ancients used to recite the whole Qur'an every day or at every inclination, but this was exceptional. If people persist in this practice, though it may be permissible, still modulation and pausing are preferred by the learned. The Prophet said: He will acquire no sound knowledge who takes less than three days to read the Qur'an.

The devil has deluded some Readers to recite the Qur'an on the minaret of a mosque at night all together with loud voices, to the extent of one or two Parts. These people combine public annoyance by keeping people from sleep with exposing themselves to the charge of hypocrisy. Some recite in the mosque at the time of the Call to prayer because that is the time at which the congregation assembles.

The most curious case that I have seen of this sort is that of a man who used to lead morning prayer on Friday, then turn and read the two final Surahs, and then pronounce the prayer said when a man has read the Book through, in order that people should know that he had been doing this. This was not the procedure of the ancients. They used to conceal their devotions; all such acts of al-Rabi' b. Khaitham were performed in secret. Sometimes a visitor would come when he had opened the Sacred Volume; in such a case he would cover it with his garment. Ahmad b. Hanbal used constantly to read the Qur'an, but no one ever knew when he had perused the whole.

We have now recorded various ways wherein the devil deludes the Readers of the Qur'an; God knows best what is right and He it is Who guides.

Account of the Way Wherein he Deludes them in the Matter of Fasting

He has persuaded people to fast perpetually, which is permissible provided the fast is broken on the days wherein fasting is unlawful. Only trouble arises therein in two ways. One is that the process is likely to lead to debilitation, so that the man is unable to earn for his family, and perform his conjugal duties; in both the *Sahih* there is a Tradition that the Prophet said: you have duties to your wife. Such supererogatory act often leads to neglect of the obligatory. The second is that the man misses the better way. For there is a genuine Tradition that the Prophet said: The best fast is that of the Prophet David, who used to fast and break his fast on alternate days. Fast three days in every month, and that will count as a perpetual fast.—He said: I replied: O Prophet of God, I can do more than that.—The prophet said: Then fast one day and break your fast two days.—He said: I can do better than that.—The Prophet said: Then fast one day and break your fast one day, which is the most reasonable form of fasting, being that of the Prophet david.—He said: I can do better than that.—There is nothing better than that, said the Prophet. This Tradition is to be found in both *Sahib.* If any one object that a number of the ancients are reported to have fasted continuously, the answer is that they were able to combine fasting with discharging their duties towards their families; perhaps in most cases they had no family and so need for earning. Some of them too only did this towards the end of their lives. Still the saying of the Prophet "There is no form of fasting better than that" disposes of such stories. Many among the ancients who fasted continuously, only eating coarse food and little of that, lost their eyesight or had their brains dry up. Such procedure is neglect of the soul's just claims and putting on it an intolerable burden. Hence it is not permissible.

A report sometimes gets about that a devotee fasts continually, and learning of this report he either does not break his fast at all or only does so in secret for fear of losing reputation; so this is a latent hypocrisy. If such a man meant to be sincere, and conceal his conduct, he would break his fast in the presence of those who know him to fast, and then return to his fasting without this being known. Some of them record the amount they have fasted, e.g., "To-day makes twenty years in which I have not broken fast". He is deluded into supposing that he reports this is order that he may be imitated, whereas God knows the real purpose. Sufyan al-Thauri said: A man performs an act in secret, but Satan does not leave him alone till he talks about it, so transferring it from the register of secret to that of public performances. It is the practice of some to fast on Mondays and Thursdays, and when such a man is invited to a meal he says "To-day, Thursday, is my fasting day"; if he were to say "I am fasting", it might be supposed that this was due to some affliction; the form in which he puts it means that he fasts every Thursday. Some of these people look down on other people because they break their fast; some while fasting long do not trouble with what sort of food they break fast; or while fasting do not abstain from slander, petulance, and inquisitiveness. The devil makes them suppose that their fasting will atone for it all. All this is delusion.

Account of the Way Wherein he Deludes them in the Matter of Pilgrimage

Sometimes a man discharges his obligation by a single pilgrimage, and then repeats the performance without his parents' consent, and this is an error. Or he goes on pilgrimage while in debt or having claims against him, or does so for amusement or on money from a tainted source. Many a pilgrim likes to be met and called *The Hajji,* and the majority of them neglect on their journey the obligations of purity and prayer. They assemble round the Ka'bah with impure hearts and internal uncleanness. The devil shows them the external form of the pilgrimage, deceiving them; for what is intended by the pilgrimage is proximity of heart not of body. This can be realized only by maintenance of piety. Many men go to Meccah thinking only of the number of his pilgrimages, and saying "I have stood in this place twenty times". Many men have resided long in Meccah, and not even started cleansing himself within, his mind being very likely concentrated on the favours which he will get from someone or other. Very likely he will say "I have now been a neighbour (of God) for twenty years. Many men have I seen on the Meccan road intent on pilgrimage, yet beating his companions to get at the water and jostling them on the way.

The devil has further deluded many of those who make for Meccah into omitting their prayers, and cheating when they sell, supposing that the act of pilgrimage will atone for it all. Some he has deluded into inventing ceremonies which do not belong to the pilgrimage. Thus I have seen many adopting fanciful fashions in their costume, such as baring one shoulder, and remaining whole days in the sunshine so that their skin may peel off, and their heads swell, hoping to gain credit with people thereby. Among the Traditions of Ibn 'Abbas to be found only in Bukhari there is one to the effect that the Prophet saw a man making the circuit of the Ka'bah with a halter, and cut it; or according to another account that he saw one man leading another through whose nose a ring had been passed, and cut the cord with his hand, ordering the guide to lead the other with his hand.—This Tradition indicates that religious innovation is forbidden even if the intention be to do a pious act.

He has deluded some into professing reliance on God and so starting without provision for the journey, supposing this to be "reliance." This is a grievous error. A man said to Ahmad b. Hanbal : I wish to start for Maccah in reliance without provision.—Ahmad said to him then start apart from the caravan.—The man said No, with the caravan.—Your reliance, said Ahmad, is then on other people's knapsacks.— We ask God to guide us.

Account of the Way Wherein the Devil Deludes the Raiders

The devil has deluded many people into proceeding to the sacred war with the hypocritical and vainglorious intention of being called *Ghazi;* or at times the object is to be called hero; or the quest of spoil: whereas "Acts are according to their intentions." The following Tradition goes back to Abu Musa. A man came to the Prophet and said: O Apostle of God, tell me, one man fights out of bravery, another out of patriotism, and another for display; which of these is in the path of God?—The Prophet said : When a man fights in order that God's word may be uppermost, he is on the path of God.—This Tradition is to be found in both *Sahih.*

The following is recorded as having been said by Ibn Mas'ud : Beware how ye say So-and-so died or was slain as a martyr; for a man may fight for the sake of spoil, or to obtain mention, or to exhibit his prowess.—There is also a Tradition connected by a chain of authorities with Abu Hurairah that the Prophet said : The first people to have sentence pronounced on them on the Day of Resurrection are three : A man who has died in battle, who will be brought and reminded of the benefits which he received and will acknowledge them, and will then be asked what he did in return. He will say : I fought for Thee till I was slain.—He will be told: Thou liest. Thou foughtest in order that it might be said What a brave man!—as indeed was said. An order will then be given that he be dragged on his face and cast into Hell. Next a man who has studied and acquired knowledge and read the Qur'an, who will be brought and reminded of the benefits which he received and will acknowledge them, and will then be asked what he did in return. He will say I studied and acquired knowledge on Thy account, and read the Qur'an.—he will be told: Thou liest; thou didst study in order that it might be said What a learned man!—as indeed was said. And thou didst read the Qur'an in order to be called a Reader, as indeed thou wast. An order will then be given that he be dragged on his face and cast into Hell. Next a man to whom God has been bountiful, bestowing on him every sort of wealth, who will be brought, reminded of the benefits which he received, which he will acknowledge, and then be asked what he did in return. He will say I left no object whereon Thou wouldst have money spent but spent in thereon for Thy sake.—He will be told: Thou liest. Thou didst do this in order that it might said What a generous man!—as indeed was said. An order will then be given that he be dragged on his face and cast into Hell.—This Tradition is found only in Muslim.

There is a Tradition which goes back to a Companion of the Prophet reported by Abu Hatim al-Razi. I heard, he said, 'Abadah b. Sulaiman narrate as follows : We were on an expedition with 'Abdallah b. Mubarak in Byzantine territory, when we came across the enemy. When the two armies met, one of the enemy came forward and challenged to single combat. A man on our side came forward, engaged the other for a time, then thrust him and killed him. The same thing happened with another champion and a third. Then our champion challenged to single combat, and the challenge was accepted by a man who engaged our champion for a time and then slew him. The men thronged round him, I being one of them; we found that our champion had veiled his face with his sleeve. I lifted a corner of the sleeve, and lo and behold, he was 'Abdallah b. Mubarak, who said : You too, then, Abu 'Amr, are among those who disgrace us!—So consider, I said, this sincere hero, who feared lest his sincerity should be trained through his sincerity should be trained through his being seen by men and winning their praise, and so hid himself!—Ibrahim b. Adham used to fight, but when booty was procured would take none of it in order that his reward in heaven might be all the greater.

The devil also deludes the religious warrior when he takes

booty; often-times he takes what it is unlawful for him to take. Possibly he may be so ignorant as to suppose that the goods of Unbelievers may be taken by any one, or not to know that embezzlement of spoil is sinful. The following Tradition of Abu Hurairah is to be found in both *Sahih.* We marched (he said) against Khaibar with the Prophet, and God granted us the capture thereof; we did not take as booty gold or silver, only furniture, food, and clothing. Then we proceeded to the Wadi. The Prophet was accompanied by a slave of his and when we alighted this slave started loosening his saddle, when he was hit by an arrow which caused his death. When we were felicitating the man on his martyrdom, the Prophet said Not so, by Him in whose hand in Muhammad's soul. His garment will burst into flames upon him, since he took it out of the plunder on the day of Khaibar, when it had not been apportioned to him.—The people, he said, were frightened, and a man brought a shoestrap (or a pair of them), saying I got this on the day of Khaibar. A strap (or a pair of straps) of fire—said the Prophet.

The raider may indeed know of the prohibition, but seeing a great quantity of booty be unable to restrain himself. Or he may think that his having fought in the sacred war will atone for his act. And here we may see the effect of faith and knowledge. It is recorded by a chain of authorities ending with Hubairah b. al-Ash'ath after Abu 'Ubaidan al-Anbari. When, he said, the Muslims entered Mada'in and collected the spoil, a man came forward with a casket which he gave to the officer in charge of the spoil. Those who were present said : We have never seen any object like this; all that we have got would not equal it or approach it in value. The man was asked whether he had taken anything from it. He said : You may be sure that were it not for God, I would never have brought it to you.—They saw that the man was of some importance and asked him who he was. He said : I will not tell you in order to be praised by you nor will I encourage you to eulogize me; I will praise God and be satisfied with His reward.—They sent a man to follow him, and when he had joined his comrades, the follower asked about him, and found that he was

'Amir b. 'Abd Qais.Account of the Way Wherein he Deludes Many of Those Among them who have a Reputation for Virtue

They are of two classes, the knowing and the ignorant. He approaches the knowing in two ways. The first is ostentation, seeking fame and admiration for their conduct. There is a Tradition with a chain of authorities going back to Ahmad b. Abi'l-Hawari who heard Abu Sulaiman say that he had heard Abu Ja'far al-Mansur sob in his sermon on a Friday. Anger, he said, overtook me, and I intended to rise up when he descended from the pulpit and admonish him with reference to what I knew of his conduct. Only, he said, I did not like to stand up and admonish a Caliph while the people were sitting looking at me, so that I would be guilty of ostentation, and be executed without being in the right. So I sat quiet.

The second way is anger on one's own account. This may be at the start, but often comes on in the course of enjoining right owing to the contumely which the censor endures, leading to personal hostility. So 'Umar b. 'Abd al-'Aziz said to a man : Were I not angry, I should punish you. He meant: You have made me angry, so that I was afraid the punishment would be out of wrath for God mingled with wrath for myself.

When the person who enjoins right is ignorant, Satan plays with him, and his injunction does more harm than good. For he may well forbit some act which is agreed to be legitimate, or censure some school. Such a man may break open a door or climb over a wall and beat and abuse the wrongdoers; if they retort with language which annoys him, he becomes angry on his own account. He is likely to reveal what the code bids him conceal. Ahmad b. Hanbal was asked about people who had in their possession forbidden articles covered up, e.g., a harp or some intoxicant; he said, is such a thing be, do not smash it; but according to another Tradition he said Do smash it. This is to be interpreted as meaning that the article is covered with some thin material through which its outline can be seen, whereas the former Tradition deals with the case inwhich it is not visible. He was asked about a man who heard the sound of drum or lyre, not knowing what it was; he answered You are under no obligation with regard to what is out of your ken, so do not enquire about it. It may happen that such a censor may refer the culprits to someone who will deal unjustly will them. Ahmed b. Hanbal said : If you are sure that the Sultan will inflict the legal punishments, then refer the matter to him.

Among the delusions which the devil practises on the censor is causing him, when he censures, to sit in an assembly describe what he has been doing and boast of it, and further revile the culprits in the style of an angry man, and curse them; yet they may have repented, and may be better men than he, being penitent, whereas he is proud. His talk may involve exposure of the Muslims, by giving information to the ignorant, whereas it is his duty to hide the failings of Muslims so far as it is possible to do so. I have heard how a certain ignorant censor would assault people about whose conduct he had no certain knowledge, beat them mercilessly, and smash vessels—performances all due to ignorance. When a man who has knowledge censures, you are quite safe with him. The ancient used to show delicacy in censuring. Silah b. Ashyam seeing a man talking to a woman said : Verily God shields; may He shield us and you!—Passing by some people he said: My brethren, what say ye of a man who, meaning to travel, sleeps all night and plays games all day? When will he do his travelling?—The attention of one of them was aroused and he said : Friends, this man means us.—So he and his companions repented.

The people who have the best right to be censured with delicacy are princes. The proper way to speak to them is as follows : Truly God has exalted you, so recognize the extent of His benefits, for gratitude ensure their continuance, and they ought not to be requited with transgressions.

The devil deludes some devout persons so that when they see wrong they fail to censure it, saying: Enjoining and forbidding are for saints; I am no saint, so how can I command any one else?—This is a mistake, for it is his duty to enjoin and forbid, even if he were guilty of the same offence; only when a person who is innocent of an offence censures it, his censure is effective, whereas if he be not innocent, it is ineffective. Hence the censor ought to keep himself innocent in order that his censure may have effect. Ibn Aqil said: We have seen in our time Abu Bakr al-Aqfali in the days of al-Qa'im, who when he set about censuring wrongdoing took with him a number of Shaikh who supported themselves entirely by the labour of their hands, such as the saintly shaikh Abu Bakr al-Khabbaz (the baker), who was taken from his inspection of the oven and followed him, with others, no one of whom accepted alms, or soiled himself by taking presents, men who fasted all day and kept vigil all night, shedders of tears. If any dishonest man tried to follow him, he would be rejected. Al-Aqfali would say: If we meet an army with untrustworthy troops, we shall be routed.

Revised and edited; originally published in Islamic Culture, in a series of articles, in 1930s and 1940s.

15

Al-Ghazzali on Repentance

M. S. STERN

Al-Ghazali's theological principles are of no mean importance in understanding his concept, treatment and variation of repentance.

Abu Hamid Muhammad al-Ghazzali (1058-1111) was one of the most significant personalities of classical Islam. He helped to reintroduce 'fear' into divine service. His efforts in the fields of philosophy and theology brought these disciplines a clarity essential for their availability to the greater number of Muslims. He created a framework within which Sufism attained solid acceptability within Orthodox Islam. Nor are his achievements limited to these.

Al-Ghazzali was a very prolific author. His magnum opus is the *Ihya Ulum ad-Din, Revival of the Religious Sciences*. This work, encyclopedic in scope, was written over a period of years beginning in 1095. Its intended purpose is to effect a fundamental redirection of the believer's attitude and to impart a knowledge of those internal aspects of piety which will lead to the opening of the supernal realm. The work is divided into four quarters, each containing ten books. The first book of the fourth quarter is the *Book of Repentance*. It is here al-Ghazzali gives his fullest treatment of the various aspects of the penitential process.

Al-Ghazzali views Repentance as an inherently valuable state for the religious personality. Also, in his view it is the first requisite stage in the pilgrim's search for proximity to God. Understanding the fundamental priority which al-Ghazzali assigns to Repentance requires as analysis of his theological first principles. It is to this question that this paper is directed.

The goal of worldly life, asserts al-Ghazzali, is the attainment of salvation. The understanding of the substance of this salvation would vary, according to him, based on the sophistication of the individual believer's grasp of religious truth.

The uninitiated masses (awamm) view salvation as the enjoyment of the pleasures of Paradise as portrayed in the Koran. Damnation, the converse, is the enforced suffering of the torments of hellfire. Upon man's death, at the threshold of the hereafter, his worldly life is judged and its vindication or condemnation results in such as assignment to Paradise or Hell. For such people the major theme of life and the motivation for serving God is fear; fear of being denied the joys of Paradise and fear of the agonies of hellfire.

Al-Ghazzali accepts the value of this approach considering the comprehension limits of the vulgus. It can be effective as a motivation to normative behaviour. He does not agree, however, that such an understanding reflects, objectively, the true nature of salvation.

Al-Ghazzali understands the reality of salvation to lie in the proximity to and encounter of God. Fear, for the true gnostic (arif), is only a preliminary stage which is overtaken by that of Love. Neither the sensual pleasures of Paradise nor the agonies of Hell interest such a man. His only fear is of being separated from the Beloved (i.e. God).

In some mystic traditions the purpose and end of the pilgrim's search is to become one with God. In the monotheistic tradition of Islam, from which al-Ghazzali does not depart, such a goal is unacceptable and unattainable. The gulf that separates God and Man cannot be bridged. Yet, man is capable of attaining knowledge of God. This knowledge, the striving for which becomes intuitive and experiential (marifa). Through such illumination the gnostic achieves a portion of the divine substance and finds salvation.

This idea, that the greatest bliss in the encounter with God, is not unique to the mystical tradition. It is found both in the Koran and the talmudic tradition of Judaism. Yet, in those sources, the expectation of intuitive knowledge or experience of God's presence is viewed as possible solely in the context of the hereafter. Maimonides, for example, who asserts that knowledge of God is man's prime duty, is dealing with an intellectual phenomenon. When he treats the bliss of Encounter (i.e. the equivalent of marifa) as the reward of the righteous, he is clearly dealing with the rewards of the hereafter. The mystics, al-Ghazzali included, understood this experience to be attainable, through ectasy, in this life. Indeed, it is only through gnosis that man can, in this world, gain a clear and direct image of the life to come.

What function, then, does this world (dunya) serve in al-Ghazzali's concept of salvation?

This world, which he terms the World of the Material and the Evident (*alam al-mulk wa-sh-shahada*), compares to the hereafter, termed the World of the Hidden the Transcendent (*alam al-ghayb wa-l-malakut*), as sleep compares to the waking state. The literal form of a dream cannot yield a knowledge of the true state of things. Truth, however, can be revealed by the proper interpretation of the content or meaning of a dream. Thus, in this world, man is limited in his apprehension of the true state of things in the hereafter by his ability to properly interpret the parables and allegories presented him by prophecy. Man can directly experience and know God only by gnosis. This, however, is also strictly limited. Man, by his very nature, cannot achieve perfect and lasting gnosis in this life. So long as man's state of mortality and knowledge is imperfect, a condition whose inevitability will be treated below, he cannot aspire to salvation, i.e. full knowledge and proximity to God, in this life. Salvation is only to be found in the hereafter.

This world is an antechamber to the hereafter. Al-Ghazzali often makes reference to the tradition which asserts that this world is a field for the cultivation of the hereafter. Man's life in this world plays a preparatory role in which he can assure for himself either salvation or consignment to domination. The possibility of achieving some measure of gnosis in this life allows man a foretaste, as it were, of the saved state in the hereafter. He can then be in a position to appreciate the rewards of the good life.

The relationship between this world and the hereafter is, in al-Ghazzali's thought, much more complex than just an antechamber leading into the great hall. Man, he asserts, will experience nothing new in the hereafter. Man receives, in the hereafter, only as he has provided himself in this world. If man wishes to find salvation in the hereafter, he must struggle to achieve gnosis, salvation's forestate, while still in this ephemeral life. This concept is very similar to the one expressed in the rabbinic dictum which states that only he who has prepared on the eve of the Sabbath will eat on the Sabbath. The parallel is very apt. In the rabbinic tradition, the Sabbath is spoken of as a forestate of the life to come.

It is of interest to note that al-Ghazzali points, in this regard, another parallel between this world and the hereafter. In different contexts he calls his reader's attention to the fact that the Master of both worlds is one and the same and, furthermore, that His order (sunna) is constant. In trying to thus connect this world and the hereafter he is not asserting that both are exactly alike. Such an assertion would be grossly inconsistent with his projections on the nature of the hereafter. He is asserting, however, that there exists of a man's life in this world from what he can expect in the hereafter. Thus, while the nature of man's life in the hereafter is unique, its roots and causes are to be found in his temporal existence.

The last two points explain al-Ghazzali's firm conviction that salvation, i.e. proximity to God, has various degree. It is not an absolute state that one either succeeds or fails to attain. Rather, whatever degree of closeness one attains by means of efforts in the world express the range of salvation. This finds expression, in al-Ghazzali's writings, in the traditional imagery of a multi-levelled Paradise and the different terms that are used to refer to the people of Paradise.

Al-Ghazzali, finally, views this world not merely as a preparation for the hereafter, but as a test. This world (dunya) is the prime cause of sin and, therefore, man's alienation from God. This world is not intrinsically evil but if man begins to live it for its own sake, it will lead him to perdition. For al-Ghazzali all sin can be traced to a man's finding excessive delight in the pleasures of this world. This life should be valued only for its functional use in aiding man to achieve salvation. Al-Ghazzali does not advocate extreme asceticism. Such behaviour, in his view, makes man as much a slave to this world as its opposite. Rather, man must learn to use this world to meet his primary goal and he prepared to renounce that which is neither useful nor desirable to that end. This moderate asceticism should not be confused with the denial that al-Ghazzali prescribes for individual as self-castigation for specific sins. If an individual finds himself so attracted to an aspect of the temporal world that it is leading him to sin, he should renounce it even though, for most men, it would be permissible.

In sum, therefore, this world (dunya) is a preparation for the hereafter. It is a test of man's worthiness and, in fact, a context within which he can gain a foothold on or preclude himself from salvation. Salvation, however, belongs to the hereafter. Only in the hereafter can the success of a man's efforts in this life truly be validated.

Al-Ghazzali sees man as being endowed, as part of his basic nature, with two hostile forces: appetite and intellect. They are not, however, equal or co-temporal. These forces develop progressively as a man grows older. The first to develop are the impulses leading man to desire the delights of this world (dunya). Only later, over a span of some thirty-three years beginning at age seven, does the intellect develop as a control on the appetites. Its function is to limit man's devotion to the mundane and direct him to knowledge of God and, thereby, to salvation.

Al-Ghazzali considers the unbridled pursuit of one's appetites as the basic road to alienation from God, i.e. sin. It follows, then, that with a person's appetites developing before the formation of the intellect, sin is inevitable. Even after the intellect has emerged it requires many years of development before it fully matures. If the appetites are allowed to gain control, the development of the intellect may be stunted and never reach full maturity. In such a case of sin becomes impervious to conquest as well as inevitable. This view of sin's inevitability in man is shared by both later Christianity and Judaism. The view, moreover, that man's moral position is strongly affected by the development of impulses during his early years is reflected in the biblical tradition.

Man's appetites and impulses, according to al-Ghazzali, also develop progressively and sequentially. First, man develops an animal disposition. Then he moves on to a predatory, a satanic, and finally, an egotistic disposition. Each of these stages, separately and in combination, leads man to different traits, and therefore, the tendency to different sins. At the first stage a man might sin by robbery. At the last stage his sin might consist of tyranny over his fellows. Just as a man's intellectual growth may be retarded by the force of his passions, so might his intellect limit the development of sinful tendencies. Al-Ghazzali asserts, therefore, that each person will have a proclivity to different sins.

Al-Ghazzali maintains that man is created with a sound heart (qalb salim). Furthermore, only a person who, at the end of his life, presents himself to God with a sound heart, will be granted salvation in the hereafter. This position seems to indicate that man starts life with salvation assured and must only ensure that he does nothing to forfeit it. Yet al-Ghazzali also asserts that sin is not an act that counters man's natural disposition. Indeed, sin is inevitable. Moreover, in the parable of the conquering kind, the parable by which al-Ghazzali explicated the various states of the hereafter, he has a specific classification for the likes of the feeble-minded and the children; those who are, for various reasons not under their control, beyond obedience or disobedience. al-Ghazzali does not assign them to Paradise. They are not rewarded with salvation, neither are they condemned to hellfire. The sound heart which brings salvation is, for al-Ghazzali, only such as has become pure through refinement. His position that every man is born with a sound heart would seem to indicate his conviction that every man has, in his very nature and constitution, the potential for attaining salvation. Notwithstanding the inevitability of sin, no man is inherently evil. This understanding is consistent with al-Ghazzali's statement at the beginning of the *Book of Repentance* that total evil is not the nature of man but Satan. The nature of man, he asserts there, is to sin but afterward to return to good through sincere repentance. Each man has the potential to return the heart God gave him in trust, refined by his deeds, and thereby be worthy of salvation.

In light of the above it is pertinent to note that al-Ghazzali did not accept the concept of infallibility (isma). In the biographies of the Prophet (sira) and in Koranic exegesis (tafsir) there exists a tendency, much akin to rabbinic Midrash, to create a more perfect personality for the faith's model. This led to a widespread acceptance among the Sunni dogmatists of the concept of prophetic immunity from sin and error. Among the Shia, of course, infallibility was attributed to the imam to a greater degree than to the prophets. In al-Ghazzali's view no man is free of sin, it is part of man's fundamental make-up. Al-Ghazzali, in many of his writings, makes clear is attitude of opposition to this basic aspect of Shi'ism. Furthermore, as regards the Sunni tradition, in discussing the requisite qualities and attributes of the community's leadership he explicitly denies infallibility as a requirement. In fact, al-Ghazzali advocated, for pedagogical purposes, the public discussion of the Prophets' sins and their consequent punishment. All men are fallible but they are also given the potential to overcome the weakness of their nature and achieve salvation.

The ground of sin is the pursuit and love of the mundane world. Such pursuit diverts man from the search for the hereafter and leads to the loss of salvation. The nature of sin is disobedience and its effect is the alienation of man from God. The specifics of any particular act of sinning are important in the process of correction but are almost irrelevant in defining that act as sinful. It is the disobedience to God, in whatever form it is manifested, that removes one from proximity to God.

It has already been noted that man's nature, combining appetites and intellect, make his sinning inevitable but also provides the wherewithal for over-coming the consequences of sin and achieving salvation. This comes through the intellect's gaining control over the appetites. The intellect masters the appetites by gaining knowledge and leading to gnosis. When it fails, totally or partially, it leaves the man with active appetites and ignorance (jahl), and such a state leads inexorably to sin. Knowledge, then, is the key to avoidance of sin.

Belief, according to al-Ghazzali, is of two types. Firstly, there is the belief in God, His attributes and deeds. The belief belongs to the category al-Ghazzali refers to as the Science of Revelation (ilm al-mulashafa). To be lacking in such faith is to be left with sheer unbelief and, therefore, perdition. It is the root of all belief and knowledge without which there can be no other. Secondly, there is the belief, termed faith (iman), in the practical duties and states of a man's heart. This al-Ghazzali refers to under the heading of the Science of Behaviour ('ilm al-mu'amala). This belief is equated, in his writings, with knowledge. If one's belief in the practical sciences is defective, therefore, he is ignorant. Ignorance, again, is the condition that brings man to sin. It follows, then, that a person may indeed sin while being a believer. A defect in the latter belief does not necessitate a defect in the former.

Al-Ghazzali understood, however, as did others in the Christian and Jewish traditions, that sin is an inner process of disease and decay. Continuing sinfulness, which of itself is a defect only in the context of the practical sciences, must, little by little, erode the belief in the science of revelation. Eventually, if sin is left unchecked, the erosion of basic belief will lead of spiritual death, the loss of the heart. If one loses the heart, salvation is precluded. In this context al-Ghazzali is fond of using the parable of the mirror which was originally brought to a high polish (i.e. man is born with a sound heart). If he sins he allows vapour and filth to encrust itself upon the surface of the mirror. If this process is not controlled and reversed the metal becomes so dull as to preclude the possibility of reburnishing. Once the mirror begins to dull it must immediately be cleansed and polished. Thus a man, after sinning, must proceed forth-with to attain the knowledge that counteracts the dulling effect of ignorance and defective faith; if not, the course of the decay will proceed apace. This process of correction is repentance. It emerges from the confrontation between knowledge and ignorance. This is constant and enduring. Thus repentance is a life-long obligation flowing from the imperfection of man.

In pre-Islamic pagan Arabia the Gods were worshipped, with certain centering on public sacrifice, and the morality of the age seems to have had limited religious sanction or relevance. The pagan, insofar as he went beyond the mundane, lived in world filled with magical forces to be propitiated and neutralised. Muhammad, in preaching the message of Islam, cancelled public sacrifice and relegated such ritual to a private and secondary status. He instituted public worship through prayer and taught obedience to God through the fulfilment of the religious commandments. This parallels, to significant degree, a process of change in rabbinic Judaism just before and following the destruction of the second Temple of Jerusalem. In Judaism the sacrificial cult was slowly losing ground to the institution of the synagogue so that, with the destruction of the Temple, a smooth transition to obligatory public prayer was possible. The developments of the later biblical tradition in which the sacrificial practices were increasingly limited by the prophetic call to worship through good works and piety were decisive in the development of both talmudic Judaism and Christianity.

The centrality of the pious life of obedience to the divine commandments was challenged by the proponents of Sufism. The mystics believed that perfection and salvation could be achieved only by the search for knowledge and experience of God. Worship, on its various levels, was to be defined by its utility in the quest for the unitive state. Many of those travelling on the mystic Way developed an indifference to the observance of the commandments. They viewed the commandments, all normative piety, as a lower form of spirituality designed for the uninitiated masses. Al-Ghazzali found this attitude to be fundamentally deficient. Al-Ghazzali sought to inculcate the mystics with an appreciation of the basic importance of obedience to God through the commandments as an ongoing requisite of salvation.

Maimonides, representative in this matter of many medieval thinkers, viewed the religious commandments as a means by which man, through control of his bestial impulses and the discipline of virtue, could perfect himself, morally and intellectually. Having thus perfected himself, man would be prepared for the ultimate knowledge of God. This knowledge, for Maimonides, was philosophical. After attaining to this perfection, the commandments are no longer functional. Al-Ghazzali's position is, to a great extent, parallel. The purpose of the commandments is to help man master his appetites, educate himself in virtuous living, and deepen his religious experience. Al-Ghazzali does not, however, view the intellectual knowledge of God to be the highest objective. Man's goal is knowledge, intuitive and experiential. In this world such experience is only attainable through deeds of obedience. Observance of the commandments, then, lead to knowledge ('ilm). This knowledge further refines his deeds which allow him to experience gnosis (ma'rifa). Man's nature, furthermore, is such that there are always forces working to dull the surface of his heart. The result, for the pilgrim (salik), is a continuous need for further commitment to the pursuit of obedience through the observance of the commandments. Moreover, the higher a man is able to reach in his knowledge, the more he is able to infuse his observance with depth of intent. In the 'way of the hereafter' the proper observance of the commandments requires the combination of knowledge and action ('ilm wa-'amal). The process creates a spiral of expanding knowledge leading to deeper observance which, in turn, brings man to greater knowledge. Clearly al-Ghazzali was addressing himself to both the shallow religiosity of the mechanically pious and rootless spirituality of the libertine mystics.

During the early formative years of classical Islam there emerged a number of debates whose development and resolution were decisive in forming the body of doctrine that became accepted as orthodox. Among these was the debate over the individual and communal consequences of sin. The Koran indicates that sin leads man to hellfire. The questions that arose in this context concerned which sins or types of sin are those that result in damnation and, following such a determination, what status does such a sinner have within the community of believers.

The Koran differentiates, as to punishment or forgiveness, between two categories of sin: grave (kabira) and minor (saghira). This can be seen in the verse: If you avoid the heinous sins that are forbidden you we will acquit you or your evil deeds and admit you by the gate of honour. Thus it follows that minor sin does not, of itself, carry the punishment of hellfire. The people of Hell are those who commit grave sins. The ensuing debate concerned itself, then, with the immediate and ultimate disposition of such as commit sins considered grave

The Khariji sectarians believed, to use Watt's terminology, in the 'charismatic community. Salvation was tied into membership in the community of believers which alone was the source of the people of Paradise. Moreover, salvation was seen as dependent on the integrity of the community. A person who committed a grave sin was, therefore, to be excited from the community. Such a man is an unbeliever and of the people of Hell. These people, posing a threat to the salvation of the entire community, must be fought, killed if necessary. There were, however, variations within the Khariji movement. The Azariqa, for example, were extreme in the application of this principle. They never succeeded in forming large or stable communities and were constantly in armed conflict with the established political and social order. The Najdiyya, however, did succeed in establishing their own political unit. The practical demands of government were, no doubt, responsible for a more moderate approach. They asserted that isolated instances of sin did not make one an unbeliever or threaten the salvation of the community. Such a threat only followed persistent grave violations. In any case, all the Khariji factions held the position that grave sin was unbelief and its consequence was eternal punishment.

The Mu'tazila, like most other Islamic groups, did not concur in this attitude toward a salvational community. They held that one who commits a grave sin is neither, believer or an unbeliever. Rather, he occupies an intermediate position (manzila bayna 'l-manzilatayn). Their outlook, as with most other early Islamic theologies, was more individualistic. They did concur with the Khariji, however, that the consequence of grave sin is eternal punishment.

A third group, important for the emergence of the orthodox view, was the Murjia. They believed that the status of the grave sinner, both as to his being a believer and his ultimate fate, were matters that could not be judged by men. They are questions best left for God at Judgement. Man should, to be considered a believer in this temporal setting, make the profession of faith. This latter consideration evokes the question of the relative importance, as regards man's ultimate disposition, of faith versus works.

The orthodox position, as articulated by al-Ash'ari and his school, posits that all unbelievers will be assigned to eternal damnation. Those attaining the status of believer, however, have done so as a result of their profession of faith and not as a result of their works. If a man has faith, if he accepts the Islamic creed, he will gain entrance to Paradise. The Ash'ari schools did not ignore the effects of sin. Indeed, man may be purged in the fires of Hell for a time. Ultimately, however, all who profess the faith will be saved.

Al-Ghazzali's position is very close to that of the Ash'ari school. He does, however, refine this position in light of his understanding of both belief and sin. Polytheism (shirk), which is unbelief in the sphere of the revealed sciences, precludes pardon and condemns the unbeliever to perdition, eternally. If, on the other hand, a person is a believer he is assured of salvation. If a man commits a sin, a defect in the practical sciences, he is punished with hellfire for a time. Only the sound heart is accepted by God. If the surface of the heart is dirtied, it must be cleansed by fire. After death the only fire is that of Hell. In such a case the function of hellfire is purgative. After the heart is restored to its purity, entrance to some level of Paradise is effected. In this there is no real variation from the Ashari doctrine. However, al-Ghazzali's understanding of sin, as previously expounded, is much more sophisticated. It is difficult for a man to continue in sin without an erosion of his belief in the revealed sciences. There is an intimate relationship, that of root and branch, between the areas known as faith and works. It is difficult for al-Ghazzali to envision a man persisting unrepentant in sin and remaining uncorrupted in faith. These two are not easily divisible.

Furthermore, while profession of faith is sufficient to preclude exclusion from the community and temporal punishment as an unbeliever, al-Ghazzali is emphatic that ultimately it is of no avail if it is merely verbal. Al-Ghazzali believes that it is beyond human competence to judge the sincerity or veracity of another's profession of faith. Also, he does not believe that a man's faith can, in this life, be confirmed or denied by his sins. All of these judgments are beyond human ken. God, however, will indeed make these judgments.

Al-Ghazzali does not consider the community as the basic reference for or source of salvation. In line with the Koran, al-Ghazzali is committed to an individualistic approach. Each man stands for judgment as an individual. Also, each person's struggle for salvation must be based on his own strength and weaknesses as an individual. Al-Ghazzali, as Islam in general, does not present an institutionalised atonement procedure as might be found in Judaism and Christianity. Public confession is neither required or encouraged except in the case of social offense. Indeed, since sin is derived from the pursuit of the appetites, the specific development of which varies from individual to individual, the quest for integrity of faith and works must differ from one person to another. The covenantal relationship in Islam is between the individual Muslim and God.

In rejecting the community as the source of salvation al-Ghazzali does not lose sight of the societal environment in which man lived out his temporal life. Ignorance, for example, can only be removed by the spread of knowledge. As God entrusted the people's education to the prophets, so it falls to the lot of the learned doctors, the prophets heirs, to continue this work. Yet, in terms of ultimate responsibility each learned doctor will be judged as an individual, as will his charges. His communal work is a personal obligation imposed by his level of knowledge or appointed position. That all men have social responsibilities for which they are answerable to God is attested to by the fact that injustices against one's fellows are also transgressions against God and are breaches of the belief in the practical sciences. The community is not the source of salvation but rather it is, by divine will and command, an area of responsibility in which man can pursue either obedience or disobedience.

There is another interesting element in al-Ghazzali's treatment of sin. Sins, according to al-Ghazzali, may be measured in two ways: objectively or subjectively. Objective assessment may be made by recourse to the Law. Yet, this alone would be insufficient. Al-Ghazzali insists that the measurement of a sin must take into account the spiritual level (i.e. knowledge and perception) of the sinner. The transgression of an ignoramus is not the same violation as the identical infraction perpetrated by a learned doctor. Incidentally, the social or communal stature of the sinner, as well as the attendant publicity of the sin, are also important variables. The learned doctor, for example, is a model whose public actions will be emulated. A sin he commits publicly could lead others to sin. He would then be doubly culpable.

In discussing the division of sins into those grave and those minor, al-Ghazzali has recourse to a number of different standards based on the legal tradition. He is able, finally, to indicate that some sins are definitely known as being grave, others as minor, while some are in doubt. Yet, in continuing his analysis he introduces a subjective element asserting that a minor sin may become grave notwithstanding its status according to the objective sources of tradition through a person's persistence or faulty attitude.

A determination of sin is based on a code of morality whose violation is an offence against God. The Mu'tazila conceived of an autonomous morality which followed from rational premises. Al-Ghazzali rejects this conception out of hand. It is evident from the aforementioned that, for al-Ghazzali, the ethical is secondary to the religious. Revelation is the sole source of morality. The basis of that morality is God's command. Sin is no more and no less than rebellion against God. This does not mean that reason has no function in al-Ghazzali's system. To the contrary, even the sciences of the hereafter are categorised by him as rational sciences. Nonetheless, al-Ghazzali is insistent that morality is revelatory.

Salvation, then, is to be found in proximity to and experience of God the Beloved. It is a constant state attainable only in the hereafter. It must, however, be cultivated in the life which is proving ground of man's worthiness. Sin, the disobedience to God, leads directly to man's alienation from God. If the sin is in the sphere of the practical sciences, it is debilitating. If, on the other hand, it ends as a defect in the revealed sciences, it becomes damning. Man can, however, enhance his knowledge of God, intellectual and intuitive, by continued and ever more intensified observance of the divine commandments.

One of the most fundamental and contested issues in the formative years after the establishment of Islam was that of defining the implications of the Prophet's assertion of God's omnipotence. An early and most basic question that emerged from this issue pertained to a determination of man's basic nature as regards violation. Does man act as a free agent or are his actions predetermined by God?

The Khariji movement, influenced to no small degree by their political philosophy and goals, were among the earliest advocates of the free will position. They were followed in this by the Mu'tazila. On the other extreme were many in the traditionalist camp who, feeling that the assertion of human freedom impinged upon the absoluteness of God's omnipotence, upheld a position of pure and total determinism.

Al-Ashari, reflecting the orthodox position, affirmed the determinists position while adding that man was nonetheless responsible for his actions. He explained that God creates all of the component elements that lead to an action and then man chooses the act into which he is compelled. While the act is totally of God's creation, man acquires it (kasab, iktisab). This formulation is quite obscure, proverbially so. Yet it is clearly an attempt to reaffirm God's absolute freedom while preventing fatalistic indifference to proper moral behaviour. Man's subjective feeling of choice is given formal status while, at the same time, there is a recognition of God's acting out His will through men. This conception is foreign to Jewish thought as it is, in general, to Christianity. There does, however, exist a similar idea in the New Testament.

This conception is echoed by al-Ghazzali. Man, he says, is compelled into that choice which is his. He goes to great length to show how God creates the various sequential elements that lead man into acting in a predetermined manner. Yet, al-Ghazzali also promotes ideas that do not seem to harmonise with this position. The very idea of repentance implies man's ability to choose and act upon that choice. In fact, al-Ghazzali asserts that the ability to turn from evil and correct one's mistakes is a fundamental characteristic of human nature. Al-Ghazzali, moreover, states that God does not require of man more than that of which he is capable. If so, God's commanding man presupposes his ability and volition. Finally, al-Ghazzali often emphasises the ability of all men, at least potentially, to raise themselves to the ranks of the saints, prophets, and angels.

The basic paradox inherent in the various writings of al-Ghazzali on this subject is explicitly rendered in his presentation of the parable of the blond men and the elephant. In this parable of buddhist origin, al-Ghazzali tells of a group of blind men who examine, by touch, different parts of an elephant in order to ascertain its nature. Each man, having felt a different part of the animal, describes it differently. All of the men spoke truthfully, yet none of them was able to encompass, in his description, the totality of the animal. Thus, says al-Ghazzali, those who take the positions of determinism, acquisition (kasb), and free will, have each stated a part of the truth but, if taken singly as embracing the totality, each position is only a distortion of reality.

Al-Ghazzali, the teacher and spiritual physician, had, it seems, a basic functional commitment to the position that man has the ability to make choices and act freely. He also understood that creation's order, as well as man's previous actions, limit his freedom. The elements requisite for any choice must also exist. Moreover, al-Ghazzali no doubt felt the need, as did some of those who preceded him (e.g. al-Ash'ari), to protect the theological integrity of God's omnipotence. Man is required to understand that nothing can be accomplished, even for the gnostic ('arif), without divine grace. Yet as dependent as man is on God, he is not simply a vessel or automation. He does, in a real sense, have the ability to exercise choice (ikhtiyar).

Man, especially such as for whom al-Ghazzali wrote the *Revival*, should be left with the mystery and paradox unresolved. It was, for him, mystery in pursuit of which the unenlightened would stumble and which the illumined are forbidden to reveal.

The debate about man's free volition was intimately tied to two other issues: Order and Justice. Does there exist, in God's creation, ordered causality? Do defined causes beget constant and predictable results? Most of the early Muslim theologians, in the context of their attitudes on the question of God's omnipotence, were atomistic in their view of the world. There does not exist a potence, were atomistic in their view of the world. There does not exist a necessary cause-effect relationship. Rather, each moment is a fresh creation and an expression of divine will. If man stands witness to the fact that a particular cause has always resulted in the same effect, he cannot, with certainty, project this as having a bearing on the next instance of that cause.

Al-Ghazzali rejects this position. Happiness or misery in the hereafter are directly attributable to man's actions, good or bad. In fact, this causal relationship can be reduced to the lowest measurable degree. The scales of judgment are tipped to salvation or perdition even by weight of an atom. His previously cited parable of the conquering king is eloquent testimony to this belief in causality. Each man's station in the hereafter, as in the newly conquered territory, is defined directly by the measure of his service or disservice. Again, in a different context, al-Ghazzali indicated that a person's fate is decided, in the minutest detail, by the quantity, quality, duration, and intensity of his faith and works. This is not an insignificant statement of fact. The acceptance of the reality of this causal order was, in his view, the very foundation of the belief in the divine origin of the commandments and the revelation *shar'*).

This causal order does not relate to the hereafter alone. Remaining in the moral sphere, al-Ghazzali also viewed the struggle for moral correction to be a natural outcome of the maturation of the intellect. If the intellect is allowed to develop, it will naturally confront the appetites and induce man to repentance. According to Obermann, moreover, al-Ghazzali feels that acceptance of repentance is necessary in the sense that the very act of repentance results, causally, in the effect of acceptance (i.e., purification of the heart).

Al-Ghazzali, in treating the ideas of Mercy and Wrath, makes it clear that the causal order is not always manifest to man. At times, says he, a man will be granted salvation or condemned to hellfire when all the apparent causes point to a different disposition. The condemnation of an apparently righeous man or the saving of an evil one would argue, one might think, for a lack of order and causality. Al-Ghazzali, however, emphatically asserts that there is always a cause even, as in such a case, if it be hidden and secret. These hidden causes (asbab hafiya), however, that result in mercy or wrath are not comprehensible through the rational science. While there exists a causal order, it is God's order (sunna) and as such it is comprehensible only through revelation.

The other issue was that of Justice. There is order in creation, can this order be termed equitable? The Mutazila held, as one of their two most basic propositions, that it was part of the very nature of God that He be just and, according to some of their theorists, act in man's best interests. Thus they could speak of justice as being an obligation of God. Al-Ashari was convinced, no doubt, of God's being equitable. This concern is probably one of the motives for his struggling with man's responsibility in the face of the doctrine of determinism. Yet, he could not reconcile the idea of obligation with God's omnipotence, a concept that assumes absolute freedom of will.

Al-Ghazzali follows and elaborated al-Ash'ari's position. Is God just? His response is a resounding affirmative. God does not reward evil or punish obedience. Man's actions are requited with absolute equity. There exists almost infinite variety, among men, in the quantity and quality of their obedience or disobedience. God, then, prepares innumerable levels both in Paradise and Hell. A man's fate is measured according to his faith and works. These are, therefore, examined even to the measure of an atom. If a man realises genuine repentance it will surely be accepted. Even in the working of the mysterious elements of mercy and wrath al-Ghazzali explicitly insists on their being just. Can this justice, which is clearly an absolute, he termed an obligation or a necessity? Here al-Ghazzali responds with an emphatic negative. Justice, in his view, is a part of God's order and practice (sunna). This order is itself an act of God's will, He could have willed otherwise. Being a part of His order, however, it is not wholly comprehensible to man except insofar as God wills it to be son. The dimension of justice must also be one in which, for man, mystery remains a part.

All in all, these basic theological issues: salvation, the nature of man, the nature and consequence of sin, and Free Will, are the keys by which to properly understand the place of Repentance in al-Ghazzali's conception, he did not place high value on theology and theological peculation as such. On the contrary, he perceived theological speculation as a grave danger to the spiritual well-being of the believer and most theologians as part of the 'vulgus', albeit more articulate than most. As explicated above, authentic religious truth can be secured only intuitively through the experience of gnosis. Reliance on theology could, therefore, act so as to obscure these truths and preclude their apprehension.

There is, according to al-Ghazzali's view, input that is productive for all believers, no matter their state. This constitutes the nutriments required for the support and furtherance of their religious quest.

Others are merely remedies, correctives for particular weaknesses or maladies, the indiscriminate utilisation of which could actually prove destructive. Theology falls into this latter category. Its development and use, nonetheless, are important, and positively valued, insofar as they are functional in treating malaise among Muslims.

To understand his general approach and his rejection of theology, while appreciating his sophisticated knowledge and use of theological principles, it is necessary to note al-Ghazzali's own penitential 'conversion' and the insights it afforded him.

When al-Ghazzali's mentor al-Juwayni died in 1085, he joined the entourage of the Seljuq vizier Nizam al-Mulk. He remained with the vizier until Nizam appointed him to a professorship at the Baghdad Nizamiyya college in July of 1091. He continued in his professorship for four years until his spiritual crisis led to his resignation and withdrawal from public life in 1095.

Al-Ghazzali, in the semi-autobiographical *Deliverance*, describes his un-relenting search for certainty and truth. This quest, to which al-Ghazzali attributes his crisis, brought him to study the four major intellectual and spiritual approaches of his day: theology, philosophy, Isma'ili authoritarian instruction (ta'lim) and sufism. Yet, a critical analysis of his work and behaviour must lead to the conclusion that his crisis, and therefore his conversion, needs be viewed as personal, immediate and non-academic.

What caused the eruption of his crisis? Authoritarian instruction does not seem to have been an acceptable personal option. When he refers to it, he is totally polemical. Sufism, on the other hand, was not a new experience. The family friend, in whose care he had been placed as a child, was himself a sufi. Rather, al-Ghazzali's crisis flowed from his increasing disenchantment with his colleagues in Baghdad. They were not the great religious models he had thought them to be. In his view, they were not the great religious models he had thought them to be. In his view, they were using their scholarship to further worldly ambitions. In all probability al-

Ghazzali became alarmed because, seeing himself falling into that same state, he became increasingly uncertain of his salvation. This uncertainty, coupled with a feeling of personal worthlessness, caused a progressive functional breakdown until al-Ghazzali finally resolved to withdraw from public life and follow the sufi Way in search of personal salvation. That there were other factors, political ones among them, which encouraged his departure from Baghdad is not to be discounted. Yet, they can only have been secondary. In all probability the other factors were decisive only in highlighting for him the worldliness of his status.

Al-Ghazzali spent the next ten years in retirement. Part of the time was spent in Syria, some on pilgrimage, and it seems, some in Baghdad itself. He returned to teaching, however, at the Nizamiyya college of Nishapur in 1106.

He later went into semi-retirement in Tus where he established a small circle among whom he taught.

His undertaking of renewed public duties is indicative of the direction in which his penitential search led him. The answer to his previous worldliness was not in withdrawal but rather in reorientation, and in a way, intensification of his pedagogical work. His sensitivity to the responsibility of the 'ulama' class brought him to the realisation that a 'return' on his part necessitated him working towards a general return, and therefore, a revival of the religious sciences.

While theology as a discipline and methodology (kalam) was, to al-Ghazzali's mind, vulgar, the malaise of his generation required its judicial use by such, as himself, who would function as spiritual physicians. Just as his own back-ground in the study of theology helped prepare him to embark, with Repentance as the first (and continuing) stage, on the quest for personal salvation, so also could it be used, medicinally, to treat the weaknesses of his contemporaries. Al-Ghazzali's theological principles, therefore, are of no mean importance in understanding his concept, treatment and valuation of Repentance.

REFERENCES

1. Al-Ghazzali, Ihya Ulum ad-din, Cairo, n.d.
2. Maimonides, Yad Ha Hazaqa: Mishna Torah, Jerusalem, 1955.
3. S M Watt, Muslim intellectual: A study of al-Ghazzali, Edinburgh, 1971.
4. Al-Ghazzali, "The beginning of guidance", The faith and practice of al-Ghazzali: Translated, by W M Watt, London, 1953.

Revised and edited; originally published in Islamic Quarterly.

16

Az-Zamakhshari and Al-Baydawi: On Reason and Revelation

KUTPI IBRAHIM

The aim of this article is to investigate the relation of reason and revelation in az-Zamakhshari and al-Baydawi. Topics discussed include the question of good and evil, the nature of the karamat of the saints, and God's giving of sustenance.

The problem of the relation between Reason (*'aql*) and Revelation (*shari'a*) is the point of conflict between the Mu'tazilites and the Ash'arites in pursuing the knowledge of God (*ma'rifat Allah*), since "knowledge" in the Mu'tazilite view means "rational insight religion."

The question at issue now is whether knowledge of God becomes incumbent upon man as soon as he acquires a mature-capacity (*mukallaf*) for reasoning; or whether it becomes incumbent upon him only after a messenger has been sent to his community to inform it of all that is necessary for a man to know. To this, az-Zamakhshari supports the former, saying that the knowledge of God is obligatory upon man since he is a rational being. He maintains that Reason is a guide to the truth and capable of comprehending the knowledge of God. Therefore, Reason, in accordance with az-Zamakhshari, is self-sufficient in making the knowledge necessary. However, it is implied that the "sending of the prophets" is not necessary since Reason alone can grasp what is there to be grasped intellectually (i.e., the knowledge of God). So what is the purpose of sending the prophets? To find out the answer let us examine az-Zamakhshari's viewpoint concerning the following Qur'anic verses:

'17: 15' "We never punish until We have sent a messenger." (*Wa ma kunna mu'adhdhibina hatta nab'atha rasulan*).

Az-Zamakhshari says that the purpose of "sending the prophets" was to remind people of what they had forgotten about the necessity of reflection (*nazar*). This verse, however, has little implication for az-Zamakhshari, in denying the occurrence of divine punishment before the coming of the law, since he states that, "Even if God does not send the prophet, it is till incumbent upon man to believe in God and His unity," because Reason has the potentiality to know Him through His sign '64 : 10'. "But those who disbelieve and deny Our signs (*ayati-na*) are the inmates of the fire, they will abide therein—a hapless journey's end." Another reason for the sending of the prophets, according to az-Zamakhshari', is as a refutation to disbelievers' presupposed argument against God after the messengers. The more extreme views of az-Zamakhshari regarding Reason can be seen from his interpretation of the verse '3 : 50'. "I come unto you with signs from your Lord" that the prophets themselves deduced the truthfulness of their message through Reason in which God created for them signs leading them to know their own message. According to az-Zamakhshari, Reason can even conceive the need of repenting the sin even though it was committed by the unbeliever, but Revelation restricts it to the believer only. The tradition, the consensus and the analogy, however, should come after the proofs of Reason (*adillat al-'aql*).

Az-Zamakhshari's main emphasis as far as Reason is concerned is that Reason has the potentiality to know the creator of this world even though there is no Revelation. And his view that the "sending of the prophets was to remind their people" cannot be considered as of secondary importance to Reason since the two are inevitably relevant to each other, because the performance of the orders of the *shari'a* such as *as-salat* (the prayer), according to him, is dependent upon *iman*. By *iman*, he means Revelation.

Perhaps what he means by reflection (*nazar*) is to know the creator of this universe grossly. If a man dies without hearing about the messenger and consequently has not believed in God, according to az-Zamakhshari, he will be punished because in his lifetime there has been the condition necessitating *imam*, and that condition is Reason.

Another question is, "what is the value of *iman* based merely on the authority of others rather than on reasoning and logical proof, such as the common people who were not trained at all in reasoning and the art of dialectics?"

Before going any further it is, perhaps, relevant to quote the important passage from al-Baghdadi concerning the Mu'tazilite views on the belief in the authority of others:

The Mu'tazilites are divided on this point. Those who consider knowledge as being of a primary nature say that he who believes the truth, believing it as something axiomatic, and not marring this condition by mortal sins is faithful. If such a one should, however, mar his condition by mortal sins, he would be *fasiq*, that is, neither faithful nor infidel. Whoever believes the truth, but does not regard it as something of a primary nature, is under no obligation to believe. Those Mu'tazilites, however, who way that knowledge regarding Allah, His books and His Apostle, is knowledge acquired by reasoning and deduction, are of different opinions concerning him who believes the truth on the authority of others. Some way that he is *fasiq*, according to them, is neither faithful nor infidel. Others say that he is an infidel, whose repentance is invalid through his neglect of one of his legal obligations.

As far as *taqlid* is concerned, az-Zamakhshari, however, is in opposition to it since from the very beginning he emphasises that reason is capable of comprehending the knowledge of God. In strengthening his view, he alludes to the Qur'anic verse '20:16': "Let none bar thee from it, that believes not in it but follows after his own caprice, or thou wilt perish," saying that the destruction (*al-halak*) and the peril are always due to *taqlid* and its followers. Az-Zamakhshari, however, conceives that not all people can avoid the *taqlid*. By this he means that *taqlid*, to some extent, is permissible. For instance, he opposes the *muqallid* who does not know what he does '17:36' "(O man), Follow not that whereof thou hast no knowledge." For az-Zamakhshari, a *muqallid* is obliged to some extent to use his reason (i.e., to know whom he follows) in order to follow the right *'alim (al-alim al-muhtadi*).

As an advocate of al-Ash'ari, al-Baydawi, however, maintains that the knowledge of God is made obligatory by Revelation or the divine law. The obligatory nature of the knowledge of God, al-Baydawi asserts, has nothing to do with Reason. The most important proof-text for al-Baydawi is the verse '17:15', "We never punish until We have sent a messenger." This verse evidently denies the occurrence of divine punishment before the coming of the law. Al-Baydawi argues that as far as this verse is concerned, there can be no obligation at all before God's sending a messenger and before the prophetic call reaches people's ears.

Concerning the Qur'anic verse '4:165', al-Baydawi in strong opposition to az-Zamakhshari, says that the sending of the prophet is necessary (*darura*) since Reason has insufficient potentiality to know God, (i.e., especially the native belief of the common people). Therefore, the sending of the prophets, according to al-Baydawi, is a completion of God's Revelation since obligatoriness is based solely on the evidence of divine words.

Al-Baydawi emphasises that the prophets did not know the truthfulness of their message except through Revelation. For al-Baydawi, this Quranic verse '52:52', "Thou (Muhammad) knewest not what the scripture was, nor what the faith" provides strong proof to criticise az-Zamakhshair's argument that the prophets knew their message by means of Reason. A question arises that if the prophets themselves, according to al-Baydawi, did not testify their message except through Revelation, what about the common folk? Did they know God before the "sending of the prophet" through Reason?

According to al-Ash'ari, he who believes the truth on the authority of others (*taqlidan*) is neither a polytheist nor an infidel. Yet al-Ash'ari does not in general apply the qualification "faithful" to such a one, and his doctrine compels him to admit that the sins of such a one may be forgiven, since he is neither a polytheist nor an infidel.

Al-Baydawi maintains that the belief in the authority of others is not permissible for a *mukallaf* who is capable of reflection (*nazar*) '7:36', but he does not consider the *mukallaf* who follows a prophet or a *mujtahid* as *muqallid.* In fact, he calls him the "follower of what was been revealed. It is very clear that al-Baydawi does not wholly share al-Ash'ari's view, since he affirmatively declares that the following of the right *alim* is permissible.

Good, evil and the best

As we already know, the problem of reason and revelation is one of the most persistent problems in theological discussion between the Mu'tazilites and the Ash'arites, since the opinions differ as to the right precedence of the criterion of reason and revelation.

According to the Mu'tazilites, reason is the criterion of good and evil. God is good. He is all-wise. The wise can only do what is best for His servants. Therefore, evil (*qabih*) cannot be the negation of His wisdom, since the existence of it (i.e., evil) is incompatible with a God who is at once omnipotent and benevolent.

Az-Zamakhshari is in line with the view held by the majority of the Mu'-tazilites when he says that a thing is good or bad in itself (*qabihun aw hasanun bi dhitihi*) through the judgment of reason. For instance, to fill up the measure (*al-mizan*) is good, while to decrease it unjustly is bad according to reason. Similarly, lying (*al-kidhb*) is also bad in itself as even the unbelievers realised who did not know the law *shari'a.*

Even the goodness of God is judged by the same standard as that of men. He maintains that God's deeds (*af'al Allah*) are all good and wise, even if there are some aspects of the goodness still hidden to human intellect. Az-Zamakhshari alludes to the Qur'anic verse '2:30-31:' "He said surely I know that which ye know not.

And He taught Adam all the names." God does not will polytheism (*ash-shirk*) and disobedience (*al-ma'sia*). In contrast, He encourages them to do good things (*jamiliha*).

As regards evil *(al-qabih)*, az-Zamakhshari maintains that God did not even will evil acts, it was only the Mujbirites who attributed such acts to God." He interprets the Qur'anic verse '7:180' ".... and leave those who blaspheme His names...." by saying leave those who attribute the evil acts to God alone", since it is inadmissible for God to do any act of evil *(li yajuzu 'alay-hi l-qabih)*. The inadmissibility of Him to do such an act is due to His having no inventive (*ad-da'i*).

Taklif (The imposition of duty)

Does God impose some responsibility on man in consideration of the principle of good and evil?

In order to avoid attributing of evil to God, az-Zamakhshari, like other Mu'tazilites, maintains that God does not impose duty on man beyond his capacity. He bases his view on the Qur'anic verses such as '50:29': "I wrong not my servants." Of course, for az-Zamakhshari, God's praising Himself that He can do no evil, would be useless if He imposed duty on man beyond his capacity. Another point given by az-Zamakhshari refers to the Qur'anic verse '16:90' "Surely Allah bids to justice and good doing..." in which he maintains that contained in the justice of God is the non-imposition of duty beyond His servants' capacity (*fawqa taqatihim*).

As regards "the best," az-Zamakhshari in defending his Mu'tazilite view, maintains that God would not do anything for His servants but the best. He alludes to some Qur'anic verses as follows:

I '16:9' "And Allah is the direction of the way (*wa'ala-llahi qasdu s-sabil*), and some (roads) go not straight (*wa min-ha ja'irun*). And had He willed He would have led you all aright."

Az-Zamakhshari says that the direction of the way leading to the truth is necessary for God. He clarifies the passage by citing '92:12'. "Lo! Ours it is (to give) the guidance (*huda*)."

Az-Zamakhshari places emphasis on the words *wa min-hl ji'irun*. A question arises, why did God not say *wa' alayhi ja'irun*? In answer to this, az-Zamakhshari states that such words are to declare that the way that is not straight should not be attributed to God. If it were true, as the Mujbirites said, he continues, God would say *wa'aly-ha ja'irun*. As far as the proof-text is concerned, az-Zamakhshari seems to have considered himself in this respect as a victory against the Mujbirites. Furthermore, he interprets the verse, "And had He willed He would have led you all aright" as meaning "by force" *(qasran)*, but God did not will to do so, since He granted them "free will" to distinguish between the right and the wrong as clearly stated in the verse. Therefore, God does only what is good for His servants.

II "21:23' "He will not be questioned as to that which He doeth, but they will be questioned." (*La ysu'alu `amma yaf `alu wa hum yus'alun*).

As far as this verse is concerned, az-Zamakhshari tries to draw out attention to every-day life. He says that if it is customary not to question kings concerning their rules even if they do injustice (*fasad*), God the Almighty would not be questioned as to that which He does. It is especially conceivable that His deeds are reasonable (*ma'qul*) and are motivated by His wisdom (*al-hikma*). Therefore, any mistake or act of evil cannot be attributed to Him.

III '64:2' "He it is who created you, but one of you is a disbeliever and one of you is a believer." (*Huwa-lladhi khalaqa-kum fa-min-kum kafirun wa min-kum mu'minun*).

Az-Zamakhshari maintains that human beings are the authors of their unbelief (*al-kufr*) and their being unbelievers should not be attributed to God, since He is the wise, the knower of all evils, then all His deeds should be considered good. Therefore, His creation the the author of evil should be considered good and even if the aspect of goodness still cannot be conceived by human intellect, yet it does not impair His goodness. In order to make it clear, az-Zamakhshari sets forth an example by saying that "Likewise our ignorance of knowing God's motivation in creating some beautiful creatures, does not impair their goodness."

IV '91:7-8' "By the soul, and that which shaped it and inspired it to lewdness and Godfearing!" (*Wa nafsin wa ma sawwa-ha fa-alhama-ha fujura-ha wa taqwa-ha*).

Az-Zamakhshari states that the right and the wrong have been inspired (*alhama*) by God. so it is up to Reason to distinguish between the two, and choose willingly. In supporting his view, he refers to the Qur'anic verses '91: 9-10' "Prosperous is he who purifies it, (*qad aftaha man zakka-ha*), and failed has he who seduces it" (*wa qad khaba man dassa-ha*). He says that Reason is the cause of growth or the stunting of it, not God. The basis of his argument is that the "doer" (*al-fa'il*) in "*zakka-ha* and *dassa-ha*" is Reason (*al-'aql*) not God. Furthermore, he says that only the Mujbirites attributed such a thing a God who is the exalted.

According to the Ash'arites, Revelation is the criterion of good and evil. Reward and punishment are only the consequences of God's being well pleased or displeased.

Al-Baydawi maintains that a thing is good or bad when it is proved by law (*shari'a*) and not judged by Reason.

As regard the *taklif*, al-Baydawi maintains that God can impose duty on man beyond his capacity (*taklif ma la yutaq*). He bases this view on the second part of the Qur'anic verse '2:285' "... our lord, do Thou not burden us beyond what we have the strength to bear." He says that if *taklif* is inadmissible, the invocation (*du'a*) in the verse would be useless, while in his interpretation of the first part of the verse "Allah charges no soul save its capacity" he maintains that God will not impose the *taklif* on man beyond his capacity, although He could.

Judging from his two statements, al-Baydawi tries to balance his view between the attributing of evil to God by means of imposing duty on man beyond his capacity and the "rationale" of the *taklif* itself as understood by az-Zamakhshari.

Al-Baydawi strongly attack az-Zamakhshari's view regarding "the best" (*al-islah*) by saying '16:9' that it is not necessary for God to guide people to the right way (*tariq mustaqim*). If He does so, it is a mere grace (*fahl*) and mercy (*rahma*) from Hi, because if He had willed, He would have guided them collectively to the right way. Al-Baydawi argues that it is God's unwillingness that made them disbelieve, and not any misuse of their Reason. Therefore, God is not bound to do what "is best."

As far as verse '21:23' is concerned, al-Baydawi says that God will not be questioned as to what He does because He is almighty and is the sole agent of power. Hence, He can do what He wills even if the act involves evil (i.e., the creation of unbelief). For al-Baydawi, it seems that good and evil are relevant only to human acts and cannot be attributed to God whether the consequence of His deed is good or not for His creatures since He will not be questioned about what He does.

Concerning the Qur'anic verse '64:2', al-Baydawi believes that God already created human being whether disbelievers or not. If God willed some-one to be a believer, He would have created something which would lead him to become a believer and so on. Therefore, the principle of "the best" according to al-Baydawi, remains as no obligation to God.

As regards verse '91:7-8', al-Baydawi, however, maintains that the inspiration of the wrong (*fujur*), and right (*taqwa*) is dependent upon Revelation, not Reason, since the "doer" (*al-fa'il*) in the said verses refers to God, while az-Zamakhshari believes that it should refer to Reason.

In the light of the above arguments between az-Zamakhshari and al-Baydawi, it can be concluded that az-Zamakhshari, who was a supporter of the Mu'tazilites, believes that human reason is capable of knowing the *hasan* and the *qabih* without the assistance of any prophetic revelation. In order to correspond to this principle, az-Zamakhshari has to say that God is bound to do what is best to human beings. Goodness, according to az-Zamakhshari, is a real quality inherent in things which are rationally known to be good. Similarly badness is a quality that is inherent in things which are rationally known to be bad. Al-Baydawi, however, believes that goodness and badness are determined things (i.e., by God). Furthermore, the goodness or badness of a thing is not a real quality of things inherent in them but a function of the divine will. Therefore, the principle of "the best" has no place in al-Baydawi's theology.

Sustenance (rizq)

As far as "sustenance" is concerned, az-Zamakhshari maintains that God would not produce an "unlawful sustenance," since He attributes the *rizq* to Himself, and it is only that sort of thing (i.e., lawful sustenance) which is called "sustenance." `2:3' "... and spend of what We have bestowed upon them." Az-Zamakhshari argues that God has granted everyone his own "sustenance" including food, drink, etc., in the right way so that sustenance can only be called "lawful sustenance." Az-Zamakhshari's argument, therefore, is taken to imply that God can grant no "unlawful sustenance.' It is very clear that az-Zamakhshari's strong defence that only "lawful sustenance" can be attributed to God, is to avoid attributing evil things to Him science He is the wise, and the wise always does what is best. On the other hand, his treatment of the subject is rather peculiar, which can be seen through his interpretation of the verse `11:6' "And there is not a beast in the earth but the sustenance thereof dependeth on Allay" (*ala-llahi rizquha*).

The obvious meaning of the verse is that it is necessary for God to sustain His servants. Az-Zamakhshari, however, tries to explain the text by saying that the words "*ala-llahi rizquha*" mean a "grace" from God. Having assured that He would sustain them gracefully, however, it became obligatory (*wajiban*) as when someone makes a vow. Of course, its obligatory nature, according to az-

Zamakhshari, is due to His promise that He would sustain them gracefully, since God is truthful, az-Zamakhshari argues, He will fulfil His promise.

Al-Baydawi, however, maintains that "sustenance" can be both lawful and unlawful sustenance, since it is God who sustains them both. God's attribution of sustenance to Himself, does not mean that only the lawful ones can be considered as "sustenance." Moreover, he says that the attributing of sustenance to God is merely for exaltation (*ta'zim*), and encouraging people towards "charity". As far as the verse `11:3' is concerned, al-Baydawi admits that the sustenance is taken to mean "lawful sustenance" because God admires it. Thus what really concerns al-Baydawi is not verse itself, but the concept of *rizq* in general applied to both the "lawful" and the "unlawful sustenance." He alludes to a prophetic tradition saying that "God has sustained you by what is good (*tayyiban*), then you have chosen what has been prohibited by God from His *rizq* in place of what has been made lawful to you."

Al-Baydawi argues that if it were not called *rizq* (sustenance), the consumer in the whose of his life, would not also be called "on sustained" (*ghayra marzuqin*), since God said `11:6' "And there is not a beast in the earth but the sustenance thereof dependeth on Allah." For al-Baydawi as far as *rizq* is concerned, there is nobody who will escape from being sustained by God whether the *rizq* is lawful or not.

More evidence given by al-Baydawi is that '5:88' "Eat of that which Allah has bestowed on you as food lawful (*halalan*) and good (*tayyiban*).

Al-Baydawi says that if the *rizq* does not imply "unlawful" (*al-haram*) the mention of the word *halalan* (lawful) in the verse would be useless.

The miracles of the saints (karamat)

In fact, the Mu'tazilites strongly oppose the view that the

karama is possible for the saints (*awliya'*). They say that if the *karama* is granted, it will be confusing to distinguish between the prophets and the non-prophets. On the other hand, *karama* is against the natural course of things, and no human being can cause any disorder in the course of nature; while the Ash'arites affirmatively maintain that the *karama* is possible for the *awliya* since it is not meant to silence opponents. Therefore it is quite different from the *mu'jiza* as the *mu'jiza* sought to silence opponents, and it was usually faced with opposition (*tahadda*) and *da'wa* (claim). On the other hand, for the Ash'arites, *karama* is a favour from God which He can bestow on the *awliya.*

In order to investigate az-Zamakhshari's view regarding the *karama*, we had better refer to his interpretation of some Qur'anic verses related to this point:

I '3:42' "And when the angels said: O Mary! Lo! God has chosen thee and made thee pure, and has preferred thee above (all) the women of creation."

Az-Zamakhshari places emphasis on the incident which took place between the angel and Mary. He says that the incident was the result of Zachariah's miracle or the sign foretelling the prophecy of Jesus, and not Mary's *karama.*

II '3:37' "Whenever Zachariah went into the sanctuary where she was, he found that she had food. He said: O Mary! Whence cometh unto thee this (food)? She answered: It is from God. God giveth without stint to whom He will."

As far as this verse is concerned, az-Zamakhshari tried to explain away the verse, and left it without referring to whether or not the food which came to Mary was a result of her miracle or Zachariah's.

III '72:26, 27' "He is the knower of the unseen, and He revealeth unto none His secret, save unto every messenger (*rasul*) whom He hath chosen, and then He maketh a guard to go before him, and a guard behind him."

Commenting on this verse, az-Zamakhshari, however, emphasises the words "Save unto every messenger whom He hath chosen" (*illa man irtada min rasul*). He points out that though the saints were chosen by God, yet they were not His messengers. Therefore, they are excluded from the obvious meaning of the verse. Moreover, he says that this verse was to repudiate the miracles of the saints, since they were not the messengers of God, and God gives the miracles only to His messengers.

In order to make it clear, az-Zamakhshari proceeds to give us an example by saying that this verse is also to repudiate the divination (*al-kahana*) and the astrology (*at-tanjim*). The reason for God's repudiation, according to az-Zamakhshari, is that both the diviner and the astrologer have not been granted the sanction of God (*al-irtida'*), instead, they are subject to the wrath of God.

Al-Baydawi, in agreement with the Ash'arites concerning the miracles of the saints, maintains that the *karama* is possible for the saints.

Concerning the Qur'anic verse '3:42', al-Baydawi maintains that the angels "talking to Mary fact to face" was the result of her *karama* and not Zachariah's miracle as claimed by az-Zamakhshari. However, he asserts that the *karama* is not impossible for the saints.

Al-Baydawi's criticism regarding the Qur'anic verses '3:37' is obvious. He says that the verse itself, however, is indicative of the possibility of *karama* for the saints.

Al-Baydawo, in his interpretation of the Qur'anic verse '72:26-27', strongly repudiates az-Zamakhshari's view. He points out that the word *rasul* (messenger) in the verse means the angel (*al-malak*), and not the prophet as claimed by az-Zamakhshari. On the other hand, he argues that the significance of using the words "*illa man irtada min rasul*" is to show that there is no intermediary (*bi-ghayri wastin*) between God and the angels if He has chosen them to know the unseen (*al-ghayb*). In order to make his view clear, he states that the *karama* of the saints on the unseen *(al-mughayyabat)* is through the intermediary of the angels. Likewise, out knowledge of the eschatological matters, he continues, is dependent no the intermediary of the prophet. Inevitably al-Baydawi's interpretation of the word *rasul* to mean the angel, however, implies that the *karama* is not impossible for anyone who has been chosen by God even though he is not a prophet.

Concluding Remarks

Concerning Reason and Revelation, as-Zamakhshari maintains that the knowledge of God is made obligatory upon man by Reason without the assistance of Revelation, since Reason is self-sufficient, a guide to the truth. The coming of the prophets, in accordance with az-Zamakhshari, is only to remind people of what they have forgotten about the necessity of Reflection, while al-Baydawi opposes this view, saying that the knowledge of God is made obligatory by Revelation. The obligatory nature of the knowledge of God has nothing to do with Reason, since the verse '17:15' evidently denies the occurrence of divine punishment before the coming of the prophetic call. Therefore, the sending of the prophets, according to al-Baydawi, is a completion of God's revelation.

Az-Zamakhshari's view that human reason is capably of knowing the right and the wrong, leads him to believe that God is bound to do what is best for man. Goodness and badness are real qualities inherent in things which are rationally known to be good or bad. Al-Baydawi, however, rejects the principle of "the best" and considers that the goodness or badness of a thing is not a real quality inherent in them, but a function of the divine will.

Az-Zamakhshair's view that God would not produce "unlawful sustenance' since God has attributed the *rizq* to Himself, is criticised by al-Baydawi who maintains that God's attribution of *rizq* to Himself is for glorification. Further-more, al-Baydawi argues that if it were not called *rizq*, the consumer would not be called "one sustained" at any time in his life.

The basis of az-Zamakhshari's denial of the miracles of the

saints refers to his interpretation of the word *rasul* in the verse '72:27-27,' in which he interprets it as meaning "messenger," therefore, the miracle is only for the prophets. Al-Baydawi, on the other hand, interprets it as angel (*malak*); hence, it implies than the *karama* is not impossible for anyone who has been chosen by God, even though he is not a prophet. Therefore, the *karama* based on al-Baydawi's argument is also possible for the saints.

REFERENCES

1. az-Zamaksshari, Jar-Allh Mahmud b. Umar, al-Kashshaf an-Haqaiq ghawamid at-tanzil wa uyun al-aqwal fi wujuh at-tawil, Cairo, 1307 AH.
2. az-Zamakhshari, ATwaq adh-dhahab fi mawaiz wal kitab, Cairo, 1328.
3. al-Baghdadi, Usul ad-din, Istanbul, 1346.
4. al-Baydawi, Anwar at-tanzil wa asrar at-tawil. Cairo, n.d.,

Revised and edited; originally published in Islamic Quarterly.

Bibliography

The Ka'ba, Maj. Al-Mushir, (May 1966), pp. 10-11. Moslem sermons preached in constantinople, Hibbert J., 8 (1910), pp. 641-660.

Religious freedom in Egypt, MW, 20 (1930), pp. 344-351. Can Islam be reformed The Turkish answer, MW, 16 (1926), pp. 238-252.

"ZAKIR" Concept of "adl" or justice of God as a cardinal principle of Islam, Alserat, 5 i (1979), pp. 25-31.

The works of Professor Uriel Heyd, Asian and Afr. Studs., 5 (1969), pp. 203-207.

Abstracta islamica. 27 serie. pp. 158, REI, 41 (1973).

The Omani manuscript collection at Muscat. Part I. A general description of the MSS., G.R. Smith; Part 2, The early Ibadi figh works, Arabian Studies, 4 (1978), pp. 161-191-208.

Abstracta Islamica 31e serie 1977, REI, 45 (1977), pp. 289-370.

Summary of a report on a conference on Arabic documents held at the University of Ghana. 26 and 27th February, 1965, Research Bull. Ibadan, 1 iii (1965), pp. 8-25.

A list of academic periodicals published in the Sudan, Sudan Notes and Records, 43 (1962), pp. 158-160.

Obituary. Dr. Mohammad Shafi, Islamic Studies, 2 (1963), pp. 141-142.

Department of Manuscripts. Acquisitions, January to June 1963, BMQ, 27 (1963), pp. 116-117.

A chronological list of J. Cassar Publicino's contributions, Maltese Folklore R., 1 (1962-1963), pp. 81-84.

"Voprosy istoril" and "Middle Eastern Studies", MES, 2 (1965), pp. 94-96.

Social Science periodicals dealing with the Middle East, Int. Soc. Sci. Bull., 5 (1933), pp. 762-765.

Lull's Mission and Message, MW, 22 (1932), pp. 1-4.

Gibb Mss. in Glasgow University Library, Trans. Glasgow Or. Soc., 6 (1929-33), p. 29.

Some libraries of Cairo, MW, 28 (1938), pp. 223-230.

Forough Farrokhzad: the bitter loss, Iranian Stud., 1 (1968), pp. 52-53.

In appreciation of Dr. Edwin E. Carverley, MW, 57 (1967), pp. 178-185.

Draft report: International Seminar and Exposition of manuscripts. Kabul July 31-August 4, 1967., Afghanistan, 30 iii 91967), pp. 91-96.

ABBERRY, A.J.

The book of knowledge, IQ, 11 (1967), pp. 123-128.

ABBOTT, N.

Maghribi koran Mss. of the 17th to the 18th centuries (in the private collection of Dr. and Mrs. Paul Hudson, Ohio State Univ.), AJSL, 55 (1938), pp. 61-65.

ABD-AL-HAMID, and ALI, Abd Ar-Raziq.

Mohammed of the newspapers, MW, 18 (1928), pp. 167-172.

ABDURRABB Subhani.

A daring utterance of Abu Yazid Al-Bistami, J. Reg. Cult. Inst., 5i(1972), pp. 19-36.

ABUSHANAB, R.E.

Two philosophically-oriented theologians. Al-Ghazali and St. Bonaventure, Miscellanea Francescana, 75 (1975), pp. 883-892.

ADAMS, C.

Islamic religion (Part I), MESA Bull., 4iii (1970), pp. 1-15; 5i (1971), pp. 9-25.

ADAMS, C.C.

Mohammed Abdul, the reformer, MW, 19 (1929), pp. 264-273.

ADAMS, C.C.

Sanusis, MW, 36 (1946), pp. 21-45.

ADATIA, A.K. and KING, N.Q.

Some East African Firmans of H.H. Aga Khan III, J. rel. Africa, 2 (1969), pp. 179-191.

AFFIFI, Hussain el-Tiby.

The attributes of 'Allah' - in the verses of the Quran, Majallat al-Azhar, 44ii (1972), pp. 7-16.

AFFIFY, Hussain el-Tiby.

The attributes of 'Allah', Majallat al-Azhar, 44i(1972), pp. 15-16.

AFSHAR, I.

The present state of Iranian studies in Iran., Abr-nahrain, 12 (1971-72), pp. 6-14.

AFSHAR, Iraj.

Iranian studies, J.Reg.Cult.Inst., 3(nos. 11-12, 1970), pp. 135-142.

AGWANI, M.S.

Religion and politics in Islamic theory and practice, Islam and the modern age, 2i (1971), pp. 45-62.

AHMED, Jamal M.

Islam in the context of contemporary socio-relgious thought of Africa, Al-Abhath, 20ii (1967), pp. 1-36.

AHMED, Manzooruddin.

Key political concepts in the Quran, Islamic stud., 10 (1971), pp. 77-102.

AHMED, Ziauddin.

Socio economic values of Islam, and their significance and

relevance to the present day world, Islamic stud., 10 (1971), pp. 343-355.

AITKEN, B.M.W.

Some impressions of books and publishing in the Middle East, RCAJ, 53 (1966), pp. 158-165.

AKBARABADI, Sa'id Ahmed.

Contribution of India to Arabic language and literature since independence, India and the Arab World, ed. by S. Maqbul Ahmed, 1969, pp. 24-28.

ALAIE, M.

The apperception of Islamic culture, Ann.Fac.Arts Ain Shame, 7(1962), pp. 85-113.

ALAWI, Anwar Ahmad.

The Jizyah or the Cpitation Tax, J. Pakistan Hist. Soc., 16(1968), pp. 182-189.

ALBRIGHT, W.F.

Islam & the religious of the ancient drient, JAOS, 60 (1940), pp. 283-301.

ALEXANDER, G.

Story of the Kaba, MW, 28 (1938), pp. 43-53.

ALI, Abdul Mukti.

Some consideration of spread of Islam in Indonesia, Proc. 9th Int. Cong. Hist. Rel., 1958, pp. 209-217.

ALI, Muhammad Basharat.

The place of religious experience in the formation and development of Islamic society, personality and culture, Pakistan Philos. J., 5 (1962), pp. 45-60.

ALI, Sayyid Rizwan.

Two great contemporaries of thirtenth century A.D.: Sultan al-Ulma al-Izz Ibn al-Salam and Ibn 'Arabi, IC, 45(1971), pp. 192-201.

ALWAYE, A.M. Mohiaddin.

The sixth conference of Islamic Research Academy of Al-Azhar

[Cairo - 1971], Majallat al-Ashar, 43iii(1971), pp.1-6.

ALWAYE, A.M. Mohiaddin.
Religion and the moral development of man, Majallat al-Azhar, 43v(1971), pp. 1-7.

ALWAYE, A.M. Mohiaddin.
Faith and moral qualities, Majallat al-Azhar, 43iv(1971), pp. 1-5.

ALWAYE, A.M. Mohiaddin.
The Holy Quran describes le commentaire coranique de Fakhr al-Din Al-Razi, Etudes philos. et litt., 3(1968), pp. 11-24.

ALWAYE, A.M. Mohiaddin.
The Holy Quran describes qualities of true believers, Majallat al-Azhar, 43ii(1971)), pp. 1-4.

ALWAYE, A.M. Mohiaddin.
The significance of 'Hijrah', Majallat al-Azhar, 43i(1971), pp. 1-4.

ALWAYE, A.M. Mohiaddin.
The role of "Hajj" strenghening equality and freternity among mankind, Maj. al-Azhar, 42 x (1970), pp. 1-5.

ALWAYE, A.M. Mohisddin.
The missionof Prophet Muhammad, Maj. al-Azhar, (June 1968), pp. 1-4.

ALWAYE, A.M. Mohisddin.
The Holy Qur'an - eternal guidance suited to all times and climes, Maj. al-Azhar, 42 ix (1970), pp. 1-5.

ALWAYE, Mohiaddin.
The principles of equality in Islam, Majallat al-Azhar, 44ii (1972), pp. 1-6.

ALWAYE, Mohiaddin.
Islam and human civilization, Majallat al-Azhar, 43ix(1971), pp. 1-3.

ALWAYE, Mohiaddin.
Islam - the religion of knowledge and wisdom, Majallat al-Azhar, 43vi(1971), pp. 1-6.

ALWAYE, Mohiaddin.
Who is the most honourable is the sight of God, Majallat al-Azhar, 43viii(1971), pp. 1-4.

ALWAYE, Mohiaddin.
The effect of Quranic moral qualities on the life of man, Majallat al-Azhar, 43viii(1970), pp. 1-5.

ALWAYE, Mohiaddin.
The duties of believers towards God - in verses from the Quran, Majallat al-Azhar, 42viii(1970), pp. 5-8.

ALWAYE, Mohiaddin.
Fasting in Islam, Ma-jallat al-Azhar, 43vii(1971), pp. 1-6.

ALWAYE, Mohiaddin.
The role of 'Hijrah' in the spread of Islam, Majallat al-Azhar, 44i(1972), pp. 1-4.

ALWAYE, Mohiaddin.
Why Makka is chosen for Hajj, Majallat al-Azhar, 43x(1971), pp. 1-4.

AMEDROZ, H.F.
Notes on some sufi lines, JRAS, (1912), pp. 551-586, 1087-1089.

AMEER, Ali.
Impressions of christianity from the points of view of non-christian religious. (iii) christianity from the Islamic standpoint, Hibbert J., 4 (1906), pp. 241-259.

AMIJI, Hatim M.
Some notes on religious dissent in nineteenth-century East Africa, Afr. Hist. Stud., 4(1971), pp. 603-616.

ANDRAE, T.
Muhammad's doctrine of revelation, MW, 23 (1933), pp. 252-171.

ANSARI, Raschid.
Eid Al-Adha (The sacrificial feast), Maj. al-Azhar, (March 1967), pp. 8-10.

ANWARULHAG,M.

The Dini Da'wat (Religious call), Proc. 27th Int. Cong. Or. 1967, (1971), pp. 397-398.

ARBERRY, A.J.

Mawaif of at-Niffari, JRAS, (1930), pp. 404-406.

ARBERRY, A.J.

Notes on the mahasin al-majalis of Ibn al-Arif, BSOAS, 12 (1948), pp. 524-532.

ARBERRY, A.J.

Two rare manuscripts, J. Arabic Lit., 1 (1970), pp. 109-116.

ARNALDEZ, R.

Trouvailles philosophiques dans le commentaire coranique de Fakhar Al-Din Al-Razi, Etudes philos. et litt., 3(1968), pp. 11-24.

ARNOLD, Sir. T.W.

The study of Arabic, BSOAS, 1 (1917), pp. 112-121.

ARRERRY, A.J.

Al-Khatib on traditionists, IQ, 14 (1970), pp. 19-21.

ASKARI, Hasan.

Modernity and faith, IMA, liii(1970), pp. 39-48.

AUSTIN, R.W.J.

Counsels of a Sufi Master, Studs. in compar. relig., 5(1971), pp. 207-214.

AVON, Earl of.

Obituary: The Earl of Scarbrougn, JRAS, (1970), p. 96.

AYOUB, Mohmoud.

The martyr of Karbala, Alserat, 4 iv (1978), pp. 3-17, 44.

AZAD, Moulana Abul Kalam.

Importance of Surat-ul-Fatiha, Majallat al-Azhar, 43ii(1971), pp.14-16.

BADSHAH, Hussain A.F.

English sliah koran commentary, MW, 19 (1929), pp. 31-40.

BAIG, M. Safdar Ali.

Sufism in Persian poetry, Indo-Iranica, 23iv(1970), pp. 15-24.

BAKKER,D.
Sin & grace in Mohammadanian, MW, 6 (1916), pp. 394-400.

BALL, J.
Schweinfurth and the cartography of Egypt, Bull. Soc. Geog. Egypte, 14 (1926-27), pp. 139-144.

BARAKAT, Soliman.
Thanksgiving and patience, Maj. al-Azhar, (Jan. 1967), pp. 13-16.

BARCLAY, H.B.
The parpetuation of Muslim tradition in the Canadian north, MW, 59 (1969), pp. 64-73.

BARNETT, L.D.
Oriental Mss, BMQ, 4 (1929), pp. 8-9.

BARNETT, L.D.
Recent acquisitions of oriental Mss, BMQ, 4 (1930), pp. 112-113.

BARNETT, L.D.
Gift of oriental Mss, BMQ, 3 (1929), pp. 105-106.

BARNETT, L.D.
Newly acquired Arabic Ms, BMQ, 3 (1928), pp. 71-72.

BARNETT, L.D.
Some oriental Mss, BMQ, 8 (1934), pp. 138-139.

BARNETT, L.D.
Treasure of Rubies, BMQ, 6 (1931-32), pp. 96-97.

BARNETT, L.D.
Persian & Arabic Mss., BMQ, 6 (1931-32), pp. 78-79.

BARNETT, L.D.
Persian poetical Mss., BMQ, 9 (1934), pp. 20-21.

BARNETT, L.D.
Oriental Mss & printed books, BMQ, 6 (1931-32), pp. 55-56.

BARNETT, L.D.
Early Arabic grammer, BMQ, 10 (1935), pp. 30-31.

BARNETT, L.D.
Illustrated Divan of Khatai F., BMQ, 8 (1933), pp. 13.

BARNETT, L.D.
A Ms. of the Dastur i Ushshak, BMQ, 7 (1932-33), p. 27.

BARNETT, L.D.
Oriental Mss., BMQ, 10 (1935-36).

BECKA, J.
Jan Rypka: Czechoslovak Iranist and Turkologist, 28th June 1886-29th December 1968, Arch. Or., 37 (1969), pp. 309-317.

BECKINGHAM, C.F.
Hakluyt's description of the Hajj, Arabian Studies, 4 (1978), pp. 75-80.

BEDDIE, J.S.
Some notices of books in the East in the period of the crusades, Speculum, 8 (1933), pp. 240-242.

BELL, R.
Muhammad & divorce in the Quran, MW, 29 (1939), pp. 55-62.

BELL, R.
Muhammad's pilgrimage proclamation, JRAS, (1937), pp. 233-244.

BELL, R.
Who were the Hanifs, MW, 20 (1930), pp. 120-124.

BELL, R.
Duplicate in the Koran the composition of surah XXIII, MW, 18 (1928), pp. 227-233.

BENTWICH, N.
Oriental studies at the Hebrew University of Jerusalem, Indian Art and Letters, N.S. 17 (1943), pp. 20-23.

BERNUS, M.
In memorian Henri Masse., BAEO, 6(1970), pp. 12-13.

BERSON, A.
The Muslim Republics of the U.S.S.R., RCAJ, 48 (1961), pp. 56-66, 253-262.

BIJLEFELD, W.A.

A prophet and more than a prophet? Some observations on the Qur'anic use of the termn 'prophet' and 'apostle', MW, 59 (1969), pp. 1-28.

BIRGE, J.K.

Turkish translations of the Koran, MW, 28 (1938), pp. 394-399.

BIRGE, J.K.

Printing of books in Turkey in the 18th century, MW, 33 (1943), pp. 292-294.

BISHAI, W.B.

A possible Coptic source for a Quranic text, JAOS, 91(1971), pp. 125-128.

BISHOP, E.F.F.

Shubhiha lahum: A suggestion from the New Testment (Surahiv, 156, 157), MW, 30 (1940), pp. 67-75.

BISHOP, E.F.F.

Forty - (two) traditions of an-Nawawi, MW, 29 (1939), pp. 163-177.

BISHOP, E.F.F.

From criticism & the forty-two tradition of an-Nawawi, MW, 30 (1940), pp. 253-261.

BLACK, M.

Paul Ernst Kahle, 1875-1965, Proc. Brit. Acad., 51 (1965), pp. 485-495.

BLACKWOOD, P.

Viewes of a Chinese Moslem, MW, 26 (1936), pp. 68-78.

BLASDELL, R.A.

Use of the drum for Mosque services, MW, 30 (1940), pp. 41-45.

BLASDETI, R.A.

Muslim attitude toward, sin, MW, 28 (1938), pp. 272-278.

BOARDMAN, F.

Recent AUB publications on economic research, MEJ, 15 (1961), pp. 329-353.

BOSWORTH, C.E.

Manuscripts of Tha'alibi's Yatimat ad-dahr in the Sulleymaniye Library, Istanbul, JSS, 16(1971), pp. 41-49.

BOTHAM, O.M.

Moslem womenof China, MW, 16 (1926), pp. 172-175; 28 (1938), pp. 360-364.

BOUSQUET, G.H.

Islam in the balkans, MW, 27 (1937), pp. 65-71.

BOWMAN, J.

British museum Arabic eschatological fragment, MW, 38 (1948), pp. 198-217.

BOYD, E.I.M.

Ricoldus a dominion missionary to Muslms in the 13th century, MW, 8 (1918), pp. 45-51.

BRADLEY, Julia.

A Sufi approach, Theoria to theory, 12 (1978), pp. 229-236.

BRAVMANN, M.M.

The phrase in Kuntum fa'ilina in Surat Yusuf, v.10, Islam, 48(1971), pp. 122-125.

BRAVMANN, M.M.

Allah's liberty to punish or to forgive, Der Islam, 47(1971), pp. 236-237.

BREASTED, J.H.

Oriental Institute of the University of Chicago, AJSL, 35 (1918-19), pp. 196-204.

BREASTED, J.H.

Place of near orient in the career of man and the tsak of American orientalist, JAOS, 39 (1919), pp. 159-184.

BREASTED, J.H.

Oriental institute of the University of Chicago - a beginning & a program, AJSL, 38 (1921-22), pp. 233-328.

BRETSCHNEIDER, E.

Chinese medieval notices of Islam, MW, 19 (1929), pp. 52-61.

BRONSTEIN, L.
Some laistonical problems raised by a group of Iranian Islamic potteries, Bull. Am. Inst. Iran Art, 5 (1938), pp. 225-235.

BROOMFIELD, G.
Psychology of Mohammed, MW, 16 (1926), pp. 37-58.

BROWN, K., ROLLMAN, W.J. and WATERBURY, J.
Research facilities in Morocco, MESA Bull., 4iii (1970), pp. 55-67.

BROWNE, E.G.
Further notes on the literature of the Hirrafis and theri connection with the Bektashi order of dervishes, JRAS, (1907), pp. 533-581.

BROWNE, E.G.
Persian Mss of the late Sir Albert Houtum-Schindler KCIE (now in Cambridge), JRAS, (1917), pp. 657-694.

BROWNE, L.E.
Religious in Turkey, today & tomorrow, MW, 19 (1929), pp. 14-24.

BRUNSCHVIG, R.
Joseph Schacht, SI, 31 (1970), pp. v-ix.

BURGBY, J.H.
Moslems in London, MW, 28 (1938), pp. 76-79.

BURGESS, J.
Orientation of mosques, JRAS, (1906), pp. 454-458.

BURKE, E.
III Recent books on colonial Algerian history, ME studies, 7(1971), pp. 241-250.

BYKL, A.R. and SPRENGLING, M.
Hebraes - sufic poem, AJSL, 46 (1929-30), pp. 203-204.

C.N.
Short bibliography of books on Iran published in 1963, Persica I, (1963-1964), pp. 86-87.

CALVERLY, E.D.
Doctrins of the soul (Nafs & Ruh) in Islam, MW, 33 (1943), pp. 254-264.

CALVERLY, E.E.

Fundamental structure of Islam, MW, 29 (1939), pp. 364-384.

CARTER, T.F.

Islam as a barrier to printing, MW, 33 (1943), pp. 213-216.

CHANDRA Dilip.

Islam in modern Indonesia. A historical survey of its social and political role in Indonesia, Islam and the modern age, 2iv(1971), pp. 96-108.

CHEIKHO, L.

Some moslem opocryphal legends, MW, 2 (1912), pp. 47-59.

CHITTICK, W.C.

The last will and testment of Ibn 'Arabia's foremost disciple and some notes on its author, Alserat, 5 i (1979), pp. 32-44.

CLEMONS, J.T.

some oriental manuscripts in the Friedsam Library of St. Bonaventure University, Oriens Christianus, 51 (1967), pp. 101-105.

COOKE, E.T.

Ibn at Qaiyim's kitab-al-Ruh, MW, 25 (1935), pp. 129-144.

CORBIN, H.

Le theme de la resurrection chez molla sadra Shirazi (1050/1640), commentateur de Sohrawardi (587/1191), Studies in mysticism and religion presented to G.G. Scholem, (1967), pp. 71-115.

CORKE, F.T.

Sins & their punishment in Islam, MW, 28 (1938), pp. 272-278.

COURY, M.

Further notes on research facilities in the U.A.R., MESA Bull., 5ii(1971), pp. 92-94.

CRABITES, P.

Is Turkey a Mohammedan Country?, MW, 20 (1930), pp. 125-137.

CRAGG, K.

Contance K. Padwick, 1886-1968, MW, 59 (1969), pp. 29-39.

DAFTRY, Farhad.

Bibliography of the publications of the late W. Ivanov, IC, 45(1971), pp. 55-67.

DANI, A.H.

Personalities in archaeology: Dro Muhammad Abdullah Chaghatai, Ancient Pakistan, 2 (1965-66), pp. 215-219.

DANIEL, N.

Charateristics of institutional learning in the Middle Age exemplified in the study of Islam, REI, 44 (1976), pp. 273-285.

DARBISHIRE, R.S.

Christian idea of Islam in the Middle Ages, according to the "Chanson d' Antioch", MW, 28 (1938), pp. 114-124.

DATTA, Kali Kinkar.

Acharya Jadunath Sarkar and the Indian Historical Records Commission., Indo-Iranica, 24i-ii(1971), pp. 16-19.

DAVIS, A.R.

Some implications of the Hayter Report, JOS Australia, 2i(1963), pp. 2-6.

DAVIS, G.

Sufism: From its origins to al-ghazzali, MW, 38 (1948), pp. 241-256.

DESSOUKI, Ali.

Towards a comparative study of experiences. Christian and Islamic experiences, Islam and the modern age, 2i i (1971), pp. 49-56. Directory of films on the Middle East.
MESA Bull., 6ii (1972), pp. 44-45.

DMITRIJEV, N.K.

V.D. smirnov: A memoir, JRAS, (1928), pp. 408-410.

DOI, A.R.I.

The Yoruba Mahdi, J. religion in Africa, 4(1971), pp. 175-176.

DOI, A.R.I.

The reconstruction of some Islamic institutions in the twentieth century, Orita, 1 i (1967), pp. 27-36.

DONALDSON, B.A.
Belief in Jinn among the Persians, MW, 20 (1930), pp. 185-195.

DONALDSON, D.
Al-Kumait. A companion of the secret, MW, 28 (1938), pp. 249-257.

DONALDSON, D.M.
Requirements of the common people, MW, 30 (1940), pp. 358-374.

DONALDSON, D.M.
Salaman the Persian, MW, 19 (1929), pp. 338-352.

DONALDSON, D.M.
Truth & falsehood in Islam, MW, 33 (1943), pp. 276-85.

DOUGLAS, E.H.
Edwin Elliott Calverley. October 26, 1882-April 21,, 1971., MW, 61(1971), pp. 155-160.

DOUGLES, E.H.
Al-Shadhili, a North African Sufi, according to al-Sabbagh, MW, 38 (1948), pp. 257-279.

DUNLOP, D.M.
Another "Prophetic" letter, JRAS, (1940), pp. 54-60.

DVOICHENKO-MARKOFF, E.
Nicholas Iorga, a giant of Southeastern Europe, Byzantion, 17 (1944-45), pp. 423-430.

DZIERZYKRAY-ROGALSKI, T.
Scientific activities of the Research Centre of Human Ecology in Arica, Africana Bull., 7 (1967), pp. 115-122.

EDWARDS, E.
Greenfields gift of oriental Mss, BMQ, 2 (1927), pp. 76-77.

EDWARDS, E.
Divan of Zu L-Fakar, BMQ, 2 (1927), pp. 20-22.

EDWARDS, E.
Two Persian Mss, BMQ, 8 (1934), pp. 102-103.

EDWARDS, E.
Manuscript of works of Karim al-Anvar, BMQ, 8 (1933), pp. 16-17.

ELDER, E.E.
Conception of university in early Islam, MW, 17 (1927), pp. 11-30.

ELDER, E.E.
Development of the Muslim doctrine of sius & their forgiveness, MW, 29 (1939), pp. 178-188.

ELDER, J.
Family life in shiab Islam, MW, 18 (1928), pp. 250-255.

ELIASH, J.
On the genesis and development of the Twelver-Shi'i three-tenet Shahadah, Der Islam, 47(1971), pp. 265-272.

ELIASH, J.
The si'ite Qurah. A reconsideration of Goldziher's interpretation, Arabica, 16 (1969), pp. 15-24.

EVANS, H.
Soviet writing on Central Asia, RCAJ, 50 (1963), pp. 50-59, 175-184.

EVANS, H.
New Soviet books, Middle Eastern Studies, 1 (1965), pp. 382-387.

EVANS, H.
New Soviet books, Middle Eastern Studies, 1 (1965), pp. 203-207.

EVANS, H.
New Soviet books, Middle Eastern Studies, 2 (1965), pp. 73-78.

EVANS-PRITCHARD, E.E.
Aereditary succession of Shakhs of Sanuriya lodges in Cyrenaica, Man, 46 (1946), pp. 58-62.

EVANS-PRITCHARD, E.E.
Select bibliography of writings on Cyrenaica, African studies, 4

(1945), pp. 146-150; 5 (1946), pp. 189-194; 8 (1949), pp. 62-65.

FAROUK, Abdullah.
Dr. Abdus Sadeque, JAS Pak., 6 (1961), pp. 275-276.

FARRIS, N.A. and GLIDDEN, H.
Development of the meaning of Koranic hanif, JPOS, 19 (1939), pp. 1-13.

FEDERICH, R.E. and JOHNSON, D.M.
Writing of H.W. Bailey (books and articles), BSOAS, 33 (1970), pp. ix-xiv.

FIELD, C.H.A.
Christ in Mohammadan tradition, MW, 1 (1911), pp. 68-73.

FINKEL, J.
Risala of al-Jahiz, JAOS, 37 (1927), pp. 311-334.

First death anniversary of the Founder Dr. M. Ishaque.
Indo-Iranica, 23iii(1970), pp. 39-43.

FISCHEL, W.J.
The Hebrew University and the Middle Eastl Jewish scholars on Mount Scopus throw light on Arabic learning and on the speech and ways of the fews of the Orient, Bibliotheca Orientlis, (1919), pp. 129-132.

FISCHEL, W.J.
William Popper (1874-1963) and his contribution to Islamic scholarship, JAOS, 84 (1964), pp. 213-220.

FOSTER, F.H.
Autobiography of Mohammed, MW, 26 (1936), pp. 130-152.

FRANK, R.M.
Several fundamental assumptions of the Basra School of the Mu'tazila, SI, 33(1971), pp. 5-18.

FRANKE, A.H.
Islam among the Tibetans, MW, 19 (1929), pp. 134-140.

FRAYHA, Anis.
New Yezidi texts from Beled Sinjar, Iraq, JAOS, 66 (1946), pp. 18-43.

FRIEDLAENDER, I.

Hetero doxies of the shiites in the presentation of Ibn Aazm, JAOS, 28 (1907), pp. 1-80; 29 (1908), pp. 1-183.

FRYE, (R.N.).

A note on the Andarz Name, JAOS, 77 (1957), p. 48.

FRYE, R.N.

Oriental studies in Turkey during the war, JAOS, 65 (1945), pp. 204-.

FRYE, R.N.

Oriental studies in Afghanistan, JAOS, 64 (1944), pp. 144-145.

FRYE, R.N.

Notes on Islamic studies in the USSR during the war. (lst. St. in Turkey during the war), MW, 36 (1946), pp. 69-75.

FRYE, R.N.

Orientalia in Germany & Scandinavia, JAOS, 67 (1947), pp. 139-141.

FULTON, A.S.

Thomas Hunter Weir, Glasgow Univ. Or. Soc. Trans., 20 (1963-4), pp. 1-9.

FULTON, A.S.

Unique Ms. of the Amali of Ibn al-Shajari, BMQ, 8 (1933), pp. 15-16.

FULTON, A.S.

Two Arabic Mss., BMQ, 11 (1937), pp. 83-85; 12 (1938), pp. 90-91.

FULTON, A.S.

Arabic medieval Mss., BMQ, 11 (1937), pp. 81-83.

FULTON, A.S.

Obituary notice. Alexander George Ellis, JRAS, (1942), pp. 153-154.

FYZEE, A.A.

W. Ivanow (1886-1970), Indo-Iranica, 23iii(1970), pp. 22-27.

GABRIELI, F.
Apology for orientalism, Diogenes, 50 (1965), pp. 128-136.

GAIRDNER, W.H.T.
Mohammadan tradition & the gospel record, MW, 5 (1915), pp. 349-379.

GAIRDNER, W.H.T.
Studes of Islamics at Cairo, MW, 12 (1922), pp. 390-393.

GANICHEFF, I.
Islamin Bulgaria, MW, 16 (1926), pp. 158-160.

GARBARRI, C.
Statistical survey of Islam, MW, 27 (1937), pp. 273-293.

GEDDES, C.L.
The geographical and other works of Guy Le Strange, Islamic Studies, 4 (1965), pp. 213-218.

GEIJBELS, M.
The process of Islamisation in Pakistan, Al-Mushir, 21 ii (1979), pp. 31-51.

GEIJBELS, M.
Pakistan, Islamisation and the Christian community. Part two: The status and calling of Christians, Al-Mushir, 22 iii (1980), pp. 100-116.

GEIJBELS, M.
Islamin Pakistan, Al-Mushir, 18 (1976), pp. 147-152.

GEYOUSHI, Muhammad Ibrahim el-.
The pilgrimage (Hajj) and its significance, Majallat al-Azhar, 43x(1971), pp. 5-8.

GEYOUSHI, Muhammad Ibraheem.
Al-Tirmidh's theory of saints and sainthood, IQ, 15(1971), pp. 17-61.

GIBB, H.A.R.
The heritage of Islam in the modern world (III), IJMES, 2(1971), pp. 129-147.

GIBB, H.A.R.
Structure of religions thought in Islam, MW, 38 (1948), pp. 17-28, 113-123, 185-197, 280-291.

GIBB, H.A.R.
Obituary notice: Edward Denison Ross, 1871-1940, JRAS, (1941), pp. 49-52.

GIJBELS, M.
Christian presence and witness in relation to Muslim neighbours. The Mombasa conference, Al-Mushir, 22 (1980), pp. 29-35.

GLASSER, A.F.
Report of the North American conference on Muslim evangelization, Missio, 7 (1979), pp. 233-245.

GOITEIN, S.D.
Jewish society and institutions under Islam, Cashiers d'hist. Mondiale, 11 (1968-9), pp. 170-184.

GOLDZIHER.
Cult of saints in Islam, MW, 1 (1911), pp. 302-312.

GOODSELL, F.F.
Religious liberty in Islam, MW, 30 (1940), pp. 262-268.

GOPAL, Surendra.
Indian studies in Soviet Central Asia, Indo-Asian culture, 20ii(1971), pp. 19-33.

GORDON, C.H.
Daughters of Baal & Allah, MW, 33 (1943), pp. 50-51.

GOTTHEIL, R.J.
Mohammed Abdu, late mufti of Egypt, JAOS, 28 (1907), pp. 189-197.

GOTTHEIL, R.J.H.
Lgnazio Guidi - selected bibliography, JAOS, 55 (1935), pp. 458-463.

GRAY, B.
Obituary. Eric Schoeder., Iran, 10(1972), pp. vi-vii.

GREENSLADE, W.G.

Roman Catholic literature in Arabic on Islam. (Publications the Jesuit press in Beirut of), MW, 16 (1926), pp. 357-364.

GRIEBEROW, M.G.

Islam in Tibet, MW, 26 (1936), pp. 127-129.

GUILLAMME, A.

Version of the gospels used in Madina circa A.D. 700, Andulana, 15 (1950), pp. 289-296.

GUILLAUME, A.

Some remarks on free will & predestination in Islam, together with a translation of the kitabul Qadar from the sahih of at Bukhari, JRAS, (1924), pp. 43-63.

GUPPY, M.

Genuineness of at-Tabari's Arabic "apology" & of the Syraic document on the spread of christianity in central Asia in the John Rylands Library, Bull. J.R. Lib., 14 (1930), pp. 121-124.

GUTHNE, A.

A Ms. Quran in Glasgow University Library, Glasgow Univ. Or. Soc. Trans., 15 (1953-54), pp. 36-43.

HA'IRI, Abdul-Hadi.

Afghani on the decline of Islam, WI, 13(1971), pp. 121-125.

HABIB, M.

Some notes on the Naqshabandi order, MW, 59 (1969), pp. 40-49.

HALEPOTA, Aboul Wahid J.

Psychology of Islamic belief in God, Proc.9th Int. Cong. Hist. Rel., (1958), pp. 284-295.

HALKIN, A.S.

Hashwiyya, JAOS, 54 (1934), pp. 1-28.

HAMDANI, Abbas

"The Yamani Isma`ill Dal Hatim B. Ibrahim al-Hamidi (d. 596 H./ 1199 A.D.) and his book Tuhfat al-Qulub, Proc.27th Int. Cong. Or. 1967, (1971), pp. 270-272.

HAMDANI, Viqar Ahmed.
Some rare Mss. in Istanbul, JRAS, (1938), pp. 561-564.

HAMDANI, 'Abbas.
Evolution of the organisational structure of the Fatimida'wah. The Yemeni and Persian contribution, Arabian Studies, 3 (1976), pp. 85-114.

HAMIDULLAH, Muhammad.
Devotional life and religious practices of Islam, Majallat al-Azhar, 42viii(1970), pp. 6-11; 43i(1971), pp. 5-11.

HAMIDULLAH, Muhammad.
The cultivation of spiritual life, Majallat al-Azhar, 43ii(1971), pp. 254.

HAMIDULLAH, Muhammad.
The Prophet of Islam: His biography, Maj. al-Azhar, (Oct. 1969), pp. 12-16; (Nov. 1969), pp. 11-16; (Dec. 1969), pp. 11-16.

HAMIDULLAH, Muhammed.
The system of morality, Majallat al-Azhar, 43v(1971), pp. 8-16.

HAQ, Mushir U.
Indian Muslims and personal law, Islam and the modern era, 2i(1971), pp. 75-93.

HARLEY, A.H.
Musnad of Umar B. Abdil Azeez, Trans. Glasgow Or. Soc., 5 (1923-28), p. 7.

HARRIS, G.K.
Rebellion in kansu, MW, 19 (1929), pp. 291-298.

HARRIS, R.
New text of the Kuran, Bull. J.R. Lib., 10 (1926), pp. 219-222.

HARTMAN, S.S.
Secrets for Muslims in Parsi scriptures. Islam and its cultural divergence. Studies in honor of Gustave E. von Grunebaum, 1971, pp. 63-75.

HASAN, Ahmad.
Social justice in Islam, Islamic Stud, 10(1971), pp. 209-219.

HASAN, S.M.

Jadunath Sarkar's collection of Persian manuscripts, BPP, 90i(1971), pp. 118-121.

HASAN, Syed.

Dr. Muhammad Ishaque as I knew him., Indo-Iranica, 23i-ii(1970), pp. 113-115.

HASANN, Abdul Hamid.

Patronage of Islam to human values and ideals, Majallat al-Azhar, 43iii(1971), pp. 7-15.

HASKINS, C.H.

Adelard of Bath and Henry plantagenet, Engl. Hist. Rev., 28 (1913), pp. 515-516.

HASKINS, C.H.I.

Adelard of bath, Engl. Hist. Rev., 26 (1911), pp. 491-498.

HAYWARD, H.D.

Han & Hwei in the kansu-Sinking marches, MW, 26 (1936), pp. 62-67.

HEARD, W.B.

Notes on the Yezidis, JRAI, 41 (1911), pp. 200-219.

HEGGOY, W.N.

Mozabites of Algeria, MW, 37 (1947), pp. 192-207.

HERBERT, F.W. Von.

Moslem traditon of Jesus second visit on earth, Hibbert J., 7 (1909), pp. 27-48.

HETHERWICK, A.

Islam & Christianity in Nysaland, MW, 17 (1927), pp. 184-186.

HEYD, U.

The Congress of Orientalists in Istanbul, MEA, 3 (1952), pp. 60-61.

HICKIN, L.

Advance of Islam in Nigeria, MW, 26 (1936), pp. 400-403.

HIDAYAT, Hosain M.

Tadhkirat at Talib at mu'allam of Silt Ibn al-Ajami, JASb, N.S. 24

(1928), pp. 363-365.

HILL, R.L.
Recent Italian literature concerning the Sudan, Sudan Notes and Records, 22 (1939), pp. 167-169.

HILLELSON, S.
Aspects of Muhammadanism in the Eastern Sudan, JRAS, (1937), pp. 657-677.

HILLELSON, S.
Tabaqat wad dayf Allah: Studies in the lives of the scholars & saints, Sudan Notes & Records, 6 (1923), pp. 191-230.

HILMI, Omer Bees.
Some considerations with regard to the Hamif question, MW, 22 (1932), pp. 72-75.

HIRSCHBERG, H.Z.
The works of Professor L.A. Mayer, Ars Orientalis, 4 (1961), pp. 455-462.

HIRSCHBERG, H.Z. (J.W.).
The works of Professor L.A. Mayer, Eretz-Israel, 7 (L.A. Mayer memorial volume, 1964), pp. XIX-XXVII.

HISCHFELD, H.
Hebraes sufic poems, JAOS, 49 (1929), pp. 168-169.

HITTI, P.K.
Arabic & Islamic studies in Princeton University, MW, 31 (1941), pp. 292-294.

HITTI, P.K.
First book printed in Arabic, Princeton Univ. Libr. Chron, 4 (1942), pp. 5-9.

HOBALLAH, M.
The contribution of the religion of Islam to mutual understanding, Proc. 9th Int. Cong. Hist. Rel., 1958, pp. 736-739.

HOFFMANN, H.
Manichaeism and Islam in the Buddhist Kalacakra system, Proc. 9th Int. Cong. Hist. Rel., 1958, pp. 96-99.

HOLMES, M.C.
Islam in America, MW, 16 (1926), pp. 262-266.

HOLWAY, J.D.
The Quran in Swahili: Three translations, MW, 61(1971), pp. 102-110.

HONSA, V.
Alois Richard Nykl (1885-1958), Arabist and Hispanist: A biography and bibliography, Orbis, 16 (1967), pp. 295-305.

HOPWOODD, D.
The Islamic Arabic manuscripts in the Mingana Collection, JRAS, (1961), pp. 100-105.

HOURANI, G.F.
Middle Eastern studies in Italy today, MEJ, 18 (1964), pp. 313-319.

HOWARD, H.N.
Preliminary materials for a survey of the libraries and archives of Istanbul, JAOS, 59 (1939), pp. 227-246.

HOWARD, H.N.
The Middle East in paperback, MEJ, 18 (1964), pp. 355-366.

HOWARD, H.N.
The Middle East in paperback II (1964-1969), MEJ, 23 (1969), pp. 383-391.

HOWARD, I.K.A.
Great works of Shi'i Islam: al-Kąfi by Al-Kulaini, Alseraat, 2 i (1976), pp. 28-32.

HUBBALLAH, Mahmoud.
Islam: the religion of unity and universal brotherhood, Kajallat al-Azhar, 43i(1971), pp. 12-16.

HUME, W.F.
Contributions of Dr. Schwein-furth to the knowledge of Egyptian geology, Bull. Soc. Geog. Egypte, 14 (1926-27), pp. 135-137.

HUNTER, G.W.
Islam in central Asia, MW, 20 (1930), pp. 20-23.

HUSAINI, Ishak M.

Christ in the Quran and in modern Arabic literature, Proc. 9th Int. Cong. Hist. Rel., 1958, pp. 642-648.

IBRAHIM, Asma and NASRI, Abdel Rahman el.

Sudan bibliography 1959-1963, Sudan Notes and Records, 46 (1965), pp. 130-160.

INAYATULLAH, Dr.

"Amelie Sedillot" (1808-1875 A.D.), J. Pak. Hist. Soc., 9 (1961), pp. 30-35.

IVANOW, W.

Notice on the library attached to the shrine of Imam Rim at Mesched, JRAS, (1920), pp. 535-583; (1921), pp. 248-250, 480.

IVANOW, W.

Pro. C. Salemann. A letter to the editors, Islamica, 3 (1927), pp. 271-272.

IVANOW, W.

Pro. C. Salemann. A second letter to the editors, Islamica, 4 (1931), pp. 109-112.

IWARSON, J.

Islam in eriterea & Abyssinia, MW, 18 (1928), pp. 356-364.

J.G.A.

Arthur Lane, Oriental Art, N.S. 9 (1963), p. 174.

JAWED, Nasim Ahmad.

Religion and modernity: some nineteenth and twentieth-century Indo-Pakistani ideas, MW, 61(1971), pp. 73-89.

JAZAYERY, M.A.

Persian language instruction, MESA Bull., 6i(1972), pp. 9-29.

JEFFERY, A.

Variant text of the Faliha, MW, 29 (1939), pp. 158-162.

JEFFERY, A.

Quran readings of Zaid B. Ali, RSO, 16 91936), pp. 249-289.

JEFFERY, A.

Further Quran readings of Zaid B. Ali, RSO, 18 (1940), pp. 218-236.

JEFFERY, A.
Abu Ubaid on the vesses missing from the Quran, MW, 28 (1938), pp. 61-65.

JEFFERY, A.
Islam in Yunnan today, MW, 30 (1940), pp. 292-294.

JEFFERY, A.
Prophet of Islam, MW, 28 (1938), pp. 180-186.

JEFFERY, A.
Quest of the historical Mohammed, MW, 16 (1926), pp. 327-348.

JEFFERY, A.
Anti-christions literature, MW, 17 (1927), pp. 216-219.

JEFFERY, A.
Was Muhammed a prophet from his infancy, MW, 20 (1930), pp. 226-234.

JEFFERY, A. and MENDELSOHN, I.
Orienthography of the Somarqand Quran codex, JAOS, 62 (1942), pp. 175-195.

JENKINSON, E.J.
Jesus in Moslem tradition, MW, 18 (1928), pp. 263-269.

JENKINSON, E.J.
Moslem anti-Christ legend, MW, 20 (1930), pp. 50-55.

JERKINSON, E.J.
Rivers of paradise, MW, 19 (1929), pp. 151-155.

JOHNS, A.H.
From Buddhism to Islam: An interpretation of the Javanese literature of the transition, Comp. Stud. Soc. Hist., 9 (1966-7), pp. 40-50.

JONES, W.L.
Moslem catechism (Transl. from text used in East Affrica & at Aden), MW, 35 (1945), pp. 1945), pp. 324-236.

JOSEPH, I.
Yezidis texts, AJSL, 25 (1908-1909), pp. 111-156, 218-254.

JUNG, L.

Fallen angels in Jewish, Christian & Mohammedan literature, JQR, N.S. 15 (1924-25), pp. 467-502; 16 (1925-26), pp. 287-336.

JURJI, E.

Khadijah, Mohammed's first wife, MW, 26 (1936), pp. 197-199.

JURJI, E.J.

Pre-Islamic use of the name Muhammad, MW, 26 (1936), pp. 289-391.

KASOZI, A.B.K.

Some varying and common aspects of Islam in Africa, Makere Hist. J., 2 i (1976), pp. 101-110.

KEDDIE, N.R.

Islamic philosophy and Islamic modernism: the case of Sayyid Jamal ad-Din al-Afghani, Proc.27th Int. Cong. Or. 1967, (1971), pp. 190.

KEKLIK, Nihat.

The Bulgha Fi'l-Hikma of Ibn 'Arabi, Proc. 27th Int. Cong. Or. 1967, (1971), pp. 5-13.

KENSDALE, W.E.N.

The Arabic manuscript collection fo the Library of the University College of Ibadan, Nigeria, Wala News, 2 (1955), pp. 1-4.

KENT, F.L.

Librarie in developing countries - the Arab world, Libri, 14 (1964), pp. 290-294.

KERR, M.H.

Moral and legal judgment independent of revelation, Proc.27th Int. Cong. Or. 1967, (1971), pp. 176-178.

KHACHAB, Y.El.

Some aspects of "values" in the Islamic heritage: Traditions, Imama, and Consensus, Proc. 27th Int. Cong. Or. 1967, (1971), pp. 178.

KHAN, M.A. Saleem.

Religion and politics in Turkey. Survey of contemporary

developments in the Muslim world, Islam and the modern age, 2i(1971), pp. 94-108.

KHAN, Mu'In-ud-Din Ahmad.

A diplomat's report on Wahhabism of Arabia, Islamic Stud., 7 (1968), pp. 33-46.

KHAN, Qamaruddin.

Islamic research, Iqbal, 16 i (1967), pp. 1-20.

KHATIB, 'abd al-Karim al-.

Christ in Quran, the Taurat, and the Injil: Translated and annotated by Kenneth E. Nolin, MW, 61(1971), pp. 90-101.

KHUNDMIRI, S. Alam.

A critical examination of Islamic traditionalism, Ilam and the modern age, 2ii(1971), pp. 1-18.

KHURI, Fuad I.

Work in Islamic thought, Al-Abhath, 2lii-iv(1968), pp. 3-13.

KING, Russel.

The pilgrimage to Mecca: some geographical and historical aspects, Erdkunde, 26(1972), pp. 61-73.

KNAPPERT, J.

The Prophet Muhammad in Swahili literature, Alserat, 5 i (1979), pp. 3-6.

KOHNEL, E.

In memoriam Ernst Diez 1878-1961, Kunst des Orients, 4 (1963), p. 110.

KRAEMER, H.

Survery of the Netherlands Indies, MW, 27 (1937), pp. 44-55.

KRAEMER, H.

Modern revindication of Islam, MW, 29 (1939), pp. 141-150.

KRAUSS, S.

Moses legend, JQR, N.S. 2 (1911-12), pp. 339-364.

KUDSI-ZADEH, A.A.

Afghani and Freemasonry in Egypt, JAOS, 92(1972), pp. 25-35.

KUDSI-ZADEH, A.A.
Islamic reform in Egypt: some observations on the role of Afghani, MW, 61(1971), pp. 1-12.

KYRRIS, Costas P.
The admission of the souls of immoral but humane people into the Limbus Puerorum, according to the Cypriote Abbot Kaioumos (VIIth century A.D.), compared to the Quran's Al' Araf (Suras 744-46, 5713f) rev.et.sud-esteur., 9(1971), pp. 461-477.

LANDAU, J.M.
Russian journals dealing with thė Middle East, ME studies, 7(1971), pp. 237-239.

LANDAU, J.M.
Israeli studies on the Middle East, MEJ, 19 (1965), pp. 334-362.

LANDAU, J.M.
Soviet studies on workers movements in the Middle East, ME Studies, 6 (1970), pp. 346-349.

LATHAM, J.D.
In memoriam S.M. Stern., BAEO, 6(1970), pp. 11-12.

LAUBACH, F.C.
Matias, a son of Moropirates, MW, 19 (1929), pp. 115-124.

LAUGIER de BEAURECUEIL, S.
de La pauvrete, attitude essentielle de l'homme en face de dieu, d'apres Abdallah Ansari de Herat (Ve/XIe siecle)., Attidell VIII Cong. Int. Stor. Rel., (1955), pp. 441-443.

LAW, H.D.G.
Farewell to Aqai Minovi, J. Iran Soc., 1 (1950-), pp. 31-32.

LAZARUS-YAFEH, Hava.
Contemporary religious though among the 'Ulma' of al-Azhar, Asian & Afr. Studs., 7(1971), pp. 211-236.

LEVEEN, J.
Mohammed & his Jewish companions, JQR, N.S. 16 (1925-26), pp. 309-406; 17 (1926-227), pp. 327-485.

LEVI-DELLA VIDA, G.

Arabic block print, Scientific Monthly, 59 (1944), pp. 473-474.

LEVONIAN, L.

Doctrine of manin Islam & evangelism, MW, 30 (1940), pp. 249-252.

LEVTZION, N.

Early nineteenth century Arabic manuscripts from Kumasi (In Copenhagen), Trans. Hist. Soc. Ghana, 8 (1965), pp. 99-119.

LEVY, R.

Account of the Ismaili doctrines in the Jamial Tawarikh of Rashid al-Din Fadlallah, JRAS, (1930), pp. 509-536.

LEWIS, B.

Assassins of Syria and Ismailis of Persia, La Persia nel medievo, (1971), pp. 573-574.

LIGHTON, G.

Numerical strength of Islam in the Sudan, MW, 26 (1936), pp. 253-273.

LINGS, M.

The seven deadly sins, Stud. comp. religion, 5(1971), pp. 26-33.

LITTLE, K.L.

Moslem 'Missionary' in Mendeland, Sierra Leone, Man, 46 (1946), pp. 111-113.

LOCKHART, L.

Hasan-i-sabbah and the Assassins, BSOAS, 5 (1928-30), pp. 675-696.

LOEWENTHAL, R.

Sino-Islamica: Bibliographical notes on the Chinese Muslims, Momumenta Serica, 22 (1963), pp. 209-212.

LYONS, M.C.

In memoriam A.J., Arberry. BAEO, 6(1970), pp. 13-15.

MACCALUM, F.L.

From the vieneyard of attainment, MW, 20 (1930), pp. 286-288.

MACDONALD,D.B.
Doctrine of revetation in Islam, MW, 7 (1917), pp. 112-117.

MACDONALD,D.B.
God a unit or a unity? The answer of Islamic theology & its lesson, MW, 3 (1913), pp. 11-20.

MACDONALD,D.B.
Development of the idea of spirit of Islam, MW, 22 (1932), pp. 25-42; 153-168.

MACDONALD,D.B.
Development of the idea of spirit of Islam, Act. Or., 9 (1931), pp. 307-351.

MACDONALD,D.B.
Continuous re-creation & atomic time in Muslim scholastic theology, ISIS, 9 (1927), pp. 326-344.

MACKAY,P.A.
Certificates of transmission on a manuscript of the Maqamat of Hariri (MS Cairo, adab 105), Trans.Amer. Phil. Soc., 61iv(1971), pp. 81.

MACKEEN, A.M. Mohamed.
The early history of Sufism in the Maghrib prior to Al-Shadhili (D.656/1256), JAOS, 91-(1971), pp. 398-408.

MACKEEN, A.M. Mohamed.
The rise of al-Shadhili (D.656/1256), JAOS, 91(1971), pp. 177-190.

MACKENSEN, R.S.
Moselm libraries and sectarian propaganda, AJSL, 51 (1934-35), pp. 83-113.

MACKENSEN, R.S.
Background of the history of Muslim libraries, AJSL, 51 (1934-35), pp. 114-125; 52 (1935-36), pp. 22-33, 104-110.

MACKENSEN, R.S.
Arabic books and libraries in the Ummaiyad period, AJSL, 52 (1935-36), pp. 245-253; 53 (1936-37), pp. 239-250; 54 (1937), pp. 41-61; 56 (1939), pp. 149-157.

MAHMUD, Khalil.
The Arabic collection of Ibadan University Library, Libri, 14 (1964), pp. 97-107.

MAHMUD-UL-HAQ.
Islamic modernism. A response to the challenge of modern age, Islam and the modern age, 2ii(1971), pp. 80-86.

MAJID, M.A.
A brief resume of the activities of the Iran Society (1944-1969), Indo-Iranica, 23i-ii(1970), pp. 41-50.

MAJID, M.A.
Remembering the great savants, Indo-Iranica, 24i-ii(1971), pp. 43-47.

MAJID, M.A.
Remembering the great savants, Indo-Iranica, 24ii-ii(1971), pp. 43-47.

MAJUL, Cesar Adib.
The Muslims in the Philippines. A historical perspective, majallat al-Azhar, 42viii(1970), pp. 12-16.

MAKDISI, G.
Interaction between Islam and the West, REI, 44 (1976), pp. 287-309.

MALLOWAN, M.E.L.
Obituary. Sir Maurice Bowra., Iran, 10(1972), pp. iii-v.

MAREK, J.
Islamic studies in Czechoslovakia, J. Pak. His. Soc., 10 (1962), pp. 303-311.

MARGOLIOUTH, D.S.
Relies of the prophet Mohammed, MW, 27 (1937), pp. 20-27.

MARGOLIOUTH, D.S.
Some additions to professor Jeffery's foreign vocabulary of the Quran, JRAS, (1939), pp. 53-61.

MARGOLIOUTH, D.S.
Use of the Apocrypha by Muslim writers, MW, 5 (1915), pp. 404-408.

MARGOLIOUTH, D.S.
Ideas andideals of modernIslam, MW, 20 (1930), pp. 235-350.

MARGOLIOUTH, D.S.
On Mohdis & Mahdism, Proc. Brit. Acad., (1915-16), pp. 213-233.

MARGOLIOUTH, D.S.
Harut & Marut, MW, 18 (1928), pp. 73-79.

MARGOLIOUTH, D.S.
On "the book of religion & empire" by Ali B. Rabban at Tabari, Proc. Brit. Acad., 16 (1930), pp. 164-182.

MARGOLIOUTH, D.S.
Devil's delusion, by Ibn al-Jauzi, Trans., 19 (1945), pp. 69-81, 171-188, 272-89, 376-383; 20 (1946), pp. 58-71, 181-190, 297-310, 408-422; 21 (1947), pp. 73-79, 174-183, 394-402; pp. 22 (1948), pp. 75-86.

MARGOLIOUTH, D.S. and HOLMYARD, E.J.
Arabic documents from the monneret collection, Islamica, 4 (1931), pp. 249-271.

MARTIN, B.G.
Unbelief in the Western Sudan: Uthman dan Fodio's ta'lim al-ikhan (incl. Arabic text of the work and an English trans.), MES, 4 (1967), pp. 50-97.

MASON, I.
Future of Islam in China, MW, 30 (1940), pp. 76-84.

MASON, I.
Moslem chronology in China, MW, 27 (1937), pp. 267-268.

MASON, I.
How Islam entered China, MW, 19 (1929), pp. 249-263.

MASSIGNON, L.
Islam in USSR, MW, 17 (1927), pp. 359-369.

MATTHEWES, C.D.
Mss. and a Mamluk incription in the lansing collection in the Demer Public Library (U.S.), JAOS, 60 (1940), pp. 370-382.

MATTHEWS, C.D.
"Kitab baitu-n-rufus" of Ibm-l-Farikh, JPOS, 14 (1934), pp. 284-293; 19(1935), pp. 51-87.

MATTHEWS, C.D.
Muslim iconoclast (Ibn Taymiyyah) on the "Merits" of Jerusalem and Palestine, JAOS, 56 (1936), pp. 1-21.

MAYER, C.F.
Collection of Arabic medical literature in the army medical library, Bull. Med. Lib. Ars., N.S. 30 (1942), pp. 96-104.

MAZZAOUI, M.M.
Shi'ism in the medieval Safavid, and Qajar periods: a study in Ithna-'ashari continuty, Iran:continuity and variety, ed. by P.J. Chelkowski, (1971), pp. 39-57.

MCDONOUGH, S.
Creation from nothing and the teaching of the Quran, ZDMG, 120(1971), pp. 274-280.

MCDONOUGH, S.
Iman and Islam in the Quran, Iqbal rev., 12i(1971), pp. 81-88.

McELROY, P.S.
Ethopia: Moslem or Christian, MW, 28 (1938), pp. 125-37.

McELROY, P.S.
Islam in transition, MW, 27 (1937), pp. 164-172.

MCLEAN, W.H.
Personal experiences in the Near East, Trans. Glasgow Or. Soc., 6 (1929-33), pp. 46-47.

MEIER, F.
Hurasan und das ende der klassischen sSufik, La Persia nel medievo, (1971), pp. 545-572.

MEIER, F.
The ultimate origin and the hereafter in Islam, Islam and its cultural divergence Studies in honor of Gustave E. von Grwnebaun, (1971), pp. 96-112.

MENDELSOHN, I.
Columbia University copy of the Samarqand Kufic Quran, MW, 30 (1940), pp. 375-378.

MERTINOVITCH, N.N.
Arabic, Persian & Turkish Mss. in the Columbia University Library (U.S.), JAOS, 49 (1929), pp. 219-233.

MEULEUN, D. Van der.
Crisis in Islam, MW, 26 (1936), pp. 337-357.

MILES, G.C.
The writings of Ernst Herzfeld, AI, 7 (1940), pp. 82-92.

MILSON, Menshez.
The elusive Jamal al-Din al-Afghani, MW, 58 (1968), pp. 295-307.

MINGANA, A.
Important Ms. of Bakhani's Sahib, JRAS, (1936), pp. 287-292.

MINGANA, A.
Syriac influence on the style of the Kuran, Bull. J.R. Lib., 11 (1927), pp. 77-98.

MINGANA, A.
Important old Turki Ms. in the John Rylands Library, Bull. J. R. Libr. Z, (1914-15), pp. 129-138.

MINGANA, A.
Kitab ud-din wa-d-Danlah, Bull. J. R. Libr., 11 (1927), pp. 99-100.

MINGANA, A.
Brief notes on some of the rarer or unique Arabic & Persian-Arabic Mss. in the John Rylonds Library, Bull. J.R. Libr., 6 (1921-22), pp. 522-230.

MINGONA, A.
Notes upon some of the kuranic Mss. in the John Rylands Library, Bull. J.R. Libr, 2 (1914-15), pp. 240-250.

MINOVI, A.
Summary of Aqai Minovi's lecture on Sufism, J. Iran. Soc., 1 (1950), pp. 32-34.

MOIN, Mumtaz.
Imam Abu Hanifah (life and personality), J. Pakistan Hist. Soc., 16(1968), pp. 153-162.

MOINUL HAQ, S.
Risalah Haqqiyah of Shaykh Nizam al-Din Balkhi, J. Pakistan Hist. Soc., 19(1971), pp. 223-264.

MONDESERT, C.
In memoriam: Rene Mouterde, S.J. (1880-1961), MUSJ, 38 (1962), pp. 1-9.

MONKET, E.
Saint worship in North Africa, MW, 3 (1913), pp. 242-245.

MORGENSTERN, H.
American culture & Oriental studies, JAOS, 48 (1928), pp. 97-108.

MORRIS, G.
The Muslim Republics of the U.S.S.R., RCAJ, 49 (1962), pp. 329-342.

MOTTAHEDEH, R.
Sources for the study of Iran, Iranian Stud., 1 (1968), pp. 4-7.

MOUTSATSOS, B.
Directory of films on the Middle East, MESA Bull., 5i(1971), pp. 39-55.

MUJEEB, M.
The status of the individual conscience in Islam, Studies in Islam, 7(1970), pp. 125-149.

MUJEEB, M.
Sufis and Sufism, Dr. Adilya Nath Jha felicitation vol. III, (1969), pp. 223-264.

MULLA, P.
Koranic wisdom according to a Turk, MW, 26 (1936), pp. 274-280.

MULLICK, M.A. Hussain.

The challenge of modern development before the Muslim world, Islamic Stud., 6 (1967), pp. 225-240.

MUNDY, C.S.

Notes on thre Turkish Mss, BSOAS, 12 (1948), pp. 533-541.

MUSHIR UL-HAQQ.

Religion, secularism and secular state: the Muslim case, Religion and society, 18iii(1971), pp. 36-47.

NAISH, J.P.

Connection of oriental studies with commerce, art & literature during the 18th - 19th centuries, J. March. Ig. & Or. Soc., 15 (1930), pp. 33-39.

NAIYER, S.A. Haider.

Dr. M. Ishaque: a devotee of the temple of learning, Indo-Iranica, 23i-ii(1970), pp. 116-118.

NALDER, R.F.

Influence of animism in Islam, Sudan Notes & Records, 9 (1926), pp. 75-87.

NASR, S.H.

Al-hikmat al-ilahiyyah and kalam, SI, 34(1971), pp. 139-149.

NASR, Seyyed Hossein.

Mysticism and traditional philosophy in Persia, Pre-Islamic and Islamic, Studs. in cmpar. relig., 5(1971), pp. 235-240.

NASR, Seyyed Hossein.

The Persian works of Shaykh al-ishraq Shihab al-Din Suhrawardi, Proc. 27th Int. Cong. Or. 1967, (1971), pp. 170.

NASR, Seyyed Hossein.

The spread of the illuminationist school of Suhrawardi, La Persia nel medievo, 1971, pp. 255-265.

NEUSTUPNY, J.V.

First steps towards the conception of "Oriental languages", Arch. Or., 33 (1965), pp. 83-92.

NIAZI, Shaheer.
The destruction of the Alexandrian Library, J. Pakistan Hist.Soc., 16(1968), pp. 163-174.

NICHOLSON, R.A.
Early Arabic version of the miraj of Abu Yazid at Bistami, Islamica, 2 (1926), pp. 402-415.

NICHOLSON, R.A.
Saying of Maruf al-Karklvi, JRAS, (1906), pp. 999-1000.

NICHOLSON, R.A.
Note on the Sasabul Khirqa, JRAS, (1907), pp. 166-168.

NICHOLSON, R.A.
Historical enquiry concerning the origin & development of Sufism, with a list of definitions of the terms "Sufi" & "trasowwuf"arranged chronologically, JRAS, (1906), pp.303-348.

NIKITIN, B.
Life and work of Y.N. Marr, Georgica, 1 iv & v (1937), pp. 278-286.

NILSON, D.L.F., NUR, Fazel, and KAMAL, Sajida.
A partially annotated bibliography of Afghan lingustics, Afghanistan, 23i(1970), pp. 43-56; 23iii, pp. 65-72; 23iv, pp. 57-67.

NIMRI, N.N.
Warrior people of Djebel Druze. A military minority in the Middle East, J. Middle East Soc., 1 (1946), part I, 47-62; 1 (1947), part II, 90-96.

NOWAIHI, Mohamed al-.
Towards a re-evaluation of Muhammad: Prophet and man, MW, 60 (1970), pp. 300-313.

NYKL, A.R.
Notes on E.H. Palmer's "The Quran", JAOS, 36 (1936), pp. 77 84.

O'SHAUGHNESSY, T.
Islam in South-East Asia, Studia missionalia, 16(1967), pp. 55-74.

O'SHAUGHNESSY, T.
Creation from nothing and the teaching of the Quran, ZDMG, 120(1970), pp. 274-280.

O'SHAUGHNESSY, T.
An annotated list of selected books on Islamism appearing from 1950 to 1960, Studia Missionalia, 11 (1961), pp. 201-222 [Offpr. in SOAS].

O'SHAUGHNESSY, T.J.
Creation with wisdom and with the world in the Quran, JAOS, 91(1971), pp. 208-221.

O'SHAUGHNESSY, Th.
Man's creation from clay and from seed in the Quran, BAEO, 7(1971), pp. 131-149.

OBERMANN, J.
Political theology in early Islam. Hasan at-Basri's treatise on gadar, JAOS, 55 (1935), pp. 138-162.

OFFOR, R.
University Libraries in the British colonies and the Sudan, Libri, 5 (1954-1955), pp. 54-75.

OGILVIE, C.L.
Classified bibliography of books on Islam in Chinese & Chinese-Arabic, MW, 18 (1918), pp. 74-78.

OTUKEN, A.
The youngest national library in the world, Libri, 1 (1950-1951), pp. 171-172.

PAGLIERO, R.
Conservation of two Islamic monuments in Mosul, Sumer, 21 (1965), pp. 41-56.

PAREJA, F.M.
In memoriam Juan Busquets Mulet, BAEO, 7(1971), pp. 6-7.

PAREJA, F.M.
In memoriam Joseph Schacht., BAEO, 6(1970), pp. 9-10.

PARET, Rudi.

Islam in new Turkey, IMA, liii(1970), pp. 9-12.

PARRY, E.S.

Why copts become Moslems, MW, 26 (1936), pp. 372-379.

PELLAT, C.

Joseph Schacht, Arabica, 17 (1970), pp. 1-2.

PELLAT, Ch.

Islam and history, Islam and the moder age, 2iii(1971), pp. 36-47.

PERLMANN, M.

Ibn Hazm on the equivalence of Proofs, Jewish Qly. Rev., N.S. 40 (1949-50), pp. 279-289.

PHILLIP, W.

Need of an American school of living oriental languages, JAOS, 39 (1919), pp. 185-189.

PICKENS, C.L.

With the moras of the Philippines, MW, 30 (1940), pp. 36-40.

PICKENS, C.L.

Journey through Northwest China, MW, 27 (1937), pp. 112-114.

PICKENS, C.L.

Early Moslem leaders in China, MW, 26 (1936), pp. 232-239.

PINES, S.

"Israel, my firstborn" and the sonship of Jesus: a theme of Moslem anti-Christian polemics, Studies in mysticism and religion presented to G.G. Scholem, 1967, pp. 177-190.

PINTO, D.

Libraries of the Arabs during the time of the Abbasides, IC, 3 (1929), pp. 210-243.

POBEE, J.S. and MENDS, E.H.

Social change and African traditional religion, Sociol Analysis, 38 (1977), pp. 1-12.

POUHHADI, Ibrahim V.

Iran's public and private libraries, Q.S. Libr. Cong., 25 (1968), pp. 219-229.

PRATT, I.A.
Selected bibliography of R.J.H. Gottheil, JAOS, 56 (1936), pp. 480-489.

PROBSTER, E.
Arabic instruction in France, Islamica, 1 (1925), pp. 106-108.

PRUETT, G.E.
The escape from the seraglio: Anti-Orientalist trends in modern religious studies, Arab Studies Q, 2 (1980), pp. 291-317.

PYE, E.
Prayer and mosque attendance in Turkey, MW, 18 (1928), pp. 392-398.

QAMARUDDIN.
Sayyid Muhammad Jaunpuri, a spiritual reformer, IMA, liii(1970), pp. 91-109.

QASIMI, A.S.
Libraries in the early Islamic world, J. Univ. Peshawar, 6 (1958), pp. 1-15.

RACAGNI, M.
Research facilities in Tunisia, MESA Bull., 6i(1972), pp. 30-36.

RAMAZANI, Rouhollah K.
Research facilities in Iran, MESA Bull., 41 91970), p. 51.

RAY, Atul Chandra.
Sir Jadunath Sarkar: as a man and a historian, Indo-Iranica, 24i-ii (1971), pp. 1-15.

RIAZ, Muhammad.
A reappraisal of the sources on Shaykh Mu'in al-Din Ajmeri, J. Pakistan Hist. Soc., 16(1968), pp. 145-152.

RIAZ, Muhammad.
Mir Sayyid Muhammad Nur Bakhsh, J. Pakistan Hist. Soc, 17(1969), pp. 177-190.

RICE, W.A.
Ali in Shiah tradition, MW, 4 (1914), pp. 27-44.

RIEDL, J.O.

Maimomides & scholarticism, New Scholasticism, 10 (1936), pp. 18-29.

ROBSON, J.

Blessings on the Prophet, MW, 26 (1936), pp. 365-371.

ROBSON, J.

Muhammadan teachings about Jesus, MW, 29 (1939), pp. 37-54.

ROBSON, J.

Some Arab saints, Trans. Glasgow Or. Soc., 5 (1923-25), pp. 62-65.

ROBSON, J.

Is the moslem hell eternal?, MW, 28 (1938), pp. 386-396.

ROBSON, J.

Non-resistance in Islam, Glasg. Or. Soc. Trans., 9 (1938-39), pp. 2-11.

ROCHLIN, S.A.

Early Arabic printing at the Cape of Goodhope, BSOAS, 7 (1933-35), pp. 49-54.

RONA-TAS, A.

The Oriental Committee of the Hungarian Academy of sciences on the co-operation of Urdlic and Altaic studies in Hungary, Acta Or. Hung., 20 (1967), pp. 367-368.

RONA-TAS, A.

Julius Nemeth, life and work, Acta Or. Hung, 32 (1978), pp. 261-284.

ROSENTHA, E.I.J.

Arthur J. Arberry - a tribute, Relig. Stud., 6 (1970), pp. 297-302.

ROSENTHAL, F.

"Muslim Brethren" in Egypt, MW, 37 (1947), pp. 278-291.

RUNCIMAN, Sir St.

Muslim influences on the development of European civilization, Sarkiyat Mecmuast, 3 (1959), pp. 13-24.

RUTTER, E.
Muslim pilgrimage, Geog. J., 74 (1929), pp. 271-273.

RYCKMANS, G.
Harry St. John B. Philiby, J. Semitic Studies, 6 (1961), pp. 222-225.

RYCKMANS, J.
In memoriam Hermann von Wissmann (1895-1979), Museon, 92 (1979), pp. 387-394.

SAARDA, C.
Origins of the Mosque, MW, 28 (1938), pp. 336-344.

SAEED, Khan.
Sect of Ahl-t-Haqq (Ali Islahis), MW, 17 (1927), pp. 31-42.

SALIM, Muhammad.
Shaykh Baha al-Din Zakariyya, J. Pakistan Hist. Soc., 17(1969), pp. 1-24.

SANGAR, S.P.
Conversions of Hindus to Islam during Auranzeb's region, Panjab Univ. res. bull.(arts), 2ii(1971), pp. 61-68.

SARKAR, Jagadish narayan.
A note on International Congress of Orientalists, Canberra, Q'ly rev.hist.stud., 10(1970-1), pp. 227-233.

SARKAR, Jagadish Narayan.
Thoughts on Acharya Jadunath Sarkar, Indo-Iranica, 24i-ii(1971), pp. 1-15.

SA'ADEH, Mounir R.
Why not canonize Mohammed, MW, 27 (1937), pp. 294-297.

SCARCIA AMORETTI, B.
Lunar green and solar green: On the ambiguity of function of a colour in Islam, Acta Or. Hung., 33 (1979), pp. 337-343.

SCHACHT, J.
On some manuscripts in the libraries of Morocco, Hesperis Tamuda, 9 (1968), pp. 5-55.

SCHOONOVER, K.
Al-Muhasibi & bis al-Riya, MW, 39 (1949), pp. 26-35.

SCHUTZ, E.
In memoriam, Jan Reychman (1910-1975). Acta Or. Hung., 30 (1976), pp. 251-253.

SCHUTZ, E.
The 11th session of the Permanent International Altaistic Conference (PIAC) in Horsholm, Denmark, 2-6 June, 1968, Acta Or. Hung., 22 (1969), pp. 273-277.

SCOTT, R.B.
Quran courses in Turkey, MW, 61(1971), pp. 239-255.

SEGAI, J.B.
David Storm Rice, BSOAS, 25 (1962), pp. 666-671.

SHAH, Sahibzada Hasan.
Bibliography of his writings (i.e. M.A. Chaghtai's), Ancient Pakistan, 2 (1965-66), pp. 219-226.

SHAKIR, Muhammad.
Onthe translation of the Koran into foreign languages, MW, 16 (1926), pp. 161-165.

SHALABY, I.M.
The role of the [Muslim] School in America in the process of cultural renewal, Maj. Al-Mushir, (Jan. 1969), pp. 8-12.

SHAMMA, S.H.
An interpretation of the first two Suraha in the Qur'an, Bull. Coll. Arts (Baghdad), 10 (1967), pp. 37-62.

SHELLABEAR, W.G.
Exposure of counter feiters, MW, 20 (1930), pp. 359-370.

SIDDIQI, Bakhtiyar Hasan.
T.W. Arnold: LIfe and works, Iqbal, 16 iii (1968), pp. 59-67.

SILERSTEIN, T.
Darviel of moley, english cosmogonist and student of Arab science, Medieval Studies, 10 (1948), pp. 176-196.

SIMSAR, A.

Three rare manuscripts from the John Frederick Lewis collection, JAOS, 57 (1937), pp. 88-94.

SINGER, C.

Daniel of morely, an English philospher of the 12th century, ISIS, 3 (1920), pp. 263-269.

Sir Jadunath Sarkar: a bibliographical sketch.

Indo-Iranica, 24i-ii(1971), pp. 48-49.

SKILLITER, S.A.

Arthur John Arberry, BSOAS, 33 (1970), pp. 364-367.

SMITH, M.

Rabia the nuptic, MW, 20 (1930), pp. 337-43.

SMITH, M.

Women saint in the development of Islam, MW, 17 (1927), pp. 130-138.

SOMMER, F.E.

New depository of oriental Mss. in the United States (The army medical library), JAOS, 66 (1946), pp. 183-184.

SOMMER, F.E.

Material for oriental search in Cleveland (U.S), JAOS, 66 (1946), pp. 261-264; 68 (1948), pp. 68.

SOMOGGI, J.de.

Ibu al Jauzi's handbook on the Makkan pilgrimage, JRAS, (1938), pp. 541-546.

SOMOGY, J. de.

Collection of the literary remains of Iglace Goldziher, JRAS, (1935), pp. 149-154.

SOMOGYI, J. DE.

First International Congress of Arabic Studies, Cordoba, Spain, September, 1962, MW, 53 (1963), pp. 151-154.

SOMOGYI, Joseph de.

My reminiscences of Ignac Goldziher, MW, 51 (161), pp. 5-17.

SPICES, O.
Activities of the Turkish delegation in the 26th Congress of Orientalists, Islam Tetkikleri Enstitusu dergisi, 4(1964), pp. 119-127.

SPRENGLING, M.
Berlin Druze lexicon, AJSL, 56 (1939), pp. 388-417; 57 (1940), pp. 75-94.

SPRENGLING, M.
Berlin Druze texicon, AJSL, 58 (1941), pp. 91-98.

SPRENGLING, M.
Translations from the Arabic, AJSL, 39 (1922-23), pp. 192-207.

SUBHAN, J.A.
New forces of Islam, MW, 16 (1926), pp. 166-171.

SUBHAN, J.A.
The Reverend Lewis Bevan Jones, MW, 51 (1961), pp. 128-131.

SWAN, G.
Literature of the Dervish orders, MW, 16 (1926), pp. 59-65.

SWAN, G.
The Tanta Mulid, MW, 4 (1914), pp. 45-51.

SWAN, G.
Saintship in Islam, MW, 5 (1915), pp. 232-239.

SWANG, G.
Dhikr, MW, 2 (1912), pp. 380-386.

SYRDAL, R.A.
Christ in the Chinese Koran, MW, 27 (1927), pp. 72-83.

SZCZUDOWSKA, A.
The Egyptological Conference in Leipzig, Africana Bull., 9 (1969), pp. 90-92.

TAYLOR, F.
The oriental manuscript collections in the John Rylands Library, Bull. John Rylands Lib., 54(1971-72), pp. 449-478. The duties of believers towards God in verses from the Quran. II. Majallat al-Azhar, 43ix(1971), pp. 4-6. The first congress on Mediterranean

studies of Arabo-Berber influence.

THOMPSON, L.S.
Books in Turkey, MEA, 8 (1952), pp. 171-180.

THOMPSON, O.H.
Al hallaj, sairt & martyr, MW, 19 (1929), pp. 383-402.

THOMPSON, O.H.
Druzes of the Lebanon, MW, 20 (1930), pp. 270-285.

THOMSON, W.
Renaiscnce of Islam, Starward Theol. REv., 30 (1937), pp. 51-63.

THOMSON, W.
Al-ashari & his at-Ibanah, MW, 32 (1942), pp. 242-260.

THOMSON, W.
Conception of human destiny in Islam, MW, 35 (1945), pp. 281-299.

THOMSON, W.
Asceticat mystical movement in Islam, MW, 39 (1949), pp. 282-291.

THOMSON, W.
Sects and Islam, MW, 39 (1949), pp. 208-222.

THWING, E.W.
Chinese Moslem's perplexity and his way out. (Are there beautiful girls in paradise?), MW, 7 (1917), pp. 283-293.

TIBAWI, A.L.
English-speaking Orientalists. A critique of their approach to Islam and Arab Nationalism, IQ, 8 (1964), pp. 25-45, 73-88.

TIBAWI, A.L.
English - speaking orientalists. A critique of their approach to Islamand Arab Nationalism, MW, 53 (1963), pp. 185-204, 298-313.

TISDALL, (W. St. C.).
London school of oriental studies. A great oppurtunity for missionary students, MW, 7 (1917), pp. 394-401.

TISDALL, W. St. C.
Shiah addition to the Koran, MW, 3 (1913), pp. 227-241.

TISDALL, W.St.C.
"The book" of the "people of the book", MW, 2 (1912), pp. 164-170.

TOPUZOGLU, Tevfik Rustu.
Further Istanbul manuscripts of Tha'alibi's, Arabica, 18(1971), pp. 211-213.

TORREY, C.
Jeffery's "Foreign vocabulary of the Quran", MW, 29 (1939), pp. 359-63.

TORREY, C.C.
Outlook for American Oriental Studies, JAOS, 38 (1918), pp. 107-120.

TRITTON, A.S.
The camel and the needle's eye, BSOAS, 34(1971), pp. 139.

TRITTON, A.S.
Man, nafs, ruh, 'aql, BSOAS, 34(1971), pp. 491-495.

TRITTON, A.S.
Theology in the making, JRAS, (1945), pp. 82-86.

TRITTON, A.S.
Foreign influences on Muslim theology, BSOAS, 10(1940-42), pp. 837-842.

TRITTON, A.S.
Muslim theology & Arabic literature, Glasgow Univ. Or. Soc. Trans., 12 (1944-46), pp. 46-47.

TRITTOR, A.S.
Islam & the protected religious, JRAS, (1927), pp. 479-484, (1928), pp. 485-508.

TRITTOS, A.S.
Islam andthe protected religion, JRAS, (1931), pp. 311-338.

TRITTOS, A.S.
An-Nabita, JRAS, (1932), p. 37.

TROTTON, A.S.
Theological text, BSOAS, 12 (1947), pp. 1-4.

TROWBRIDGE, S. Van. R.
Alevis, N. Difiers of Ali, Harvard Theol. Rev., 2 (1909), pp. 340-353.

TRYJARSKI, E.
In memoriam Ananiasz Zajaczkowski, BAEO, 7(1971), pp. 7-9.

TSERETELI, E.
Training of Orientalists in the USSR, AION, N.S. 17 (1967), pp. 349-354.

TUR-SINAI, N.H.
Remembering a fine man (L.S. Mayer), Eretz-Israel, 7 (L.A. Mayer memorial volume, 1964), pp. XVI-XVII.

TURNER, Sir. R.L.
Obtiuary: Sir Edward Denison Ross, BSOAS, 10 (1940-42), pp. 832-836.

UKPABI, S.C.
Christianity and Islam and change in African society and religion, Afirica qly., ll(1971), pp. 126-135.

ULLENDORFF, E.
A letter from Th. Noldeke to E. mittwoch., BSOAS, 34(1971), pp. 5-8.

USMANI, Nassem ul-Islam.
Letter to Muslim 'Ulamas', Majallat al-Azhar, 43x(1971), pp. 14-16; 44i(1972), pp. 8-14.

UTAS, Bo.
Notes on some public and semipublic libraries in the Near and Middle East containing Persian and other Moslem manuscripts (situation as of summer 1965, Acta Or., 33(1971), pp. 169-192.

VAHIDUDDIN, Syed.
Professor Kenneth Cragg's approach to the Quranic consciousness of man, Studies in Islam, 7(1970), pp. 19-28.

VALIUDDIN, Mir.
The way to control anger - the Quran builds, IC, 45(1972), pp. 63-73.

VALIUDDIN, Mir.
The screts of Hajj (Pilgrimage to K'aba): the Sufi approach, Islam and the modern age, 2iv(1971), pp. 42-70.

VALIUDDIN, Mir.
Cleansing of the heart: the Sufi approach, Studies in Islam, 7(1970), pp. 29-61.

VALIUDDIN, Mir
Righeousness (a Sufi approach), IC, 45(1971), pp. 157-170.

VALIUDDIN, Mir.
Illumination of the spirit, Iqbal Rev., 9 iii (1968), pp. 119-140.

VALSAN, M.
Notes on the Shaikh al-'Alawi(1869-1934), Studs. in compar relig., 5(1971), pp. 145-150.

VALUI'D-DIN, Mir.
The character that the Quran builds, IC, 45(1971), pp. 1-23.

VAN ESS, J.
A new source of Muslim heresiography, Proc. 27th Int. Cong. Or. 1967, (1971), pp. 269-270.

VAN ESS, J.
Umar II and his epistle against the Qadariya, Abr-Nahrain, 12(1971-2), pp. 19-26.

VAN ESS, J.
Skepticism in Islamic religious thought, Al-Abhath, 2 ii (1968), pp. 1-18.

VERNET, J.
In memoriam Jose M. Millas Vallicrosa., BAEO, 7(1971), pp. 5-6.

VOCHT, H. de.
Oriental languages in Louvain in the 17th century, Museon, 59 (1946), pp. 671-688.

VON GRUNEBAUM, G.E.
Islam in humanistic education. The traditional Near East, ed. by J. Stwart Robinson, 1966, pp. 36-68. Reprinted from the,

Journal of General Education, IV (1949), pp. 12-31.

WAARDENBURG, J.
Massignon: notes for further research, MW, 56 (1966), pp. 157-172.

WAKKAD, Mahmoud el-.
Arabic manuscripts in Ghana, Ghana Notes and Queries, 2 (1961), p. 11.

WALKER, F.D.
Islam & Christianity in West Africa, MW, 19 (1929), pp. 129-133.

WALKER, J.
Asiya: The wife of pharaoh, MW, 18 (1928), pp. 45-48.

WALKER, J.
Who is Dhrl-kifl, MW, 16 (1926), pp. 399-401.

WALKER, J.
Who is Idris, MW, 17 (1927), pp. 259-260.

WALKER, J.
Who is 'Uzair', MW, 19 (1929), pp. 303-306.

WALTZ, J.
Historical perspectives on early missions" to Muslims. A response to Allan Cutler, MW, 61 (1971), pp. 170-186.

WAMSBROUGE, J.
Samuel Milkos Starn, BSOAS, 33 (1970), pp. 599-602.

WARDENBURG, J.D.J.
Two lights perceived: medieval Islam and Christianity, Ned. Theol. Tijds., 31 (1977), pp. 267-289.

WATERMAN, L.
Half-century of biblical & semitic investigation, AJSL, 32 (1915-16), pp. 219-229.

WATSON, W.J.
Ibrahim muteferrika and Turkish incunabule, JAOS, 88 (1968), pp. 435-441.

WATT, W. Montgomery.
Beiief in a "High God" in pre-Islamic Mecca, JSS, 16(1971), pp. 35-40.

WATT, W. Montgomery.
Some Muslim discussions of anthropomorphism, Glasg. Or. Soc. Trans., 13 (1947-49), pp. 1-10.

WATT, W.M.
Origin of the Islamic doctrine of acquisition, JRAS, (1943), pp. 234-247.

WATT, W.M.
Free will & predestination in early Islam, MW, 36 (1946), pp. 124-152.

WAZI, Nabibakhsh.
German contribution to Islamic studies, J. Asiat. Soc. Pakistan, 9 i (1964), pp. 71-83.

WEIR, T.H.
Persian & Turkish Mss. in the Hunterian Library British Isles of the Univ. of Glagsow, JRAS, (1906), pp. 595-609.

WENSINCK, A.J.
Bar Hebraene's spiritual ancestors, JRAS, (1920), pp. 231-232.

WENSINCK, A.J.
Wine in Islam, MW, 36 (1946), pp. 189-192.
What kind of nation Muslims must be? - in verses from the quran. Majallat al-Azhar, 44i(1972), pp. 5-7.

WHEELER, G.
Middle Eastern studies in the USSR, Middle Eastern Studies, 1 (1964), pp. 84-90.

WHEELER, G.E.
Russia and Asia in 1960. The Moscow Congress of Orientalists and a visit to Central Asia, RCAJ, 48 (1961), pp. 17-28.

WHWED, Munir ud-Din.
The Institution of al-Mudhakara, XVII, Deutacher Orientalisstentag, 1968 teil 2 (ZDMG Supplementa I, 1969), pp. 595-603,

WILES, J.W.
Moslem women in Yugoslavia, MW, 18 (1928), pp. 61-65.

WILLIAMS, L.F. Rush Brook.
Ninth century defence of Islam, IC, 1 (1927), pp. 109-110.

WILTON, A.J.
The Middle East Centre for Arab Studies, RCAJ, 52 (1965), pp. 260-262.

WINNETT, F.V.
Daughters of Allah, MW, 30 (1940), pp. 113-130.

WINRETT, F.V.
Allah before Islam, MW, 28 (1938), pp. 239-248.

WOLFSON, H.A.
The Hatirani in the Kalam and Ghazali as inner motive powers of human actions, Studies in mysticism and religion presented to G.G. Scholem, 1967, pp. 363-379.

WOODWORTH, W.S.
Moslem mind in Turkey today, MW, 17 (1927), pp. 139-146.

WOOLWORTH, W.S.
Bibliography of Koran texts & translations, MW, 17 (1927), pp. 279-289.

WORREL, W.H.
Account of schools for living oriental languages established in Europe, JAOS, 39 (1919), pp. 189-195.

WORRELL, W.H.
Case of Muhammed, JAOS, 48 (1928), pp. 136-146.

WORRELL, W.H.
Kolonial Institute of Hamburg, MW, 4 (1914), pp. 303-307.

WWEMER, S.M.
Allah of Islam & the God revealed in Jesus Christ, MW, 36 (1946), pp. 306-318.

YATES, D.E.
Sir Richard Francis Burton, J. Gypsy Lore Soc., 3rd ser., 43 (1964), pp. 1-2.

YOHANNAN, A.
Some Persian references to Zoroaster & his religion, JAOS, 28 (1907), pp. 182-188.

YOUNG, H.B.
Near East in South America, MW, 30 (1940), pp. 168-170.

YUSUF, K.M.
My impressions of Dr. Muhammad Ishaque, Indo-Iranica, 23iii(1970), pp. 106-112.

ZARRINKOOB, A.H.
Persian Sufism in its historical perspective, Iranian studs., 3(1970), pp. 139-220.

ZEMER, S.M.
Working library on Islam, MW, 2 (1912), pp. 32-36.

ZOECKLER, G.E.
What the shiaks teach their children, MW, 16 (1926), pp. 378-398.

ZTTESTEN, K.V.
Preliminary report on the Orintal Mss. in the library of Uppsala University (Sweden), IC, 3 (1929), pp. 244-248.

ZUKOVSKY, V.A.
Persian sufism, BSOAS, 5 (1928-30), pp. 475-488.

ZWEMBER, S.M.
Attonement by blood sacrifice in Islam, MW, 36 (1946), pp. 189-192.

ZWEMER, S.M.
Islam in Ethiopia & Eritrea, MW, 26 (1936), pp. 5-15.

ZWEMER, S.M.
Surat at ikhles, MW, 26 (1936), pp. 325-328.

ZWEMER, S.M.
Return to the old Qibla, MW, 27 (1937), pp. 13-19.

ZWEMER, S.M.
Use of alms to win converts, MW, 19 (1929), pp. 141-150.

ZWEMER, S.M.

Islamin Southern Europe, MW, 17 (1927), pp. 331-357.

ZWEMER, S.M.

Animism in the creed & in the use of the book & the rosary, MW, 10 (1920), pp. 13-24.

ZWEMER, S.M.

Animism in Islam (Hair, finger nails & the hand), MW, 7 91917), pp. 245-255.

ZWEMER, S.M.

Two Moslem catochisms (published at Capetown), MW, 15 (1925), pp. 349-360.

ZWEMMER, S.M.

A survey of Islam in South Africa, Int. Rev. Missions, 14 (1925), pp. 560-571.

'ABDUR RABB, Muhammad.

Abu Yazid al-Bistami's contribution to the development of sufism, Iqbal rev., 12iii (1971), pp. 49-73.

Islamic modernism, Hibbert Jl., 62 (1963), pp. 71-73.

Religion today: 6. Islam in Africa, Hibbert Jl., 61 (1963), pp. 57-60.

Where do Muslims and Christians differ?, Maj. al-Azhar, 42 v (1970), pp. 5-8.

Religion today: II. America's Black Muslims, Hibbert Jl., 61 (1963), pp. 109-111.

Religion today: Filipino Muslims, Hibbert Jl., 63 (1964), pp. 39-41.

The meaning of Kufr. (A study from the July, 1959, Summer School, Jerusalem), MW, 49 (1959), pp. 315-322.

The Muslim-Christian dialogue of the last ten years, Pro Mundi Vita Bull., 74 (1978), pp. 2-52.

Islam: Its origin and its future, Maj. al-Azhar, 31 (1960), pp. 205-236; 32 i (1960), pp. 65-72.

AAYAT, Ahmed Hassan el-.
The three powers of Islam, Maj. al-Azhar, 32 ii (1959), pp. 33-36.

ABBAS, Mohammad Galal.
Islam and African thought, Maj. al-Azhar, (Apr. 1969), pp. 14-16.

ABBOTT N. WAHBB MUNABBBIH.
A review article, Jnes, 36 (1977), pp.103-112.

ABBOTT, F.
The transformation of the Jihad Movement, MW, 52 (1962), pp.288-295.

ABDEL FATTAH, Afifi.
Dr. Mohamad Abdullah Draz (La morale du Koran), Maj. al-Azhar, (Oct. 1964), pp. 12-16; (Nov. 1964), pp. 13-16; (Jan. 1965, pp. 14-16; (Feb. 1965), pp. 15-16.

ABDEL-MALEK, Anouar.
Orientalism in crisis, Diogenes, 44 (1964), pp. 103-140 [Offprint in SOAS]; letter by C. Cahen, 49 (1965), pp. 135-138.

ABDUL KARIM.
Shah Gharib Allah of Chittagong, JAS Pak., 11 (1966), pp. 73-80.

ABDUL KHALIQ.
Social teachings of the Qur'an, Iqbal, 11 (1962), pp. 12-38.

ABDUL MALIKI, H.E.
Alhaji,, Islam in Nigeria, IQ, 9 (1965), pp. 30-36.

ABDUL, Musa.
The role of Abraham in the formation of Islam, Orita, 5 i (1974), pp. 58-70.

ABDUR Rabb, M.
Abu Yazid Bistami's contribution to development of Sufism, Iqbal Re., 12 iii(1971), pp. 49-73.

ABN AL-TAFAHUM.
"City of wrong", MW, 46 (1956), pp. 132-143, 225-236.

ABSIL, Ibrahim M. el-.
Al-Hajj (Piligrimage). An Islamic world conference, Maj. al-Azhar, (Feb. 1965), pp. 11-12.

ABU SHANAB, N.R.
The philosophical significance of al-ghazzali, Iqbal Rev., 13 i (1972), pp. 51-70.

ABUL HASHIM.
The effects of the belief in the oneness of God, Maj. al-Azhar, (Dec. 1966), pp. 5-8.

ABUN-NASR, Jamil.
Some aspects of the Umari branch of the Tijaniyya, J. Afr. Hist., 3 (1962), pp. 329-331.

ADAMS, C.J.
The history of religions and the study of Islam, ACLS news l., 25 iii-iv.

AFFIFI, A.E.
The works of Ibn 'Arabi in the light of a memorandum drawn up by him, Bull. Fac. Arts Alexandria, 8 (1954), pp. 109-117.

AGAHI, Abbas.
Some names and practices in the Druze system of beliefs, Bull. BAO, N.S. 9 (1977), pp. 14-21.

AHMAD, Al-Hafis Basheer.
A glimpse into Islam in Britain, Maj. al-Azhar, (June 1969), pp. 14-16.

AHMAD, Shabbir.
The "Addurrat ul-Thaminah" of Mullla Abdul Hakim of Sialkot, J. Research Soc. Pakistan, 1 ii (1964), pp. 47-78.

AHMED, Manzooruddin.
Sovereignty of God in the constitution of Pakistan: A study in the conflict of traditionalism and modernism, Islamic Studies, 4 (1965), pp. 201-212.

ALI, Mohammed.
Sayid Jamal-ud-Din Afghani, Afghanistan, 17 i (1962), pp. 1-9.

ALI, Mubarak.
The Khutba: A symbol of royality in Islam, Sind. U. Research Arts Ser., 17 & 18 (1978-9), pp. 89-96.

ALWAYE, A.M. Mohiaddin.
The conception of human responsibility in Islam, Maj. al-Azhar, (Oct. 1969), pp. 4-7.

ALWAYE, A.M. Mohiaddin.
Islam and human rights, Maj. al-Azhar, (Dec. 1968), pp. 1-8.

ALWAYE, A.M. Mohiaddin.
Fasting: Its definition and objective, Maj. al-Azhar, (Dev. 1967), pp. 1-5.

ALWAYE, A.M. Mohiaddin.
The conduct of Muslims in a war, Maj. al-Azhar, (Aug. 1967), pp. 1-3.

ALWAYE, A.M. Mohiaddin.
The effects of Hajj on the life of man, Maj. al-Azhar, (Feb. 1970), pp. 1-3.

ALWAYE, A.M. Mohiaddin.
The concept of 'Jihad' in Islam, Maj. al-Azhar, (March 1967), pp. 1-4.

ALWAYE, A.M. Mohiaddin.
Fasting and its values, Maj. al-Azhar, (Nov. 1969), pp. 5-8.

ALWAYE, A.M. Mohiaddin.
Al-Hajj - the pilgrimage: The significance, object and rites, Maj. al-Azhar, (March 1968), pp. 1-7.

ALWAYE, A.M. Mohiaddin.
Importance of the Prayer, Maj. al-Azhar, (April 1969), pp. 1-5.

ALWAYE, A.M. Mohiaddin.
The significances of "Hajj", Maj. al-Azhar, (March 1966), pp. 9-11.

ALWAYE, A.M. Mohiaddin.
Fasting in Islam, Maj. al-Azhar, (Nov. 1966), pp. 1-4.

ALWAYE, A.M. Mohiaddin.
Hostility of the Jews against the Prophet, Maj. al-Azhar, (Oct. 1967), pp. 1-6.

ALWAYE, A.M. Mohiaddin.
The applicability of Islam in varying conditions of life, Maj. al-Azhar, 42 vi (1970), pp. 1-4.

ALWAYE, A.M. Mohiaddin.
The effects of the belief in the Oneness of God, Maj. al-Azhar, (March 1965), pp. 3-4.

ALWAYE, A.M. Mohiaddin.
Islam resists fanaticism and isolation, Maj. al-Azhar, (Jan. 1970), pp. 1-4.

ALWAYE, A.M. Mohiaddin.
The world Prophet, Maj. al-Azhar, (may 1969), pp. 1-8.

ALWAYE, A.M. Mohiaddin.
The Prophet of light and guidance, Maj. al-Azhar, 42 v (1970), pp. 1-3.

ALWAYE, A.M. Mohiaddin.
The role of Islam in spread of knowledge, Maj. al-Azhar (Sepg. 1968), pp. 3-4; 13,

ALWAYE, A.M. Mohiaddin.
Islam and life, Maj. al-Azhar, (April 1965), pp. 5-6; Sept. 1965, pp. 6-7; Oct. 1965, pp. 7-8.

ALWAYE, A.M. Mohiaddin.
History of the Ka'ba, Maj. al-Azhar, (Feb. 1969), pp. 1-4.

ALWAYE, A.M. Mohiaddin.
The 'Ascent' of the Prophet connected the Islamic world with Jerusalem, Maj. al-Azhar, (Oct. 1968), pp. 1-6.

ALWAYE, A.M. Mohiaddin.
'Jamaluddin Al-Afghani' on the occasion of his 70th anniversary (d. 1897 A.D.), Maj. al-Azhar, (April 1967), pp. 1-4.

ALWAYE, A.M. Mohiaddin.
The mosque in Islamic society, Maj. al-Azhar, (Jan. 1968, pp. 1-4.

ALWAYE, Mohiaddin.
True religion, Maj. al-Azhar, Feb. 1965, p. 13.

ALWAYE, Mohiaddin.
Prophet Muhammad: The perfect example for humanity, Maj. al-Azhar, (Oct. 1964), pp. 10-11.

ALWAYE, MOHIADDIN.
Quran and freedon of belief, Maj. al-Azhar, (Jan) 1965, p. 12.

AMER, Abdul Khaliq.
The effects of Islam in the development of Africa, Maj. al-Azhar, (May 1966), pp. 12-15.

AMIJI, H.M.
Some notes on religion dissent in 19th century East Africa, Afr. Hist. Stud., 4 (1971), pp. 603-616.

ANDRZEJEWSKI, B.W.
The roobdoon of Sheikh Aqib Abdullahi Jama: A Somali prayer for rain, Afr. Lang. Stud., 11 (1970), pp. 21-34.

ANSARI ZAFAR ISHAQ.
Some reflections on Islamic bases for dialogue with Jews and Christains, J. Ecumen. stud, 14 (1977), pp. 433-447.

ANSARI, Raschia al-.
My experience of Islam. The right path, Kan. al-Azhar, Dec. 1965, pp. 4-9; Jan. 1966, pp. 7-8; Feb. 1966, pp. 4-6; Mar. 1966, pp. 12-16.

ANSARI, Raschid.
A story of the Prophet, Maj. al-Azhar, (May 1966), pp. 8-9.

ANSARI, Raschid Al-.
Al-Qur'an - a living miracle of the Prophet., Maj. al-Azhar, (Oct. 1967), pp. 7-11.

ANSARI, Raschid Al-.
Al-Madinah, Maj. al-Azhar, (May 1967), pp.12-14,5.

ANSARI, Raschied al-.
Jerusalem (Al-Kuds), Maj. al-Azhar, (Jan. 1967), pp. 6-8.

ANSARI, Raschied Al-.
The significance of 'Ramadan', Maj. al-Azhar, (Nov. 1966), pp. 5-7.

ANSARI, Rashhid al-.
Fundamentals of Islam, Maj. al-Azhar, (April 1965), pp. 12-13.

ANSARY, Raschid.
The magnificent man, Maj. al-Azhar, (Oct. 1965), pp. 3-4, 6.

ANTOUN, R.T.
The social significance of Ramadan in and Arab village, MW, 58 (1968), pp. 36-42; 95-108.

AQQAD, Abbas Mahmoud el-.
Equality in Islam and subversive doctrines, Maj. al-Azhar, 31 (1959), pp. 139-142.

ARAFAT, W.N.
Fact and fiction in the history of pre-Islamic idol-worship, IQ, 12 (1968), pp. 9-21.

ARBERRY A. J.
Bistamiana, Bsoas, 25 (1962), pp. 28-37.

ARBERRY A.J.
The diine colloquy in Islam, Bull J.R. Lib., 39 (1956), pp. 18-44.

ARBERRY, A.J.
Al-Ashari's tract on faith, BSOAS, 19 (1957), pp. 160-162.

ARBERRY, A.J.
Jami's biography of Ansari, IQ, 7 (1963), pp. 57-82.

ARBERRY, A.J.
The vita of Ahmad-i Jam, BSOAS, 26 (1963), pp. 420-425.

ARBERRY, A.J.
The teachers of Al-Bukhari, IQ, 11 (1967), pp. 34-49.

ARBERRY, A.J.
Traditions by three liaks, IQ, 13 (1969), pp. 169-182.

ARBERRY, A.J.
Synonyms and homonyms in the Qur'an, IQ, 13 (1969), pp. 135-139.

ARBERRY, A.J.
Two Sufi biographies, IQ, 12 (1968), pp. 219-225

ARBERRY, A.J.
A Hanbali tract on the eternity of the Qur'an, Islamic Q., 3 (1956), pp. 16-41.

ARBERRY, A.J.
Bistamiana, BSOAS, 25 (1962), pp. 28-37.

ARKOUN, Mohammed.
Islam facing development, Diogenee, 77 (1972), pp. 71-91.

ARMAJANI, Yahya.
What the US needs to know about Islam, Worldiew, 22 (1979), pp. 13-19.

ARNETT, M.
The Trinidad Muslim League, MW, 48 (1958), pp. 52-62.

ARO, J.
Dialogue between religions in the past and at the present day, Temenos, 12 (1976), pp. 105-116.

ARRAMADI, Gamal Addin.
Virtues from the Quran, Maj. al-Azhar, 32 vii (1960), pp. 24-27.

ARRAMADI, Gamal Addin.
The influence of Sufism on the human literature and thought, Maj. al-Azhar, 32 ii-iv (1960), pp. 20-21.

ARRAMADI, Gamal Addin.
The birthday of Mohammed through history, Maj. al-Azhar, 32 v (1960-61), pp. 14-18.

ASAD, Talal.
Politics and religion in Islamic reform: A critique of Kedourie's, Afgani and Abduh. RMES, 2 (1976), pp. 13-22.

ASSIL, Ibrahim M. el-.
Tradition is the second source of Islamic law, Maj. al-Azhar, (March 1965), pp. 13-14.

ASSIL, Ibrahim M. el-.
Fasting in Islam, Maj. al-Azhar, (Jan. 1965), p.13.

AUSTIN, R.W.
A letter to desciples in prison, Studies in Comparative religion, 8 (1974), pp. 39-41.

AUSTIN, R.W.
"Iseek God's..." [on Au Madyan], Stud. in Comp. Religl, 7 (1973), pp. 92-94.

AUSTIN, R.W.J.
Some key words in the Islamic concept of man, Studies in Comp. Rel., 10 (1976), pp. 46-57.

AUSTIN, R.W.J.
Connsels of Sufi master, Studies in Comp. Rel., 5 (1971), pp. 207-214.

AUSTIN. R.
Sufism and its world view, Ultimate reality and meaning, 3 (1980), pp. 50-69.

AWAD, B. A.
The moderation of Islam, IQ, 7 (1963), pp.83-89.

AWAD, B.A.
The universal religion, IQ, 8 (1964), pp. 64-72.

AWANG, Omar.
The Um al-Barahin of Sanusi, Nusaritara, 2 (1972), pp. 157-168.

AWN, P.J.
Master, dsciple and devil: A look at Islamic spirituality, New R. Books Rel., 3 (1979), p. 3.

AYYAD, M. Gamaluddin.
The merits of labour in Islam, Maj. al-Azhar, (Oct. 1965), pp. 5-6; (Dec. 1965), pp. 10-12; (April, 1966), pp. 7-10.

AYYAD, M. Gamaluddir.
The meaning of "Amal" in Islam, Maj. al-Azhar, Sept. 1965, pp. 11-12.

AZAD, Mauians Abul Kalam.
The Qur'an leads humanity to the path of progress, Maj. al-Azhar, 42 ix (1970), pp. 13-16.

AZAD, Moulana Abul Kalam.

The Quran's conception of God, Maj. al-Azhar, (April 1966), pp. 1-4; May (1956), pp. 1-7.

AZMA, Nazeer el-.

The Qur'an and poetry, Al-Arabiyya, 13 i & ii (1980), pp. 65-79.

BABSMALA, S.

Self-realization in the mystical thought of Al-Kubra: An interpretation, Orita, 12 (1978), pp. 51-65.

BADEAU, J.S.

Religion in the Middle East, Social Education, 25 i (1961), pp. 37-40.

BADEAU, J.S.

Islam and the modern Middle East, Foreign affairs, 38 (1959), pp. 61-74.

BAGLEY, F.R.C.

The Azhar and Sldism, MW, 50 (1960), pp. 122-129.

BAHAY MUHAMMAD EL-.

How to make the youth adhere to religion, Maj. sl-Azhar, 31 (1959), pp. 197-204.

BAHAY, Mohammad el-.

Islam as a system of life, Maj. al-Azhar 31, 31 (1959-60), pp. 45-57; (1959), pp. 45-57.

BAHAY, Mohammad el-.

Islam the religion of the virtuous standard of humanity, Majallat al-Azhar, 31 (1959), English suppl., pp. 11-25.

BAHAY, Muhammad el-.

The duty of the learned (al-Ulammaa), Maj. al-Azhar, 31 (1960), pp. 169-182.

BAHAY, Muhammad el-.

Religion in the life of man, Maj. al-Azhar, 31 (1959), pp. 106-128.

BAHAY, Muhammad el.

Islam and social development, Maj. al-Azhar, 32 iii-i (1960), pp. 12-19.

BAHAY, Muhammmad el.
Belief in God, Maj. al-Azhar, 32v (196O), pp. 10-13.

BAKARAT, Soliman.
Faith, Maj. al-Azhar, (March 1968), pp. 14-16; (April 1968), pp. 14-16.

BALJON, J.M.S.
The 'Amr of God' in the Koran, Acta Or., 23 (1958), pp. 7-18.

BALOGUN, I.A.
The concept of ahd in Islam, Orita, 12 ị (1978), pp. 3-11.

BANETH, D.E.N.
What did Muhammad mean when he called his religion "Islam"? The original meaning of Aslama and its derivitives, Israel Oriental Studies, 1 (1971), pp. 183-190.

BANKS D.J.
Islam and inhritance in Malaya: culture conflict or revolution?, Amer. Ethnologist, 3 (1976), pp. 573-586.

BARAAT, Soliman.
The ways of good and evil, Maj. al-Azhar, (Dec. 1966), pp. 15-16.

BARAKAT, Soliman.
Observance of Jihad, Maj. al-Azhar, (Sept. 1967), pp. 9-13.

BARAKAT, Soliman.
Prayer, II, Maj. al-Azhar, (Nov. 1967), pp. 14-17.

BARAKAT, Soliman.
Selected prayers of the Prophet, Maj. al-Azhar, (Dec. 1967), pp. 14-16; (Jan. 1968), pp. 12-16.

BARAKAT, Soliman.
Intent, the Muslim's Inward, Maj. al-Azhar, (Sept. 1968), pp. 14-16.

BARAKAT, Soliman.
Al-Fatihah. The opening chapter of the Qur'an, Maj. al-Azhar, (Oct. 1968), pp. 14-16.

BARAKAT, Soliman.
Two sorts of intimates, Maj. al-Azhar, (March 1967), pp. 14-16.

BARAKAT, Soliman.
Significances of the prayer, Maj. al-Azhar, (Oct. 1967), pp. 12-16.

BARAKAT, Soliman.
The true believer, Maj. al-Azhar, (May 1969), pp. 15-16.

BARAKAT, Soliman.
Tell of the merits of your dead, Maj. al-Azhar, (April 1967), pp. 14-16.

BARCLAY, H.B.
A Sudanese religios brotherhood: al-Tariqa al-Hindiya, MW, 53 (1963), pp. 127-137.

BARCLAY, H.B.
Muslim religious practice in a village suburb of Khartoum, MW, 53 (1963), pp. 205-211.

BARKAT, Anwar M.
Church-state relationships in an ideological Islamic state, Ecumenical R., 29 (1977), pp. 39-51.

BARKOW J.H.
Hausa womaen and Islam, Can. J.Afr. Stud, 6 (1972), pp. 317-328.

BASETTI-SANI G.
Muhammad and St. Francis, MW, 46 (1956), pp. 345-353.

BASETTI-SANI, J.
For a dialogue between Christian and Muslims, MW, 57 (1967), pp. 126-137, 186-196.

BASHARAT ALI, M.
Sociology and sociological analysis of the Quran, Pakistan Philos J., 6 ii (1962), pp. 70-84.

BASHARAT ALI, M.
The sociology of the science of the Quran, Pak. Philos J., 8 (1964), pp. 53-73.

BASHARAT ALI, M.
The Qura'nic sociology of knowledge, Pakistan Philos. J., 7 iv (1963), pp. 65-84.

BASR, Seyyed Hossein.
The interior life in Islam, Religious Traditions, 1 (1978), pp. 48-55.

BASSIOUNI, M. Cherif.
Protection of diplomats under Islamic law, AJIL, 74 (1980), pp. 609-633.

BATTON, J.M.S.
Pakistan views of Hadith, WI, N.S. (1958), pp. 219-227.

BAUSANI A.
On some recent translations of the Qur'an, Numen, 4 (1957), pp. 75-81.

BEAURECUEIL, S.de.
Khwadja Abdullah Ansari of Herat (1006-1089), Adab [Kabul], 24 ii (1976), pp. 1-4.

BEESTON, A.F.L.
An ancient Druze manuscript, Bodl. Libr. Rec., 5 (1956), pp. 286-290.

BEESTON, A.F.L.
The "Men of the Tanglewood" in the Qur'an, J. Semitic Stud., 13 (1968), pp. 253-255.

BELLAMY, J.A.
The makarim al-Akhlaq by Ibn Abi l-Dunya, MW, 53 (1963), pp. 106-119.

BEN-SHEMESH, A.
Some suggestions to Qur'an translators, Arabica, 16 (1969), pp. 81-83; 17 (1970), pp. 197-204.

BENDA, H.J.
Continuity and change in Indonesian Islam, Asian and African Studies, 1 (1965), pp. 123-138.

BENNETT, J.G.
Sufi spiritual techniques, Systematics, 7 (1969-70), pp. 244-260.

BENOIST, L.
Work of Frithjof Schuon, Etudes Traditionneles, 79 (1978) no. 461, pp. 97-101.

BERGER, M.
The Blac Muslims, Horizon, 6 (Winter 1964), pp. 49-64.

BERGER, M.
The Mosque: Aspects of governmental policy towards religion in Egypt today, MES, 6 (1970), pp. 3-34.

BERKES, Niyazi.
Ethics and social practice in Islam, Philosphy East and West, 9 (1959), pp. 60-62.

BETHMANN, E.W.
Muslim-Christian relationships, MW, 51 (1961), pp. 259-264.

BHALABY, Abdul Wadood.
The fundamental halief in Islam, Maj. al-Azhar (Nov. 1964), pp. 8-11; (Dec. 1964), pp. 6-9; (Jan. 1965), pp. 8-11; (Feb. 1965), pp. 8-10,

BIECHLER, J.E.
Christian humanism confornts Islam: Shifting the Qur'an with Nicholas of Cusa, J. Ecumenical Studies, 13 (1976), pp. 1-14.

BIRDS J.S.
Oerland pilgrimage from West Africa to Mecca: anachronism or fashion?, Geography, 62 (1977), pp. 215-217.

BIRKELAND, H.
The interpretation of Surah 107, SI, (1958), pp. 13-29.

BIRKS J.S.
The Mecca pilgrimage by West Afrcan pastoral nomads, JMAS, 15 (1977), pp. 47-58.

BISHOP, D.H.
Forgieness in religious thought, Stud. Compar. Relig., 2 (1968), pp. 31-44.

BISHOP, E.F.F.
Jerusalem byways of memory, MW, 50 (1960), pp. 199-206.

BISHOP, E.F.F.
Islam in the Psalter, MW, 55 (1965), pp. 19-27.

BISHOP, E.F.F.
The reasonableness of Christ, MW, 55 (1965), pp. 346-356.

BISHOP, E.F.F.
Is Pontius Pilate's aqueduct referred to in the Qur'an?, MW, 52 (1962), pp. 189-193.

BISHOP, E.F.F.
Jerusalem byways of memory III "Some teachers", MW, 51 (1961), pp. 265-273.

BISHOP, E.F.F.
Some New Testament occurrences of Monos with Theos, MW, 51 (1961), pp. 123-127.

BISHOP, E.F.F.
Jerusalem: Byways of memory VII. Characters on the high way., MW, 57 (1967), pp. 33-41.

BISHOP, E.P.F.
Gates and doors in the New Testment and the Qur'an, Glasgow Or. Soc. Trans., 22 (1967-8), pp. 39-45.

BIVAR, A.D.H.
A dated Kuran from Bronu, Nigeria Mag., 65 (1960), pp. 199-205.

BLANC, H.
Druze particularism: Modern aspects of an old problem, MEA, 3 (1952), pp. 315-321.

BODROGLIGETT, A.
The Persian translation of the Koran in Latin letters, Acta Or. Acad. Sci. Hung, 13 (1961), pp. 261-276.

BOGERT, E.A.
The desolation and solitude of Job, MW, 52 (1962), pp. 322-330.

BOISARD, M.A.

Contributing to a better mutual understanding between Islam and the West, J. Inst. Muslim Minority Affairs, 1 ii & 2 i (1979-80), pp. 194-201.

BORRMANS, M.

The doctrinal basis common to Christians and Muslims and diffferent areas of conergence in action, J. Ecumenical Studies, 14 (1977), pp. 32-50.

BOSWORTH, C.E.

Al-Hwarazmi on theology and sects: The chapter on kalam in the Maf-atih al-ulum, BEO, 29 (1977), pp. 85-95.

BOSWORTH, C.E.

The Prophet vindicated: A restoration treatise on Islam and Muhammad, Religion, 6 (1976), pp. 1-12.

BOSWORTH, C.E.

Dr. S.M. Stern M.A., D. Phil, Iran, 8 (1970), p. ix.

BOSWORTH, C.E.

A dramatisation of the prophet Muhammad's life: Henri de Bornier's Mahamet, Numen, 17 (1970), pp. 105-117.

BOSWORTH, E.

The rise of the Karamiyyah in Khurasan, MW, 50 (1960), pp. 5-14.

BOWKER, J.

The problem of suffering in the Qur'an, Relig. Stud., 4 (1968), pp. 183-202.

BOWKER, J.W.

Intercession in the Qur'an and the Jewish tradition, J. Semitic studies, 11 (1966), pp. 69-82.

BOWMAN, J.

Banu Islail in the Qur'an, Islamic Studies, 2 (1963), pp. 447-455.

BRADEN, C.S.

Islam in America, Int. R. Missions, 48 (1959), pp. 309-317.

BRADMAH, B.A.R.
Morality in Islam, Ghand Bull. Theology, 4 iii (1972), p. 45-53.

BRADMAH, B.A.R.
Concept of sin in Islam, Ghana Bull. Theology, 4 i (1971), pp. 31-40.

BRADY, D.
The Book of Revelation and the Qur'an is there a possible relationship?, JSS, 23 (1978), pp. 216-225.

BRAIMAH, B.A.R.
Morality in Islam, Ghana Bull. Theol, 4 iii (1972), pp. 45-53.

BRAMANN, M.M.
Allah's liberty to punish/forgie, Aer. Is., 47 (1971), pp. 236-237.

BRAMANN, M.M.
The phrase in untum fa ilina in S. Yusuf, v.10, Islam, 48 (1971), pp. 122-125.

BRASWELL, G.W.
Iran and Islam, Theology today, 36 (1980), pp. 523-533.

BRASWELL, G.W.
Civil religion in contemporary Iran, J. Church and State, 21 (1979), pp. 223-246.

BRASWELL, G.W. Jr.
Iran and Islam, Theology today, 36 (1979-80), pp. 523-533.

BRAVMANN, M.M.
The 'Completion' or 'Improvement' of a Laudable Deed: An ancient Arab ethinic motif, Der. Islam, 49 (1972), pp. 273-276.

BRAVMANN, Mefr M.
The Ancient Arab background of the Qur'anic concept al-gizyatu gan yadin, Arabica, 13 (1966), pp. 307-314; 14 (1967), pp. 90-91, 326-327.

BRENNER, L.
The Sufi teaching of Tierno Bokar Salif Tall, J. Religion in Africa, 8 (1976), pp. 208-226.

BREWSTER,, D.P.
The study of Sufism; towards a methodology, Religion, 6 (1976), pp. 31-47.

BROADRIBB, D.
The self-image in Islam, Abr-Nahrain, 9 (1969-70), pp. 66-80.

BROWN, L.C.
The Islamic Reformist Movement in North Africa, J. Mod. Afr. Studies, 2 (1964), pp. 55-63.

BRYER, D.R.W.
The origins of the Druze religion Chapter four, Der. Islam, 53 (1976), pp. 5-27.

BUCHANAN, J. Robertson.
The Druzes: Their origins and development to the zenith of their power under Fakhr-al-Din II, Trans. Glasgow Univ. Or. Soc., 19 (1961-62), pp. 41-51.

BURCKHARDT, T.
Islamic surveys: Four works by Seyyed Hossein Naar, Stud. Compar. Relig., 2 (1968), pp. 171-177.

BURCKHARDT, T.
The prayer of ibn Mushish (As-salat al-Mashishiyah), Studies Comp. Rel., 12 i-ii (1978), pp. 8-16.

BURCKHRDT, T.
The symbolism of chess, Stud. Compar. Relig, 3 (1969), pp. 107-112.

BURNS, P.
Islam in Idonesia: The unconsummated marriage, Milla wa-milla, 17 (1977), pp. 24-26.

BURNS, W.H.
The Black Muslims in America: A reinterpretation, Race, 5 (1963), pp. 26-37.

BURTON, J.
"Those are the high-flying cranes", J. Semitic Stud., 15 (1970), pp. 246-263.

BUSHANAK, Adil A.
The Hajj transportation system, Hajj Studies, 1 (178), pp. 87-115.

CACHIA, P.J.E.
Baydawi on the Fawatih, J. Semitic Stud., 13 (1968), pp. 218-231.

CAGATAY, Neset.
The outline of Islamism and Turkish retromations, Hahiyat Fak. Dergisi, 9 (1961), pp. 141-146.

CALVERLEY E.E.
The grammar of Suratu 'l-Ikhlaṣ, SI, 8 (1957), PP. 5-14.

CALVERLEY, E.E.
Negro Muslims in Hartford, MW, 55 (1965), pp. 340-345.

CALVERLEY, E.E.
Al-Baydwi's Matali' al-Anzar. A systematic theology of Islam, MW, 43 (1963), pp. 293-297.

CALVERLEY, E.E.
Sumaniyyah, MW, 54 (1964), pp. 200-202.

CALVERLEY, E.E.
Christian theology and the Qura'an, MW, 47 (1957), pp. 283-289.

CAMMANN S.V.R.
Religious symbolism in Persian art, History of religions, 15 (1976), pp. 193-208.

CAMPS, A.
The cult of Khwaji Khizi in Sind. A legendary saint, Franciscan Echoes, 2 i (1962), pp. 30-32, (Offprint in SOAS).

CAMPS, A.
Pir Fazl Shah Jilani Goth. A mental hospital in Sind., Framciscan Echoes, 1 v (1961), pp. 24-25 [Offprint in SOAS].

CANTEINS, J.
Koranic initials, Etudes Traditionnelles, 79 (1978), p. 102.

CARSWELL, John.
China and Islam: A survey of the coast of India and Ceylon,

Trans. Or. Ceramic Soc., (1977-8), pp. 25-68.

CAVENDISH, M.W.
The custom of placing pebbles on Nubian graves, Sudan Notes and records, 47 (1966), pp. 151-156.

CEHAJIC, dzemal.
Bektashis and Islam in Bosnia and Hercegovina, Anali Gazi Husrevbegove Bibl., 5-6 (1978), pp. 83-90.

CHEJNE, Anwar G.
Mu'ammar Ibn 'Abbad al-Sulami, a leading Mu'tazilite of the eigth-ninth centuries, MW, 51 (1961), pp. 311-320.

CHITTICK, W.C.
The last will and testament of Ibn 'Arabi's foremost disciple and some note on its author, Sophia perennis, 4 i (1978), pp. 43-58.

CHITTICK, W.C.
Ibn 'Arabi's own summary of the Fusus: "the imprints of the bezels of wisdom" (conclusion), Sophia Perennis, 1 ii (1975), pp. 88-128; 2 ii (1976), pp. 67-106.

CHITTICK, W.C.
A Shadhili presence in Shiite Islam, Sophia Perennis, 1 i (1975), pp. 97-100.

CLARKE, P.B.
Islamic millenarianism in West Africa: A revolutionary ideology?, Religious Studies, 16 (1980), pp. 317-339.

CLARKE, P.B.
The Islamilis: A study of community, Brit. J. Sociol, 27 (1976), pp. 484-494.

CLARKE, P.B.
The Ismaili sect in London: Religion institutions and social change, Religion, 8 (1978), pp. 68-84.

CLAUSON, G.
Nostratic, JRAS, (1973), pp. 46-55.

CLINTON, J.W., CROLL, D.C., DAVIS, E.W. and LUTHER, A.
On the feasibility of an automated bibliography of Iranian studies,

Iranian Stud., 2 (1969), pp. 151-169.

COMSTOCK, G.L.

The Yoruba and religious change, J. Religion Africa, 10 (1979), pp. 1-12.

CONSTANTELOS, D.J.

The "Neomartyrs" as evidence for methods and motives leading to conversion and martydom in the Ottoman Empire, Greek Orth. Theol. R., 23 (1978), pp. 216-234.

CRAGG K.

Ramadan prayers, MW, 47 (1957), pp. 210-223.

CRAGG, K.

The Qur'an and the Christian reader, MW, 46 (1956), pp. 61-68.

CRAGG, K.

Religious developments in Islam in the 20th century (with special reference to the pressures of the modern, secular world, J. World Hist., 3 (1956), pp. 304-324.

CRAGG, K.

West African catechism, MW, 48 (1958), pp. 237-247.

CRAGG, K.

Being Christian and being Muslim: A personal debate, Religion, 10 (1980), pp. 196-208.

CRAGG, K.

How not Islam?, Religious Studies, 13 (1977), pp. 387-394.

CRUISE O'BRIEN D.A.

A versatile charisma: the Mouride brotherhood 1967-1975, Archeurop sociologie, 18 (1977), pp. 84-106.

CUTLER, A.

The ninth-century Spanish martyrs' movement and the origins of Western christian missions to the Muslims, MW, 55 91965), pp. 321-339.

CUTLER, A.

Who was the "Monk of France" and when did he write? A note on D.M. Dunlop's "A christian mission to Muslim Spain in the

11th century, and., 28 (1963), pp. 249-269.

DANNER, V.
Islamic mysticism, Studies in Comp. Rel., 10 (1976), pp. 25-37.

DAR, B.A.
The growth of early Sufism, Iqbal, 2 i (1953), pp. 88-100.

DE JONG, F.
Materials relatie to the history fo the Darqawiyya order and its branches, Arabica, 26 (1979), pp. 126-143.

DE JONG, F.
The works of Tantawi Jawhari (1862-1940). Some bibliographical and biographical notes, Bibl. Or., 34 (1977), pp. 153-161.

DENNY, F.M.
Some religio-communal terms and concepts in the Qur'an, Numen, 24 (1977), pp. 26-59.

DODGE, B.
Al-Ismailiyyah and the origin of the Fatimids, MW, 49 (1959), pp. 296-305.

DOLAN, J.P.
Medieval Christian tolerance and the Muslim world, MW, 51 (1961), pp. 280-287.

DONALDSON, D.M.
The study of Muslim ethics, MW, 48 (1958), pp. 286-294.

DROUBIE, Riadh El-.
A Muslim looks at Christianity and the Church living in a multicultural society, Expository Times, 88 (1976-7), pp. 264-268.

DUL, Musa.
The Ramada fasts, Nigerian Islam, 2 ii (1972-74), pp. 33-39.

EBERHARD, W.
Modern tendencies in Islam in Pakistan, Sociologus, 10 (1960), pp. 139-152.

EBIED, R.Y. and YOUNG, M.J.L.
An exposition of the Islamic doctrine of Christ's second coming,

as presented by a Bosnian Muslim scholar, Orientalia Lovaniensia periodica, 5 (1974), pp. 127-137.

EBIED. R.Y. and YOUNG, M.J.I.
An unpublished refutation of the doctrines of the Wahhabis, RSO, 50 (1976), pp. 377-397.

EDMONDB, C.J.
The beliefs and practices of the Ahl-i Haqq of Iraq, Iran, 7 (1969), pp. 89-101.

ELIAṢH, J.
The Ithna ashari-shi'i juristic theory of political and legal authority, SI, 29 (1969), pp. 17-30.

ENDE, W.
The flagellations of Muharram and the Shi'ite 'Ulama!, Der Islam, 55 (1978), pp. 19-36.

FADEL, Aly Omar.
Estimation of mankind in Islam, Maj. al-Azhar, (Nov. 1966), pp. 13-14, 12.

FADEL, Aly Omar.
Universality of Islam, Maj. al-Azhar, (Jan. 1967), pp. 9-12, 16.

FAKHRY MAJID.
The classical Islame arguments for the existence of God, MW, 47 (1957), pp. 133-145.

FAROQHI, Suraiya.
Agricultural activities in Bektashi center: The takke of Kizil Deli 1750-1831, Sudostforschungen, 35 (1976), pp. 69-96.

FARRAN, C.D.O.
The Nile waters question in international law, Sudan Notes and Records, 41 (1960), pp. 88-100.

FARUKI, Kemal.
Tawhid and the doctrine of 'Ismah, Islamic Studies, 4 (1965), pp. 31-43.

FARUKI, Kemal.
Al-Ahkam al-khamah: The five values, Islamic Stud., 3 (1966), pp. 43-98.

FARUQI, Islmail Ragi A. al-.
History of religions: A nature and significance for Christian education and the Muslim-Christian dialogue, Numen, 12 (1965), pp. 35-65, 81-86.

FARUQI, Isma'il Ragi al-.
Towards a new methodology for Quranic exegesis, IS, 1 (1962), pp. 35-52.

FARUQI, Ismafi, R. al-.
The essence of religious experience in Islam, Thumen, 20 (1973), pp. 186-201.

FARUQI, Ismail al-.
On the nature of Islamic da'wah, Int. Rev. Mission, 65 (1976), pp. 391-409.

FASHOLE-LUKE, E.
Christianity and Islam in Freetown, Sierra Leone Bull. Religion, 91 (1967), pp. 1-16.

FATIMI, S.Q.
A new light on the Hijrat to Habashah, J. Pak. Hist. Soc., 9 (1961), pp. 109-115.

FATIMI, S.Q.
In quest of Kalah, J. Southeast Asian Hist., 1 (1960), pp. 62-101.

FISHER, A.W.
Enlightened despotism and Islam under Catherine II, Slavic Rev., 27 (1968), pp. 542-553.

FISHER, H.
The early life and pilgrimage of al-Hajj Muhammad al-Amin the Soninke (d. 1887), J. Afr., 11 (1970), pp. 51-69.

FITZGERALD M.L.
Christian-Muslim dialogue in South-East Asia, Islamochristiana, 2 (1976), pp.171-185.

FLETCHER, J.
The Naqshbandiyya and the Dhir-i arra, J. Turkish Studies, 1 (1977), pp. 113-119.

FORBES, A.D.W.

The Muslim national minorities of China, Religion, 6 (1976), pp. 67-87.

FRANK, R.M.

The structure of created casuality according to Al-As'art, SI, 25 (1966), pp. 13-15.

FRANK, R.M.

The Kalam, an art of contradiction making or theological science? Some remarks on the quetion, JAOS, 88 (1968), pp. 295-309.

FRANK, R.M.

The divine attributes according to the teaching of Abu l-Hudhayl Al-'Allaf, LE Museon, 82 (1969), pp. 451-506.

FRANK, R.M.

Al-ma'nd: Some reflectiosns on the technical meanings of the term in the Kalam and its use in the physics of Muammar, JAOS, 87 (1967), pp. 248-259.

FRAZEE, C.A.

Ibn al-'Arabi and Spanish mysticiam of the sixteenth century, Numen, 14 (1967), pp.229-240.

FRYE, R.N.

Islam in Iran, MW, 46 (1956), pp. 5-12.

FRYZEL, T.

Thedoctrine of jihad in Islam and its contemporary interpretation, Dialectics and humanism, 6 (1979), pp. 141-152.

FUDA, Abdul Rahim.

The Holy Quran. Eternal miracle of the Prophet, Maj. al-Azhar, (Oct. 1969), pp. 1-3.

FUDA, Abdul Rahim.

Faith and action, Maj. al-Azhar, (Jan. 1970), pp. 14-16.

FUDA, Abdul Rahim.

Why Ramadan is important?, Maj. al-Azhar, (Nov. 1969), pp. 1-4.

FUDA, Abdul Rahim.
Al-Aqas Mosque ....O Muslims!!, Maj. al-Azhar, (Sept. 1969), pp. 1-3.

FUDA, Abdul Rahim.
The 'ascent' of the Prophet, Maj. al-Azhar, (Dec. 1964), pp. 4-5.

FUDA, Abdul Rahim.
The greatnesof the apostle, Maj. al-Azhar, (Nov. 1964, pp. 5-7.

GALINDO AGUILAR, E.
The second international Muslim-Christian congress of Cordoba (March 21-27, 1977),, Islamochristiana, 3 (1977), pp. 207-218.

GARDET, I.
Towards a renewal of Islamic humanism, Islamic Studies, 1 iv (1962), pp. 25-39.

GEDDES, C. L.
The Messiah in South Arabia, MW, 57 (1967), pp. 311-320.

GEERTZ, C.
Modernization in a Moslem society: the Indonesian case, Quest, 39 (1963), pp. 9-17.

GELLNER, E.
Allah and caesar, Hibbert J., 59 (1960), pp. 54-58.

GHAZALI, Abdul Karim.
Sierra Leone Muslims and sacrificial rituals, Sierra Leone Bull. of religion, 2 (1960), pp. 27-32.

GHAZALI, Abdul Karim.
A Muslim propaganda play, with a commentary by L: Proudfoot, Sierra Leone Bull. Rel., 3 (1961), pp. 72-79.

GHAZANFAR, Habibullah.
Ma'ali al Himam of al-Junaid, Iqbal R., 6 (1965), pp. 49-74.

GHORABA, Hammouda.
The dilemma of religion and philosophy, ii. The problems of God's attributes, Islamic Qly., 3 (1956), pp. 4-15, 74-87.

GIBB, Sir H.A.R.
Unitive and divisive factors in Islam, Civilisations, 7 (1957), pp. 507-514.

GIBB, Sir H.A.R.
Pre-Islamic monotheism in Arabia, Harvard Theol. Rev., 55 (1962), pp. 269-280.

GIBSON, J.I.
The framework for Hajj simulation models; a preliminary report, Hajj. Studies, 1 (1978), pp. 39-57.

GILSENAN, M.D.
Some factors in the decline of the Sufi Orders in modern Egypt, MW, 57 (1967), pp. 11-18.

GIUNASVILI, D.
A further note on the ta'rik-i sistan manuscripts, East and West, 21 (1971), pp. 345-346.

GLASSNER, M.I.
The Bedouin of Southern Sinai under the Israeli administration, Geog. R., 64 (1974), pp. 31-60.

GOITEIN, S.D.
The origin and nature of the Muslim Friday worship, MW, 49 (1959), pp. 183-195.

GOLDFELD, I.
'Umyanis the idol of Khawlan, Israel Or. Studies, 3 (1973), pp. 108-119.

GOLDFELD, I.
The illiterate Prophet (nabiummi). An inquiry into the development of a dogma in Islamic tradition, Der Islam, 57 (1980), pp. 58-67.

GORIAWALA, Muizz.
Worship Islam, Orita, 11 (1977), pp. 160-168.

GOTTEIN, S.D.
Muhammad's inspiration by Judaism, J. Jewish Studies, 9 (1958), pp. 149-162.

GOUDIE, A.S.

George Nathaniel Curzon - superior geographer, Geog. J., 146 (1980), pp. 203-209.

GOWING, P.G.

Past and present postures in Christian-Muslim relations in insular Southeast Asia, S.E. Asia J. Theol., 18 i (1977), pp. 38-54.

GOWING, P.G.

Muslim Filipinos today, MW, 54 (1964), pp. 112-121.

GOWING, P.G.

Islam: The contemporary scene, Philippine Studies, 12 (1964), pp. 639-647.

GRACILL. J.L.

Missionary influence on American relations with the Near East, 1914-1923, MW, 59 (1968), pp.43-56; 141-154.

GRAGG, K.

Christian-Muslim dialogue (Review article), Anglican Theol. R., 57 (1975), pp. 109-120.

GREEN, A.H.

The Sufi orders in 19th century Tunisia: Sources and prospects, Rev. Hist. Maghreb., 13-14 (1979), pp. 61-68.

GREYLING, C.

Schech Yusuf, the founder of Islam in South Africa, Religion in Southern Africa, 1 i (1980), pp. 9-22.

GUENON, R.

The science of hand-reading in Sufism, Stud. Compar. Relig, 1 (1967), pp. 120-123.

GUENON, R.

The language of the birds, Stud. Compar. Relig., 3 (1969), pp. 94-106.

GUEVERA BAZAN, R.

Muslim immigration to Spanish America, MW, 56 (1966), pp. 173-187.

GUHIAUME, A.
A note on the Sira of Ibn Ishaq, BSOAS, 18 (1956), pp. 1-4.

GUILLAUME A.
Al-Lum'at al-saniya fi-tahqiq al-ilqa' fi-l-umniya by Ibrahim al-kurani, Bsoas, 20 (1957), pp. 291-303.

GUILLAUME, A.
The first book to come out of Arabia, Islamic Studies, 3 (1964), pp. 151-166.

GUILLAUME, A.
The pictorial background of the Qur'an, Annual Leeds Univ. Or. Soc., 3 (1961-62), pp. 39-59.

HADDAD, H.S.
"Georgic" cults and saints of the Levant, Numen, 16 (1969), pp. 21-39.

HADJIBEYLI, Djeihun.
Anti-Islamic propaganda in Azerbaidzhan, Cauc. Rev., 7 (1958), pp. 20-65.

HAINES B.L.
Islamic fundamentalism and Christian responsibility, Christian century, 96 (1979), pp. 365-366.

HAJJ, Muhammad al-.
The Fulani concept of Jihad: Shahu Uthman dan Fodio, Odu, 1 (1964), pp. 45-58.

HAMID, Irfan A.
Islamic eschatology, Al-Mustanairiya Univ. Rev., 1 (1969-70), pp. 143-157.

HAMIDULLAH, M.
Two Christians of Pre-Islamic Mecca 'Uthman ibn al-Huwairith and Waraqah ibn Naufal, J. Pakistan Hist. Soc., 6 (1958), pp. 97-103.

HAMIDULLAH, M.
The Christian monk Abu 'Amir of Medina of the time of the Holy Prophet, J. Pakistan Hist. Soc., 7 (1959), pp. 231-240.

HAMIDULLAH, Muhammad.
Faith and belief, Maj. al-Azhar, 42 vi (1970), pp. 9-12; 42 ii (1970), pp. 9-12.

HAMIDULLAH, Muhammad.
The Islamic conception of life, Maj. al-Azhar (English section), 42 i (1970), pp. 10-16; 42 iv, pp. 5-81 42 v, pp. 9-13.

HANNA, Sami and GARDNEN, G.
Khayr ad-Din (1822-1890) and Muhammad 'Abauh (1849-1905) did they or didn't they?, AJAS, 2 (1974), pp. 22-52.

HANNA, Suhail ibn Salis.
Biographical acholarship and Muhammad 'Abdul, MW, 59 (1969), pp. 300-307.

HARRIES L. MAULID BARZANJI.
The Sqahili abridgement of Seyyid Mansab, Afrika and Ubersee, 42 (1958), pp. 27-39.

HARVEY, L.P.
A Morisco manuscript in the Godolphin Collection at Wadham College,, Oxford and., 27 (1962), pp. 461-465.

HASSAN, Abdul Hameed.
The spirit of Islam is the chief factor in reforming contemporary society, Maj. al-Azhar, (Oct. 1966), pp. 20-26, (Nov. 1966), pp. 8-12.

HASSAN, Hassan Ibrahim.
Aspects of Shiah history, MW, 47 (1957), pp. 271-287.

HASSAN, S. Mahdi.
The garb of the Sufi and its significance, Iqbal, 8 (1960), pp. 72-81.

HASSAN, Y. F.
The penetration of Islam in the Eastern Sudan, Sudan Notes and Records, 44 (1963), pp. 1-8.

HEER, N.A.
Sufi psychological treatise. A translation of the Bayan al-Farq bayn al-Sadr wa al-Qalb wa al-Fuad wa al-Lubb of Abu

'Abd Allah Muhammad ibn 'Ali al-Hakim al-Tirmidhi, MW, 51 (1961), pp. 25-36, 83-91, 163-172, 244-258.

HELLWIG, M.K.
Bases and boundaries for interfaith dialogue: A Christian viewpoint, J. Ecumen Stud., 14 (1977), pp. 419-432.

HENRRY, K.H.
Glimpses of Turkish opinion, MW, 48 (1958), pp. 315-321.

HISKETT, M.
An Islamic tradition of reform in the Western Sudan from the sixteenth to the eighteenth century, BSOAS, 25 (1962), pp. 577-596.

HISKETT, M.
The 'community of grace' and its opponents, the 'rejecters': A debate about theology and mysticism in Muslim West Africa with special reference to its Hausa expression, Afr. Lang. Stud., 17 (1980)

HJARPE, J.
The holy year or the harranian. Some remarks on the festival calendar of the Harranian Sabins, Orientalia Suecana, 23-24 (1974-5), pp. 68-83.

HODGKIN, T.
Islam and national movements in West Africa, J. Afr. Hist., 3 (1962), pp. 323-327.

HODGSON, M.G.S.
A comparison of Islam and Christianity as a framework for religious life, Diogenes, (1960), pp. 49-74.

HODGSON, M.G.S.
Islam and image, History of religions, 3 (1964), pp. 220-260.

HODGSON, M.G.S.
Al-Darazi and Hamza in the origin of the Druze religon, JAOS, 82 (1962), pp. 5-20.

HOFFMANN, H.H.R.
Kalaoakra studies I. Manichaeism, christianity, and Islam in the

Kalaoakra Tantra, Central Asiatic J., 13 (1969), pp. 52-74.

HOOKER, M.B.
Adat and Islam in Malaya, BTLV, 13 (1974), pp. 69-90.

HOURANI, A.
Rashid Rida and the Sufi orders: a footnote to Laoust, BEO, 29 (1977), pp. 231-241.

HOWARD, I.K.A.
Al-Mufid's account of the imamate of 'Ali b. al-Hussayn Zayn al-Abidin, Alserat, 4 i (1978), pp. 18-32.

HUNWICK, J.G.
Further light on Ahmad Baba al-Tinbuktf, Res. Bull. CAD Ibadan, 2, no.2 (1966), pp. 19-48.

HURI, Sofi.
Yunus Emre: In memoriam, MW, 49 (1959), pp. 111-123.

HUSAINMUHAMMADKAMIL.
The Exodus: an Egyptian view, MW, 49 (1959), pp.30-40.

HUSAIN, Muhammad Kamil.
The meaning of Zulmin the Qu'an (Summary of points in the Academy's discussion by Kenneth Cragg, pp. 205-212), MW, 49 (1959), pp. 196-212.

HUSAIN, Syed Muazzam.
Effect of Tauba (repentance) on penaltyin Islam, Islamic Stud., 8 (1969), pp. 189-198.

HUSAINI, Ishaq Musa al-.
What is revelation?, Maj. al-Azhar, (March 1966), pp. 1-5.

HUSAYNIISHAQMUSAAL-.
Christ in the Qur'an and in modern Arabic literature, MW, 50 (1960), pp. 297-302.

HUSINI, Ishaq Musa al-.
The position of Jerusalem in Islam, Maj. al-Azhar, (Nov. 1968), pp. 25-30.

HUSSAIN, J.M.
New light on the activities of the imamates during the time of

Musa al-Kazim (148-183 A.H.), Alserat, 4 iv (1978), pp. 36-43.

IBISH, Yusuf.
Life and works of al-Baqillanf, Islamic Studies., 4 (1965), pp. 225-236.

IBRAHIM, Lutpi.
The concept of Ihbat and Takfir according to az- Zamakhshari and al-Baydawi, WO, 11 (1980), pp. 117-121.

IKRAM, S.M.
An unnoticed account of Shaikh Jalal of Sylheṭ, J.A.S. Pakistan, 2 (1957), pp. 63-68.

IMBER, C.H.
The persecution of the Ottoman Shiites according to the muhimme defterieri, 1565-1585, Der. Islam, 56 (1979), pp. 245-273.

IMOTO, Eiichi.
The Ka'ba-i Zardust, Orient (Tokyo), 15 (1979), pp. 65-69.

ISRAELI, R.
Ahung and Literatus: A Muslim elite in Confucian China, WI, N.S. 19 (1979), pp. 212-219.

ISRAELI, R.
Islam and Judaism in China: The merger of two cultural sub-systems, Asian Profile, 5 (1977), pp. 31-42.

ISRAELI, R.
The Muslims under the vianchu reign in China, SI, 49 (1979), pp. 159-179.

ISRAELI, R.
Muslims versus Christians in China, Asia Q., (1976), pp. 327-335.

ISRAELI, Raphael.
Established Islam and marginal Islam in China. From electicism to syncretism, JESHO, 2 i (1978), pp. 99-100.

IVANOW, W.
Sufism and Ismailism: Chiragh-nama, Rev. Iran. Anthrop, 3 i-vi (1959), pp. 13-17.

IZUTSU, Toshihiko.

The theophanic ego in Sufism. An analysis of the Sufi psychology of Najm al-Din Kubra, Sophia Perennis, 4 i (1978), pp. 23-42.

J.B.

Dated ivory box of hispano-Arabic origin, Bull. Met. Mus. Art, 18 (1923), pp. 6-8.

JACOB, J.R.

The authorship of "An account of the rise and progress of Mahometanism", Notes and Queries, NS 26 (1979), pp. 10-11.

JAMALI, Fadil.

The theological colleges of Najaf, MW, 50 (1960), pp. 15-22.

JAMIL, K.N.

Modern theories of evolution and the problems of creation in the holy Quran, Bull. College Arts, Baghdad, 6 (1963), pp. 23-44.

JANSEN, J.J.G. Ibrahim Abduh (b. 1913).

His autobiographies and his political polemical writings, Bibl. Or., 37 (1980), pp. 128-132.

JAWED, Nasim Ahmad.

Principles of movement in modern Islam: An analysis of some ideas developed in the 19th and 20th centuries by Indo-Pakistani Muslims in justification of change in religious thought and structure, Islamic Stud., 9 (1970), pp. 295-315.

JEFEERY, A.

Ibn Al-Arabi's Sha-jarat al-awn, SI, 40 (1959), pp. 43-77.

JEFFERY, A.

Ibn Al-'Arabi's Shajarat Al-awn (Concluded), SI, 11 (1959), pp. 113-160.

JISH, Sheikh Nadin Al-.

Our cultured youth and religiousness, Maj. al-Azhar, (May 1965 1965, pp. 19-21; Sept, 1965, pp. 2-5; Dec. 1965, pp. 13-16.

JOHNS, A.H.

Sufism as a category in Indonesian literature and history, J. Southeast Asian Hist., 2 (1961), pp. 10-23.

JOHNS, A.H.

Qur'anic translation some remarks and experiments, Milla wa-milla, 18 (1978), pp. 37-51.

JOHNSON, L.A.

Cresent and consciousness: Islamic orthodoxies and the West African novel, Research in African Literature, 11 i (1980), pp. 26-49.

JOMIER, J.

The idea of the prophet in Islam, Bull. Secretariatus pro non Christianis, 6 (1972), pp. 149-163.

JONES, A.

The mystical letters of the Qur'an, SI, 16 (1962), pp. 5-11.

JUNUS, U.

The payment of Zakat al-Fitrah in a Minangkabau community, BTLV, 122 (1966), pp. 447-454.

JURJI, E.J.

The Islamic setting in the history of religions, Islamic Stud., 8 (1969), pp. 301-317.

JUYNBOLL, G.H.A.

The Qur'an in early Islamic history, JESHO, 16 (1973), pp. 113-129.

JWYNBOLL, G.H.A.

Fighting angels, Ohio J. Relig. Stud., 2 i (1974), pp. 85-87.

KAGAYA, Kan.

Islam as a modern social force, Developing Econ., 4 (1966), pp. 70-89.

KAHANE, Reuven.

Religous diffusion and modernization: A preliminary reflection on the spread of Islam in Indonesia and its impact on social change, Arch. Europ. Sociol, 21 (1980), pp. 116-138.

KAMALI, Abdul Hameed.

Sufism and the modern European thought, Pakistan Philos J., 2 (1959), pp. 65-73.

KAMALI, Sabih Ahmad.
The moral basis of faith. An Islamic interpretation, MW, 55 (1965), pp. 112-116.

KAMALI, Sahib Ahmad.
The moral basis of faith. An Islamic interpretation, MW, 55 (1965), pp. 9-18.

KAMEL ABDUL AZIZ.
Islam in the light of its sources, Cultures, 4 (1977), pp. 131-163.

KARKLINS, R.
Islam: How strong is it in the Soviet Union? Inquiry based on oral interviews with Soviet Germans repatriated from Central Asia in 1979, Cah. Monde Russe Sov., 21 (1980), pp. 65-81.

KARMI, H.
The Ecumenical Movement and Islam, RCAJ, 52 (1965), pp. 263-266.

KARMI, Hasan al-.
Prayer in Islam, IQ, 9 (1965), pp. 37-45.

KARMI, Hasan al-.
The prophet Mahammad and the spirit of compromise, IQ, 8 (1964), pp. 89-94.

KAZI, A.K. and FLYNN, J.G,
Sharistani kitab: Al Milal Wal Nihal: the KKharijite and Mearjites, Al. Naharain, 10 (1970-71), pp. 47-75.

KAZI, A.K. and FLYNN, J.G.
The Mu'tazilites, Abr- Nahrain, 8 (1968-9), pp. 36-68.

KAZI, A.K. and FLYNN, J.G.
Shahrastani Kitab al-milal wa'l-Nihal: The Kharijites and the Murji'items, Abr-Nahrain, 10 (1970-1), pp. 49-75.

KAZI, A.K. and FYNN, J.G.
The Jabarites and the Sifatiya, Abr-Nahrain, 9 (1969-70), pp. 81-107.

KAZI, Abdul Khaliq.
The meaning of Iman and Islam in the Qur'an, Islamic Stud., 5

(1966), pp. 227-237.

KEDDIE, M.R.
Sayyid Jamal al-Din al-Afghani's first twenty-sevens years: the darkest period (Biographical review), MW, 20 (1966), pp. 517-533.

KEDDIE, N.R.
Afghani in Afghanistan, Middle Eastern Studies, 1 (1965), pp. 322-349.

KEDDIE, N.R.
Symbol and sincerity in Islam, SI, 19 (1963), pp. 27-63.

KEDOURIE, Elie.
Further light on Afghani, Middle Eastern Studies, 1 (1965), pp. 187-202.

KEDOURIE, Elis.
"The elusie Jamal al-Ida al-Afghanf". A comment, MW, 59 (1969), pp. 308-314.

KELLY, C.
The RGS archives: A handlist, Part IV: Asia. Geog. J., 143 (1977), pp. 73-85.

KENNY J.
Christian-Muslim relations in Nigeria, Islamochristian, 5 (1979), pp. 171-192.

KERR, M.
Rashid Rida and Islamic legal reform: An ideological analysis, MW, 50 (1960), pp. 99-108, 170-181.

KESBY, J.D.
Islam in Senegal, IQ, 7 (1963), pp. 40-50.

KHALAFALLAH, M.
Qura'nic studies as an important factor in the development of Arabic literary criticism, Bull. Fac. Arts Alexandria, 6-7 (1952), pp. 1-6.

KHALID, DETLE.
'Ubayd-Allah Sindhi - modern interpretation of Muslim uniersalism,

Islamic Stud., 8 (1969), pp. 97-114.

KHALID, Detlev.
Some aspects of Neo-Mu'tazilism, Islamic Stud., 8 (1969), pp. 319-347.

KHALID, Detlev.
Ahmad Amin and the lagacy of Muhammad 'Abduh, Islamic Studies, 9 (1970), pp. 1-31.

KHALID, Detlev.
Ahmad Amin - modern interpretation of Muslim uniersalism, Islamic Stud., 8 (1969), pp. 47-93.

KHALIDI TARIF.
Mu'tazilite historiography: Maqdisi's Kitab al-bad' wa'l ta'rikh, JNES, 35 (1976), pp. 1-12.

KHALIL, M.I.
A plea for a shorter L.L.B. course in Khartoum, J. Afr. Law, 7 (1963), pp. 125-132.

KHAN, Ghulam Mustafa.
Some unpublished works of Hazrat jalal of Herat, Sind. U. Res. J. Hum. Soc. Sci., 6 (1967), pp. 1-14.

KHAN, Mohamed Samin.
Religion state in Turkey, Pakistan Horizon, (1958), pp. 146—155, 221-244.

KHAN, Mu'in-ud-Din.
Ahmad Successors of Dudu Miyan, J. Pak. Hist. Soc., 11 (1963), pp. 278-289.

KHAN, Muin-ud-Din.
Ahmad Muhsin al-Din Ahmad alias Dudu Miyan (A.I.) 1819-1862), J. Pak. Hist. Soc., 11 (1963), pp. 234-258.

KHAN, Qamaruddin.
Incidence of abrogation (Naekh) in the Qur'an, Iqbal, 15 i (1966), pp. 8-46.

KINGSBURY, J.A.T.
Character studies in contemporary Turkish Islam, MW, 48

(1958), pp. 29-39.

KISTEN, M.J.
'A bag of meat': A study of an early badith, BSOAS, 33 (1970), pp. 267-275.

KISTER, M.J.
'An yadin (Qur'an IX/29). An attempt at interpretation, Arabica, 11 (1964), pp. 272-278.

KISTER, M.J.
"A booth like the booth of Moses ..." A study of an early Hadith, BSOAS, 25 (1962), pp. 150-155.

KNAPP, B.L.
The Kaliph Hakim and history as a cyclical happening, Nineteenth-century French Studies, 5 (1976-7), pp. 79-93.

KNAPPERT, J.
Wilada Nabil: A praise poem on the Prophet Mohammed, Afrika U. Ubersee, 50 (1967), pp. 34-40.

KNAPPERT, J.
The Qisau'l-anbiyai as moralistic stories, Proc. Arabian Studies, 9 (1976), pp. 103-116.

KNAPPERT, J.
Al-Husain ibn Ali in the epic tradition of the Swahili, Alseraat, 2 i (1976), pp. 20-27.

KOENIG, F.C.
The monotheism in the contemporary world, Travaux at jours, 16 (1965), pp. 23-42.

KOHLBERG, E.
The development of the Imami Shii doctrine of Jihad, ZDMG, 126 (1976), pp. 64-86.

KOHLBERG, E.
Some shil views of the antediluvian world, SI, 52 (1980), pp. 41-66.

KOHLBERG, E.
An unusual Shii isnad, Israel Or. Studies, 5 (1975), pp. 142-149.

KOHLBERG,E.

Manahij al-arifin, a treatise on Sufism by Abu' Abd al-Rahman al-Sulami, JSAI, 1 (1979), pp. 19-39.

KRAEMER,H.

Islamic culture and missionary adequacy, MW, 50 (1960), pp. 244-251.

KRITZECK,J.

Moslem-Christian understanding in mediaeal times, Comp. Stud. Soc. Hist., 4 (1961-1962), pp. 388-401.

KRITZECK,J.

A mission to Islam, N.Z. Missonswis, 20 (1964), pp. 42-49.

KROEF, J.M. van der.

Recent trends in Indonesian Islam, MW, 52 (1962), pp. 48-58.

KRYMSKY,A.E.

A sketch of the development of Sufism up to the end of the third century of the Hijra, IQ, 5 (1959), pp. 109-125.

KUDST-ZADEH,A.A.

Jamal al-Din al-Afghani: A select list of articles, ME Studies, 2 (1965), pp. 66-72.

LAMBTON A. K. S.

Areconsideration of the position of the Marja' sl-Taqlid and the religious institution, SI, 20 (1964), pp. 115-135.

LAMBTON A. K. S.

A reconsideration of the position of the Marja's al- Taqlid and the religious institution, SI, 20 (1964), pp. 115-135.

LAMBTON,A.K.S.

A reconsideration of the position of the Marja' al- Taqlid and the religious institution, SI, 20 (1964), pp. 115-135.

LANDAU,R.

The Karaouine at Fez., MW, 48 (1958), pp. 104-112.

LANDAU,R.

The philosophy of Ibn Arabi, MW, 47 (1957), pp. 46-61, 146-160.

LANFRY J.
Islamic-Christian dialogue approaches tothe obstacles, J. Ecumen. stud., 14 (1977), pp. 484-500.

LAUNAY, R.
The birth of a ritual: The poltics of innovation in Dyula Islam, Savvanah, 6 (1977), pp. 145-154.

LAZAROFF, A.
Babya's asceticism against its Rabbinic and Islamic background, J. Jewish Stud., 21 (1970), pp. 11-38.

LAZARUS-YAFEH, H.
Muslim festivals, Numen, 25 (1978), pp. 52-64.

LAZARUS-YAFEH, Hava.
Contemporary religious attitudes of Muslim Arabs toward the Ka'ba and the Hajj. (The revival of Muslim fuundamentalism), AAS (Haifa), 12 (1978), pp. 173-201.

LESLIE, D.D.
Islam in China to 1800: A bibliographical guide, Abr-Nahrain, 16 (1975-6), pp. 16-48.

LEWIS, B.
Gibbon on Muhammad, Daedalus, 105 (1976), pp. 89-101.

LEWIS, I.M.
Sufism in Somaliland: A study in tribal Islam, BSOAS, 18 (1956), pp. 145-166.

LIBRANDE, L.
A reconsideration of Ibn Khallad's place in the Buwayhid lands, Der Islam, 57 (1980), pp. 1-8.

LIBRANDE, L.
The calligraphy of the Qur'an how it functions for Muslims, Religion, 9 (1979), pp. 36-58.

LIBTSNFR, L.
The categories high and low as reflections on the Rihlah and Kitabah in Islam, Der Islam, 55 (1978), pp. 267-280.

LICHTENSTADTER, I.
A note on the gharaniq and related Qur'anic problems, Israel Or. Studies, 5 (1975), pp. 54-61.

LINDBECK, G.
Christians between Arabs and Jews: A report from Jerusalem on a theological debate, Worldview, 22 (1979), pp. 25-26, 35-39.

LINGS, M.
Sufi answers to questions on ultimate reality: Writtenin the margin of R.W. J. Austin's 'Sufism', Ultimate Reality and Meaning, 3 (1980), pp. 70-77.

LINGS, M.
"With all thy mind, Studies in Comp. Rel., 10 (1976), pp. 13-25.

LINGS, M.
Extract from the letter of Shaikh al- 'Arabi ad-Darqewi. Translated by Titus Borckhardt, Studies in Comparative Religion, 1 i (1967), pp. 13-21.

LITTMANN, D.
Jews under Muslim rule in the late nineteenth century, Wiener Libr. Bull., 28 (N.S. 35/36, 1975), pp. 65-76.

LUDIN (Muhammad Kabir).
The miracle of the holy Qur'an, IQ, 8 (1964), pp. 57-64.

LUDIN, Muhammad Kabir.
Faith and intellect in Islam, IQ, 7 (1963), pp. 90-95.

MA'SUMI, M.S.H.
Ibn Hazm's allegations against the leading Imams, Islamic Stud., 7 (1968), pp. 113-128.

MA'SUMI, Muhammad Saghir Hasan.
Shykh 'Ali al-Muttaqi's Risalah Tabyin al-Turuq, Islamic Studies, 3 (1964), pp. 339-373.

MA'SUMI, S.H.
The concept of society in Islam, Pakistan Philos. J., 7 iv (1963), pp. 42-50.

MACDONALD J.
Ikslamic doctrines in Samaritan theology, MW, 50 (1960), pp. 279-290.

MACDONALD J.
Joseph in the Qur'an and Muslim commentary, MW, 46 (1956), pp. 113-131, 207-224.

MACDONALD, J.
The preliminaries to the resurrection and judgement (Islamic eschatology, IV), Islamic Studies, 4 (1965), pp. 137-179.

MACDONALD, J.
The Samaritans under the patronage of Islam, Islamic Studies, 1 iv (1962), pp.91-110.

MACDONALD, J.
The twilight of the dead (islamic eschatology, III), Islamic Studies, 4 (1965), pp. 55-102.

MACDONALD, J.
Paradise, Islamic Stud., 5 (1966), pp. 331-383.

MACDONALD, J.
The Angel of Death in late Islamic tradition, Islamic Studies, 3(1964), pp. 485-519.

MACDONALD, J.
The creation of man and angels in the eschatological literature. (Translated excerpts from an unpublished collection of traditions) [Leeds MS. 264], Islamic Studies, 2 (1964), pp. 285-308.

MACDONALD, J.
The day of resurrection, Islamic Stud., 5 (1966), pp.l 129-197.

MACKEEN, A.M.M.
The Sufiqawm movement, MW, 53 (1963), pp. 212-225.

MADELUNG, W.
Some notes on non-Ismaili Shiism in the Maghrib, SI, 44 (1976), pp. 87-97.

MAHAMUN, Ali Ghul.
Was the ancient South Arabian night the Islamic mihrab?,

BSOAS, 25 (1962), pp. 331-335.

MAHDIHASSAN, S.

The kalimah of the Muslims in the light of terms as understood before Islam, Milla wa-milla, 17 (1977), pp. 3-7.

MAHMOUD ABDEL HAMID HAMDY.

The Western attitude to Islam as viewed by Arnold of Lubeck, Bull. Fac. Arts. Cairo, 10 (1956), pp. 77-84.

MAHMOUD, Mohammad Fatthy.

The Muslims in the Philippines: A bibliographic essay, Asian Studies, 12 ii-iii (1974), pp. 173-197.

MAJU, Cesar Adib.

The Muslims in the Philippines. A historical perspective, Maj. al-Azhar (English section), 42 v (1970), pp. 14-16; 42 vi, 13-16; 42 vii, 13-16.

MAJUL, C.A.

An historical background on the coming andspread of Islam and Christianity in Southeast Asia, Asian studies, 14 ii (1976), pp. 1-14.

MAJUL, C.A.

An historical background on the coming and spread of Islam and Christianity in Southeast Asia, Asian Studies, 14 ii (1976), pp. 1-14.

MAKAREM, Sami N.

The philosophical significance of the Imam in Ismailism, si, 27 (1967), PP. 41-53.

MAKDISI, G.

Ashari and the Ash'artes in Islamic religious history, SI, 17 (1962), pp. 37-80; 18 (1963), pp. 19-39.

MALIK, Abdul Qayyum.

The Prophet of Islam, Iqbal, 5 iii (1957), pp. 71-81.

MALLICK, M. Tahir.

Life and works of Ibrahim B. Tahman (a traditional of 2nd/8 century), J. Pak. Hist. Soc., 24 i (1976), pp. 1-30.

MALTIDOUCLAS, Fedwa.

Controversy and its effects on the biographical tradition of al-Khatib al-Baghadi, SI, 46 (1977), pp. 115-131.

MARDIN, Serif.

Religion in modern Turkey, Int. Soc. Sci. J., 29 (1977), pp. 279-297.

MARRISON, G.E.

Islam and the Church in Malaya, MW, 47 (1957), pp. 290-298.

MARTIN, J.D.

The religious belief of Abu'l-'Atahiya, Glasg. Or. Soc. Trans., 21 (1965-6), pp. 56-67.

MASON, H.

A memory of Massignon., MW, 57 (1967), pp. 321-322.

MASUD, MUHAMMAD KHALID.

Al-Hakim al-Tirmidhi's Budiaw Sha'n, Islamic Studa, 4 (1965), pp. 315-343.

MAYER, A.C.

Pir and Murshid: An aspect of religious leadership in West Pakistan, MW Stud., 3 (1966-7), pp. 160-169.

MCCARTHY, R.J.

Al-Baqillani's notion of the Apologetic Miracle, Studia Biblica et Orientalia III, (Analecta Biblica, 12), 1959, pp. 247-256.

McCLAIN, E.G.

The Ka'ba as archetypal ark, Sophia perennis, 4 i (1978), pp. 59-75.

MCKANE W.

A manuscript on the Mi'raj in the Bodleian, J. Semitic Stud, 2 (1957), pp. 366-376.

MELAND, B.E.

In response to Dr Faruqi, Numen, 12 (1965), pp. 87-95.

MERAD ALI.

Reformism in modern Islam, Cultures, 4 (1977), pp. 108-127.

MEREDITH-OWENS G. M.
Qasim Efendi, JRAS, 1961, PP. 36-38.

MEREDITH-OWENS G.M.
Notes on an old Ottoman translation of the Qur'an, Oriens, 10 (1957), pp. 258-276.

MEYENDORFF, J.
Byzantine views of Islam, Dumbarton Oaks Papers, 18 (1964), pp. 113-132.

MILLER, R.E.
Renaissance of the Muslim spirit: The sun is rising again over the world of Islam as it begins another century, Christianity Today, 23 (1979), pp. 16-21.

MILSON, Manahes.
"The elusive Jamal al-Din al-Afghani. A rejoindar, MW, 59 (1969), pp. 315-316.

MIRZA, Mohd. Sakhawat.
Maktubat i Amir Abu al-'Ula, J. Pak. Hist. Soc., 10 (1962), pp. 331-343.

MIRZA, N.
The Syrian Ismailis and the doctrine of metempsychosis, Milla wa-Milla, 4 (1964), pp. 48-51.

MIRZA, Nasseh.
The Isma'ilis and their belief in the universal divine order, Glasgow Univ. Or. Soc. Trans, 20 (1963), pp. 10-22.

MOHANNA, Ahmad I.
Psychological moties used by the Holy Qur'an, Maj. al-Azhar, (Nov. 1969), pp. 9-10, 16.

MOHANNA, Ahmad I.
Islam and human dignity, Maj. al-Azhar, (June 1969), pp. 8-9.

MONTGOMERY, J.W.
The apologetic approach of Muhammad Ali and its implications for Christian apologetics, MW, 51 (1961), pp. 111-122.

MOREAUL.
The chances of a dialogue between Christianity and Islam in Back Africa, Concilium, 106 (1977), pp. 112-118.

MORGAN, H.L.
A Turkish text-book on Islam, MW, 46 (1956), pp. 13-23.

MORRIS, H.S.
The divine kingship of the Aga Khan: A study of theocracy in East Africa, SWJA, 14 (1958), pp. 454-472.

MUBARAKALI.
The Khutba: A symbol ofroyalty in Islam. Sind U. Res. J. Arts Series, Humanities and Social Science, 17-18 (1978-9), pp. 89-96.

NAQVI, Syed Sibte Nabi.
The Quranic cosmology, Iqbal R., 6 (1964), pp. 85-96.

NASH, M.
Islam in Iran: turmoil, transformation or transcendence?, World Deelopment, 8 (1980), pp. 555-561.

NASR S.H.
Contemplation and nature in the perspective of Sufism, Iqbal, 12 iii (1964), pp. 14-21.

NASR SEYYED HOSSSEIN.
A Muslim reflection on religion and theology, J. ecum. stud, 17 (1980), pp. 112-120.

NASR, S.H.
Contemplation and nature in the perspective of Sufism, Iqbal, 12 iii (1964), pp. 14-21.

NASR, Sayyed Hossein.
Who is man? The perennial answer of Islam, Stud. Compar. Relig, 2 (1968), pp. 45-56.

NASR, Seyyed Hossein.
The sufi master as exemplified in Persian Sufi literature, STud. Compr. Relig., 4 (1970), pp. 140-149; also in Iran 5 (1967), pp. 35-40.

NASR, Seyyed Hossein.
Sufism and the perennity of the mystrical quest, Milla wa-milla, 10 (1970), pp. 4-18.

NASR, Seyyed Hossein.
Islam and the encounter of religions, IQ, 10 (1966), pp. 47-68.

NASR, Seyyed Hossein.
Shi'ismand Sufism: Their relationship in essence and in history, Relig. Stud., 6 (1970), pp. 229-242.

NASR, Seyyed Hussein.
Sufism and the perennity of the mystical quest, Stud. Compar. Religon, 4 (1970), pp. 231-246.

NASR, Seyyed Hussein.
Seventh century Sufism and the school of Ibn 'Arabi; Pakistan and Turkey, J. Reg. Cult. Inst., 1 i (1967), pp. 450-50.

NETTLER, R.
Ibn 'Arabi's notion of Allah's mercy, Israel Oriental Studies, 8 (1978), pp. 219-229.

NETTLER, R.
Ibn 'Arabis notion of Allah's mercy, Israel Or. Studies, 8 (1978), pp. 219-229.

NIEUWENHUIJZE, C.A.O. van.
The legacy of Islam in Indonesia, MW, 59 (1969), pp. 210-219.

NIEUWENHUIJZE, C.A.O. van.
The Qur'an as a factor in the Islamic way of life, Islam, 38 (1963), pp. 215-257.

NIEUWENHUIJZE, C.A.O. Van.
The prophetic function in Islam: An analytic approach, Corresp. d'Orient Etudes, 3 (1963), pp. 99-119.

NIEUWENHUIJZK, C.A.O. van.
The prophetic function in Islam: An analytic approach, Correspondance, d' Orient: Etudes.

NOLIN, K.E.
The story of Adam. Translation, with introduction and notes, of

Dr. Muhammad Kamil Husayn's "Qissat Adam" from his collection of essays entitled: Mutanawwi'at pub. 1961, pp. 38-42, MW, 54 (1964), pp. 4-13.

NOLIN, K.E.
Al-ustadh al-haddad, MW, 60 (1970), pp. 170-177.

NOWAIHI, Mohamed al-.
The religion of Islam. A presentation to Christians, Int. Rev. Missions, 65 (1976), pp. 216-225.

NOWAIHI, Mohamed al-.
Some recent attempts towards a more liberal interpretation of the Quran and modernization of Islamic jurisprudence, J. Middle East, 3 (1976), pp. 59-70.

NURI-ALA, Ismail.
Some observations on the necessity of a non-essentialist analysis of religious developments in Iran, Zaman, 2-3 (1980)l, pp. 45-50.

O'LEARY, De L.
Al-Hallaj, Philosophy East and West, 1 i (1951), pp. 56-62.

O'SHAUGHNESSY, T.
The seven names for Hell in the Quran, BSOAS, 24 (1961), pp. 444-469.

O'SHAUGHNESSY, T.
Sin as ahenation in Christianity and Islam, BAEO, 14 (1978), pp. 127-135.

O'SHAUGHNESSY, T.J.
Filipino Muslims and national identity, Omnis Terra, 25v (1970), pp. 135-140 [Offprint in SOAS].

O'SHAUGHNESSY, T.J.
Islam - surrender to God, Phil. Stud., 15 (1967), pp. 108-129.

OWEN, J.E.
Religion and society in Pakistan, MW, 50 (1960), pp. 291-296.

PANJWANI, Ibrahim A.G.
Muslims in Malawi, J. Inst. Muslim Minority Affairs, 1 ii & 2 i (1979-80), pp. 158-168.

PARET R.

Recent European research on the life and work of Prophet Mahammad J. Pakistan Hist, Soc, 6 (1958), pp. 81-96.

PARET, Rudi.

Islam and Christianity, Islamic Studies, 3(1964), pp. 83-95.

PARKIN, D.

Politics of ritual syncretism: Islam among the non Muslim Giriama of Kenya, Africa, 40 (1970), pp. 217-233.

PARRINDER E. G.

Islam and West African indigenous religion, Numen, 6 (1959), pp. 130-141.

PASTNER, S. and C. McC.

Aspects of religion in Southern Beluchistan, Anthropologica, 14 (1972), pp. 231-241.

PELLAT, C.

Seriousness and humour in early Islam (Al-jidd wa'l-hazl fi sadr al-Islam), Islamic Studies, 2 (1963), pp. 353-362.

PERIMANN, M.

Samau'al al-Maghribi ifham al-yahud Silencing the Jews, Proc. Amer. Acad. Jewish Research, 32 (1964), pp. 15-102.

PERLMAN, M.

Ibn Khaldun on Sufism, Bibl. Or., 17 (1960), pp. 222-223.

PERRY, W. N.

Orhodory andthe master, Stud. compar. relig., 1 (1967), pp. 59-68.

PERRY, W.N.

Reincarnation: New flesh on old bones, Stud. Compar. Relig., 1 (1967), pp. 84-94.

PETERS, R. and DE VRIES, G.J.J.

Apostasy in Islam, WI, N.S. 17 (1976), pp. 1-25.

PINES, S.

Some traits of Christian theological writing in relation to Moslem kalam and to Jewish thought, Proc. Israel. Acad. Sci. Humanities,

5 (1976), pp. 105-125.

PLESSNER, M.
Muhammed's clandefine umra in the Du'l-Qa'da 8 H. and Sura 17. I., RSO, 32 (1957), pp. 525-530.

POLITELA J.
Al-Ghazali and Meister Eckhart two giants of the spirit, MW, 54 (1964), pp. 233-244.

POLITELLA, J.
Sufism as a bridge between Eastern and Western religious thought, MW, 53 (1963), pp. 50-58.

POURJAVADY, N. and WILSON, P.L.
A Sufi fable: Shah Da'i i Shirazi's "Tale of the fish", Studies in Comp. Rel., 10 (1976), pp. 98-105.

POWELL, A.J.
The Qur'anic view of other scriptures. A translation of sections from writings by 'Afir 'Abd al- Fattah Tabbara and al-Ustadh al-Haddad, MW, 59 (1969), pp. 95-105.

PRINS, J.
Some notes about Islam and politics in Indonesia, WI, N.S. 6 (1959), pp. 117-129.

PROUDFOOT, L.
Mosque-building and tribal separatism in Freetown East, Africa, 29 (1959), pp. 405-416.

PROUDFOOT, L.
Towards Muslim solidarity in Freetown, Africa, 31 (1961), pp. 147-157.

QAGATAY, Neset.
The tradition of Maulid recitations in Islam particularly in Turkey, SI, 28 (1968), pp. 127-133.

QAZI, Nabi Bakhsh.
Significance of "Light" in the pre-Tasawwuf literature, Sind Univ. Res. J., 3 (1963), pp. 62-71.

QUELQUEJAY C.

Anti-Islamic propaganda in Kazakhstan since 1953, MEJ, 13 (1959), pp. 319-327.

QURESHI, Saleem.

Islam and deelopment: The Zia regime in Pakistan, Wolrd Deelopment, 8 (1980), pp. 563-575.

RAHBAR, Daud.

Christian apologetic to Muslims, Int. Rev. Missions, 54 (1965), pp. 353-359.

RAHBAR, Daud.

The relation of shi'a theology to the Quran, MW, 51 (1961), pp. 92-98, 211-216; 52 (1962), pp. 17-21, 124-128.

RAHBAR, Daud.

Reflections on the tradition of Quranic exegesis, MW, 52 (1962), pp. 269-307.

RAHBAR, Muhammad Daud.

The challenge of modern ideas and social values to Muslim society, MW, 48 (1958), pp. 274-285.

RAHBAR, Muhammad Daud.

"The call of the Minaret". A review, MW, 48 (1958), pp. 40-51.

RAHIM, Hussein A.

The Prophet of God the deliverer of mankind, Alseraat, 2 i (1976), pp. 3-5.

RAHIM, M.A.

The Baul mystic order, J. Research Soc. Pakistan, 2 (1965), pp. 49-61.

RAHMAN, Fazlur.

Islamic modernism: Its scope, method and alternatives, IJMES, 1 (197), pp. 317-333.

RAHMAN, Fazlur.

Qur'anic concept of God, the universe and man, Islamic Studs., 6 (1967), pp. 1-19. s

RAHMAN, Fazlur.
Sunnah and Hadith, Islamic Studies, 1 ii (1962), pp. 1-36.

RAHMAN, Fazlur.
The post-formative developments in Islam, Islamic Studies, 1 iv (1962), pp. 1-2; 2 (1963), pp. 279-316.

RAHMAN, Fazlur.
Currents of religious thought in Pakistan, Islamic Stud., 7 (1968), pp. 1-7.

RAMAḌI, Gamal El Din El.
Prophet Muhammad's family life, Maj. al-Azhar, (Sept. 1965), pp. 13-15.

RAMADI, Gamal Eldin El-.
Social security in Islam, Maj. al-Azhar, (March 1965), pp. 9-12.

RAMADY, Gamal El-Din El-.
The foundations of Islam and their psycholigical effects, Maj. al-Azhar, (Apr. 1968), pp. 11-13.

RAMADY, Gamal Eldin el-.
A battle against the enemies of life and religion, Maj. al-Azhar, (Nov. 1967), pp. 10-13.

RAMADY, Gamal Kl-Din El-Din el-.
Islam: The origin of human rights, Maj. al-Azhar, (Mar. 1967), pp. 11-13.

RAMAN, Fazlur.
The impact of modernity on Islam, Islamic Stud., 5 (1966), pp. 113-128.

RASJIDI, Muh and BARWANI, Ali Muhsin.
Christian mission in the Muslim world. Two case studies: Indonesia and Tanzania, Int. Rev. Misssion, 65 (1976), pp. 427-447.

RAUF, M.A.
The Qur'an and free will, MW, 60 (1970), pp. 207-217, 289-299.

RAUF, M.A.
Some notes on the Qur'anic use of the terms Islam and Iman,

MW, 57 (1967), pp. 94-102.

RESCHER, N.

Nicholas of Cusa on the Qur'an. A fifteenth-century encounter with Islam, MW, 55 (1965), pp. 195-202.

RIEMER, C.L.

Qur'anic concept of retaliation, S.E. Asia J. Theol, 18 ii (1977), pp. 46-51.

RINGGREN H.

The initiation ceremony of the Bektashis, Initiation (Studies in the history of religions, supplements to Numen x), 1956, pp. 202-208.

RINGGREN, H.

The pure religion, Oriens, 15 (1962), pp. 93-96.

RIPPIN, A.

A Qur'an 21: 95 "a ban is upon every town", JSS, 24 (1979), pp. 43-53.

RIVERA, G.F.

The Maranac Muslims in Lumbayao, Lanso, Philippine sociol Rev., 14 (1966), pp. 127-134.

ROBINSON, R.D.

Mosque and school in Turey, MW, 51 (1961), pp. 107-110.

ROBSON J.

The transmission of Ibn Majah's "Sunan", J. Semitic Stud, 3 (1958), pp. 129-141.

ROBSON J.

The form of Muslimtradition, Glasgow Univ. Or. Soc. Trans., 16 (1955), pp. 38-50.

ROBSON J.

Some of la and lam in the Qur'an, J. Semitic stud, 4 (1959), pp. 139-144.

ROBSON, J.

Traditions from individuals, J. Semitic Studies, 9 (1964), pp. 327-349.

ROBSON, J.

The transmission of Nasa'i's 'Sunan, J. Semitic Stud, 1 (1956), pp. 38-59.

ROBSON, J.

A shi's collection of divine traditions, Glasgow Or. Soc. Trans, 22 (1967-8), pp. 1-13.

RONDOT, P.

Islam, Christianity, and the modern state, MEA, 5 (1954), pp. 341-345.

ROSENTHAL P.

The empty Throne, ST, 31 (1970), pp. 233-238.

ROSENWTHAL, F.

"Life is short, the art is long": Arabic commentaries on the first Hippocratic aphorism, Bull. Hist. Med., 40 (1966), pp. 226-245.

RUBIN, U.

Pre-existence and light. Aspects of the concept of Nur Muhammad, Israel Or. Studies, 5 (1975), pp. 62-119.

RUBIN, U.

Prophets and progenitors in the early Sha tradition, JSAI, 1 (1979), pp. 40-65.

RUDVIN A.

The concept and practice of Christian mission (in relationship to Islam, Int. rev. mission, 65 (1976), pp. 374-390.

RYAN, P.J.

The descending scroll: A study of the notionof revelation as apocalypse in the Bible and in the Qu'an, Ghana Bull. Theol, 4 viii (1975), pp. 24-39.

RYMSY, A.E.

A sketch of the development of Sufism down to the end of the third century of the Hijra, IQ, 6 (1961), pp. 79-106.

SAAH, Hassan.

Communication between Christianity and Islam, MEJ, 18 (1964), pp. 41-62.

SABAH, Rasha al-.
Inferno XXVIII: The figure of Muhammed, Yale Ital. Studies, 1 ii (1977), pp. 147-161.

SACHEDINA, Abdulaziz.
A treatise on the occultation of the twelfth Imamite Imam, SI, 48 (1978), pp. 109-124.

SACHEDINA, Abdulaziz.
Al-Khums: The fifth in the Imami Shii legal system, JNES, 39 (1980), pp. 275-289.

SADLER, A.W.
Islam: The parish situation and the virtuoso community, MW, 51 (1961), pp. 197-210.

SAITOH, Abdul Karim.
The historical journey of Islam eastward and the Muslim community in Japan today, J. Inst. Muslim Minority Affairs, 1 i (1979), pp. 117-126.

SALEH, Awang Had.
Modern concept of Hajj management: The experience of Malaysia, Hajj Studies, 1 (1978), pp. 73-86.

SALEM, Elie.
Arab reformers and the reinterpretation of Islam, MW, 55 (1965), pp. 311-320.

SALINGER, G.
A christian Muhammad legend and a Muslim Ibn Tumart legend in the 13th century, ZDMG, 117 (1967), pp. 318-328.

SAMARAWEERA, Vivaya.
some sociological aspects of the Muslim revivalism in SriLanka, Social Compass, 25 (1978), pp. 465-475.

SANDERSON, L.
The Sudan Interior Mission and the Condominium Sudan, 1937-1955, J. Religion Africa, 8 (1976), pp. 13-40.

SANNEH, Lamin.
Christian experience of Islamic da'wah, with particular reference to Africa, Int. Rev. Mission, 65 (1976), pp. 410-426.

SANNEH, Lamin.
The domestication of Islam and Christianity in African societies, J. Religion Africa, 11 (1980), pp. 1-12.

SARDAR, Ziauddin.
The spiritual and physical dimensions of Hajj: A systems overview, Hajj. Studies, 1 (1978), pp. 27-38.

SAUNDERS, J.J.
The Muslim Christ, Milla wa-milla, 8 (1968), pp. 3-10.

SCANLON G.T.
Leadership in the Qarmatian Sect, Bifao, 59 (1960), pp. 29-48.

SCHACHT, J.
Islam in Northern Nigeria, SI, 8 (1957), pp. 123-146.

SCHACHT, J.
An early Murci'ite treatise: The Kitab al 'Alim wal-Muta'llim, Oriens, 17 (1964), pp. 96-117.

SCHACHT, J.
Notes on Islam in East Africa, Studia Islamica, 23 (1965), pp. 91-136.

SCHACHTER, Zalman M.
Bases and boundaries of Jewish, Christian and Moslem dialogue, J. Ecumen. Stud., 14 (1977), pp. 407-418.

SCHIMMEL, A.
The martyr-mystic Hallaj in Sindhi folk-poetry. Notes on a mystical symbol, Numen, 9 (1962), pp. 191-200.

SCHIMMEL, A.
Translations and conmentaries of the Qur'an in Sindhi language, Oriens, 10 (1963), pp. 224-243.

SCHIMMEL, A.
The origin and early development of Sufism, J. Pakistan Hist. Soc., 7 (1959), pp. 55-67.

SCHOEN, U.A.
Christian theology in a Muslim context: The spiritual pilgrimage of Jean Faure, NE School Theol Theol. R., 1 i (1978), pp. 27-35.

SCHUB, M.B.

Its is easier for a cable to go through the eye of a needle than for a rich man to enter God's kingdom, Arabica, 23 (1976), pp. 311-312.

SCHUB, M.B.

Three syntactic discussions in al-Zamahsari's commentary on the Qur'an, And., 42 (1977), pp.465-469.

SCHUON, F.

Understanding the Qur'an, Islamic Q., 5 (1959), pp. 12-20.

SCHUON, F.

The Wisdom of the Virgin, Stud. Compar, Relig, 2 (1968), pp. 130-140.

SCHUON, F.

Paradoxical aspects of Sufism, Stud. Comp. Rel, 12 (1978), pp. 131-175.

SCHUON, F.

Understanding and believing, Stud. Compar. Relig., 3 (1969), pp. 130-138.

SCHUON, Fr.

Alternations in Semitic monotheism, Studies in Comparative religion, 11 (1977), pp. 166-187.

SCHUON, Fr.

The mystery of the veil, Studies in Comp. Religon., 11 (1977), pp. 66-83.

SCHUON, Fr.

The three dimensions of Sufism, Studies in Com. Rel., 10 (1976), pp. 5-13.

SCHUON, Fr.

Celestial apparitions: An elementary criteriology, Studies in Com. Rel., 10 (1976), pp. 67-73.

SCHWARZ, M.

The Qadi 'Abdal-Gabbar's refutation of the As'arite doctrine of 'acquisition' (Kasb), Israel Oriental Studies, 6 (1976), pp. 229-263.

SCHWARZ, M.
The letter of al-Hasan al-Basri, Oriens, 20 (1967), pp. 15-30.

SEALE, M.S.
The ethics of Malamatiya Sufism and the Sermon on the Mount, MW, 58 (1968), pp. 12-23.

SELMS, A. van.
Siggin and siggii in the Qur'an, WO, 9 (1977), pp. 99-103.

SERAJULHAQUE.
A poem of Imaṃ Ibn Taymiyya on predestination, J. Asiat. Soc. Paistan, 1 (1956), pp. 1-17.

SERAJULHAQUE.
Some aspects of tasawwuf, Pak. Philos J., 9 (1965), pp.63-68.

SERJEANT, R.B.
Recent marriage legislation from al-Mukalla with notes on marriage customs, BSOAS, 25 (1962), pp. 472-498.

SERJEANT, R.B.
Saint Sergius, BSOAS, 22 (1959), pp. 574-575.

SERJEANT, R.B.
Mihrab, BSOAS, 22 (1959), pp. 439-453.

SERJEANT, R.B. Professor A.
Guillaume's translation of the Sfrah, BSOAS, 21 (1958), pp. 1-14.

SHACK, W.A.
Black Muslims: A nativistic religious movement among Negro Americans, Race, 3 i (1961), pp. 57-67.

SHACKLE, C.
The Multani marsiya, Der Islam, 55 (1978), pp. 281-311.

SHAFAQ, S. R.
Religion and religious study today, MW, 46 (1956), pp.99-103.

SHAFFER, J.G.
Origins of Islam: A generative model, Eastern Anthropoligist, 31 (1978), pp. 355-364.

SHAIKH, M. Saeed.
Mutazilism: Its historical development, Iqbal, 8 (1960), pp. 46-58.

SHAITOUT, Mahmoud.
Islam: The religion of mind and knowledge, Maj. al-Azhar, 32 iii-iv (1960), pp. 4-11.

SHAITOUT, Mahmoud.
The source of immortality in Islam, Maj. al-Azhar, 31 (1959-60), pp. 37-42, 69-75.

SHALABI, Abdul Wadood.
The basis of the ethical system in Islam, Maj. al-Azhar, (Apr. 1968), pp. 7-10; (may 1968), pp. 11-14; (June 1968), pp. 14-16; (Sept. 1968), pp. 9-13.

SHALABY, Abdul Wadood.
Principles of Islam, Maj. al-Azhar, (Oct. 1964), pp. 4-9.

SHALABY, Abdul Wadood.
Pillars of Islam, Maj. al-Azhar, (March 1965), pp. 5-8, (Apr. 1965), pp. 7-11.

SHALABY, Ibrahim.
What does the school in the nation of Islam in America teach?, Maj. al-Azhar, 42 vi (1970), pp. 5-8; 42 vii (1970), pp. 5-8.

SHALABY, Ibrahim M.
The black man in America, Maj. al-Azhar, (Dec. 1967), pp. 10-13; (Jan. 1968), pp. 9-11, 16.

SHALABY, Ibrahim M.
Ethnocentrism and Islam, Maj. al-Azhar, (Feb. 1968), pp. 8-12.

SHALTGUT, Mahmoud.
An introduction to Islam, Maj. al-Azhar, 31 (1960), pp. 158-162.

SHALTOUT, Mahmoud.
Religion is how to deal with prople, Maj. al-Azhar, 31 (1959), pp. 133-138.

SHALTOUT, Mahmoud.
The reform of humanity in Islam, Maj. al-Azhar, 31 (1959),

English suppl. pp. 6-10.

SHAMMA, S.
The source of morality in the Meccan period of the Qur'an., Bull. Coll. Arts, 7 (1964), pp. 43-51.

SHAMMA, S.R. al-.
An interpretation of Sura III, the house of Imran, Bull. Coll. Arts (Baghdad), 11 (1968), pp. 32-45.

SHARIF, M.M.
Islam and spiritual alues, Philosophy East and West, 9 (1959), pp. 41-43.

SHEIKHOLESLAMI, Assad.
Succession in Islamic law according to the Shafi school, Maqalat va barrasiha, 1 (1976), pp. 16-39.

SHINAR, Pessah.
Ibadiyya and orthodox reformism in modern Algeria, Studies in Isl. Hist. and Civilization (Seripta Hierosolymitana, IX (1960), pp. 97-120.

SICARD, S. von.
Christian and Muslim in East Africa, Africa Theol. J., 7 (1978), pp. 53-67.

SIDDIQ, Mazharuddin.
General characteristics of Muslim modernism, Islamic Stud., 9 (1970), pp. 33-68.

SIDDIQI, Abdul Hamid.
Religion of the pre-Islamic Arabs, Iqbal, 16 i (1967), pp. 73-83.

SIDDIQI, Aslam.
Jihad, an instrument of Islamic revolution, Islamic Studies, 2 (1963), pp. 383-398.

SIDDIQI, Mazharuddin.
Intellectual bases of Muslim modernism - I, Islamic Studies, 9 (1970), pp. 149-171.

SIDDIQI, Mazher-u-din.
Some aspects of the Mu'tazili interpretation of the Qur'an,

Islamic Studies, 2 (1963), pp. 95-120.

SIDDIQI, Mazheruddin.
Islamic conception of destiny, Iqbal, 2 i (1953), pp. 49-59.

SIMMONS, W.S.
Islamic conversion and social change in a Senegalese village, Ethnology, 18 (1979), pp. 303-323.

SIRAJ AD-DIN, Abu Bakr.
The spiritual function of civilisation, Stud. Compar. Relig., 2 (1968), pp. 234-23.

SIRAJ AD-DIN, Abu Bakr.
The origins of Sufism, Islamic Q, 3 (1956), pp. 53-64.

SIRAJ AL-DIN, Abu Bakr.
Pilgrimage to Mecca, Stud. Compar. Relig., 1 (1967), pp. 171-181.

SIRRIYA, E.
Ziyarat of Syria in a rihla of 'Abd al-Ghani al-Na abulusi (1050/1641 - 1143/1731), JRAS, (1979), pp. 109-122.

SKINNER, D.E.
Mande settlement and the development of Islamic institutions in Sierra Leone, Int. J. Afr. Hist. Stud., 11 (1978), pp. 32-62.

SKINNER, E.P.
Christianity and Islam among the Mossi, Am. Anthr., 60 (1958), pp. 1102-1119.

SMITH JANE I.
Concourse between the living and the dead in Islamic eschatological literature, History of religions, 19 (1980), pp. 224-236.

SMITH, G.R.
A Muslim saint in South Africa [Shah Ghulam Muhammad Habibi], African Studies, 28 (1969), pp. 267-278.

SMITH, Jane I.
Women in Islam: Equity, equality, and the search for the natural order, J. Amer. Acad. Religion, 47 (1979), pp. 517-537.

SMITH, Janet.
Reflections on aspects of immortality in Islam, Harvard Theol. R., 70 (1979), pp. 85-98.

SOPER J.
Jnofficiall Islam: a Muslim minority in the USSR, Religion in communist lands, 7 (1979), pp. 226-231.

SPEIGHT, H.M.
The opening verses of the chapters of the Qur'an. An attempt at classification, MW, 59 (1969), pp. 205-209.

SPEIGHT, R.M.
Some bases for a Christian apologetic to Islam, Int. R. Missions, 54 (1965), pp. 193-205.

SPEIGHT, R.M.
Islamic reform in Morocco, MW, 53 (1963), pp. 41-49.

SPOONER, H.J.
The function of religion in Persian society, Iran, 1 (1963), pp. 83-95.

SPULER, B.
Gustav Edmund von Grunebaum (1909-1972), Der. Islam, 49 (1972), p. 248.

SPULER, B.
Russia and Islam, Slavic R., 22 (1963), pp. 650-655.

STERN, M.S.
Al-Ghazzali, Maimonides, and Ibn Paquda on repentance: A comparative model, J. Amer. Acad. Religion, 47 (1979), pp. 589-607.

STERN, S.M.
Abu'l-Qasim al-Busti and his refutation of Isma'ilism, JRAS, 1961, pp. 34-35.

STERN, S.M.
The early Ismaill missionaries in North-West Persia and in Khurasan and Transoxania, BSOAS, 23 (1960), pp. 56-90.

STEVENSON, R.C.
Some aspects of the spread of Islam in the Nuba mountains, Sudan Notes and Records, 44 (1963), pp. 9-20.

STEWART, C.C.
Notes on North and West African manuscript material relating to the West African Qadiriyya Tariqa, Res. Bull. CAD Ibadan, 4, no.1&2 (1968), pp. 1-25.

STONE, F.A.
The Muslim "faith and reason" discussion and its implications for Islamic education, MW, 60 (1970), pp. 314-320.

SWANTZ, M.L.
Interaction of Islam and the African society on the East African coast, Temenos, 12 (1976), pp. 136-148.

SYRJANEN, S.
Dialogue between Muslims and Christians - obstacles in the Pakistani situation, Temenos, 12 (1976), pp. 117-124.

TABIBI, Heshmatollah.
Influences of the seven Amshasepand on the religious beliefs of the Ahl-e Haqq Kurds, Historical Studies of Iran, 3 (1975), pp. 95-100.

TAYLON, John.
An approach to the emergence of heterodoxy in mediaeval Islam, Relig. Stud., 2 (1967), pp. 197-210.

TAYLOR, John B.
Some aspects of Islamic eschatology, Relig. Stud., 4 (1968), pp. 57-76.

THOMSON, R.M.
William of Malmesbury and some other Western writers on Islam, Medievalia et humanistica, N.S. 6 (1975), pp. 179-187.

TIBAWI, A.L.
Is the Qur'an translatable?, MW, 52 (1962), pp. 4-16.

TIBI, Bassam.
Islam and secularization: Religion and the functional differentiation

of the social system, Archiv Rechts-Socialphilos, 66 (1980), pp. 207-222.

TIGNOR, R.L.
Lord Cromer on Islam, MW, 52 (1962), pp. 223-233.

TRIMINGHAM J.S.
The formative stages of the Islamic religious order, Glasgow. Univ. Or. Soc. Trans, 18 (1959), pp. 65-76.

TRIMINGHAM, J.S. and FYFE, C.
The early expansion of Islam in Sierra Leone, Sierra Leone Bull. Religion, 2 (1960), pp. 33-40.

TRITTON, A.S.
"Debate" between a Muslim and a Jew (BM. Or. 12485), Islamic Studies, 1 ii (1962), pp.60-64.

TRITTON, A.S.
Ibn Hazm and al-fisal fi'l-milal, Eretz-Israel, 7 (L.A. Mayer memorial volume, 1964), pp. 116-117.

TRITTON, A.S.
Ibn Hazm: The man and the thinker, Islamic Studies, 3 (1964), pp. 471-484.

TRITTON, A.S.
The Old Testmentin Muslim Spain, BSOAS, 21 (1958), pp. 392-395.

TRITTON, A.S.
False prophets and others, JRAS, (1957), pp. 1-9.

TRITTON, A.S.
Notes on religion in early Arabia, Museon, 72 (1959), pp. 191-195.

TRITTON, A.S.
An early work from the school of al-Maturidi, JRAS, (1966), pp. 96-99.

TRITTON, A.S.
The speech of God: A tract of the eighth fourteenth century, BSOAS, 31 (1968), pp. 377-382.

TURNER, B.S.
Conscience in the construction of religion: A critique of Marshall G.S. Hodgson's "The venture of Islam", RMES, 2 (1976), pp. 95-112.

TURNER, B.S.
Origins and traditions in Islam and Christianity, Religion, 6 (1976), pp. 13-30.

UTAS, B.
Notes on Afghan Sufi orders and khanaqahs, Afg. J., 7 (1980), pp. 60-67.

VACCA, V.
Social and political aspects of Egyptian and Yamani sufism, J. Pakistan Hist. Soc., 8 (1960), pp. 233-259.

VANESS, J.
Ibn ar-Rewandi, or the making of an image, al-Abhath, 27 (1978-9), pp. 5-26.

VAPORIS, N.M.
The price of faith: some reflections on Nikodemos Hagiorites and his struggle against Islam, together with a translation of the "Introduction" to his New Martyrologion, Greek Orth. Theol. R., 23 (1978), pp. 185-215.

VON GRUNEBAUM, G.E.
Islam: experience of the holy and concept of man, Diogenes, 48 (1964), pp.81-104.

VON GRUNEBAUM, G.E.
Byzantine iconoclasm and the influence of the Islamic environment, History of religions, 2 (1962), pp. 1-10.

VREDENBREGT, J.
The haddj. Some of its features and functions in Indonesia, BTLV, 118 (1962), pp. 91-154.

WAARDENBURG, J.
Official and popular religion in Islam, Social Compass, 25 (1978), pp. 315-341.

WAFI, Aly Abdul Wahid.
Islamic socialism, the best safeguard against Communism, Maj. al-Azhar, 31 (1959-60), pp. 58-64, 91-93.

WAIDA, Manabu.
Notes on sacred kingship in Central Asia, Numen, 23 (1976), pp. 179-190.

WALDMAN, M.R.
The development of the concept of Kufr in the Qur'an, JAOS, 88 (1968), pp. 442-455.

WALL MALEFIJT, A. de.
Animism and Islam among the Javanese in Surinam, Anthropol. Q., 37 (1964), pp. 149-155.

WANSBROUGH, J.
Majan al-qur'an: periphrastic exegesis, BSOAS, 33 (1970), pp. 247-266.

WANSBROUGH, J.
Arabic rhetoric and Qu'anic exegesis, BSOAS, 31 (1968), pp. 469-485.

WARREN, M.
Christian minorities in Muslim countries, Race, 6 (1964), pp. 41-51.

WATT W. M.
Some mystics of the later third/ninth century, Islamic,

WATT, M.M.
Sidelights on early Imamite doctrine, SI, 3 i (1970), pp. 287-298.

WATT, W.
Montgomery, on interpreting the Qur'an, Oriens.

WATT, W. Montgomery.
The place of religion in the Islamic and Roman empires, Numen, 9 (1962), pp. 110-127.

WATT, W. Montgomery.
The logical basis of early Kalam, IQ, 6 (1961), pp. 3-10; 7 (1963), pp. 31-39.

WATT, W. Montgomery.
The Rafidites: a preliminary study, Oriens, 16 (1963), pp. 110-121.

WATT, W. Montgomery.
Created in his image. A study in Islamic theology, Glasgow Univ. Or. Soc. Trans., 18 (1959-60), pp. 38-49.

WATT, W. Montgomery.
Some problems before West African Islam, IQ, 4 (1957), pp. 43-51.

WATT, W. Montgomery.
Shfism under the Umayyads, JRAS, (1960), pp. 158-172.

WATT, W. Montgomery.
The early development of the Muslim attitude to the Bible, Glasgow Univ. Or. Soc. Trans., 16 (1955-6), pp. 50-62.

WATT, W. Montgomery.
The conception of the charismatic community in Islam, Numen, 7 (1960), pp. 77-90.

WATT, W. Montgomery.
The dating of the Qur'an: a review of Richard Bell's theories, JRAS, (1957), pp. 46-56.

WATT, W. Montgomery.
The Qur'an and belief in a "High God", Der Islam, 56 (1979), pp. 205-211.

WATT, W. Montgomery.
The political attitudes of the Mu'tazilah, JRAS, (1963), pp. 38-57.

WATT, W.M.
Some mystics of the later third/ninth century, Islamic Stud., 7 (1968), pp. 309-316.

WATT, W.M.
The conception of iman in Islamic theology, Islam, 43 (1967), pp. 1-10.

WATT, W.Montgomery.
Suffering in Sunnite Islam, SI, 50 (1979), pp. 5-19.

WEIGHTMAN, S.C.R.
The significance of Kitab Burhan ul-Haqq, Iran, 2 (1964), pp. 83-103.

WESSELS, A.
Speaking about Jesus Christ in dialogues with Muslims, NE School Theol. R., 1 ii (1978), pp. 3-17.

WILBER, D.N.
The structure and position of Islam in Afghanistan, Afghanistan, 10 ii (1955), pp. 7-14.

WILKS, I.
The growth of Islamic learning in Ghana, J. Hist. Soc. Nigeria, 2 (1963), pp. 409-417.

WILLIS, J.R.
Jihad fi sabil Allah - its doctrinal basis in Islam and some aspects of its evolution in nineteenth century West Africa, J. Afr. Hist., 8 (1967), pp. 395-415.

WILSON, R.T.
The 'gizu': winter grazing in the South Libyan desert, J. Arid Environments, 1 (1978), pp. 327-344.

WINTER, M.
Sheikh 'Ali ibn Maymun and Syrian Sufism in the sixteenth century, Israel Or. Studies, 7 (1977), pp. 281-308.

WOLF, C.U.
Muslims in the American Mid-West, MW, 50 (1960), pp. 39-48.

WOLFSON, H.A.
Philosophical implications of the problem of divine attributes in the Kalam, JAOS, 79 (1959), pp. 73-80.

YAHYA, Uthman.
Man and his perfection in Muslim theology, MW, 49 (1959), pp. 19-29.

YOUNIS, M. Abdel Moneim.
The religious significance of Mi'raj, Maj. al-Azhar, (Nov. 1967), pp. 5-9.

YOUNIS, M. Abdel Moneim.
Fasting in Islam, Maj. al-Azhar, (Nov. 1968), pp. 9-12.

YOUNIS, M. Abdel Moneim.
The religion of Islam, Maj. al-Azhar, (Dec. 1967), pp. 6-9; (Jan. 1968), pp. 5-8; (Feb. 1968), pp. 6-7, 16.

YOUNIS, M. Abdul Moneim.
Zaketu'l Fitr, Maj. al-Azhar, (Dec. 1968), pp. 13-16.

YUSUF, S.M.
The Sunnah: Its place in Islam, Islamic Studies, 1 iv (1962), pp. 41-50.

ZAYAT, Ahmad Hassan Al-.
Jihad: The equipment of Islam and the strength of Muslims, Maj. al-Azhar, (May 1967), pp. 1-5.

ZAYAT, Ahmed Hassan el-.
The memory of the Prophet's birth-day, Maj. al-Azhar, 32 iii-iv (1960), pp. 1-3.

ZAYAT, Ahmed Hassan el-.
Muhammad the messenger of God. The first to declare human rights, Maj. al-Azhar, 31 (1959-60), pp. 185-188.

ZAYAT, Ahmed Hassan el-.
Out threefold revolution needs a fourth one, Maj. al-Azhar, 32 vii (1960), pp. 1-5.

ZAYAT, Ahmed Hassan el-.
From the dark cradles the light of God dawned, Maj. al-Azhar, 31 (1959-60), pp. 65-68.

ZAYAT, Ahmed Hassan el.
The three powers of Islam, Maj. al-Azhar, 31 (1959-60), pp. 33-36.

ZAYAT, Ahmed Hassan el-.
How Islam tackles poverty, Maj. al-Azhar, 31 (1960), pp. 153-157.

ZAYAT, Ahmed Hassan el-.
Al-Jihad an Arab virtue and a religious injunction, Maj. al-Azhar,

31 (1959), pp. 97-105.

ZAYAT, Ahmed Hassan el-.
The month of Rabi Al Awal in the life of the Prophet, Maj. al-Azhar, 32 v (1960-61), pp. 1-4.

ZAYAT, Ahmed Hassan el-.
The adent of Islam ushered in a new world, Maj. al-Azhar, 31 (1959-60), pp. 129-132.

ZAYYAT, A.H. El-.
Man in the law of Mohammad (in the context of racial discrimination), Maj. al-Azhar, (Oct. 1964), pp. 1-3.